Education, Training and Employment Dynamics

LABOUR MARKETS AND EMPLOYMENT POLICY

General Editor: Günther Schmid, *Director of the Research Unit on Labour Market Policy and Employment, the Social Science Research Center (WZB) and Professor of Political Economics, Free University of Berlin, Germany*

This volume is part of a series arising from an international research network on 'Social Integration Through Transitional Labour Markets' that was funded under the European Commission's Fourth Framework Programme of Targeted Socio-Economic Research (TSER) 1996–9. This project focused on the potential of a new regulatory idea – 'transitional labour markets' – for building institutional bridges which support individual transitions between various employment statuses (unpaid and voluntary civil work, part-time and full-time work, continuous education or training, dependent employment and self-employment). A basic premise of the series is that 'making transitions pay' enhances the employment intensity of growth and avoids the dilemma of growing segmentation of the labour market into 'insiders' and 'outsiders', thereby fostering social integration in a world of rapid structural change.

Education, Training and Employment Dynamics

Transitional Labour Markets in the European Union

Edited by

Klaus Schömann

Senior Research Fellow, Social Science Research Center Berlin (WZB), Germany

and

Philip J. O'Connell

Senior Research Officer, Economic and Social Research Institute, Dublin, Ireland

LABOUR MARKETS AND EMPLOYMENT POLICY

Edward Elgar

Cheltenham, UK • Northampton, MA, USA

Published by
Edward Elgar Publishing Limited
Glensanda House
Montpellier Parade
Cheltenham
Glos GL50 1UA
UK

Edward Elgar Publishing, Inc.
136 West Street
Suite 202
Northampton
Massachusetts 01060
USA

A catalogue record for this book
is available from the British Library

Library of Congress Cataloguing in Publication Data

Education, training and employment dynamics : transitional labour markets in
the European Union / edited by Klaus Schömann and Philip J. O'Connell.
    p.   cm. — (Labour markets and employment policy)
  Includes index.
  1. Occupational training — European Union countries. 2. Manpower policy
— European Union countries. I. Schömann, Klaus, 1961– II. O'Connell,
Philip J., 1956– III. Series.

HD5715.5.E85 E38 2002
331.26′92′094–dc21   2001055510

ISBN 1 84064 278 5

Printed and bound in Great Britain by MPG Books Ltd, Bodmin, Cornwall

Contents

Figures

Tables

Foreword

Günther Schmid

The reasons to look for new institutional arrangements to cope with structural change are straightforward. Unemployment in most post-industrial societies has risen to levels unprecedented in post-war history. In countries that face this phenomenon, rising levels of unemployment have led to persistent long-term unemployment. The economic and social problems related to this development are clear: the longer the exclusion from gainful employment, the higher the risk of being also excluded from full participation in social and political life; this holds especially true for women and for young people with low skills. This threat to social integration may even undermine the trust in the basic institutions of our democratic societies. An *underlying assumption* of this series is that a return to full employment in the traditional sense is highly unlikely, or only at unacceptable social cost. If some countries have succeeded in recent years in reaching levels of unemployment similar to those in the 1960s, it has either been at the cost of high income differentials and increasing numbers of working poor or many precarious employment relationships, especially for women, and more or less involuntary massive early retirement for many older workers. The objective of this project, therefore, is to seek alternatives to such ill-conceived responses to 'globalization' and 'individualization' which in different ways can generate forms of social exclusion.

It is not only structural unemployment that is of concern, although this is the most visible change. More importantly, the underlying forces of balancing supply and demand on the labour market seem to be quite different from the past. The aim of our common effort was, therefore, also to understand these new dynamics and to ask which institutional arrangements would be able to prevent or to alleviate the high flows into unemployment and to mitigate the concomitant adverse selection mechanisms during the subsequent difficult processes of reintegration, which often result in the unemployed also becoming victims of social exclusion. Social exclusion is the counterpart of social integration, which erodes the 'cement of societies'. Social integration in modern societies, therefore, means not just having a permanent job and being protected by social rights such as unemployment benefits. It also means having the perspective of evolutionary job careers, having access to the means of ensuring employability by lifelong learning, and being able to participate fully in all relevant areas of social life. The risk of unemployment is always a risk of reducing substantially the freedom of choice for a significant minority of people concerned, as well as the range of social participation.

The project was subdivided into three modules around the following topics: social integration through working time transitions, social integration through training and human capital investment, and social integration through active labour market policy. Outside the formal contractual support, a fourth module was set up to work on a larger theoretical and empirical framework of employment systems. The common underlying argument of the four modules is based on *the concept of transitional labour markets*. Transitional labour markets (TLMs), as an *analytical concept*, relate to the observation that the borderlines between gainful employment and other productive activities are becoming increasingly blurred. The 'standard labour contract' is eroding, but we do not know yet which new standards will develop. People transit more and more between different employment statuses, for instance between different working time regimes, between unemployment and employment, between education or training and employment, between unpaid family work and gainful labour market work, and between work and retirement. Thus, as an analytical concept, TLMs emphasize the dynamics of labour markets, which means focusing the analysis on flows rather than purely on stocks, and applying methodologies that find out and explain patterns in the many transitions during the life cycles of individuals or groups in different societies.

Some of these transitions are critical in the sense that they may lead to downward spirals of job careers (*exclusionary transitions*), ending in recurrent unemployment or (finally) in long-term unemployment, poverty, discouraged inactivity or violent protest. We identified five major critical transitions during a life cycle: (1) the transition from school to work, (2) the transition from part-time to full-time work or vice versa, (3) the transition between family work and labour market work, (4) the transition between employment and unemployment, and (5) the transition to retirement. As a *normative concept*, TLMs envisage new kinds of institutional arrangements to prevent those transitions from becoming gates to social exclusion and to transform them into gates to a wider range of opportunities for the employed (*maintenance transitions*) as well as for the inactive or unemployed people (*integrative transitions*). 'Making transitions pay' requires institutions that realize in one way or the other the following: *work organizations* which enable people to combine wages or salaries with other income sources such as transfers, equity shares or savings; *entitlements or social rights* which allow choices to be made between different employment statuses according to shifting preferences and circumstances during the life cycle; and *policy provisions* which support multiple use of insurance funds, especially the use of income (unemployment) insurance for financing measures that enhance employability.

The following research institutions were involved in the joint venture to search for solutions to these problems: Economic and Social Research Institute (ESRI), Dublin; Hugo Sinzheimer Institute at the University of Amsterdam, Amsterdam; Economic Faculty of the Universidad de Alcalá, Madrid; Institute for Employment Studies (IES), University of Sussex, Brighton; Manchester School of Management (UMIST), Manchester; Netherlands Economic Institute (NEI), Rotterdam; The Centre for European Labour Market Studies (CELMS), Gothenburg, in cooperation with the University of Växjö; Modélisations Appliquées, Trajectoires Institutionnelles et Stratégies SocioEconomiques) (MATISSE), Centre National de la Recherche Scientifique (CNRS) Université Paris 1; Sociological Faculty at Tilburg University (Tilburg); and as coordinating institution the Labour Market Policy and Employment Research Unit at the Social Science Research Center Berlin (WZB).

Acknowledgments

The contributions to this book are based on a three-year research project which was funded under the Fourth Framework Programme by the European Commission (Target Socio-Economic Research TSER, Contract number SOE2-CT95-3007, Project Number: CT 953007 PL 953442). The project made it possible to collaborate with our colleagues in the research network for a much longer time than was officially financed. We are happy to say that we have moved on to new projects which involve largely the same partners and some additional ones in various contexts and research collaborations. The amount of own resources in terms of time and effort contributed to this endeavour by the authors has been well beyond initial commitments. We hope the readers will find this worthwhile.

Special thanks are due to Jacqueline O'Reilly, Christoph Albrecht and Hannelore Minzlaff at the WZB who handled the financial management and coordination of the project with the European Commission and the individual partner institutes in a very pleasant and friendly manner. Karin Reinsch organized the workshops and conferences as well as providing excellent secretarial support for the book production and supported the editors in her efficient, reliable and joyful manner. Thanks are due to Andrew Wilson who accompanied the manuscript as an excellent copy editor and improved the clarity of our arguments and English style. We would also like to thank Bernard Gazier (Paris) and Luis Toharia Cortés (Alcalá de Henares) for hosting interim meetings and providing additional support for the training module of this project.

The editors and authors of this volume would also like to express their gratitude to Günther Schmid for both his intellectual inspiration and continuous feedback on the topics dealt with in this volume.

Klaus Schömann, Berlin
Philip O'Connell, Dublin
February 2001

Contributors

Cecilia Albert is Professor of Economics at the University of Alcalá (Madrid). Her research has mainly focused on the analysis of the economics of education, human capital and labour market. Her PhD was awarded the premium National Education Research. She has recently published a book with Luis Toharia and others about the Spanish labour market as a part of the series of Labour Market Studies edited by the EC, and has articles on the Spanish labour market in a number of journals.

Florence Audier is a French economist. She belongs to the MATISSE-University Panthéon-Sorbonne/CNRS). She has published several articles concerning education and vocational training, as well as youth integration into the labour market.

Rolf Becker is Assistant Professor at Dresden University of Technology Department of Sociology. His fields of research are life course analysis, social stratification and mobility, labour market analysis, social inequality of education and further training, social methodology and statistics.

Maria A. Davia is Lecturer in Economics at the University of Castilla–La Mancha. She has worked as a researcher at the University of Alcalá, Madrid, on European projects in the fields of human capital, transitions among different working-time schedules and active labour market policies. Her current research interest is in youth labour market insertion in a European context. She has been a Visiting Fellow at the WZB (Social Science Center Berlin) and the European Work and Employment Research Centre at UMIST (University of Manchester Institute of Technology).

Arie Gelderblom is a senior staff member of SEOR (Social Economic Research Institute, Rotterdam), which is linked to the Erasmus University Rotterdam. In a former job he worked for the Netherlands Economic Institute (NEI). His background is in economics. He is a specialist in the economics of training and education. For part of the time he is also working for the Institute of Labour Market Policy which concentrates on the effects of ICT (information and communication technologies) on the labour market, training and education.

Olivier Giraud gained his PhD in Political Science in 1968, and has been engaged at different research centres focusing on the study of socioeconomic regulations (WZB, Berlin; Matisse–CNRS; Paris). He is working for the CNRS at the CURAP (Université d'Amiens, France). As a policy analyst, he specializes in the field of training and employment.

Virginia Hernanz is Assistant Lecturer in Economics in the University of Alcalá, as well as a research assistant at FEDEA (Fundación de Estudios de Economía Aplicada). She is interested in labour market transitions, human capital, employment policies and youth labour markets. She is currently working on segmentation in the Spanish labour market and on the links between temporary jobs and segmentation. She has been a Visiting Fellow in the European Work and Employment Research Centre at UMIST (University of Manchester Institute of Technology) and the WZB (Social Science Center Berlin), among other centres.

Annie Jolivet is an economist researcher at the Institute of Economic and Social Research (IRES). Her areas of research are employers' practices towards ageing workers, in particular age management and age discrimination, and European employment policy.

Jaap de Koning is Professor of Labour Market Policy at the Erasmus University, Rotterdam. He is also a director at the Social Economic Research Institute (SEOR) at the same university. He was previously director of the labour and education division and member of the management team of the Netherlands Economic Institute. He has been active in the field of the economics of education and training for more than 15 years. He has also done extensive research in the related field of evaluation of labour market policy in which training plays an important role.

Ruurd Kunnen is a sociologist. He is director/proprietor of swob De Kade, a small private institute for social scientific research. In former jobs he worked for OSA (Organization for Strategic Labour Market Research) and NEI. His specialities are labour and the labour market in the knowledge society.

Frances McGinnity is a post-doctoral research fellow in sociology at the Max-Planck-Institute for Human Development in Berlin. She did her doctorate at Nuffield College Oxford, and previously worked at the Economic and Social Research Institute in Dublin. Her research interests are active labour market policy, comparative welfare states and longitudinal data analysis.

Philip J. O'Connell is a Senior Research Officer at the Economic and Social Research Institute (ESRI) in Dublin. His recent publications include *Working Schemes? Active Labour Market Policy in Ireland* (Ashgate, 1997) (with Frances McGinnity), and he is joint editor of *Labour Market Studies: Ireland* (European Commission, 1996) and of *Astonishing Success: Economic Growth and the Labour Market in Ireland*, (ILO, 1999). He is on the editorial boards of *Work, Employment and Society*, *The Journal of Youth Studies* and *The Irish Journal of Sociology*.

William Praat was a senior staff member of OSA (Organization for Strategic Labour Market Research). In that framework, he was involved in issues such as labour demand-side economics, social security, retirement, pensions, education and training. He has an econometric background. At the present time he is working as a technical consultant for Cap Gemini Ernst & Young.

Sophie Rouault is a research fellow in the labour market and employment research unit at the Wissenschaftszentrum Berlin für Sozialforschung (Social Science Research Center Berlin: WZB) and is working on her doctoral dissertation in political science at the Institut d'Etudes Politiques in Paris. Her research interests are in EU integration and comparative policy analysis; her research focuses on social and training policies and on the regulation of local labour markets.

Klaus Schömann is a senior research fellow in the labour market and employment research unit at the Wissenschaftszentrum Berlin für Sozialforschung (Social Science Research Center Berlin: WZB). His research focuses on transitions in the labour market, employment contracts, training and evaluation methodology.

Luis Toharia is Professor of Economics at the University of Alcalá (Madrid). He has published his research on various aspects of the labour market in Spain, including the measurement of employment and unemployment, the causes and consequences of unemployment, the nature of employment growth and the rise of fixed-term and part-time employment, the cost of dismissals, the unemployment benefit system and active labour market policies. He directed the study on the labour market in Spain published by the European Commission (1997). He has acted on several occasions as expert and consultant for the Spanish government as well as for the European Commission.

Marian de Voogd-Hamelink is working as a data analyst at the Organization for Strategic Labour Market Research (OSA) in Tilburg. There she is jointly responsible for the management and analysis of the panel data that OSA has within its own management, the OSA Labour Force Panel and OSA Labour Demand Panel.

Pieter van Winden is a senior researcher at the Netherlands Economic Institute (NEI), which is part of the ECORYS group. He studied econometrics at the Erasmus University in Rotterdam and is a specialist in quantitative economic research in the field of the labour market, social security and education.

1. Introduction

Klaus Schömann and Philip J. O'Connell

It is now a well established fact that education and training are of critical importance to individual labour market prospects. This insight into the importance of human capital has meant that education and training have become central issues in the social science research agenda and it has brought education and training to the fore in many recent policy debates and policy recommendations. This volume of the series on transitional labour markets addresses the issues of education, training and employment dynamics from the perspective of whether policies in these fields facilitate or inhibit social integration. The basic argument pursued throughout this volume is that, in order to respond to a lack of employment opportunities, and to risks of unemployment and social exclusion, individuals need to be enabled to organize and pass through multiple transitions between working and learning throughout their life course.

Modern democratic societies attempt to achieve social integration by promoting equal opportunity and occupational choice to their citizens to the extent possible. The institutional frameworks governing education and training systems and regulating labour markets entail a balance between basic rights and obligations that varies between countries. At the level of the individual, education and training systems and labour market institutions provide a framework within which individuals enjoy the right to a basic education and, in the majority of European Union countries, also a right to work. These rights are counterbalanced by the obligation to accept a suitable job offer or, among those dependent on unemployment compensation, retraining. In order to achieve social, or at least, labour market, integration it is necessary for individuals to accomplish a series of transitions between learning and work during the life course. The role of the modern welfare state therefore does not just consist of guaranteeing these rights but also entails the formation and implementation of interventions to support individual choices and transitions.

Most existing work in the area has, however, concentrated on the impact of the 'front end' of the education and training system – initial education and training – and has adopted a static approach to the analysis of the impact of education and training on subsequent events and transitions over the life course. Analyses of the impact of continuing education and training on employment dynamics (for example, about market-related training programmes for the employed and unemployed) are still scarce and many analyses have remained rather static in character in the sense that only a few attempts have been undertaken to capture medium- or longer-term effects of educational choices for major areas of the life course.

This book adopts a dynamic approach to the analysis of the impact of education and training across the life course. We draw on transitional labour market theory (Schmid, 1993, 2000; Schömann in this volume) which was developed in response to emerging trends of flexibility of work and precarity of careers in the labour markets of the advanced societies. The dynamic approach of the book derives from its concern with important labour market transitions: those from education to the labour market, from employment to unemployment, from unemployment back to employment, from domestic to paid work and finally the gradual transition from employment to retirement.

Our central focus is on whether, and to what extent, education and training plays a preventive or curative role in facilitating positive labour market outcomes and thus promotes social integration (O'Connell, 1999; OECD, 1999; Schömann, 1998). The order of chapters follows the sequence of the life course. The empirical chapters start with an analysis of parental influence on children's educational choices and exits from initial full-time education. This is followed by first entry to the labour market and employment–unemployment transitions, and extending to early labour market exit and retirement transitions. Throughout we are concerned with the extent to which education and training choices, decisions and experiences influence subsequent labour market outcomes and their implications for social integration or exclusion over the life course. With regard to continuing training of adult workers, our focus is confined to job-related education and training. While we recognize that more general adult education, including access to adult education facilities and public libraries, may have implications for social integration, our focus on job-related training is dictated by resource and space constraints. Moreover, we believe that future research into the impact of adult education more broadly conceived would be valuable.

The concepts of the life course (Mayer, 1997) and transitional labour markets (Schmid, 2000) are combined in an attempt to develop a theory of transitional labour markets and the life course which has its roots in the work of James Coleman (Coleman, 1990) in the sense that social integration across the life course is a multi-level phenomenon where both individual decisions and societal opportunity structures determine actual outcomes over the life course. To capture the effects of institutional arrangements on the life course we also adopt a modelling strategy based on systems theory to capture the interdependent institutional factors which then influence individual-level processes. The life course perspective requires a largely microanalytic research design based on individual and household surveys as well as micro-level analysis of the demand side of the labour market, that is firms' employment strategies.

Institutional factors may intervene as explanatory variables in micro-level analyses either directly, by affecting a specific outcome, or indirectly by influencing a process or relationship. Where institutional context is believed to influence an outcome directly, this can be analysed by comparing outcomes before and after a policy shift. To examine whether the institutional context influences processes or relationships, it is often necessary to undertake historical or cross-sectional comparisons in order to allow for variation in the institutional context: for example, by means of comparisons across countries. The latter approach has been applied throughout this volume either in comparative analyses of several countries within a single chapter or by comparing results from different countries across chapters.

The sequence of chapters runs from the influence of parents on children's education and labour market choices to first entry into the labour market, youth labour markets, employment and unemployment transitions, further training transitions to training an ageing workforce and early retirement transitions due to lack of marketable skills. Education and training as well as labour market policies are rarely defined as policies which address particular phases of the life course, but the analyses presented in this volume do suggest that differing policy domains are of varying importance at different stages of the life course. So initial education and training may be of greatest importance early in the life course, while continuing training may have greater influence later in life. Nevertheless, there is no one-to-one correspondence, since, as several chapters demonstrate, initial educational attainment may have lasting consequences for an individual's entire career prospects.

In general, the book draws upon the theoretical and empirical approaches of three social science disciplines: the economics of education and the labour market, the sociology of education and inequality, and the actor-centred approach of multi-level governance from political science. In Chapter 2, rather than outlining three separate approaches of social science analysis to the problems of social integration and social exclusion, we develop a theoretical framework which combines the insights of the differing approaches. Of course other approaches to the issue of social integration, including social psychology, public health, labour law and criminology, are also relevant. However, we consider that the attempt to integrate just three broad perspectives is itself a sufficient challenge for the present volume. Individual contributions to the volume typically argue from a particular disciplinary perspective. The concluding chapter then attempts to bring together the differing approaches and findings from the empirical chapters.

This volume combines quantitative longitudinal analyses based on individual- as well as firm-level data, complemented by in-depth case studies of institutional factors in the development and negotiation of training policies. Each of the four parts of the book has at least one comparative chapter, explicitly comparing similar data sets across countries. The main countries analysed are France, Germany, Ireland, the Netherlands and Spain. In the country-specific chapters the authors have sought to present results in a manner that permits comparison with the results from other country-specific chapters dealing with similar issues using comparable methodologies and analytic techniques.

The empirical part of the volume has four major parts. Part I produces individual-level analyses of selectivity within the education system and the labour market segmentation at entry to the transitions into the labour market. Part II examines micro-level evidence on participation in further training, including differential access to training by age and educational attainment, as well as the impact of training on transitions between unemployment and employment. Part III looks at the incidence and impact of enterprise-based training, the role of state intervention in training of workers, as well as the complex relationship between enterprise-based training and social exclusion of older workers. Part IV focuses on actors in the training field, using case study approaches to differentiate the differing roles of social partners and local, national and European policy makers. Finally, conclusions attempt to derive guidelines for policy making in this field for the local, national and the European level.

This volume on training and human capital investment strategies deals with investment-oriented labour market processes concerning individuals, households, firms and political actors. Policy interventions to advance social integration have generally been recognized as achieving their targets, although often the returns to training and other forms of human capital investments tend to be small and to be realized rather slowly. Exceptions are training programmes for target groups in fields of precisely identified skill shortages. The specific approach of this book has been to pursue a theory-driven research agenda based on the analysis of labour market transitions rather than static labour market outcomes. This means that we developed a series of guiding hypotheses relating to processes of labour market integration derived from Schmid's theory of labour market transitions and transitional labour markets (Schmid, 2000; Schömann in this volume) and individual chapters examined those hypotheses across five

European countries. A second set of hypotheses, mainly addressing institutional aspects, also put to the test in the course of this project, suggests that education and training can serve as a form of individual or societal insurance against the risk of social exclusion. We believe that further comparative research is warranted into these fundamental institutional differences between national education and training systems and labour market regulations.

The concept of transitional labour markets stresses the multiple dimensions of processes of social integration and exclusion. The major dimensions are related to each of the five major transitional labour markets corresponding to a life course perspective on labour market transitions. The theory of labour market transitions developed in this module highlights the fact that there are important multi-level relationships which intervene in labour market processes so that individual transitions, for example into the labour market or back into employment, may turn out to be very hard to accomplish in specific macroeconomic, macrosocial or country-specific institutional arrangements. The two major hypotheses tested are: that (a) initial investments in education and training, as well as the early experience of transitions, have lasting effects on entry into the labour market and subsequent labour market transitions; and (b) segmentation early in the education system, and particularly at the time of entry and re-entry into the labour market, has a strong tendency to persist unless mitigated through transitional labour market arrangements which confer additional qualifications.

PLAN OF THE BOOK

Chapter 2 gives a definition of what constitutes training transitions and explains why training transitions are an important policy instrument to avoid social exclusion. It relates the policy issues of lifelong learning to the theory of transitional labour markets. Our central concern is with the role of investment in human potential in preventing social exclusion and promoting social integration, and with the institutional mediation of basic labour market processes that constitute transitional labour markets which allow for the combination of learning and working. Our dynamic focus includes, not only the impact of initial education and training on the first transition from school to work, but also the impact of continuing training on transitions from unemployment to employment, as well as the potential for training to prevent the undesirable transition from employment to unemployment or involuntary early retirement. A second major aspect addresses the importance of early preparation for transitions later in the life course, in effect learning to accomplish transitions. How can this be achieved? How well prepared are the different national education and training systems to meet these new challenges? What type of new institutional arrangements are needed to facilitate transitions related to training and further training? This concerns both the education system and labour markets and we argue for the need to analyse both systems jointly.

The first empirical part of the volume identifies important features of the institutional background for training transitions in the major European countries. This section focuses on an analysis of transitions within the education system and the first entry into the labour market based on individual level analyses. Here we try to answer the question of what kind of institutional arrangements tend to facilitate socially integrative transitions or increase the chances of subsequent social integration.

Part II deals with the evaluation of training interventions. Active labour market policies aimed at the unemployed have come to play a central role in the response to unemployment in Europe. Why is this the case? What are the effects in terms of equity and efficiency of such government intervention? If there is market failure what are the outcomes in terms of social integration and social exclusion? What type of policy measure works, what are the components of a policy evaluation framework which reflects upon social integration and social exclusion? These issues are addressed by four chapters which analyse individual-level data covering several different countries.

In Part III we shift the focus to the firm's rationale for training. Models based on the perspective of the firm emphasize the close relationship between wages and productivity in influencing training decisions. In practice, the link between age and productivity can dominate firms' training rationale and this can lead to differential access to training and thus increase the risk of social exclusion facing older employees. Alternatively, seniority rules can adversely affect the employment prospects of young labour market entrants and other labour market outsiders such as women seeking to return to work after a period of domestic work. Differential returns to general versus firm-specific training imply various forms of cost sharing between firms and the individual, as well as the need for state interventions to organize and finance training in order to overcome market failures leading to under-investment – either in overall training or in the training of particular groups.

The aims and strategies of political actors are dealt with in Part IV. Who are the actors in the field of training and what are their strategies? The two chapters in this section adopt case study approaches to investigate the formulation and implementation of training policies in negotiations between the social partners at the level of the enterprise, and in the relationship between local, regional and national actors and the institutions of the European Union. Finally, the concluding chapter provides a summary of results and of what we can learn about the impact of education and training on social integration from the approaches of the different social sciences in this volume. Here we attempt to unite the differing perspectives and findings into an integrated framework which sets out the potential for a transitional labour market of learning and working to promote social integration.

BIBLIOGRAPHY

Coleman, J.C. (1990), *Foundations of Social Theory*, Cambridge, Mass.: Belknap Press, Harvard.

Mayer, K.U. (1997), 'Notes on a comparative political economy of life courses', *Comparative Social Research*, 16, 203–26.

O'Connell, P.J. (1999), 'Adults in Training: An International Comparison of Continuing Education and Training', WD(99)1, OECD Center for Educational Research and Innovation, Paris: OECD.

OECD (1999), *Employment Outlook*, Paris: OECD.

Schmid, G. (1995), 'Is Full Employment Still Possible? Transitional Labour Markets as a New Strategy of Labour Market Policy', *Economic and Industrial Democracy*, 16 (3), 429–56.

Schmid, G. (2000), 'Transitional labour markets: A new European Employment Strategy', in B. Marin, D. Meulders and D. Snower (eds), *Innovative Employment Initiatives*, Aldershot: Ashgate, pp. 223–54.

Schömann, K. (1998), 'Access to life-long learning and implications for strategies of organisational learning in the European Union', in Horst Albach, Meinolf Dierkes, Ariane Berthoin Antal and Kristina Vaillant (eds), *Organisationslernen institutionelle und kulturelle Dimensionen*, WZB-Jahrbuch 1998, Berlin: edition sigma, pp. 443–6.

2. The theory of labour market transitions applied to the transitional labour market of education and training

Klaus Schömann

1. INTRODUCTION

Micro-level labour market theories, policy recommendations and evaluations of labour market policies continue to be based on rather static assumptions and analyses of education, earnings, employment and unemployment. The macroeconomic literature on the flow approach to the labour market is one of the few exceptions to date (Burgess, 1994; Schettkat, 1996). Despite some innovative theoretical approaches and empirical analyses of labour markets, there is a tendency to focus on either the individual or the aggregate macro level of analysis, with few attempts being made to address the link between the levels. Transitional labour market theory, combined with the theory of transitions over the lifetime, offers several ways of bridging this gap. This extension of the theory goes hand-in-hand with a concern to revise the concept of full employment through improved institutional arrangements, legal reforms, changes to governance structures and new kinds of labour market policies.

   In focusing on the field of education and labour market transitions, this volume explicitly addresses the link between the different levels of analysis and stresses the importance of dealing with the links between different institutions rather than analysing them in isolation from each other. We analyse the initial education system, further training arrangements, labour markets and employment insurance systems in greater detail. We propose a general theory of transitions, in particular of labour market-related transitions, and apply this theory to the transitional labour market of education and employment (Schmid, 1993, 1998; Schmid and Gazier, 1998; Schömann, 1998). On the basis of the theoretical advances made in this chapter, we derive testable hypotheses for the empirical analyses carried out in the other chapters of the book.[1]

The issue of social integration and social exclusion is the overarching subject of the series of which this book is a part (DeKoning and Mosley, 2001; O'Reilly *et al.*, 2000; Schmid and Gazier, 2002) and it is the particular concern of each chapter in this volume. Thus we briefly define the terms 'social exclusion' and 'social integration' as used throughout this volume in the light of their application to education and labour market transitions.[2] It is difficult in general to disentangle the multiple links between the micro and macro levels of analysis, and the field of education and labour market transitions is no exception to this rule. Nevertheless, the present volume attempts to advance understanding in this area. It takes as its starting point Coleman's seminal work on the foundations of social theory (1990),[3] which argues for a more comprehensive analysis of macro-level phenomena at different points in time and for an analysis of macrosocietal change that includes micro-level explanations.

Thus a change in the 'propensity for social inclusion' in a macrosocietal system is broken down into Coleman's three basic explanatory steps: (a) the explanatory impact of macro or systemic influences upon individual-level explanations, which constitutes the macro to micro link; (b) the explanation of individual actions through individual characteristics and individual behaviour, as in micro-level theories such as human capital theory; and (c) explanations of how individual actions in their sum, or collective action, determine macro or system-level outcomes, for example a change in the 'propensity for social inclusion'. In testing the impact of different institutional settings on the macro/micro link, we refer mainly to country comparisons.

This chapter is structured as follows. Section 2 outlines the multidimensional and multi-level issues around social integration and presents the key elements of the transitional labour market approach to countering social exclusion. Section 3 deals with the links between social integration and social exclusion from a theoretical perspective. Section 4 states some basic elements of a general process-oriented theory of transitions and derives hypotheses from this theory, mainly with a view to dealing with education and labour market transitions. In section 5 we combine this theory and its application to education and training transitions with the more general debate on social integration through transitional labour markets. In the same section, we discuss the implications for transitional labour markets and the potential for developing the theory of transitional labour markets into a broader theory of social integration.

2. SOCIAL INTEGRATION: A MULTIDIMENSIONAL AND MULTI-LEVEL ISSUE

In the absence of a generally accepted theory of social integration, we start the analysis by presenting some stylized facts about social integration and exclusion. Two phenomena will suffice to demonstrate the multi-level challenge embodied in the issue of 'social exclusion and its obverse, social integration' (Cousins, 1998, p. 129).

Firstly, a person might be socially integrated by virtue of one individual characteristic but socially excluded because of a characteristic ascribed to the particular group to which they belong. For example, a person with an individual or household income well above the poverty line might still suffer social exclusion because they belong to a group which is largely excluded from full active participation in society. This might apply, for example, to family members working on family farms, to disabled persons in countries where the public infrastructure is inadequate for them or to sex workers in societies that take a hostile moral stance to their activity.[4]

Secondly, a person might be socially excluded because of an individual characteristic, although they might at the same time be integrated into society by virtue of a characteristic ascribed to the group to which they belong. For example, a person with an individual or household income below the poverty line might suffer from social exclusion because their standard of living in terms of purchasing power is below the societal average. However, that same person may still belong to a group that is socially respected, such as poorly paid workers providing family or personal care in non-profit organizations, or those engaged in voluntary work more generally.

This multi-level aspect of social integration necessitates a comprehensive research design that combines individual-level analysis with group or country-level analyses. Thus what is required here is a combination of qualitative and quantitative approaches. The major problem to be overcome is the choice of pertinent indicators and dependent variables in the analysis of social integration. A narrow focus on just one dependent variable, such as income, as is largely the case in the economic analysis of poverty, is insufficient, since it neglects the social components of poverty and societal effects on individuals.

Social exclusion and, particularly, social integration are a multidimensional (Fagan and Lallement, 2000) and multi-level issue. Over and above the economic aspects of social integration, the social dimension deals with civic rights and entitlements and the interpersonal or psychosocial aspects of social integration. To some extent, this reflects the different approaches adopted by academic disciplines, as in the differentiation between human capital and social capital (Coleman, 1990); that is, the societal aspect of human capital acquisition and the network resources available to individuals.

In our analysis of the processes of social integration, allowance will be made for multi-level influences and multiple feedback structures between the levels. A number of societal institutions[5] play an important mediating role in both the group and individual aspects. In the course of our analysis, we pose the following questions. To what extent do institutions reduce or contribute to social exclusion at the individual or group level? How effectively do labour market, education and further training institutions join forces on the different levels in order to further social integration? Is there a specific role for the social partners as mediators between conflicting interests and exclusionary outcomes? Should governments intervene in these processes, and if so at what level and how?

Since we are still lacking a generally accepted labour market theory of transitions,[6] the analysis of transition dynamics has been driven largely by empirical research (Blossfeld 1996), much of it propelled by evaluations of specific labour market policies (Schmid *et al.*, 1996). In particular, the development of techniques for longitudinal data analysis, such as transition rate models and specific panel estimators, has made it possible to construct a suitable empirical basis for tackling dynamic research issues. At the same time, huge efforts have been made to collect longitudinal data on individuals and firms, with specific efforts being made on the European level to improve the comparability of country-specific data.[7] Despite these improvements in the availability of longitudinal data and in longitudinal methods, empirical tests of transitions are still based largely on labour market theories developed by reference to the analysis of educational level, earnings or labour market status. There have been few attempts, on the theoretical level, to take issue with this longitudinal revolution in empirical social science research.[8] We shall try to bridge this gap, at least partially, by proposing a theory of transitions over the lifetime to complement the institutional theory of transitional labour markets. This theoretical approach to transitions between education and employment over the lifetime is applied in the following chapters of this book.

In our own previous work on labour law, particularly employment protection, and labour market processes, we find that few labour market theories deal appropriately with labour market transitions and the relevant social institutions (Schömann, Rogowski and Kruppe,1998). At best, most labour market theories seem merely to acknowledge the presence of institutional arrangements, such as individual labour contracts or collective agreements, that affect the levels of pay or recruitment and dismissal processes under study. This might be acceptable in analyses dealing with historical phases, in which the relevant institutional arrangements appear rather time-invariant or can reasonably be assumed to be temporarily constant. In comparative research, however, these bridging assumptions become more and more difficult to defend. The theory of reflexive labour law (Rogowski and Wilthagen, 1994) has been fruitfully applied in earlier work to the analysis of country comparisons of labour market regulation, and particularly employment protection, in order to disentangle the multiple feedbacks between various parts of the regulatory framework. In this volume, we focus on the links and feedbacks between education and further training as well as on those between training, employment and earnings.

The theory of transitions over the lifetime questions the usual 'bridging' assumptions made in comparative research (the main tenet of which is 'other things being equal') and transforms them into testable hypotheses suitable for comparative scrutiny. Different institutional arrangements and institutional changes relevant to the processes under investigation are more likely to emerge as the number of countries compared increases. Similarly, the process of labour market integration in the early stages of the lifetime takes place in a way that is inextricably linked to the institutions of national education, training and further training systems (Müller and Shavit, 1998; Schömann *et al.*, 1995) and to central labour market institutions, such as labour law, employment insurance and the broader framework of social protection.

Thus there is a need for a labour market theory that deals with transition processes over the lifetime in addition to the institutional aspects of transitions that are dealt with more explicitly in transitional labour market theory. This is particularly evident in cases where a transition involves exit from one institutional arrangement and entry into another, as in the school-to-work transition or the transition into retirement. Such transitions are referred to as 'critical transitions' in the lifetime (Behrens and Voges, 1996). Research on social integration through transitional labour markets examines five kinds of transitional labour markets (Schmid, 1998, 1993): (1) transitions between dependent employment and self-employment, part-time versus full-time employment or fixed-term employment versus more permanent employment relationships, (2) transitions between unemployment and employment, (3) transitions between education/training and employment, (4) transitions between private and labour market activity, and (5) transitions between employment and retirement. On the individual level, these 'bridges' can be crossed in both directions, and in some cases several times within a year. On the level of society as a whole, there are choices to be made as to the institutional arrangements applying to such transitions. For example, individuals who opt to leave full-time education at an early stage in the lifetime might be given opportunities to reverse that decision.

Four principles characterize transitional labour markets. Firstly, they combine paid employment with other useful social activities; secondly, they combine various income sources, such as wages and transfer payments; thirdly, there are legally enforceable entitlements to a choice of transitional employment; and, fourthly, fiscal incentives operate in such a way as to finance employment rather than unemployment (Schmid, 1998, p. 9). In addition to the principles underpinning the governance structure of transitional labour markets, Schmid defines four criteria against which specific institutional arrangements can be evaluated in order to ascertain whether a distinction can be made between favourable and unfavourable transitional arrangements. These are empowerment of individuals, sustainability of both employment and income, flexible coordination between decision-making levels and cooperation in networks.

These principles and criteria need to be viewed in conjunction with previous work on labour market policies and evaluation (Schmid *et al.*, 1996). Taken together, these two strands constitute a comprehensive research agenda for developing new forms of active labour market policies and innovative institutional arrangements in order to promote employment, together with a detailed framework for empirical evaluation of the outcomes.

3. ON THE RELATIONSHIP BETWEEN SOCIAL INTEGRATION AND SOCIAL EXCLUSION

The main motivation for the development of a theory of labour market transitions linked to transitional labour markets and life cycle research (Mayer and Müller, 1986) is concern about the processes of social integration and social exclusion. The 'regulative idea of transitional labour markets' (Schmid, 1998) views such specific markets as a way of facilitating social integration. Most analysts who have tackled these two topics have been content to establish the meaning of these terms. Few attempts have been made to construct a theory of social integration. One exception is the theory of poverty and social exclusion developed by Jordan (1996), which is based largely on Buchanan's theory of clubs and Olson's theory of collective action. This theory cannot be applied directly to the question of social integration, since an absence of social exclusion does not necessarily mean social integration, as we shall argue in this chapter.

Most research efforts are confined to identifying groups of more or less excluded or integrated people, like the long-term unemployed or persons in marginal employment. Although institutional arrangements such as unemployment or social insurance systems were originally put in place in order to counter risks of exclusion, some authors consider them to be at least partly responsible for today's forms of persistent exclusion from the labour market (OECD, 1996, 1999, p. vii), since the high non-wage labour costs required to finance social expenditures might lead to lower aggregate levels of employment.

The risk of labour market exclusion arises for individuals who fall into the 'unemployment or poverty trap' or who remain in poorly-paid, insecure and temporary forms of employment for large parts of their lifetime. The theory of transitional labour markets suggests many specific escape routes that might be used to avoid or lower the risks of social exclusion, as well as strategies for improving labour market integration. The strength of the theory lies in the identification of major issues and the development of detailed proposals for facilitating the social integration of persons with only marginal attachment to the labour market. Empirical tests of the functioning of such new institutional arrangements, in accordance with the regulative notion of transitional labour markets, are dealt with in the following chapters of this book,[9] as well as in the other books in this series.

Clues from the History of Ideas

There is a huge literature on both theoretical and empirical approaches. Most of it addresses the issue of social exclusion rather than attempting to develop positive, solution-oriented approaches to social integration. The notion of social class has its roots in the early writings of Karl Marx and, as Schumpeter (1950, pp. 40–41; 1964, p. 116) claims, is rather static, since it assumes little mobility between the classes. A more pertinent early reference to theoretical approaches is the process of social closure as introduced by Max Weber (1980). The term 'social closure' denotes the desire of one group of persons to distinguish itself from another group. By definition, membership of one group means exclusion from the other (dependent employee versus self-employed or capitalist, for example). Parkin (1974) introduced the notion of twofold or dual strategies of social closure. For example, membership of a trade union implies both non-membership of the capitalist or employer's group and a tendency towards social closure in respect of unemployed or inactive persons. This latter form of social closure is developed further in the insider–outsider theory developed by Lindbeck and Snower (1988, p. 3), who distinguish insiders, recent entrants and outsiders as the three basic groups in conflict over wages and job opportunities.

In Norbert Elias's seminal work (1991, pp. 37–9, 44) on 'the society of individuals', the integration of individuals into a society is analysed from the perspective of interpersonal relationships. These relationships between persons and groups open up the possibility of analysing the operation of social integration from a different perspective, making it possible to incorporate the role of specific actors and their networks into the analysis. This is not an easy task, since social integration is a multidimensional process which operates on multiple levels[10] embedded in institutions and networks of social actors. Although in semantic terms social integration figures as the antonym of social exclusion, we do not consider a person who is not suffering social exclusion as one who is automatically socially integrated, in the sense of fully participating in social and community life. In other words, the distinction between social integration and social exclusion is not a simple binary relationship of the either/or type.[11]

The Challenge to Comparative Research

Because of the individual–group distinction, it appears more appropriate to apply a 'multidimensional indicator', or a composite definition of social integration and exclusion, in theoretical and empirical analyses incorporating both economic and social dimensions. In the two-level case described in the introduction, which is similar to Parkin's (1974) basic notion of twofold social closure, a two-by-two matrix (Table 2.1) produces four types of social exclusion.[12] Allowing for institutional variation, as is standard practice in international comparative research, or the addition of a regional level (East/West or North/South) of potential social exclusion, produces at least two matrices like that in Table 2.1 What then needs to be clarified is whether the two matrices of social exclusion for two regional entities have to be considered as theoretically distinct patterns of social exclusion. Alternatively, there is just one more general theoretical pattern with two distinct empirical patterns.

Table 2.1   Combinations of individual and group-level social exclusion

		Social exclusion on level of society	
		Yes	No
Social exclusion on individual level	Yes	Income and network poor (frequently related to old age)	Income poor, persons working in the voluntary sector
	No	Child labour/family members Non-poor sex workers	Most people in society in standard employment relationships over sufficiently long periods

If informed comparisons are to be made, substantial amounts of information about very specific institutional arrangements are required in order to allow comparisons of individual and group-level social exclusion between countries. The challenge to comparative research becomes more obvious from a comparison of, for example, two long-term unemployed persons from countries with very different social protection arrangements, such as Spain and Germany. Even though, individually and on the group level, neither of the long-term unemployed persons would consider themselves to be socially excluded, a simplified comparison of the level of unemployment compensation in the two countries would label the unemployed person in Spain as socially excluded in national terms relative to the average level of unemployment compensation in Europe (OECD, 1998; see also Chapter 3 in this volume).[13]

We have confined ourselves so far to a simple static analysis of social exclusion and integration. If we are to shift to a dynamic analysis and begin to examine transition processes, then the matrix in Table 2.1 has to be analysed at a minimum of two points in time, with the ensuing multiplication of potential transitions. Allowing for rapid changes in national employment insurance and other social protection regulations, this would produce a rather complex set of potential transitions (including institutional changes) to analyse and to classify as favourable or unfavourable. The regulative notion of transitional labour markets allows this complexity to be reduced to a manageable number of five major transitional labour markets.[14]

There is a close link between individual life histories and the transitional labour market approach. In order to reduce the complexity of international comparisons, we can identify cases where social integration or exclusion occurs at a transition. This is less obvious in the case of the individual attributes of social exclusion, but it is quite common with group-level attributes. For example, attribution to the student category usually precludes any simultaneous claiming of unemployment benefits. The identification of critical transitions, such as that from school to work or early retirement from the labour market, allows us to choose specific transitions involving either integration or exclusion.

The following transitions over the lifetime are of greatest interest to us: transitions with a high risk of social exclusion, such as an early exit from full-time education (Chapter 3) and the departure from full-time education and first entry into the labour market (Chapter 4). Similarly, the employment/unemployment (Chapters 5–9) and employment/retirement transitions (Chapter 10) have also frequently been regarded as critical transitions in terms of social integration and exclusion. Although the research agenda for social integration through transitional labour markets is much wider, this volume can deal only with these critical transitions.

As is clear from Schumpeter's line of reasoning, the production and inclusion potential of individual firms, as well as firm-level processes, are also relevant to the social exclusion debate. This aspect is dealt with in Part III of the book, which is based on firm-level processes and data. It is also evident from the writings of Josef Schumpeter (1950, pp. 134–42) that our attempt to define processes of social exclusion should be regarded with a certain degree of caution. Only longitudinal evidence is likely to uncover the creative potential of the exclusionary tendency in the market process. He described this exclusionary tendency in the market process as 'the process of creative destruction'. In fact the liquidation of companies, or the 'implementation of new combinations', to quote Schumpeter's own words (Schumpeter, 1964, p. 110), has creative potential. Thus, in any investigation of social exclusion, it is important to study the dynamics and distribution pattern of new firms and of job creation over a period of time that is sufficiently long to reveal the whole pattern of, say, job mobility – not only job loss but also job creation and the supporting institutional arrangements and actors (Davis *et al.*, 1996; Baldwin *et al.*, 1998; Schömann, Kruppe and Oschmiansky, 1998).

4. BASIC ELEMENTS OF THE THEORY OF LABOUR MARKET TRANSITIONS

In this section we propose a theory of transitions over the lifetime that deals explicitly with the process-like nature of a transition and subsequently connects it to the theory of transitional labour markets. This is a challenge, since we are attempting to develop a theory that explains what is usually considered to be concealed within the 'black box' of a transition. It is usually assumed that transition processes are hard to study because the actual transition is difficult to observe or invisible to external observers. Researchers are frequently limited to observing various input factors and specific outcomes, without being able to observe how the transition operates and what kind of forces are at work. One strategy for overcoming this shortcoming of research in both the natural and social sciences has been to study processes at work in ever smaller entities and to capture the evolution of the relationship between input and outcome as they evolve over ever smaller units of time.

Empirical research in the social sciences has made considerable progress in dealing more precisely with the timing of events and with sequences of events in data analysis (Tuma and Hannan, 1984; Blossfeld *et al.*, 1986; Blossfeld and Rohwer, 1995). The primary focus of this chapter is to construct an empirically based theory of transitions that deals with the underlying mechanism of a transition. Thus the theory has to allow us to produce testable statements about how the transition from situation one to situation two is accomplished. Since we are dealing with social processes, we have to bear in mind that such a theory will have to contribute to the understanding of social institutions and the complex interplay of individual-level processes, macro-level phenomena and the institutional structure in which these processes are embedded.

Some Basic Assumptions

In Coleman's discussion of explanation in social sciences (Coleman, 1990, pp. 2–5), he applies the notion of transition stringently to a characterization of processes located on different levels of analysis. His major focus is on two specific levels of analysis: the micro or individual-actor level and the macro or social-system level, and the interaction between the two. In explaining the behaviour of social systems, he refers to the crucial need to consider processes internal to the system as component parts of the system. These component parts consist of institutions (such as unemployment insurance systems), any kind of societal subgroup (the excluded, for example) and individual behaviour (such as job search). The theory of transitions is presented in a general form in order that it can be applied to all forms of processes and transitions as specified by Coleman: that is, to processes occurring on just one level of analysis as well as to those transitions involving the micro and macro level of analysis.

As already stated, processes of social integration are, in our view, multidimensional and have therefore to be analysed on a number of different levels. We have also alluded briefly to the evolutionary nature of these processes, that is, they evolve over time. The theory seeks to elucidate traditional explanations of transitions and sequences of transitions, such as, for example, recurrent unemployment (Heckman and Borjas, 1980), discontinuous employment trajectories (Mutz *et al.*, 1995) and long-range processes of lifelong learning. The feature common to all three processes is that they involve multiple transitions, which the theory needs to address as processes. Each of the three processes deals with very different institutional arrangements, including the unemployment insurance system, wider social protection systems, and education and labour market arrangements. Thus the theory must make it possible to take account of the potential impact of institutional arrangements.

The basic unit of analysis is the individual. Individuals are assumed to be multidimensional entities that evolve over time and are open to external influences that are not necessarily imposed upon them. As well as using actual or observed statuses, transition theory makes use of the notion of human potentials, whereby an individual's earnings, for example, are only one element within a multidimensional notion of human potential. Our use of the notion of human potential rather than that of human capital reflects our desire to consider both individual human capital and social capital, as incorporated in individuals, as constituent components of a person's human potential. The notion of human potential allows us to construct a theory that incorporates parallel processes, such as a parallel increase or decrease in an individual's human and social capital.

Similarly, the connection between continuing learning activities and evolving careers in the labour market needs to be studied as a parallel process. Human capital theory makes an implicit distinction between learning in schools and working in the labour market. There is ample evidence now from various disciplines to suggest that learning processes do not stop on departure from the education system and that, conversely, practical work experience is frequently acquired during periods of education or training or in conjunction with learning processes. The aim of transition theory is to capture the parallel evolution of learning and working experiences. For this reason, each process is analysed firstly as an independent process modelled as a pendulum of fixed length and weight, and then with the addition of an elastic connection between the two processes.

Further, it has to be assumed that one of the two processes is triggered by an initial impetus. Because of the elastic connection between the two, the second process will start to move soon after the first one is in motion. In our model of the linked learning and working process, it is assumed either that primary education provides this impetus or that, as shown by an extensive sociological literature, it is provided by the social background of parents, which stimulates children's learning processes before they start school. As children pass through the education system, their achievement record is reset each year. For this reason, we believe that the learning process in the early years of education can reasonably be modelled in terms of a pendulum-like evolutionary process.

The link between learning and work might be established at any time in the learning process, although we consider it appropriate for modelling purposes to assume a link between the two processes from the beginning. In line with international legal conventions, however, the link could be established only from the age of 14 onwards. The elastic link between the two processes allows the influence of each process upon the other, parallel process to be taken into account. With a link of a specific elastic limit, the learning process might even come to a standstill after a series of mutual exchanges between the two processes. At this point, there would, in an extreme case, be no impetus at all for learning and maximum impetus for working. If the link retains its elasticity, however, both learning and working activities will quickly be resumed.

A society's or a group's social capital can also be incorporated in institutions. We consider social institutions as constant only for short durations, hence the need to study the influences of institutions on labour market processes. Since they are the outcome of some form of aggregation of individual-level processes, most labour market institutions are subject to these individual or group-level influences. In theory, the positive or negative impact of these processes on individual processes of social integration is indeterminate.

Transitional labour market theory (Schmid, 1993, 1998) identifies five major types of transitional labour markets and transitions between the various spheres of life, such as the transitional labour market between education and the labour market and that between unemployment and the labour market, to mention but two. In previous work (Schömann, 1998), we demonstrated the importance of personal education and training achievements in all five labour market processes in maintaining or improving social integration.

On the systemic and institutional level of analysis, we have shown that each of the transitional labour markets is closely linked to very specific institutional settings (Schömann *et al.*, 2000). The relationship of the education system to the labour market maintains the independence of each sphere as a subsystem governed by its own internally coherent set of regulations and with its own dynamic. From a systemic perspective, each subsystem seems to evolve as if in isolation, although from time to time the reconsideration of the link between the subsystems becomes a hotly debated issue, frequently turning into a crisis. In the field of education and labour market transitions, high youth unemployment constitutes such a crisis, in which the link between the two subsystems of education and the labour market is ripe for fundamental reform, which may be inspired by comparative research or the results of benchmarking activities (Schütz *et al.*, 1998).

The Core of Transition Theory

Each subsystem, the education system as well as the labour market, appears to be operating largely independently of the other or of other transitional labour markets. Nevertheless, each year, many individuals accomplish transitions such as that from school to work in an integrative way (Shavit and Müller, 1998). Even the reverse transition back to school or training is becoming more frequent in some European countries, mainly the Scandinavian ones, spurred not least by new policies designed to encourage lifelong learning, such as sabbaticals and other forms of training leave. This requires far-reaching changes in institutions (Tuijnman and Schömann,

1996), in individual behaviour and in firms' human resource management practices. The theory of labour market transitions over the lifetime addresses both of these aspects, despite the fact that they operate at a different level of aggregation.

Each subsystem is defined as a system in motion, with a specific link posited between the two. This link between the subsystems operates in two ways: it may or may not be permanent and it may exert a constant or variable force upon the two subsystems. For specific institutional reasons, the link between the two subsystems might be entirely interrupted or redesigned in order to favour particular features of the transition processes between subsystems. The theory of transitions builds on the analogy[15] to process analysis in other scientific disciplines, and in particular the analogy to the theory and modelling of coupled harmonic oscillators, with due account being taken of the need to adapt this theory and its underlying assumptions so that it can be applied to individuals, institutions and social processes.[16] Thus each subsystem or process is defined as an independent entity with its own specific characteristics. The link between the two processes does not alter the basic elements of each process. Each process will remain a process in its own right, but a continuous feedback structure is established through the link. Both parallel processes are set in motion after one of the two processes receives its initial impetus through early childhood or schooling. This initial stimulus will subsequently influence the parallel processes of transitions over the lifetime. Each of the periods spent in one subsystem (for simplicity's sake, this chapter confines itself to the case of two coupled subsystems[17]) can be figured as a pendulum in its own right which is coupled to other spells in employment by means of an elastic link. In Coleman's terminology (1990), these are micro to micro-level changes like an individual's school-to-work transition and later transitions from work to training. A first attempt to develop a formal model of the theory of transitions and transitional labour market theory is presented in the appendix.

Transition Theory Applied to the Macro Level

On the macro level, the connection between the two spells of different institutional subsystems, here the education/training system and basic labour market institutions, ensures that, once the system has received an initial stimulus, the energy is exchanged between the subsystems. The coupling of the two subsystems, which can be altered or even removed at any time, makes it possible to formulate hypotheses on the links and feedback structure between different institutional arrangements and the likely individual trajectories influenced by these institutions as they evolve over time. In the social sciences, processes cannot be started and interrupted as if the researcher were conducting a laboratory experiment. However, in testing this theory, we have the advantage of dealing with long-lasting social processes. Most of these have long histories or event histories attached to them, which can be used in empirical tests of the theory of transitions over the lifetime.

In fact, in the field of education and labour market transitions, it is common practice to study just the initial transition from school to work, as if the link between the two subsystems were broken thereafter.[18] In comparative work on the school-to-work transition, the identification of the strength, rigidity or flexibility of the link between the two subsystems becomes an important issue in its own right, since it critically determines the probability of successful transitions to the labour market and later success or integration into the labour market. Since public policies, and specifically labour-market policies directed towards young labour market entrants, seek to influence this link, it is surprising that little effort has been devoted to testing hypotheses about the link between the two subsystems on the institutional level.

Comparative studies need to identify the 'coupling coefficient' of the two subsystems for each country separately. They also need to ascertain whether this school-to-work transition is a once-in-a-lifetime event or whether multiple transitions are possible and do actually occur. In the 'coupled oscillator' model, the two subsystems exchange energy continuously, so that in a system with close to equal mass one subsystem reaches a point of apparent standstill while the other is at its maximum potential. If this is taken to represent the conversion of the impetus from initial education into labour market potential, it becomes clear that experience in the labour market will also stimulate investment in further training. If further training gives additional impetus to the entire system, and carries sufficient weight at a later point in time, then it will further stimulate labour market potential. Allowing for a country-specific time-lag structure, which is determined largely by the 'coupling coefficient' between the two subsystems, any positive impact on labour market transitions of a trend towards modularization in the education and training subsystem should be measurable.

Taking as a starting point the outline of transition theory given in the previous section, we turn now to the kind of hypotheses that can be deduced from this theory. These testable hypotheses will be examined, directly or indirectly, in subsequent chapters. A general assessment of the empirical content of the theory will be reserved for the last chapter of the book.

Hypothesis 1: a stronger impetus for the acquisition of skills and competences in the initial education system will be translated into greater labour market success. In more conventional terms this reads as follows: stronger demand for skills and competences in the initial education system leads to greater labour market success.

Hypothesis 2: a higher level of educational investment in a given society, measured in terms of wider access to higher education, or an improvement in the quality of education will lead to higher labour productivity and subsequently higher average earnings.

Hypothesis 3: each country can influence not only the duration and quality of its education process, and the likely consequences for the labour market, but also the school-to-work nexus itself, and hence the transitional labour market at entry into the labour market.

These hypotheses can be derived from the theory of transitions based on the 'coupled oscillators' analogy. They demonstrate the potential influence on macro-level performance of the institutional link between two subsystems. With regard to hypotheses 1 and 2, it becomes clear that an education system that produces graduates with no regard to the labour market is unlikely to provide a sufficiently large impetus for a high-performance, productive labour market (in terms of GNP).[19] Hypothesis 3 is probably of more importance to the policy maker, since it states that the link between the education and labour market subsystems can be influenced directly rather than just indirectly, by improving the skill content of some general education courses and thereby altering the components of the education or labour market subsystems, for example.

Neoclassical theories would leave little scope for policy makers to address the institutional link between the two systems. Transition theory, on the other hand, allows them to address the link explicitly in order to enhance labour market performance by improving the coupling of the two subsystems. The question of whether job rotation or apprenticeship-type links are the best way of constructing the institutional link between learning and the labour market is, ultimately, an empirical issue. The theory of transitions and transitional labour markets suggests that both these ways of organizing the link appear promising from our theoretical perspective.

The concern with enhancing social integration – defined more broadly than the mere avoidance of social exclusion – can also be discussed within the framework of this theory. Social exclusion is likely to result in cases where the link between the two subsystems does not exist, breaks down over time or is explicitly cut by the introduction of institutional rules restricting access to 'second-chance' education or further training and to new media such as the Internet. The theory defines social integration in terms of access to transitions irrespective of any specific group characteristic. A necessary, but still not sufficient, condition for social integration is the existence of a link between the two subsystems. A more stringent definition of social integration postulates the existence of bidirectional transitions, in other words flows from the education system to the labour market as well as back from the labour market to education or training. Hypothesis 4 postulates that the more frequently transitions between education/training and the labour market occur, the higher the level of social integration of participating groups will be. Thus it remains to be determined empirically whether social groups with frequent transitions between these statuses, such as women, really do achieve integration or whether they attempt several times without success to enter or stay in the labour market. If the latter pattern is more prevalent, traditional segmentation approaches may suffice to explain the social process at work.

On the meso level, there are trade unions and employers' organizations that are known to enjoy varying degrees of autonomy in the collective negotiation of wage levels and wage structures. Much less research has been done on the extent to which the social partners also play a part in the link between the different social spheres identified in the theory of transitional labour markets. The role of the social partners in the labour market is readily understood, but (hypothesis 5), in those countries where they play a greater role in the institutional arrangement of the link between education/training and the labour market, a more dynamic and mutually enhancing exchange between the two spheres is likely to arise.

So far, the institutional arrangements have been treated as if they operate only on a single level of analysis, mainly the country level. Activities on the regional level and on that of the European Union have been assumed to be an integral part of a country's institutional arrangements. This may be justified for the sake of simplicity, given the modelling approach chosen here, but in practice it applies to fewer and fewer policy spheres. In accordance with transition theory, therefore, we propose hypothesis 6: since policy making at the European level is likely to influence the long-established societal consensus on the link between the subsystems in each country, policy makers should proceed somewhat cautiously and in small, incremental stages, rather than introducing sweeping, large-scale reforms. Experimental policy making which starts on a small scale is likely to be the preferred method of multi-level governance, since in that way little damage is likely to be caused in the event of failure.

Transition Theory Applied to Micro-level Processes

The general applicability of transition theory, which makes it similar in that respect to investment calculus or price/quantity mechanisms, makes it relatively easy to apply it to micro-level social analyses. Although institutional arrangements and the links between subsystems are largely given or predetermined elements in individual decision making, in longer-run processes a change in the link between two subsystems and its consequences for individual actors can be analysed on the basis of micro-level observations. Since this is also relevant for most of the empirical analyses presented in the other chapters of this book, the hypotheses based on micro-level transition theory will be derived in this section.

In transitional labour market theory, education/training and the labour market are identified as two distinct subsystems of society. While this narrows down the institutional arrangements of relevance to labour market processes (according to the five transitional labour markets; cf. Schmid, 1993, 1998), micro-level transition processes may well occur within these subsystems as well as between social statuses not linked to a transitional labour market, between unemployment and education or unemployment and inactivity, for example (Schömann, Kruppe and Oschmiansky, 1998, p. 4; Pangloss, 1999). The opportunities for applying this general theory of transition processes at the micro level are manifold, but we will concentrate here on those directly linked to education and training systems or to longer-term consequences of these training-related processes.[20]

We retain the analogy of the coupled harmonic oscillator in the simple form of two pendulums joined by an elastic spring. If it is to be applied to individual-level processes, the social meaning of each entity and the nature of the link between the two entities set in motion need to be clearly defined. In order to avoid confusion with human capital theory, we prefer to define the education and training sphere as human potential to be influenced through education and training and the second sphere as an individual's labour market potential. A high potential in one sphere (education), suitably matched by means of an institutionally organized link (elastic or rigid spring) will, according to the theory, be transferred to the other sphere in the form of a high labour market potential. This high labour market potential can be understood as high earnings, similar to a return to human capital investment, or as long spells of labour market participation with few interruptions due to unemployment. The following hypotheses based on transition theory can be derived from the original model:

Hypothesis 7: the attainment of higher education levels, usually combined with longer periods of time spent in education or a better quality of education in terms of labour market relevance, will lead to higher labour productivity and higher earnings, assuming there is a well-established link between the two subsystems. In the coupled oscillators model, the longer period or higher level of education is reflected in the further elongation of the oscillator.

If hypothesis 7 holds, we expect hypothesis 8 to be confirmed as well, since the further the oscillator is elongated, the longer the period of oscillation will be, other things being equal. Thus higher levels of education will increase the duration of labour force participation and of employment over the lifetime. The same mechanism is likely to reduce levels and durations of unemployment for the more highly educated, since these individuals received a stronger initial impetus in the full-time education system.

Hypothesis 9: the initial stimulus received by pupils in the education system is dependent on the parents' educational background and their labour market experience. This parental feedback to the children from their own education and labour market potential is likely to filter through to the performance of their children in the education system and subsequently in the labour market. This longer-run impact is particularly strong in countries with a high coefficient of institutional coupling, which speeds up the transmission of a stimulus from one subsystem to another.

Transition theory allows us explicitly to model the link between the subsystems. In this way, the analysis of the parents' role can be taken beyond that usually acknowledged in human capital theory to include the transmission of their own experience rather than just their investment potential, as reflected in their financial contribution to their children's higher education.

Hypothesis 10: the amount of education/training, the quality of education and the early experience of transitions all have lasting effects on labour market entry as well as on most other subsequent labour market transitions, including exit decisions from the labour market. In this hypothesis, it is argued that 'making and mastering transitions' can be learned in the early stages of life and that this implicit knowledge is valuable in the successful management of transitions to other subsystems, such as unpaid activities or unemployment.

Hypothesis 11: segmentation tendencies at an early stage in the education system, and particularly at the time of labour market entry, will be very hard to overcome unless mitigated by transitional labour market arrangements and policies deliberately aimed at the links between subsystems. In segmented labour markets, the link between each labour market segment and parts of the education/training subsystem will need to be established separately. This is likely to lead to a 'particularization' of society and, therefore, to the erection of invisible borders between segments that will hinder social integration.

Hypothesis 12: because of the linkages between different societal subsystems and the five transitional labour markets, we expect labour market exit, whether in the form of individual retirement, decisions by firms to implement early retirement programmes and changes in legal retirement ages or pension levels, to have repercussions on labour market entry and overall mobility patterns.[21] This hypothesis shows the potential for developing other hypotheses that address issues involving more than two subsystems. However, such analyses and development of the theory will have to be deferred to a later time.

A number of issues related to the transitional labour market of education and training or lifelong learning have not been dealt with in much detail. One of these is the gender dimension. As in most other general labour market theories, the gender dimension is treated as a specific case of a general process. This is also the way in which, for example, hypothesis 4 approaches a gender-related issue. A more adequate approach, and another extension of transition theory, involves modelling the transitional labour market between paid and unpaid work more explicitly in order to introduce the influence of an additional societal subsystem into the oversimplified two-subsystem model used thus far.

The theory of transitional labour markets can build on transition theory in order to clarify the relationship between transitional labour markets and approaches to the labour market based on flows or mobility. Transition theory, in turn, follows the theory of transitional labour markets in identifying both the relevant societal subsystems and the scope for adapting institutional arrangements in order to generate detailed proposals for improving overall labour market performance by facilitating transitions.

5. SOCIAL INTEGRATION THROUGH TRANSITIONAL LABOUR MARKETS

The difference between transitions in the labour market and transitional labour markets can be explained in terms of 'exogenous' and 'endogenous' flows within the labour market. Endogenous transitions are flows or mobility processes that occur within a specific institutional setting: that is, without specific political intervention. They include the mobility processes of employees both within and between firms as they move directly from one job to another. Similarly, the first entry into the labour market, as well as exit from the market through retirement, used to be analysed largely as endogenous transition processes. The scale of political intervention is one of the exogenous factors used to explain endogenous transitions processes.

In times of slack labour demand, job-to-job labour mobility is considerably reduced (OECD, 1995) and political intervention plays a more important part in stimulating labour demand as well as supply-side behaviour, as can be observed currently in the youth labour market. Transitional labour markets are an institutionalized form of assistance for these endogenous transitions mediated through various types of carefully designed labour market measures and regulations. Labour market policy in the form of transitional labour markets supports transition processes within the labour market as well as those at the time of entry to and exit from the labour market. Attention has been focused here primarily on the much discussed transitional labour market related to education and training, otherwise known as the school-to-work transition, and on other training related to labour market processes. Less attention has been paid to the transitional labour market related to further education and training, although it is probably more important in our age of rapid technological change. Both aspects have been dealt with in this chapter, since they jointly constitute the transitional labour market for skills and qualifications with multiple feedback between employment and skill acquisition.

The theory of transitional labour markets recognizes that, basically, all labour market flows can occur in both directions: outflows from unemployment are linked to inflows into unemployment. Transition theory starts from this premise and proposes a theoretical framework that allows the formulation of micro and macro-level hypotheses that will be tested in the following chapters of this volume. The proposed transition theory allows us to focus on subsystems and the links between them. Analysing three or more subsystems at the same time is feasible but involves computational complexities for mathematical solutions and derivations of precise hypotheses.

The purpose of social integration through transitional labour markets is to prevent unemployment; innovative institutional arrangements are put in place in order to increase the chances of reintegration into the labour market. Both the theory of transitional labour markets and transition theory emphasize the importance of a deliberate and purposive shaping of the link between societal subsystems. The ability of a well-designed education and further training system to foster multiple transitions and to provide renewed stimulus through the motivating effect of learning processes should continue to play a major role in policies of social integration.

In most European countries, higher qualifications and further training have been operating as a kind of insurance against the risk of unemployment. The role of labour market policies in the prevention of mass redundancies is also important in the negotiation of social plans (Kunisch, 1989; Kirsch *et al.*, 1999) which, to some extent, rely on retraining programmes for employees and, occasionally, on combinations of short-time work and further training. Job rotation, in which work experience for an unemployed person is combined with further training leave for an employed person, is another instrument for fostering social integration through integrative transitions and transitional labour market arrangements. In identifying the institutional arrangements necessary to achieve social integration in different subsystems, the role of transitional labour markets is to search for innovative combinations of seemingly unrelated fields.

The theory of transitions over the lifetime suggests a systemic combination of transitional labour market theory and the short- and longer-run impact of education and training systems, from which can be derived not only the central role of education, training and further training in achieving or preparing successful labour market transitions but also the long-term implications of training potentials. The theoretical foundation for transitional labour markets starts with the acknowledgment that early experiences with transitions in the full-time education system will assist labour market entrants in preparing for subsequent transitions. These kinds of transitions may constitute changes from general education to vocational training or moves between different branches of the full-time education system. The higher the level of general or vocational education achieved, the greater the probability of successful transitions into and within the labour market will be. This in turn enhances the integration potential of society. Not only the length of full-time education but also the highest level achieved, as well as experiences of education transitions, both vertical and horizontal, are regarded as important determinants of labour market integration later in the lifetime.

A major assumption of this extension of transitional labour market theory is that transitions such as that between employment and unemployment and back into employment are not just experienced passively, but can also be actively managed and prepared for in the early stages of life. This can be achieved in particular through a new understanding of the role of education and training systems in preparing for transitions at later stages. This new role for an education and training system consists largely of preparing individuals for major and multiple transitions over the lifetime. Research from various social science disciplines suggests that the highest level of qualifications obtained is an important predictor of successful labour market transitions. This applies not only to the first transition into the labour market but also to the education selectivity of unemployment. In other words, more highly qualified people are less likely to become unemployed, and among the unemployed the more highly qualified leave the unemployment register more quickly (Tuijnman and Schömann, 1996; cf. also the findings presented in Part II of this volume). The same rationale applies to transitions from dependent to self-employment or from unemployment to self-employment.

Transitional labour market theory, combined with the notion of education selectivity derived from human capital theory, labour market segmentation approaches or transition theory, makes it possible to deduce new roles for education and training policies. These new roles revolve around the link between the education system and the labour market. Whereas human capital theory stresses the investment component of education and training, transitional labour market theory emphasizes the market and institutional aspects of qualifications, skills, certificates and training transitions in general. From the perspective of transitional labour markets, it is necessary to identify which components of this transitional labour market correspond more to the market sphere and which correspond more to the institutional sphere. Both these elements are constituent parts of the composite system of learning and the labour market.

Traditionally, aspects related to the certification of skills or qualifications are assumed to be part of the institutional aspects of training transitions, as are all regulations governing further training in any specific sector of the economy. Firms' practices of 'awarding' further training opportunities on the basis of merit or status within company hierarchies rather than by calculating marginal costs or benefits mean that these aspects have to be incorporated into analyses of transition processes. The purpose of the empirical sections of the book is to determine where the balance between market or institutional factors lies in any explanation of processes of training transitions. The theory of transitions over the lifetime, in combination with transitional labour markets, highlights the fact that each transitional labour market incorporates institutional features which might be considered exogenous but which, viewed from an evolutionary perspective, might be seen also to have some of the features of endogenous processes, such as frequent rule changes or redefinitions of market boundaries (Rutherford, 1994).

In particular, attempts to compare particular national systems of transitional labour markets, training transitions for example, have to be based on an approach broadly rooted in political economy if comparisons of the balance between the market and institutional components of training transitions are to be meaningful. Transitional labour markets also direct attention to the role of actors behind institutions and to the specific transitions responsible for integration or exclusion tendencies. The role and strategies of the social partners and state representatives in shaping transitions and processes of social closure are the subject of the following, largely empirical chapters of the book. Both micro- and macro-level evidence on education and training transitions is needed to test the hypotheses presented above. The concept of a specific transitional labour market for training and education raises the question of who the 'market maker' is in a transitional labour market. Is it the state, firms, the social partners or individuals, or a combination of these actors? The role of each of these potential market makers needs closer investigation or some degree of enhanced endogeneity in the comparison of integration and exclusion processes over time and between countries.

The overall trend towards increased technological innovation, and the related fact that occupational skills are becoming obsolete faster, mean that training and further training have to be distributed more equally between the employed, unemployed and the inactive in order to avoid deskilling among the unemployed and inactive populations, and the consequent risk of social exclusion. In order to avoid a widening of the skills gap between those in employment and those out of paid employment, most labour market transitions will need to include a training component that allows individuals to keep pace with the rapid evolution of skills and competences within the labour market. The systemic character of transitional labour market theory reveals the potential risk of a loss of marketable skills among those temporarily out of the labour market. In the next chapter, the process of educational attainment and the influence of social background on exits from the education system are analysed in order to assess the different conditions under which the processes of social integration operate in the earliest phase of first entry into the labour market.

NOTES

1. Most of the hypotheses are directly tested in the following chapters of the book, which is the outcome of a three-year collaboration between the authors made possible by the fourth framework programme (TSER) co-financed by the European Union. In the initial phase of the project each participating team (France, Germany, Ireland, Netherlands, Spain) prepared a country monograph on the institutional backgrounds, major policy changes and processes in initial education, further training for the employed and further training for the unemployed. These preparatory papers (Albert *et al.*, in the present volume; Audier and Giraud, 1999; Gelderblom and van Bokhoven, 1997; O'Connell and McGinnity, 1996; Zühlke and Schömann, 1999) were essential in delineating the basic features of the theories presented in this chapter.
2. For other, more general definitions and discussions of the paradigms of social exclusion and integration see, for example, Room (1995), Silver (1995) and Cousins (1998).
3. Abell (1991) provides a useful review of Coleman's work for European readers.
4. At least this is my interpretation of Elias's (1939, 1991, pp. 10–11) remarks on the evolution of shame, which he denotes in more abstract terms as the social process of conscience development
5. The term 'societal institutions' is used to highlight the fact that it is society at large that creates and changes institutions. This extends the meaning of social institution to include the 'social intention' of institutional arrangements.
6. Both insider–outsider theory and the segmentation approach appear to be rather static in their design, since neither of them deals with the underlying processes whereby individuals are allocated to specific segments or the ways in which insiders and outsiders are formed in the labour market. It is not very helpful, in developing positive approaches to fostering integration, to identify outsiders without specifying the processes at work, since it is difficult to formulate effective policy measures to counter segmentation or to overcome the negative effects of insider power on the group of outsiders. The flow approach in labour economics deals mainly with macro-economic flows.
7. Cf. Schömann (1996) for an overview. The main data collection programmes referred to here are the European Labour Force Survey (ELFS) and the European Community Household Panel (ECHP). There has also been a new initiative recently to collect and harmonize firm-level panel data.
8. Cf. also Blossfeld (1996) and Goldthorpe (1996) who make similar arguments, although both authors focus on strengthening the link between large-scale data analysis and

rational choice or rational action theory. This may also apply to theories about institutions and processes within institutional settings, which may also benefit from a more detailed juxtaposition of advanced theories and recent progress in empirical methodology and data availability (see Bäckman and Edling, 1999, for a specific perspective on improving the link between social theory and empirical approaches).

9. One such example can be found in Schömann, Mytzek and Gülker (1998). Behringer (1998) deals with the example of job rotation schemes, in which unemployed substitutes replace employees on training leave.

10. The distinction (and relationship) between individual and group-level integration combined with exclusion was mentioned in the introduction. This basic distinction can easily be extended to other levels of aggregation. For example, otherwise well-integrated individuals and groups may be excluded as a region or country from international exchange or from an economic, social or monetary union. The world's poorest countries may have a high level of social cohesion internally but are excluded from large areas of knowledge or production for lack of 'hard' currencies.

11. This is partly an outcome of the extensive debate on an absolute or relative poverty line and the many different arguments that exist to justify the various definitions of the cutoff point (Boltanski and Thévenot, 1991; Bourdieu, 1993; Bourdieu and Jacobs, 1998).

12. Parkin (1974, p. 9) stated that 'the terms of individualist and collectivist modes of exclusion always coexist, if in different combinations . . .'.

13. For a more detailed investigation of long-term unemployment and social exclusion, cf. DeKoning and Mosley (2000).

14. There is also an intertemporal link between transitional labour markets, since marginal integration into the labour market over long periods can lead to social exclusion at later stages of life (Kohli *et al.*, 1991; Allmendinger, 1992; Sackmann, 1998; Kohli *et al.*, 1999).

15. The use of the term 'analogy' is closest to the fourth sense of the term below: 1. similarity in some respect between things that are otherwise dissimilar: 'the operation of a computer presents an interesting analogy to the working of the brain'; 2. (logic) inference that if things agree in some respects they probably agree in others; 3. 'the models show by analogy how matter is built up' (examining resemblances or differences); 4 model, theoretical account, framework (a simplified description of a complex entity or process).

16. We are aware of the risks of oversimplification inherent in such an analogy to the physical sciences. The issue merits much more detailed discussion, but this chapter focuses on the potential for generating testable hypotheses related to this theory.

17. The analysis can be extended to three or more subsystems covering the whole range of labour market transitions and transitional labour markets. Preliminary findings on the macro-level links between different spheres of social protection have been published in Schömann *et al.* (2000).

18. Despite the fact that an easily accessible further training system or the modularization of higher education makes an early transition to the labour market more feasible because of the 'rational expectations' of a potential return even to full-time education.

19. This appears to be a rather naive statement, but in the light of the predominant interpretation of human capital theory, in which the duration of general or even specific education, or just the level attained, is much more important than the link between education and the labour market, this widespread intuition needs theoretical and empirical substantiation.

20. Early retirement, for example, is one such process with a longer-term link to education or training participation throughout the working life.

21. Although their validity is limited by small sample size, some findings for Western Germany presented by Sackmann (1998, pp. 174–5) appear to show that the employment dynamic, that is job creation and destruction, is more influential in determining labour market dynamics than intergenerational competition. A similar conclusion could be derived from Davis *et al.* (1996), whose findings relate to job dynamics rather than individuals. In terms of transition theory, the essential issue here is to determine the relative weight of these processes (and subsystems) rather than assuming that either one or the other is at work.

BIBLIOGRAPHY

Abell, P. (1991), 'Review article of James S. Coleman, Foundations of Social Theory', *European Sociological Review*, 7(2), 163–72.

Allmendinger, J. (1992), *Lebensverlauf und Sozialpolitik. Die Ungleichheit von Mann und Frau und ihr öffentlicher Ertrag*, Frankfurt a.M.: Campus.

Audier, F. and Giraud O. (1999), General Education, Initial & Further Training and the Prevention of Social Exclusion in France (unpublished manuscript).

Bäckman, O. and Edling, Ch. (1999), 'Mathematics Matters, On the Absence of Mathematical Models in Quantitative Sociology', *Acta Sociologica*, 42, 69–78.

Baldwin, J., Dunne, T. and Haltiwanger, J. (1998), 'A Comparison of Job Creation and Job Destruction in Canada and the United States', *Review of Economics and Statistics*, 80(3), 347–56.

Behrens, J. and Voges, W. (eds) (1996), *Kritische Übergänge. Statuspassagen und sozialpolitische Institutionalisierung*, Frankfurt a.M.: Campus.

Behringer, F. (1998), 'Job rotation – eine Patentlösung für die Probleme auf dem europäischen Arbeitsmarkt', *DIW-Vierteljahreshefte zur Wirtschaftsforschung*, 4, 326–43.

Blossfeld, H.-P. (1996), 'Macro-sociology, Rational Choice Theory, and Time – A Theoretical Perspective on the Empirical Analysis of Social Processes', *European Sociological Review*, 12(2), 181–206.

Blossfeld, H.-P. and Rohwer, G. (1995), *Techniques of Event History Modeling: New Approaches to Causal Analysis*. Hillsdale, NJ: Lawrence Erlbaum.

Blossfeld, H.-P., Hamerle, A. and Mayer, K.U. (1986), *Ereignisanalyse. statistische Theorie und Anwendung in den Wirtschafts- und Sozialwissenschaften*, Frankfurt a.M.: Campus.

Boltanski, L. and Thévenot, L. (1991), *De la justification – Les économies de la grandeur*, Paris: Gallimard.

Bourdieu, P. (ed.) (1993), *La misère du monde*, Paris: Edition du Seuil.

Bourdieu, P. and Jacobs, H. (1998), 'Das Elend der Welt. Zeugnisse und Diagnosen alltäglichen Leidens an der Gesellschaft', *Soziologische Revue*, 21(3), 346–7.

Burgess, S. (1994), 'Matching models and labour market flows', *European Economic Review*, 38, 809–16.

Coleman, J.C. (1990), *Foundations of Social Theory*, Cambridge, Mass.: Belknap Press, Harvard.

Cousins, Ch. (1998), 'Social exclusion in Europe: paradigms of social disadvantage in Germany, Spain, Sweden and the United Kingdom', *Policy and Politics*, 26(2), 128–46.

Davis, St. J., Haltiwanger, J.C. and Schuh, S. (1996), *Job creation and destruction*, Cambridge: MIT Press.

DeKoning, J. and Mosley, H. (2001), *Labour Market Policy and Unemployment: Impact and Process Evaluations in Selected European Countries*, Cheltenham, UK and Northampton, MA, USA: Edward Elgar.

Elias, N. (1991), *Die Gesellschaft der Individuen*, Suhrkamp: Frankfurt a.M.; first published 1939.

Fagan, C. and Lallement, M. (2000), 'Working-time, social integration and transitional labour markets', in Jacqueline O'Reilly, Inmaculada Cebrián and Michel Lallement (eds), *Working Time Changes: Social Integration Through Working Time Transitions in Europe*, Cheltenham, UK and Northampton, MA, USA: Edward Elgar.

Gelderblom, A. and van Bokhoven, E.F. (1997), *Training and Social Exclusion – Some First Considerations from the Dutch Case*, Rotterdam: Netherlands Economic Institute (NEI).

Goldthorpe, J.H. (1996), 'The Quantitative Analysis of Large-Scale Data-sets and Rational Action Theory: For a Sociological Alliance', *European Sociological Review*, 12(2), 109–26.

Heckman, J.J. and Borjas, G.J. (1980), 'Does Unemployment Cause Future Unemployment? Definitions, Questions and Answers from a Continuous Time Model of Heterogeneity and State Dependence', *Economica*, 47 (187), 247–83.

Jordan, B. (1996), *A Theory of Poverty and Social Exclusion*, Cambridge: Polity Press.

Kohli, M., Rein, M. and Guillemard, A.-M. (eds) (1991), *Time for Retirement. Comparative Studies of Early Exit from the Labour Force*, Cambridge: Cambridge University Press.

Kohli, M., Künemund, H., Motel, A. and Szydlik, M. (1999), 'Familiale Generationenbeziehungen im Wohlfahrtsstaat: Die Bedeutung privater inter-generationeller Hilfeleistungen und Transfers', *WSI-Mitteilungen*, 52(1), 20–5.

Kirsch, J., Knuth, M., Krone, S. and Mühge, G. (1999), 'Erster Zwischenbericht der Begleitforschung zu den Zuschüssen zu Sozialplanmassnahmen nach §§254ff. SGB III', *IAB Werkstattbericht*, 5/19.4.1999.

Kunisch, P. (1989), *Personalreduzierung. Aufhebungsvertrag, Kündigung, Sozialplan*, Stuttgart: Boorberg.

Lindbeck, A. and Snower, D.J. (1988), *The Insider–Outsider Theory of Employment and Unemployment*, Cambridge, Mass.: MIT Press.

Mayer, K.-U. and Müller, W. (1986), 'The State and the Structure of the Life Course', in A.B. Sorensen, F.E. Weiner and L.R. Sherrod (eds), *Human Development and the Life Course*, Hillsdale, NJ: Lawrence Erlbaum.

Müller, W. and Shavit, Y. (1998), 'The Institutional Embeddedness of the Stratification Process: A Comparative Study of Qualifications and Occupations in Thirteen Countries', in Yossi Shavit and Walter Müller (eds), *From School to Work – A Comparative Study of Educational Qualifications and Occupational Destinations*, Oxford: Oxford University Press, pp. 1–48.

Mutz, G., Ludwig-Mayerhofer, W. and Koenen, E.J (1995), *Diskontinuierliche Erwerbsverläufe. Analysen zur postindustriellen Arbeitslosigkeit*, Opladen: Leske and Budrich.

O'Connell, P.J. and McGinnity, F. (1996), 'What Works, Who Works? The Impact of Active Labour Market Programmes on the Employment Prospects of Young People in Ireland', *WZB-Discussion Paper* FSI 96-207, 96-207, WZB, Berlin.

OECD (1995), *Employment Outlook*, Paris: OECD.

OECD (1996), *Employment Outlook*, Paris: OECD.

OECD (1998), *Employment Outlook*, Paris: OECD.

OECD (1999), *Employment Outlook*, Paris: OECD.

O'Reilly, J., Cebrián I. and Lallement, M. (eds) (2000), *Working-Time Changes: Social Integration Through Working Time Transitions in Europe*, Cheltenham, UK and Northampton, MA, USA: Edward Elgar.

Pangloss (1999), 'Travail, Mode d'Emploi', *Fondation nationale entreprise et performance*, 29.

Parkin, F. (ed.) (1974), *The Social Analysis of Class Structure*, London: Tavistock.

Rogowski, R. and Wilthagen, T. (eds) (1994), *Reflexive labour law. Studies in industrial relations and employment regulation*, Deventer: Kluwer.

Room, G. (1995), *Beyond the Threshold: The Measurement and Analysis of Social Exclusion*, Bristol: Policy Press.

Rutherford, M. (1994), *Institutions in Economics – The Old and the New Institutionalism*, Cambridge: Cambridge University Press.

Sackmann, R. (1998), *Konkurrierende Generationen auf dem Arbeitsmarkt – Altersstrukturierung in Arbeitsmarkt und Sozialpolitik*, Opladen/Wiesbaden: Westdeutscher Verlag.

Schettkat, R. (ed.) (1996), *The flow Analysis of Labour Markets*, London: Routledge.

Schmid, G. (1993), 'Übergänge in die Vollbeschäftigung. Formen und Finanzierung einer zukunftsgerechten Arbeitsmarktpolitik', *WZB Discussion Paper* FS I 93-208, WZB, Berlin.

Schmid, G. (1998), 'Transitional labour markets: A new European Employment Strategy', *WZB Discussion Paper* FS I 98-206, WZB, Berlin.

Schmid, G. and B. Gazier (eds) (2002), *The Dynamics of Full Employment. Social Integration by Transitional Labour Markets*, Cheltenham, UK and Northampton, MA, USA: Edward Elgar.

Schmid, G., O'Reilly, J. and Schömann, K. (eds) (1996), *International Handbook of Labour Market Policy and Evaluation*, Cheltenham, UK and Brookfield, US: Edward Elgar.

Schömann, K. (1996), 'Longitudinal Designs in Evaluation Studies', in Günther Schmid, Jacqueline O'Reilly and Klaus Schömann (eds), *International Handbook of Labour Market Policy and Evaluation*, Cheltenham, UK and Brookfield, US: Edward Elgar, pp. 115–42.

Schömann, K. (1998), 'Transitional labour markets: training and education', *New Institutional Arrangements in the Labour Market. Transitional Labour Markets as a New Full Employment Concept*, Berlin: European Academy of the Urban Environment (EA.UE), pp. 78–89.

Schömann, K., Blossfeld, H.-P. and Hannan, M.T. (1995), 'Institutional Dynamics: Education and Labour Market Segmentation at Entry into the Labour Market', *Comparative Social Research*, 15, pp. 103–27.

Schömann K., Kruppe Th. and Oschmiansky H. (1998), 'Beschäftigungsdynamik und Arbeitslosigkeit in der Europäischen Union', *WZB-Diskussion Paper* FSI 98-203, WZB, Berlin.

Schömann, K., Mytzek, R. and Gülker, S. (1998), 'Institutional and Financial Framework for Job Rotation in Nine European Countries', *WZB-Diskussion Paper* FS I 98-207, WZB, Berlin.

Schömann, K., Rogowski, R. and Kruppe, Th. (1998), *Labour Market Efficiency in the European Union. Employment Protection and Fixed-term Contracts*, London: Routledge.

Schömann, K., Flechtner, St., Mytzek, R. and Schömann, I. (2000), 'Employment insurance in transitional labour markets', *WZB-Discussion Paper* FS I 2000-201, WZB, Berlin.

Schumpeter, J.A. (1950), *Kapitalismus, Sozialismus und Demokratie*, Berne: Franke Verlag, first published 1942.

Schumpeter, J.A. (1964), *Theorie der wirtschaftlichen Entwicklung – Eine Unersuchung über Unternehmergewinn, Kapital, Kredit, Zins und den Konjunkturzyklus*, Berlin: Duncker & Humblot; first published 1911.

Schütz, H., Speckesser, St. and Schmid, G. (1998), 'Benchmarking labour market performance and labour market policies. Theoretical foundations and applications', *WZB-Diskussion Paper* FS I 98-205, WZB, Berlin.

Shavit, Y. and Müller, W. (eds) (1998), *From School to Work – A Comparative Study of Educational Qualifications and Occupational Destinations*, Oxford: Oxford University Press.

Silver, H. (1995), 'Reconceptalizing social disadvantage: Three paradigms of social exclusion', in G. Rodgers, C. Gore and J.B. Figueido (eds), *Social Exclusion: Rhetoric, Reality, Responses*, International Institute for Labour Studies, Geneva: ILO, pp. 57–80.

Tuijnman, A.C. and Schömann K. (1996), 'Life-long Learning and Skill Formation', in Günther Schmid, Jacqueline O'Reilly, Klaus Schömann (eds), *International Handbook of Labour Market Policy and Evaluation*, Cheltenham, UK and Brookfield, US: Edward Elgar, pp. 462–88.

Tuma, N.B. and Hannan, M.T. (1984), *Social Dynamics: Models and Methods*, New York: Academic Press.

Zühlke, S. and Schömann, K. (1999), Investment in Training and Social Exclusion – Institutional Framework and Empirical Evidence from Germany (unpublished manuscript).

APPENDIX

For the purposes of simplification, social systems can be split into subsystems, with a link between the subsystems of varying force. In a further simplification for modelling and demonstration purposes, we assume that the subsystems can be reduced to a single dimensional unit, similar to the mass points m_1, m_2 in a coupled harmonic oscillator.* The elongation of m_1 from the initial position 0 to a distance x_1 produces the force $-c_1 x_1$, which sets in motion the subsystem, and thus the whole linked system. Similarly, we identify the force $-c_2 x_2$ operating in the second subsystem. The force emanating from the link between the two subsystems is denoted as k'; it increases as the distance between the coupled subsystems increases.

The distance between the two masses is equal to $x_2 - x_1$ where the force $k'(x_2 - x_1)$ acts on m_1 and the force $-k'(x_2 - x_1)$ acts on m_2.

From these basic definitions, the two equations of motion for the whole system and the subsystem can be derived, as

$$m_1 \ddot{x}_1 = -c_1 x_1 + k'(x_2 - x_1), \ m_2 \ddot{x}_2 = -c_2 x_2 - k'(x_2 - x_1).$$

Using the notation ω_1 and ω_2 as the cyclic frequency of the two subsystems and k_1 and k_2 as the two coupling coefficients,

---

* Subsystems with more than one dimension can be conceived, but this increases the necessary mathematical operations and deviations to a large extent.

$$\omega_1^2 = \frac{c_1}{m_1}, \ \omega_2^2 = \frac{c_2}{m_2}, \ k_1 = \frac{k'}{m_1}, \ k_2 = \frac{k'}{m_2},$$

which yields the following equations of motion:

$$\ddot{x}_1 = -\omega_1^2 x_1 + k_1(x_2 - x_1), \ \ddot{x}_2 = -\omega_2^2 x_2 - k_2(x_2 - x_1).$$

If the coefficients of coupling k_1 and k_2 are small (or large) relative to ω_t^2 we state the subsystems to be loosely (or rigidly) coupled.

If we then specify, again for simplicity's sake, that the components of the two subsystems are sufficiently identical in the elements of interest to us here, $\omega_1 = \omega_2 = \omega_0$ and $k_1 = k_2 = k$.

We can solve the system of equations of motion as independent differential equations after adding and subtracting the equations and introducing the parameters

$$z_1 = x_1 - x_2, \ z_2 = x_1 + x_2$$

to yield

$$\ddot{z}_1 + (\omega_0^2 + 2k)z_1 = 0, \ \ddot{z}_2 + \omega_0^2 z_2 = 0,$$

with the general solutions

$$z_1 = a_1 \cos \omega t + b_1 \sin \omega t \ \left(\omega = \sqrt{\omega_0^2 + 2k}\right)$$

$$z_2 = a_2 \cos \omega_0 t + b_2 \sin \omega_0 t.$$

For example, assuming certain initial conditions in the subsystems such that the initial stimulus originates from an elongation in only one subsystem (in our case the education system) by distance C from the origin of mass m_1 without initial velocity:

for $t = 0$: $x_1 = C$, $x_2 = 0$, $\dot{x}_1 = \dot{x}_2 = 0$ which transforms, using previous equations, to

for $t = 0$: $z_1 = z_2 = C$, $\dot{z}_1 = \dot{z}_2 = 0$.

Recalculating using previous equations $a_1 = a_2 = 0$, $b_1 = b_2 = 0$; and

$z_1 = C \cos \omega t$, $z_2 = C \cos \omega_0 t$ and, using the original parameters x_1, x_2 from previous equations,

$$x_1 = \frac{1}{2}(z_1 + z_2), \ x_2 - \frac{1}{2} = (z_1 - z_2);$$ using the transformation $\cos \alpha \pm \cos \beta$

yields:

$$x_1 = C \cos\frac{\omega - \omega_0}{2} t \cos\frac{\omega + \omega_0}{2} t, \quad x_2 = C \sin\frac{\omega - \omega_0}{2} t \sin\frac{\omega + \omega_0}{2} t.$$

From this equation we can derive a more detailed application of this general theoretical model under the initial conditions specified above.

A loose coupling of the subsystems (small value for k) leads to a process called 'beating', where the range (amplitude) of the oscillation of m_1 has the largest value, the oscillation of m_2 is zero, that is, at standstill, and vice versa. The energy of the system is exchanged periodically between the two components or subsystems. This is in fact the social science interpretation of the following solution to the system's equations of motion:

$$\omega - \omega_0 \equiv \sqrt{\omega_0^2 + 2k} - w_0 < w + w_0.$$

A graphical representation of the link between the subsystems and the evolutionary pattern of varying elongations x_1, x_2 of the two subsystems over time can be depicted in a simple two-dimensional figure, with time being represented on the x axis and the elongation on the y axis.

An exception to the rule of the exchange of gradual transfer of elongation needs to be mentioned, although it is rare in the social science application chosen here. The exchange of energy does not occur if, in the initial condition, the oscillators start at the same distance from the origin, moving either in the same or in opposite directions.

PART I

Education Systems and First Entry into the Labour Market

3. Choosing between education, training and labour market entry

Cecilia Albert, María A. Davia, Virginia Hernanz and Luis Toharia[1]

1. INTRODUCTION

The demand for education can be studied from two points of view. Firstly, a social perspective can be adopted, in which attention is focused on the need for education in society at large. Secondly, the viewpoint may be an individual one, in which education is regarded as an economic good and the demand for education is the sum of all individual demands. In this chapter, the second perspective will be adopted and it will be assumed that those who either have already achieved a certain educational level or are still striving for it constitute the demand for that particular level of education. Decisions on education determine job opportunities, wages, occupational status and even retirement conditions. Our aim here is to understand better the determinants of the demand for education and the differences in demand patterns among three European countries, Spain, Germany and Ireland. This is a first step towards extending our knowledge of the other transitions individuals make in the course of their lives. Although this subject has already been much investigated, the novel aspect of the present study is that it draws on the first wave of European Community Household Panel data (hereafter ECHP) in order to compare the situation in various European countries.

Young people's decisions on education are taken within the structure of the education and training system as it exists in each country. Given that there are significant differences between the systems in the various countries we wish to compare (data availability has limited our sample to Germany, Ireland and Spain), our chosen starting point is a classification of educational levels that has the merit of being homogeneous, even at the risk of excessive simplification. Thus provision has been divided into post-compulsory education, tertiary education and vocational training. The reason for aggregating levels in this way is twofold. Firstly, it has already been used in international studies (OECD, 1997); secondly, the ECHP database does not permit the use of anything other than very broad classifications of educational levels, in order to facilitate Europe-wide comparisons. This is a limitation from the analytical point of view, but an advantage from the comparability perspective.

Our research work draws on transitional labour market theory, which focuses on institutionalized forms of assistance for endogenous transitions effected through carefully designed labour market measures (see Chapter 2). Endogenous transitions are those flows or mobility processes that occur naturally without any policy intervention (initial labour market entry, retirement, and so on). Our concern in this study is with earlier transitions, within the education system and towards the labour market.[2] In fact, education systems are already being designed in such a way as to facilitate internal mobility (entries and exits from different levels). To quote Schömann (Chapter 2 of the present volume): 'Transitions within the education system frequently prepare later transitions related to training or education. Therefore, there is a "training of transitions" which is a stepping stone into the basic principle of social integration by transitional labour markets.' Within this theoretical framework, our primary objective is to identify those factors that lead to earlier transitions being effected within the education system rather than out of the education system into the labour market.

The chapter is organized as follows. Section 2 is devoted to a description of the database used in our analysis and an explanation of how it can be used to examine educational issues. Section 3 compares the institutional framework (that is, the education system) in Germany, Ireland and Spain. It also includes some observations on youth labour markets and household formation patterns. Section 4 describes the samples used to analyse the demand for education. The analysis is completed in Section 5, where the main results derived from the models of education demand are presented. Section 6 offers some conclusions. The chapter is supplemented by two appendices. Appendix 1 deals with methodological issues and contains a presentation of the model of education demand used in the analysis. This model takes account of the selection bias that is usual in this kind of study. Appendix 2 consists of descriptive tables of relevance to the analysis.

2.   STUDIES OF EDUCATION DEMAND USING THE ECHP

Education-related decisions are taken over time and thus contain a dynamic component. This means that a very considerable amount of information is required if a deep understanding of such decisions is to be reached. More specifically, information on the same set of individuals over time would be required – in other words, longitudinal data. As already noted, the database used here is the ECHP. Since only the first wave of data is currently available, our methodology has had to be adapted to the use of cross-sectional information, which can at least be used to address the issues involved at any one point in time.

The European Community Household Panel is a standardized, multi-response and longitudinal survey. It was launched and is managed by Eurostat. It provides information comparable across the member states on income, work and employment, poverty and social exclusion, housing, health and a range of other social indicators relating to the living conditions of private households and individuals. It involves an annual interview with a representative panel of households and individuals in each country.[3] The survey covers 60 000 households throughout the European Union.

Since the major aim of the survey is to provide an up-to-date and comparable data source on personal and household incomes, certain other aspects are not studied in any great depth. One of these is education. The ECHP includes two main sets of variables on educational issues. Firstly, those interviewees who report their main activity status as being in education, training or apprenticeship are then asked what kind of education or training they are currently involved in. The answers to this question cover education, vocational training and other employment-related training schemes. Secondly, all the interviewees are asked about their highest completed level of education. We have classified the answers to this question in the simplest possible way: tertiary education, secondary education and lower than secondary. Finally, all the individuals are also asked whether they have ever attended a vocational training course. If the answer is yes, they are asked about the kind of vocational or occupational training they have received. A combination of the two sets of questions has been used to define three main education decisions.

1. When compulsory education is completed, the decision to be taken is between completing secondary education or leaving the education system, either to enter the labour market or for other reasons.
2. For those completing secondary education, the choice is between entering some form of tertiary education or leaving the education system, presumably in order to enter the labour market.
3. The third decision may be taken either after decisions (1) and (2) or instead of them. Once the individual leaves the formal education system, at whatever level, he or she can enter the labour market immediately or develop some more marketable skills through a vocational training programme.

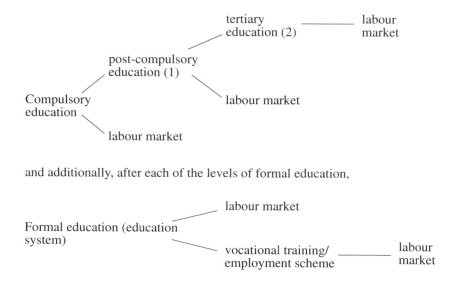

Figure 3.1   Main educational decisions

These decisions can be represented diagrammatically, as in Figure 3.1. In other words, at the end of each stage, a choice has to be made between going on to the next stage of education or leaving the system. These decisions will be analysed ex post, as the transitions are more difficult to observe. Taking the first decision as an example, for young people under 22 who have completed compulsory education a comparison between those who have gone on to complete secondary education and those who have given up before will provide a good proxy for the first decision defined above. Similar statements could be made for other decisions.

Our dependent variable is the decision about the demand for education. The ideal way of observing it would be through rich longitudinal data, which would make it possible to track individuals through the paths depicted in Figure 3.1. Since we are using cross-sectional data, however, we are forced to measure it through a combination of highest completed educational level and current course of study (where applicable). Thus, if somebody is undertaking a certain course of study, he or she is already demanding it, and in the case where he or she is not a student we consider his or her highest level of education as the level he or she has demanded (see Table 3.1). As far as the demand for vocational training is concerned, we consider two sets of responses. Current trainees/apprentices are defined as demanders for vocational training, as are those who state that

Table 3.1   Definition of demand for secondary and tertiary education

Highest completed level	Current studies		
	Tertiary	Secondary	Non student
Tertiary	—	—	Demander of tertiary
Secondary	Demander of tertiary	—	Demander of secondary
Less than secondary	—	Demander of secondary	Demander of compulsory

they have completed a vocational programme of any kind. (See Figure 3.2)

We have restricted our sample to young people aged under 22,[4] because of the very different structures of the households in which young people live in the three countries of our study, which is a hindrance to solid comparative work. Our first intention was to include young people up to 27 years old, for two reasons. Firstly, our demand for education variable is a

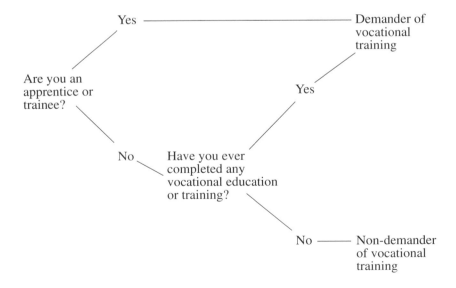

Figure 3.2   Definition of demand for vocational training

compound of highest completed level of education and current studies. Thus it includes youngsters who have either finished a particular level of education or are still studying to achieve it. Secondly, we wanted to observe as high a proportion of young people in their parental homes as possible, since family background is used as an explanatory variable in our analysis. It is clear from the distribution of the young population by relationship to the head of the household (Table 3.3) that to take the older age group in the German sample would be to lose a considerable amount of information on the family variables. Thus our study focuses on the first age group, that is, young people under 22, in order to obtain three roughly comparable samples.

3.   THE SPANISH, GERMAN AND IRISH INSTITUTIONAL FRAMEWORKS

This chapter is concerned primarily with a comparison of the determinants of educational decisions in three countries, on the basis of labour market and family background. Nevertheless, the institutional framework within which this set of decisions is taken, that is the education system and its links to the labour market, should not be left out of the analysis. Why are we interested in comparing the national education systems? Firstly, education systems are a decisive factor in determining the demand for education. People choose their course of study on the basis not only of what they want to do but also of what is available. Secondly, in highly selective systems, there will be a demanding selection process for applicants, which will act as an initial screening for the young labour force. Thirdly, some education systems have stronger links to the labour market than others, which could influence the decision to take the vocational rather than the academic route. A very interesting analysis of the influences of institutions on labour market outcomes (Allmendiger, 1989) argues that 'educational opportunities, and the very specific structures of the education systems, are as consequential for mobility in labour markets as are the attributes of the individuals who make careers in those markets'. Allmendiger identifies an important shortcoming in many empirical studies of the relation between education and mobility: educational attainment is almost always treated as an individual characteristic and empirical analyses too often overlook the fact that individual choices about schooling are significantly shaped and constrained by the opportunities the environment offers. The main features of the education system this author stresses are stratification and standardization, and he develops an empirical analysis of the way these features affect first transitions to the labour market and the initial stages of careers.

In highly stratified systems, there is a strong relationship between educational attainment and occupational status, whereas in stratified systems this is not always the case.

After this brief reference to the literature on the relevance of education systems, we now turn to the main differences between the three national institutional configurations (education systems, labour markets and household formation patterns). All three education systems have distinctive characteristics at all levels.[5] In Spain, post-compulsory secondary education, which begins at the age of 16, is divided into two main streams, general academic programmes and vocational training.[6] The general academic programmes (*bachillerato*) are the commonest option, and they lead to tertiary education. Vocational training has traditionally been considered as a path for unsuccessful students unlikely to benefit from a university education. The links between the Spanish education system and the labour market are still weak but under reform.

In Germany, post-compulsory secondary education is provided in three different types of school, namely lower, intermediate and upper secondary schools,[7] each of which leads to different educational destinations (vocational for the first and academic (university) for the last two). Even though the different types of school prepare pupils for different kinds of education or training, it is theoretically possible to switch from one path to another. The wider range of secondary education provision is also linked to a higher degree of stratification within the German system.

In Ireland, secondary education is also provided in three types of establishment: secondary schools, which have an academic profile and the highest share of the pupil population, vocational schools and comprehensive and community schools. The junior certificate can be obtained in any of these schools, and around 90 per cent of pupils then go on to obtain the senior certificate, which also may be obtained through general or vocational programmes.

Young people wishing to go on to tertiary education in Spain have not only to have completed the second stage of secondary education but also to take a national entry examination. However, this examination is not a great barrier to entry, since most students pass it. Available places are then allocated on the basis of grades obtained in the entry examination and on completion of secondary education. The supply of university places has increased considerably in recent years and access to university, even in medium-sized towns, is now easier. In terms of Allmendiger's classification, therefore, the Spanish system would seem to be characterized by a low level of stratification.

In Germany, access to university is conditional not on an entry examination but rather on possession of the upper secondary leaving certificate, or

Abitur. In practice, restrictions to entry are quite considerable, and applicants holding the *Abitur* may be unable to obtain places because their overall marks are too low. As Müller *et al.* (1995) note, 'access to tertiary education has been relatively restricted (. . .) by the rigid and highly stratified structure of secondary education. In consequence, tertiary education has been an area of exclusion and high privilege'.

In Ireland, access to tertiary education is provided by the Leaving Certificate Course in the general programmes or the Leaving Certificate Vocational Programmes, both of which are obtained on completion of the senior cycle of secondary education. Tertiary education is provided in a wide range of institutions. In addition, the post-leaving certificate courses have become a sort of intermediate level between secondary and tertiary education.[8] They are vocational programmes which encourage direct entry into the labour market.

One of the main differences between the Spanish, Irish and German vocational systems is the importance of the link to training in the workplace. In Germany, more than 90 per cent of those seeking to acquire an occupational qualification do so through an apprenticeship scheme in the dual system, and the high degree of credibility the institution of apprenticeship has acquired over time has led to the development of an idiosyncratic pattern of labour market entry. This stands in marked contrast to the weakness of the school–work link in the Spanish and Irish systems.[9] The German dual system provides apprentices with a nationally recognized qualification. In Spain, on the other hand, on-the-job training is still not given wide official recognition, while in Ireland apprenticeship programmes have an even lower profile. Thus the German vocational training system is the most standardized of the three, with the Irish the least standardized and, probably, the least stratified of them all.

As far as Allmendiger's hypothesis of a link between career patterns and the characteristics of education systems is concerned, we have been unable to compare them since this was not the aim of our research work here. Nevertheless, the good and bad patterns of labour market entry in each education system could be inferred from analysis of the youth labour market. The key figures in this area will be presented, with comments, in the next few paragraphs.

The other two main institutional arrangements that should also be kept in mind when describing the profiles of demanders for education are the youth labour market and household structures (measured on the basis of the proportion of young people in each position in the household). Table 3.2 below shows activity and unemployment rates for different age groups, together with educational attainment levels. This makes it possible to ascertain the relative positions of young people and of those with qualifications.

Table 3.2 *Activity and unemployment rates for different age groups and educational attainments*

Activity	Tertiary			Secondary			Less than secondary			Average		
	Spain	Germany	Ireland	Spain	Germany	Ireland	Spain	Germany	Ireland	Spain	Germany	Ireland
16–25	39.26	25.91	46.61	59.44	75.37	70.25	81.65	54.08	68.90	56.53	66.41	63.87
26–40	89.98	86.25	90.91	81.25	86.13	75.88	72.83	72.01	57.45	80.90	85.84	74.83
41–65	84.28	82.01	83.05	63.65	61.92	60.01	46.59	48.35	48.93	54.37	65.68	57.31
Average	71.81	77.53	71.85	69.68	72.46	69.45	55.99	55.05	53.01	64.13	73.03	64.85
16–25	46.81	16.25	17.28	40.71	8.70	25.02	40.76	39.24	33.03	42.06	10.06	24.72
26–40	16.55	5.84	4.66	22.06	7.43	14.18	26.23	15.83	36.22	21.48	7.16	15.52
41–65	4.26	5.42	1.78	13.70	9.36	9.00	17.53	15.87	19.30	14.36	8.50	12.09
average	19.02	6.02	6.79	24.99	8.45	15.97	23.24	19.55	25.26	22.93	8.15	16.53

Source: ECHP, Spanish, German and Irish first wave (1994); Eurostat.

Table 3.2 shows clear differences in unemployment and activity rates in the three countries. The unequal activity levels among young people with qualifications may give some indication of the length of time young people remain in full-time education in each country. In Germany, the highest youth activity rates are found among those who have completed either secondary education or a vocational training programme. This may be related to the higher availability of part-time and short-term jobs that provide students with work experience of great value for their future entry into the labour market proper. In fact, this group has the lowest youth unemployment rate in the three countries. Activity patterns in Spain and Ireland are fairly similar for the other two levels of education considered.

As far as unemployment is concerned, this is not only higher in Spain than in the other two countries but is also a more generalized or shared problem, since the differences in unemployment rates by level of education are less marked than in Germany and Ireland. In terms of Allmendiger's hypotheses on mobility, the most stratified education system enhances adjustment in the labour market, since it increases differentiation among individuals and prepares them in a more specific way for the labour force. In our study the German labour market, which is associated with the most highly stratified education system, is also the one which has the lowest level of mobility.

The superior patterns of labour market entry among young people in Germany are related to the so-called dual system of apprenticeship, which evolved out of the tradition of training and labour recruitment that characterized the guilds and developed into an institution which still today shapes the link between the labour market and the education system (Müller *et al.*, 1995). It combines in-plant training for the acquisition of practical knowledge and know-how and vocational training in educational establishments that focuses on more general skills. Firms are allowed to hire apprentices, subject to certain regulations, and they are in charge of the selection process. In Spain, the apprenticeship system is still very weak and only a very small proportion of young people receive their training through this route. Most young people opt for general secondary education and those who continue their studies do so through the university system, whose links to the labour market are still ill-defined. In Ireland, apprenticeships provide training in a range of crafts or trades and is the traditional path to skilled jobs in those trades. Apprentices are recruited by employers and are employed for the entire duration of the apprenticeship, usually four years. The formal educational requirement for entry to apprenticeship training is the junior certificate, but in practice most hold the leaving certificate. In 1994 there were only about 2000 apprentices in Ireland.

As far as patterns of household formation are concerned, their very

Table 3.3   Young people, by relationship to head of household

Age groups	16/21			22/27		
	Spain	Germany	Ireland	Spain	Germany	Ireland
HOH	0.60	7.80	1.79	8.90	36.60	18.66
Spouse/partner of HOH	0.80	3.00	1.25	13.10	23.80	14.80
Child of HOH	95.20	87.20	94.47	73.50	37.10	60.70
Other	3.40	2.00	2.49	4.50	2.50	5.83
Total	1913	671	1372	2078	909	1213

Note: Data are not weighted.

Source: ECHP, Spanish, German and Irish first wave (1994); Eurostat.

diversity means that the influence of family background has different implications in the three countries in our study. In order to illustrate this diversity, Table 3.3 shows the distribution of young people according to the role
they play in their families. The Spanish family model follows a
Mediterranean pattern, with most children living with their parents until
they finish their studies, and even until they have entered the labour market.
Access to the labour market has been delayed in recent years as a result
both of poor employment prospects and of the prevailing strategy of
accumulating human capital in order to avoid unemployment. Thus young
people tend to stay in the parental home until their late twenties and even
early thirties. In Germany, the exit takes place much earlier, motivated
either by earlier entry into the labour market or by the need to move away
in order to find work or attend university or college. In Ireland, the exit
from the parental home takes place at a midpoint between the other two
models.[10]

Taking household income as a measure either of the financial resources
available for education or of the family status individuals may seek to
attain, a first approximation to this variable is presented here. Table 3.4
shows the distribution of young people by the kind of education they have
demanded or are demanding and by levels of household income. The table
should be read as follows: 25.6 per cent of young people in Spain who have
demanded or are demanding post-compulsory education belong to households in the first quartile of the income distribution (that is, the poorest
group).

The average column shows the distribution of households with young
people by income quartiles. Taking this into account makes it clear that
demand for tertiary education in Spain and Ireland is more concentrated in

Table 3.4 Household income distribution, by demand for education variable

	Post-compulsory			Tertiary			Vocational training			Average		
	Spain	Germany	Ireland	Spain	Germany	Ireland	Spain	Germany	Ireland	Spain	Germany	Ireland
1st quartile	25.6	18.60	13.8	16.9	39.50	13.6	37.2	15.53	16.7	27.0	21.94	14.0
2nd quartile	25.1	15.38	23.9	24.5	5.19	21.5	24.6	19.48	21.4	25.2	16.53	23.3
3rd quartile	24.8	27.86	31.5	26.3	20.54	30.0	23.9	29.10	22.3	24.8	25.16	31.9
4th quartile	24.5	38.15	30.8	33.5	34.77	34.9	14.4	35.89	29.7	23.0	36.37	30.9
Total	1913	643	1346	1521	499	1094	1913	643	1346	1913	643	1346

Note: Data are not weighted.

Source: ECHP, Spanish, German and Irish first wave (1994); Eurostat.

higher income groups than it is in Germany, while the distribution of household income for those demanding post-compulsory education does not differ from the distribution of income across the whole population in all three countries. The distribution of demand for vocational training is very interesting. In Spain, those demanding vocational training are more concentrated in the lower household income brackets, while in Germany the distribution is more evenly spread, as it is in Ireland, although the extreme positions are reversed. This may reflect the low status of vocational training in Spain, where it is an option chosen by disadvantaged and poorer groups.

These various institutional characteristics are worth mentioning because they contribute to a better understanding of the analyses in the next sections. In other words, the empirical results have to be interpreted against this institutional framework.

4.　DESCRIPTION OF THE SAMPLE

The purpose of this section is to describe the educational choices of young people in Spain, Germany and Ireland. In order to facilitate comparison, young people are here defined as those under 22 years of age, as already noted in section 3. They are classified by gender and the following family background variables: parents' educational attainment, parents' labour force status and parents' socioeconomic category.[11] We have been able to identify the following principal features. Spain and Ireland have a higher proportion of people demanding post-compulsory and tertiary education than Germany. The tables below show the gross figures for the under 22 category (18 to 21-year-olds in the case of potential demanders for tertiary education). Tables 3.5 and 3.6, as well as the data in Figures 3.3 and 3.4, must be read as follows: the figure given is the proportion of potential demanders for each level of education in each category of young people that actually demand the corresponding level.

The main difference in Table 3.5 seems to be among those demanding tertiary education and vocational training. While demand for tertiary education is high in Ireland and Spain, the main alternative to higher education in Germany is vocational training. There are few alternatives to university in Spain and the majority of tertiary-level students in Ireland attend universities. In Germany, on the other hand, there are more vocational pathways for those wishing to acquire widely recognized, marketable skills.

Table 3.5 also shows gender differences in the demand for education. In Spain, for example, demand for post-compulsory and tertiary education is higher among women. In Ireland, attainment levels for men and women are

Table 3.5   Gender differences in the demand for education

	Post-compulsory			Tertiary			Vocational training		
	Spain	Germany	Ireland	Spain	Germany	Ireland	Spain	Germany	Ireland
Male	82.2	75.3	86.62	32.8	7.7	32.48	15.5	42.1	11.95
Female	89.1	70.9	87.20	35.0	13.6	31.42	15.3	39.1	11.86
Average	85.6	73.2	86.90	33.9	10.5	31.97	15.4	40.6	11.91
Total	1878	643	1345	1494	499	1093	1878	643	1345

Note: Data are not weighted.

Source: ECHP, Spanish, German and Irish first wave (1994); Eurostat.

Table 3.6 Demanders for various levels of education, by father's educational attainment

	Post-compulsory			Tertiary			Vocational training		
	Spain	Germany	Ireland	Spain	Germany	Ireland	Spain	Germany	Ireland
Tertiary	97.8	79.7	89.3	67.7	15.0	67.5	5.3	28.3	2.5
Secondary	93.9	74.2	88.9	38.5	7.3	40.5	17.3	48.5	8.0
Less than secondary	80.7	33.9	88.4	26.1	2.6	26.5	16.4	29.0	13.5
Fatherless	79.3	65.0	81.0	26.1	13.4	17.9	17.5	37.6	17.7
Total	1878	643	1345	1494	499	1093	1878	643	1345

Note: Totals are expressed in thousands.

Source: ECHP, Spanish, German and Irish first wave (1994); Eurostat.

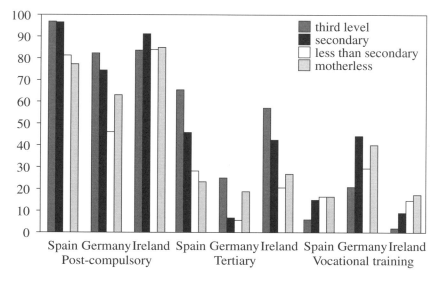

Figure 3.3   Demanders of education vis-à-vis the mother's education attainment

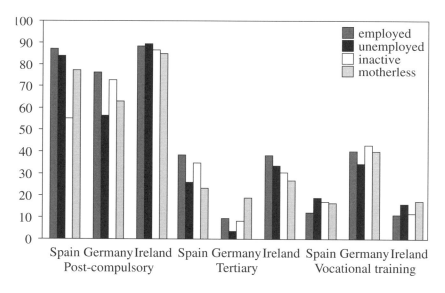

Figure 3.4   Demanders of education vis-à-vis the mother's labour force status

quite similar, but demand for both tertiary education and vocational train-ing seems to be a little higher among young men. This difference in the gender composition of higher education in Spain and Ireland may to some extent reflect differences in course content: certain tertiary-level courses in Spain would be regarded as vocational training in Ireland. It is in Germany that gender differences are most stressed. Among women, demand for post-compulsory education is lower than among men but higher than among men for university education, which suggests that once women decide to demand education they try to reach the highest level. Moreover, the female dominance of tertiary education and the male dominance of vocational training may reflect a gender segregation of disciplines and occupations, with the dual system providing training primarily for male-dominated occupations (typically skilled jobs in manufacturing industry) and the ter-tiary system focusing either on non-gendered or feminized sectors (service and public-sector workers, for instance).

The variables of demand for education are analysed in the context of family background. The focus here is on the relationship between the parents' labour market and educational characteristics and their offspring's demand for education.

The higher the parents' educational attainment is, the higher the level of demand for secondary education is among their children. In the case of Spain and Ireland, the influence is also strong for children of parents with a secon-dary or lower level attainment, while in Germany the children of parents who did not complete secondary education are much less likely to demand secon-dary education and, of course, tertiary education. Nevertheless, the average educational attainment of Spanish and Irish parents is much lower than that of their German counterparts: more than half of them have no secondary-level qualifications, while in Germany this is a residual category. This may explain the stronger duality among German demanders for education than among their Irish and Spanish counterparts. Comparison of the 'fatherless' and 'motherless'[12] categories is also interesting. Thus, in all the countries in our study, post-compulsory education tends to be demanded mainly by young people still living in the parental home; the demand for tertiary and voca-tional training, on the other hand, follows different patterns. In Ireland and Spain, tertiary education is also demanded by young people still living with their parents; in Germany, on the other hand, it seems to be a clear option for young people living independently of their parents. Vocational training also seems to be demanded by independent young people, although this may reflect different realities. In Ireland and Spain, on the one hand, it may be that young people who have undertaken vocational training entered the labour market early or that they were brought up by a single parent, which tends to be an indicator of low economic status. In Germany, on the other hand, apprenticeships may provide sufficient income to leave the parental home or may require trainees to move away from home.

Examination of parents' labour market status also reveals remarkable differences between the countries. In Germany, having one unemployed parent clearly restricts demand for tertiary education, while in Spain the negative effect is not so strong. Moreover, the demand for higher education among children of economically inactive parents is lower than among children whose parents are unemployed. Since this is particularly noticeable amidst mothers, the information displayed in Figure 3.4 refers only to them. Examination of socioeconomic category shows that children of professionals and managers in all three countries have a clear advantage when it come to taking up both post-compulsory and tertiary education.[13]

One interesting difference between the countries is the influence of mother's labour market status. In Spain, the mother's socioeconomic category is relevant only in the case of managers and professionals, among whose offspring there is considerably increased demand for higher education, while a poor labour market position (unemployment or inactivity) does not seem to affect demand. In Germany, a mother's low status has a negative effect on demand for both post-compulsory and tertiary education.

Differences in the demand for vocational training in the three countries are even more marked and reflect the different meaning of vocational training in the countries in our study. In Spain, it is regarded as a losers' option; as a result, the children of unemployed and low-skilled parents are more likely to participate in some kind of vocational training. In Germany, in contrast, apprenticeships have a higher status and apprentices come from a wider range of families. In Ireland this trend is not so strong, but the demand for vocational training is the lowest for almost all the categories of parental status.

As already described in the methodological notes, the next section will use several models of demand for education in order to examine the demander profile for each kind of education and training. The independent variables will be supplemented by the income of the household where the potential demander lives and the number of siblings whose main activity is education or training. Household income can be used as a proxy for the status the individual intends to achieve or the availability of financial resources to fund his or her studies. In addition, we will test the role of labour market indicators in determining the demand for education.

5.   THE MODELS OF DEMAND FOR EDUCATION

This section presents the preliminary results from the logit models of the demand for education in the three countries in our study. These models can be used to conduct a detailed study of the differences between these countries in the influence exerted by certain factors affecting transitions within the education system, which imply a different educational demand. The dependent variables in the models presented in this section are being (a) a demander of post-compulsory education, (b) a demander of tertiary education, and (c) a demander of vocational training, as defined in Section 2. Since this is a discrete choice model, the coefficients can be interpreted as expressing a higher probability (when $B > 0$), the same probability (when $B=0$) or a lower probability (when $B < 0$) of being a demander of each type of education relative to the reference category. Neoclassical theory has traditionally regarded the determinants of the demand for education as falling into two main categories: those derived from income and employment expectations and those related to family background. According to this theoretical framework, the coefficients in the model can be expected to have the following signs:

- the coefficient related to household income, which will be linked to the decision to go on to a higher educational level, will have a positive sign, indicating that the higher the income expectations related to a certain level of education, the higher the probability of demanding that level;
- the coefficient of the unemployment rates linked to the choice of a higher educational level that the individual observes in his or her environment is expected to have a negative sign. In other words, the higher the level of expected unemployment linked to the educational level to be achieved, the lower the probability of demanding that level;
- As far as the coefficients of the remaining variables in the model are concerned, the sign may be either positive, negative or null.

Appendix 1 contains an explanation of the way the self-selection problem is dealt with and the strategy adopted to estimate it.

Before we comment on the summary table of results, the main weaknesses of our sample and data base should be noted. Firstly, surveys of this kind have certain shortcomings when the analysis is focused on a very small part of the population, as is the case here.[14] Moreover, the use of aggregated labour market variables in these surveys may cause spurious correlation,[15] since they have been obtained from very small samples and the weight of some groups could have a negative influence on the reliability of the variable and, therefore, on the quality of the model itself. Moreover, in spite of the well-known literature on the correlation between many of the explanatory variables in our models, and in view of the fact that we have performed several tests to check their significance, we have decided to include them all in order to show the information they provide. These deficiencies are the cause of the relative lack of congruity between the results we obtain in our estimations and the ones shown in the description of the sample or those obtained in previous studies using different databases. Our findings must, therefore, be interpreted with caution.

Table 3.7 below summarizes the main results of the estimations. The most relevant explanatory variables are those that show family status, and in particular the father's educational attainment, and those that show the relevance of investment in education in the household, such as the number of student siblings. Thus the higher the parents' educational attainment is, the higher the probability of demanding both secondary and tertiary education is in all three countries, whereas the opposite is true of vocational training in Spain. The mother's educational attainment is also a status variable and is related in the same way to the probability of demanding post-compulsory and tertiary education. The educational attainments of mothers and fathers are quite closely correlated, so we did observe some improvement in the estimation when just one of the parent variables was used. Other family status variables are father's socioeconomic group and mother's labour force status. As expected, children of economically inactive and unemployed fathers are less prone to demand both post-compulsory and vocational training in Germany, while they are not a significant category in the other two countries; among the children of white-collar workers, there is a higher probability of demanding post-compulsory and tertiary education and a lower probability of demanding vocational training, as is the case in Germany. Having student siblings seems to increase the probability of demanding post-compulsory and tertiary education, but decreases the probability of demanding vocational training, which is more plausible among those who do not live in the parental home.

Wage and unemployment expectations, as measured by the regional average wage and unemployment rate of those of the level of educational attainment in question, are hardly ever significant and, even when they are, the relevant coefficients are quite low. This may reflect both problems with the data set used here and a possible correlation between family income and status and regional labour market conditions. The same applies to household income per capita.[16] Some of these variables gain significance and relevance in the model when the mother's labour force status, her educational attainment and one of the father's status variables are removed, thereby correcting the correlation between them. This is the case with income expectations in Spain. In Ireland, however, wage expectations are non-significant in respect of the demand for post-compulsory education and vocational training. Unemployment rates reflect employment expectations among those

Table 3.7 Binomial logit models: estimations of the probability of demanding each type of education

	Post-compulsory			Tertiary			Vocational training			Joint model		
	Spain	Germany	Ireland	Spain	Germany	Ireland	Spain	Germany	Ireland	Post-comp	Tertiary	Voc. train.
Gender												
Male	1.43**	−0.12	−3.07*	0.22	0.48	−0.49	0.04	−0.30	1.37	0.32**	0.32**	−0.06
Father's educational attainment												
Tertiary	1.42**	1.42*	−0.16	0.78**	5.94	1.16**	−0.85*	0.24	−1.24	0.56*	0.81*	−0.46*
Secondary	0.72**	1.42*	−0.13	0.04	5.95	0.40*	0.15	0.583	−0.40	0.35*	0.16	0.12
Fatherless	−0.12	1.11	−0.53*	−0.12	4.82	−0.40	0.26	−0.33	0.22	−0.12	−0.33*	0.09
Mother's educational attainment												
Tertiary	1.03	1.25	−0.23	0.38	10.60	0.86*	−0.41	−0.02	−1.70*	0.57*	0.77**	−0.94**
Secondary	1.24**	0.83	0.56*	0.20	7.92	0.29	−0.01	0.914	−0.32	0.71**	0.30	−0.06
Motherless	−0.09	1.455	0.79	−0.47	12.34	−0.06	0.01	1.00	0.23	0.52	0.06	0.17
Father's socioeconomic group												
Inactive	−0.04	−1.21*	−0.11	−0.38	−4.75	−0.03	−0.12	−0.41	0.18	−0.17	−0.21	−0.14
Unemployed	−0.31	−1.48*	−0.01	−0.25	−4.93	−0.18	0.47*	−1.72*	−0.53	−0.25	−0.20	−0.14
Managers and professionals	0.09	0.31	−0.03	0.36	1.92*	0.26	0.02	−1.04	−0.38	0.19	0.42*	−0.45*
Admin., services and other	0.87*	−0.38	0.22	0.27	0.53	−0.21	−0.20	−1.10	0.16	0.50*	0.23	−0.33
Mother's labour force status												
Employed	−0.18	−0.04	0.10	−0.04	−0.45	−0.03	−0.40*	−0.10	0.26	−0.05	−0.01	−0.08
Unemployed	−0.25	−0.75	0.45	−0.43	−2.80	0.20	0.13	−0.57	0.47	−0.24	−0.32	0.04
Student siblings												
One	0.72**	0.06	0.45*	0.43**	1.95**	0.52*	−0.37*	−0.64*	0.20	0.51**	0.60**	−0.25*
More than one	0.92*	−1.06	1.55*	0.91	−7.67	0.29	−0.78	−0.14	−0.28	0.96**	0.84	−0.62*

Table 3.7 (*continued*)

	Post-compulsory			Tertiary			Vocational training			Joint model		
	Spain	Germany	Ireland	Spain	Germany	Ireland	Spain	Germany	Ireland	Post-comp	Tertiary	Voc. train.
Not child of the HOH	0.01	−1.07	−0.65	0.51	−4.40	1.11*	−0.41	0.04*	−0.20	−0.39	0.76	−0.50
Wage expectations	0.00**		−0.01*	0.00		0.00	0.00		0.00			
Unemployment expectations	0.02*	0.01	−0.05	−0.01	−17.93	0.00	0.00	−1.07	0.01	0.01	−0.01	0.01
Household income per capita	0.00		2E-09	0.00*	−0.00	0.00	0.00		0.00			
Lambda				1.32		4.68					1.12	
Country												
Germany											−1.94**	1.67**
Ireland											−0.29	−0.22
Constant	−2.17*	−1.04	11.78*	−2.80*	−3.75	−3.97	−1.76*	−1.07	−6.17	−1.73**	−2.04	−1.73
N	1878	643	1345	1494	499	1093	1878	643	1345	3884	3098	3886
−2 log likelihood	1282.663	625.888	925.643	1619.817	233.472	1069.361	1478.451	715.213	863.758	2962.891	3013.218	3144.193

Notes: Woman whose parents did not attend secondary education, whose father is an unskilled worker, whose mother is employed and who has no student siblings.
* means significant at 95%; ** means significant at 99%.
Wage and unemployment expectations measure the average wage and unemployment rate in the region of residence for those who have achieved the level of education that is the dependent variable.
Lambda is the predicted probability value from the demand for secondary education.

Source: ECHP, first wave. Spanish, German and Irish data: Eurostat.

individuals demanding this level of education. Thus the higher the unemployment rate is, the lower the demand for education should be, since employment expectations are diminished. When this is not the case, it could be inferred that there is an imbalance between the demand for education and that for skilled labour or that labour market signals do not influence the demand for education.[17] This phenomenon (Albert, 2000) may have several explanations. The first and less risky one is that the unemployment rates used in the estimations are not representative, or they do not in fact measure the employment expectations of potential demanders for education. It may also be the case that education is used to mitigate the uncertainty that high levels of unemployment create among individuals. There may also be other factors that help to explain the very weak relationship observed between unemployment rates and education demand. Firstly, the results obtained may not hold for different kinds of tertiary education or vocational training. Secondly, the results might be explained in terms of the screening hypothesis, which postulates a certain, unavoidable level of overeducation among the labour force caused, not by the uncertainty produced by high unemployment rates, but by the need of the most productive individuals to send signals to the market in order to set themselves apart from the less well qualified. This effect is said to increase with rising educational levels.

Household income per capita has been used in order to control for size of household, and it has turned out to be significant (albeit with a very low coefficient) only for tertiary education in Spain. This variable is clearly correlated with the family status variables, and it becomes significant and positive when some of them are removed from the model.

The model of tertiary education has been controlled for selection bias (for a more detailed description of the process, see Appendix 1). In the specification of the model shown in Table 3.7, lambda (the predictor of the probability of demanding post-compulsory education) is not significant, but it gains significance when family status variables, which also determine the demand for post-compulsory education, are removed from the model.

Joint models have also been developed in which all the samples are pooled and a dummy added to represent the "country effect". This turns out to be quite significant for Germany when Spain is taken as the reference category and non-significant in all cases for Ireland. In the model of tertiary education, young people in Spain have a higher probability of demanding this level of education, while for vocational training the trend is completely the opposite. In the joint model there are some variables which gain significance because of the increased sample size. In the case of secondary and tertiary education, this is true of mother's educational attainment and the existence of student siblings. Despite this, the joint estimation of vocational training produces less clearly defined results, since this part of the education and training system differs so much from country to country, making the joint sample quite heterogeneous in this respect.

6.   CONCLUSIONS

The preliminary results presented here require further investigation and more extensive checking against other similar studies, since they do not seem to conform to the traditional models of demand for education. To date, some of the figures have been compared against OECD publications and an earlier version of this chapter, which was compiled on the basis of the Spanish Labour Force Survey and reflected similar trends. Many other authors have used wage equations to investigate this problem from the human capital perspective and have obtained results not far removed from ours. Examples include Duncan (1994) and Kodde (1988). In addition, Pissarides (1982) obtained similar results to ours in respect of family background and the demand for education (in other words, the higher the level of the parents' educational attainment and the better their socioeconomic status, the higher the demand for education among their children).

Our first hypotheses suggested that high parental educational attainment, income and status, together with high income and employment expectations, would necessarily mean a high level of demand for education. The level of educational attainment of the parents is a very important but not dominant variable in our analysis. Thus, even though the average educational attainment of German parents is higher than that of their Spanish and Irish counterparts, this does not mean there is a higher share of demanders for higher education among their children than among young people in Spain. The same applies to parental labour force and socioeconomic status, which seems to be less of a decisive factor in Spain and Ireland, where the impact of lower status on educational decisions is not so negative.

Labour market and income expectations variables do not have a direct impact on the demand for education in any significant way. Nevertheless, some sort of relationship may be inferred from household situation, although the exact nature of the relationship remains somewhat unclear, since the dynamics of the demand for education may respond to different incentives, one of the most important of which is the institutional framework.

Thus, although some of the trends in the demand for education we have identified could be regarded as 'normal' (that is, the relevant explanatory variables have the expected sign), there are some institutional arrangements, such as the education system or its links to the labour market, which seem to be more important. In Germany, for example, one would expect to find a higher level of demand for tertiary education; however, the highly stratified education system and the strong level of support for vocational training, together with its value in the labour market, mean that the vocational pathway is not necessarily regarded as inferior to the academic route. In the case of Spain and Ireland, the situation is radically different. On the one hand, there is no vocational training system that might offer an attractive alternative to higher education, as well as poor employment expectations. On the other hand, both countries have seen strong economic and social development in recent decades, which has brought with it a widening of access to higher education. The parental household, as another institution, also plays a different role in the three countries. While it seems to be the natural environment for those demanding higher education in Spain and Ireland, this does not seem to be the case in Germany, where young people gain economic and personal independence much earlier. In short, as was suggested in the introduction, the supply of education is a strong determinant of demand: frequently, those demanding education do not choose the kind they would ideally prefer but opt instead for what is available.

Finally, one last question: should these transitions in the education system be expected to have an effect on later transitions in the labour market? In our view, they should indeed be expected to have an effect, and the question is in fact a quite important and interesting one. In Spain, for instance, initial labour market entry has proved to be a particularly intractable problem that the education system has been unable to solve (Garrido and Requena, 1997; Albert *et al.*, 1998). Similar questions arise in Ireland and Germany concerning the mismatch between the educational and employment systems. The first transition that the demand for education is going to affect is that from school to work, which is the topic of the next chapter in this volume.

NOTES

1. We are grateful to Günther Schmid for allowing us to use to the ECHP data on Germany during the stay of two of the authors (Davia and Hernanz) at the WZB and to Philip O'Connell for providing the EHCP data and regression runs on the ECHP Irish data, as well as comments that helped us to interpret the results. Needless to say, both of them are exempt from all responsibility for any errors we may have made.
2. Transitions from the education system to the labour market are studied in depth in the next chapter of the present volume.
3. In the case of Spain, the first wave of 1994 includes 6000 households and 18 000 individual questionnaires, in that of Germany the sample size is 4800 households and 9400 personal interview, and in Ireland 4048 households and 9900 individuals were interviewed.
4. Obviously, in the case of the demand for tertiary education, the sample is restricted to those aged 18 and over, that is, the statutory age for entering university.

5. For a detailed description of these education systems, see Albert *et al.* (1997), Schömann *et al.* (1997) and O'Connell (1997) on the Spanish, German and Irish systems, respectively.
6. The Spanish education is now being reformed, and the differences between the general (academic) and vocational streams are no longer so great. Nevertheless, our empirical analysis was developed using 1994 data and takes no account of the reforms, which were at an early stage at that time.
7. The German terms are *Hauptschule, Realschule* and *Gymnasium.* Some *Länder* also have integrated comprehensive schools (*Gesamtschulen*).
8. Nevertheless, for reasons of consistency with our database, this level has been included in the post-compulsory category, since it is not tertiary education proper, and is also, of course, included in the vocational training category.
9. According to Eurostat education figures for the academic year 1993/94, the proportion of students on vocational training programmes involving both school-based and work-place training was 65 per cent in Germany and 7 per cent in Ireland. No cases were recorded in Spain, where most vocational training is provided in schools.
10. In Ireland in 1994, a significant proportion of young men were independent by age 23 to 24; for the overwhelming majority of young women, the change of status occurred at age 22 to 23.
11. Socioeconomic category is a combination of labour force status and occupation. It is intended as an indicator not of social class but of economic position.
12. The 'fatherless' and 'motherless' categories may reflect two different situations: the young person in question may be living in a single-parent household or he/she is living independently. No distinction is made here between these two situations, however, since the differences in terms of our dependent variables are not very great.
13. The information on this aspect has not been included in the text for the sake of brevity, but it is available from the authors.
14. Our interest in household variables, among others, has made it necessary to restrict the sample to the under 22 age category in the case of post-compulsory and vocational training and to the 18–21 category in the case of the demand for tertiary education.
15. We have also tried omitting this variable, but the results in terms of the sign and significance of the remaining variables do not seem to be affected by the omission.
16. No income variables have been included either in the models for Germany or in the joint model, since income variables are displayed at intervals in the German files, which makes it impossible to use them as continuous series.
17. This disparity between the employment signals sent by the market and the demand for higher education is in line with previous findings by Modrego (1986) for the Spanish case and confirms that the tendency towards overeducation is encouraged by the evolution of unemployment.

BIBLIOGRAPHY

Albert, C. (2000), 'Higher education demand in Spain: the influence of labour market signals and family background', *Higher Education*, 40(3), 147–62.

Albert, C., Davia, M.A., Hernanz, V. and Toharia, L. (1997), 'The general education system and further training in Spain', Universidad de Alcalá, Madrid, mimeo.

Albert, C., Juárez, J.P., Sánchez, R. and Toharia, L. (1998*)*, 'Las transiciones de los jóvenes de la escuela al mercado de trabajo: un análisis de flujos', WP-EC 98–24, Instituto Valenciano de Investigaciones Económicas) (IVIE).

Allmendiger, J. (1989), 'Educational Systems and Labour Market Outcomes', *European Sociological Review*, 5(3), 231–50.

Amemiya T. (1981), 'Qualitative Response Models: a Survey', *Journal of Economic Literature*, XIX(4), 1483–1536.

Duncan, T. (1994), 'Like father, like son, like mother, like daughter', *The Journal of Human Resources,* XXXIX(4), 705–15.

Eurostat (1997), 'Les Jeunes dans l'Union Européenne ou les Âges de Transition'.

Garrido, L. and Requena, M. (1997), *La emancipación de los jóvenes en España*, Madrid: Instituto de la Juventud, Ministerio de Trabajo y Asuntos Sociales.

Kodde, D.A. (1986), 'Uncertainty and the demand for education', *Review of Economics and Statistics*, 68 (3), 460–67.

Kodde, D.A. (1988), 'Unemployment Expectations and Human Capital Formation', *European Economic Review*, 32, 1645–60.

Maddala, G.S. (1983), *Limited–dependent and Qualitative Variables in Econometrics*, Cambridge: Cambridge University Press.

McFadden, D.L. (1974), 'Conditional Logit Analysis of Qualitative Choice Behaviour', in Paul Zarembka (ed.), *Economic Theory and Mathematical Economics*, New York: Academic Press.

McFadden, D.L. (1981), 'Econometric Models of Probabilistic Choice', in C.F. Manski and D.L. McFadden (eds), *Structural Analysis of Discrete Data with Econometric Applications*, Cambridge, MA, MIT Press.

Modrego, A. (1986), 'Determinantes de la demanda de educación superior: Estimación de un modelo de demanda de educación superior para la provincia de Vizcaya', PhD dissertation, Universidad del País Vasco.

Müller, W., Steinmann, S. and Ell, R. (1995), *Education and Labour Market Entry in Germany*, AB 1/Nr 10, Mannheim: Mannheimer Zentrum für Europäische Sozialforschüng.

O'Connell, P.J. (1997), 'The Irish System of Education and Training', Economic and Social Research Institute, Dublin, mimeo.

OECD (1997), *Education at a Glance*, Paris: OECD.

Pissarides, C. (1982), 'From School to University: The Demand for Post-compulsory Education in Britain', *The Economic Journal*, 92, 654–67.

Schömann, K. and Zühlke, S. (1997), 'Investment in Training and Social Exclusion – Institutional Framework and Empirical Evidence from Germany', Wissenschaftszentrum Berlin für Sozialforschung and Max Plank Institute for Human Development and Education, mimeo.

Venti, S.F. and Wise, D.A. (1983), 'Individual Attributes and Self-Selection of Higher Education', *Journal of Public Economics*, 21, 1–32.

APPENDIX 1   METHODOLOGY: A SECONDARY AND TERTIARY EDUCATION DEMAND MODEL INCLUDING LABOUR MARKET VARIABLES AND SELECTIVITY BIASES

Our purpose here is to present the model used in this chapter to estimate the demand for secondary and tertiary education. Our main references are Modrego (1986) and Kodde (1986), who incorporate the influence of labour market conditions on education demand into their model, and Venti and Wise (1983), who take into account the selection bias in the sample.

Our model, unlike that of Venti and Wise (1983), does not include either the quality of the school attended or the costs associated with each particular university, mainly because such information is not available to us.

The problem of tertiary education demand is intrinsically linked to that of self-selection, and selection is a process not studied here. In other words, the process of selection in those phases of the education system leading up to higher secondary education will have particular effects on the demand for tertiary education. Figure 3.1 depicts the series of decisions taken prior to the decision that is our concern here.

Firstly, individuals completing compulsory education have to decide whether to continue into upper secondary education ($Si > 0$) or to enter the labour market. Only those who obtain the upper secondary leaving certificate may enter tertiary education ($Ti > 0$); alternatively, they may choose to enter the labour market.

The two decisions depicted in Figure 3.1 and labelled (1) and (2) can be expressed as two choice equations:

$$Pr\,(S_i > 0) = Pr\,(X_{Mi}\beta_{0\,i} > -\varepsilon_{0i}) = 1 - F\,(X_{Mi}\beta_{0i}) \qquad (3.1)$$

and

$$Pr\,(T_i > 0/S_i > 0) = Pr\,(X_{Ui}\beta_{1i} > -\varepsilon_{1i}) = 1 - F\,(X_{Ui}\beta_{1i}), \qquad (3.2)$$

in which X_{Mi} and X_{Ui} are two vectors of exogenous personal characteristics and employment opportunities influencing the decision to continue in secondary education and tertiary education. The β terms are unknown parameter vectors and the ε terms are unobservable errors; the F is the distribution function associate.

In order to study the influence of the first decision on the decision to enter tertiary education we may write:

$$P(T_i > 0) = P(T_i > 0/S_i > 0) * P(S_i > 0). \qquad (3.3)$$

Substituting equations 1 and 2 into equation 3, the following expression is obtained:

$$Pr\,(T_i > 0\,) = (1 - F\,(X_{Ui}\beta_{1i}))*(1 - F\,(X_{Mi}\beta_{0i})). \qquad (3.4)$$

The strategy for estimating equation (3.4) consists of the estimation of a stage logit model, in which it is assumed that the error terms in equations (3.1) and (3.2) are independent, making it easy to extend Heckman–Lee two-stage estimation methods to this model (Maddala, 1983).

In the first stage, the probability of completing secondary education is estimated. In the second stage, the probability that an individual will demand tertiary education is estimated, with the previously estimated probability of completing secondary education included as an explanatory variable.

It is evident that parameters β_{0i} and β_{1i} can be estimated only if there is at least one non-overlapping variable in either X_{Mi} and X_{Ui}, (Maddala, 1983). Otherwise, it would not be known which estimates refer to β_{0i} and which refer to β_{1i} (see Amemiya, 1981; Maddala, 1983; McFadden, 1974, 1981).

The main advantage of this model is that it permits analysis of the relationship between the probability of demanding secondary-level education and the probability of demanding tertiary education.

APPENDIX 2

Table 3A.1   Descriptives of the main variables used in the analysis

	Post-compulsory and vocational training (16–21-year-olds)			Tertiary (18–21-year-olds)		
	Spain	Germany	Ireland	Spain	Germany	Ireland
Gender						
Male	51.60	53.49	51.67	51.27	55.8	51.97
Female	48.40	46.51	48.33	48.73	44.2	48.03
Father's educational attainment						
Tertiary	12.51	25.43	10.33	12.38	25.6	10.34
Secondary	21.41	52.40	28.92	19.88	51.0	27.81
Less than secondary	52.02	4.03	44.01	53.01	3.4	44.74
Fatherless	14.06	18.14	16.73	14.73	20.0	17.11
Mother's educational attainment						
Tertiary	6.60	10.70	7.88	6.49	10.4	7.78
Secondary	23.22	73.95	43.35	22.16	71.8	42.82
Less than secondary	63.31	3.41	41.64	63.59	3.4	41.90
Motherless	6.87	11.94	7.14	7.76	14.4	7.50
Father's socioeconomic group						
Inactive	12.14	3.10	8.85	12.85	3.4	8.87
Unemployed	7.61	2.79	6.47	8.23	2.4	6.22
Managers and professionals	19.65	29.30	25.28	18.61	27.4	24.79
Admin., serv. and other	7.61	3.72	4.39	7.63	3.8	4.48
Farmers and unskilled	38.92	42.95	38.29	37.95	43.0	38.52
Fatherless	14.06	18.14	16.73	14.73	20.0	17.11

Table 3A.1 (continued)

	Post-compulsory and vocational training (16–21-year-olds)			Tertiary (18–21-year-olds)		
	Spain	Germany	Ireland	Spain	Germany	Ireland
Mother's labour force status						
Employed	27.90	60.62	28.77	27.24	58.4	28.73
Unemployed	9.48	5.58	2.45	9.04	4.6	2.10
Inactive	55.75	21.86	61.64	55.96	22.6	61.67
Motherless	6.87	11.94	7.14	7.76	14.4	7.50
Student siblings						
None	62.41	74.42	63.79	61.51	70.8	61.76
One	25.61	14.42	27.06	25.77	15.2	28.36
More than one	6.92	0.47	5.35	7.10	0.6	5.67
Not child of HOH	5.06	10.70	3.79	5.62	13.4	4.21
Total	1878	645	1345	1494	500	1093

	Spain		Germany		Ireland	
	Mean	s.d.	Mean	s.d.	Mean	s.d.
Post-compulsory						
Average wage	870.74	196.05			971.56	203.49
Unemployment rate	25.76	7.50	8.77	7.36	15.93	3.51
Household income per capita	345.22	229.70			373.29	246.19
Tertiary						
Average wage	1336.32	222.38			1536.56	291.99
Unemployment rate	18.54	4.22	4.08	1.63	5.36	2.77
Household income per capita	345.26	232.09			384.97	252.25
Vocational training						
Average wage	1085.68	238.71			1069.39	206.79
Unemployment rate	23.84	5.10	7.61	7.14	15.90	6.22
Household income per capita	345.22	229.70			373.29	246.19

Notes: Average wages and household income per capita are expressed in ecu; German income data were not included since they are not available as continuous variables.

Source: ECHP, first wave, Spanish, German and Irish data; Eurostat.

4.   Segmentation in the labour market: an analysis of recruitment

Florence Audier

1.   INTRODUCTION

The purpose of this chapter is to analyse and compare the transition from school to the labour market and to show that young beginners[1] have particular modes of labour market entry which, in most European countries, are heavily influenced by their individual level of education. Rather than dealing with macro-level issues of recruitment patterns over the business cycle or relative cohort size, our analysis is focused on individual level data from the European Labour Force Survey (ELFS) and initial transitions into the labour market.

Several studies have shown that young men and women leaving school, university or any other educational institution experience difficulties in finding a job. The difficulties not only vary from country to country but also depend, within each country, on employers' strategies for recruiting manpower without any labour market experience (Audier, 1995; Elbaum and Marchand, 1993; Freysson, 1997; IRES, 1995; OECD, 1998; Shavit and Müller, 1998; Fondeur and Lefresne, 1999). Some employers prefer to hire adults able to be highly productive without delay. Others are more willing to recruit beginners, although they sometimes lay down significant preconditions as to the level of vocational training or general education, as if to counterbalance their lack of experience. In some cases, employers seem to reserve some jobs expressly for youngsters while making others quite inaccessible to them (Bilans formation-emploi, 1983–96). Depending on the sector and country in question, these 'reserved' jobs are either unskilled or, at the opposite extreme, very highly skilled ones.

Employers may indeed use a number of different criteria to sort among the labour force. Some, such as the type of vacancy, are familiar from segmentation theory. Thus some jobs may be part of the primary labour market. Such jobs will be related to the firm's core activities and be based on long-term employment contracts, good career opportunities and potential pay rises. Others will be part of the secondary market, with unstable employment contracts, weak links to the firm and low wages. Transitions between the two types of labour markets are difficult.

Even if firms' behaviour is increasingly being determined by external conditions, such as the product market and the degree of competition in the market, certain institutional features also influence the size and the stability of internal markets. The characteristics and the total number of job seekers in the labour market also matter. As a result, the various labour force categories do not seem to be equally involved in the recruitment process.

Several case studies have demonstrated that most firms' recruitment practices vary widely between different labour force categories, depending mainly on educational and skill levels. Thus in order to analyse social exclusion processes during initial contacts with the labour market, account has to be taken of the nature of the vacancies for which young people leaving the educational system are recruited.

Similarly, we need to analyse in more detail the types of activities in which young people are employed. Indeed, there are considerable disparities depending on the economic history of the various sectors in an economy, their models of labour–management relations, their skill scales, their sensitivity to market competition and other factors. Segmentation theory would also suggest that different economic sectors have different recruitment strategies for young employees, while transitional labour market theory suggests that there is a specific transitional labour market at entry into the labour market for young people. According to transitional labour market theory, however, there would be one single transitional labour market at entry, whereas segmentation theory predicts the existence of at least two different segments for young people entering the labour market. And approaches that posit the existence of widespread industrial segmentation argue that each industrial sector develops its own very specific entry patterns that will limit subsequent job mobility between economic sectors. To sum up, examination of sectoral recruitment patterns and the integration of young people into segmented labour markets yields important information on the nature of employment contracts and the career prospects offered to labour market entrants, as well as on their potential mobility (Schömann *et al.*, 1995).

Therefore we will try, in this chapter, to describe as precisely as possible what happens to school leavers when they arrive in the labour market a few months after the end of their initial full-time educational career. Our basic comparative strategy is twofold. Firstly, we will be conducting comparisons of school leavers and other categories of employees recruited at the same time and in the same country in order to ascertain whether the school leavers' situation is specific or similar to that of other employees recruited at the same time by firms in similar economic sectors.

Secondly, we will be comparing different countries in order to test whether the national situation is very specific or similar to that in other European countries. If strong similarities are found, it would be interesting to investigate whether labour management practices in these sectors are very similar in the countries in question. It would be necessary to analyse here all the consequences of these recruitment patterns, focusing particularly on the social exclusion processes connected to specific kinds of labour management practices. Six countries are examined in more detail: Germany, the Netherlands, Ireland, Spain, the UK and France.

With specific regard to young labour market entrants, the main questions we are trying to answer are the following. Who is most likely to be employed and who is at risk of social exclusion? What kind of jobs do labour market entrants find? Which sectors are relatively open to young school leavers? What is the influence of their educational level? More generally, are these characteristics of young employees linked to segmentation in the labour market, and is it common to all countries? To sum up, are these beginners allocated to a special labour market, and are there strong similarities between the different countries?

2. DATA AND DEFINITIONS USED IN THE ANALYSES

The LFS-Eurostat data (Freysson, 1996; Schömann and Kruppe, 1998) are of value in any attempt to answer these questions, since they can be used to evaluate labour market *flows* as well as *stocks*. This makes it possible to compare the labour market situation of young people to that of other employees. In fact, the data are not wholly suited to this objective, because they provide only a rather approximate description of the individual situation one year before the observation. All we can retrieve from the known data is whether the person was employed at the time of the survey; if not, his or her former situation is captured by one of four categories: non-employment, unemployment, in education or training, conscription (military or community service) and 'other'.

The data are no more precise when it comes to evaluating the flow of recruitment or the transition. We know simply whether the person was working at the time of the survey and when he or she started the current job. In the analyses presented below, the following convention is adopted. The flow of persons recruited within the year is composed of *all those recruited in the 12 months prior to the observation period, together with those recruited during the few months between the survey date and the beginning of the current year.*

The following example should clarify why the recruitment flow had to be defined in this way. The recruitment flow for 1995 is made up of all those who *had a job* in the spring of 1995 and had started their current job either during the year 1994 or during the period between January 1995 and the date of the survey (in most countries it is in March or April).[2] This flow is broken down according to the previous situation of those recruited. The European Labour Force Survey asks persons about their occupation one year before the survey: employment in *another* firm, unemployment, training, military service or some other kind of non-employment. Of course, particular attention is paid to young labour market entrants.[3]

The year 1995 was chosen as the base year for constructing comparisons between the different employment statuses and countries. In fact, the data for 1992 are not sufficiently harmonized and one rather important sample is not correctly identified. On the other hand, the most recent year available at the time was 1996, but in some countries the population is very low, as a result of changes to the national surveys themselves. All these problems preclude any comparison covering a longer period, such as the first half of the 1990s, as was intended in the original design of the analysis.

In the following, we will be examining, firstly, whether young entrants in the countries under consideration here represent only a small part of total hiring and, secondly, if the important role played by level of education in the recruitment of young people is also confirmed for other, older persons recruited at around the same time. In view of the differences between the educational level of those individuals more likely to be recruited, and comparing the economic sectors in which they find employment, we test whether young labour market entrants are in competition for the same jobs as more experienced employees. We also test whether young people go into – or are chosen for – jobs in the same kind of firms. Finally, we ask whether they are positioned in the same 'segments' in different countries.

3.   THE SHARE OF YOUNG ENTRANTS IN TOTAL NEW HIRING

On the basis of the empirical evidence from the European Labour Force Survey, we find that young labour market entrants represent only a small minority of total new hiring during the course of a year. However, the recruitment rate for young persons differs considerably across the European countries. Differences in the shares of services in total employment, in economic cycles and in cohort sizes have an impact on the hiring of young entrants in ways that are difficult to assess. Moreover, labour law, particularly employment protection legislation, might in some countries even be encouraging new, legal forms of employment, resulting in increased shares of self-employment.

In the six countries that concern us here, what might be called the 'renewal rate' (that is the proportion of employees who started their current job – as at spring 1995 – at the earliest in January 1994) is between 14 and 29 per cent of the total labour force. This also provides an indication of the relative chance of starting a new job. The lowest rate is in Germany and the highest in Spain (twice the German rate). The rates for France, the Netherlands and Ireland are not markedly different from each other, at least compared to the very high rates in the UK and Spain. In any case, it is remarkable that the renewal rate for women is higher than that for men in all the countries studied except Spain. The maximum variation was in Ireland (50 per cent greater for women, cf. Table 4.1).

Table 4.1 Proportion of employees who started in their current job (as at spring 1995) after 1 January 1994

	Men and women	Men	Women
Germany	14.3	13.5	15.4
France	15.9	15.7	16.2
NL	17.2	15.0	20.3
UK	22.4	20.5	24.7
Ireland	18.8	16.3	23.0
Spain	29.4	35.1	31.4

This raises a number of questions about these renewal rates. For instance, why are the female rates generally higher than the male ones? Is it due only to their frequent choice of inactivity (Auer, 1998), or is it the consequence of their rather fragile position in the labour market? On the other hand, is it a positive sign that women have found it easier than men to obtain jobs in recent years? More generally, do these rates reflect trends in labour market participation? What is the correct interpretation when those rates are high? Do they reflect a positive development in recruitment? Or, on the contrary, are they a symptom of a generalized tendency to offer short-term contracts, a practice that forces workers to change jobs very frequently (Schömann, Rogowski and Kruppe, 1998)? To interpret these results, it is helpful to clarify the previous labour market status of the new recruits.

Job Changers Account for the Greatest Share of Recruitment

Table 4.2 and Figure 4.1 give a general overview of the previous employment status of all those in post in spring 1995 who had been recruited for their current job after January 1994, first for men and women together and then for each gender separately.

Table 4.2   The previous situation of new recruits, 1995

Men and women	Germany	France	NL	UK	Ireland	Spain
Mobility[a]	63.3	48.6	54.8	60.3	58.9	58.7
Unemployment[a]	15.6	26.4	14.8	13.4	17.0	27.2
School[a]	13.0	11.4	14.8	13.6	17.4	5.4
Military service[a]	1.0	2.9	1.9	—	—	1.5
Other situations	7.1	10.6	13.7	12.7	6.7	7.2
Total[b]	100	100	100	100	100	100
	(5120)[c]	(3507)	(1163)	(5799)	(237)	(3774)

Men	Germany	France	NL	UK	Ireland	Spain
Mobility	67.4	51.8	59.1	62.9	61.6	60.8
Unemployment	14.1	26.7	15.1	16.7	20.8	27.7
School	12.7	9.5	14.7	13.0	16.4	4.5
Military service	1.8	5.3	3.7	—	—	2.4
Other situations	4.0	6.7	7.4	7.4	1.2	4.6
Total[b]	100	100	100	100	100	100
	(2789)[c]	(1924)	(603)	(2940)	(128)	(2319)

Women	Germany	France	NL	UK	Ireland	Spain
Mobility	58.5	44.7	50.2	57.8	55.8	55.5
Unemployment	17.3	26.1	14.4	9.9	12.5	26.5
School	12.3	13.8	15.0	14.2	18.5	6.8
Other situations	10.9	15.4	20.4	18.1	13.2	11.2
Total[b]	100	100	100	100	100	100
	(2331)[c]	(1583)	(561)	(2859)	(109)	(1454)

Notes:
[a]   *Mobility*: people who answered that they were in employment one year before the survey, but in another firm; *unemployment*: unemployed the year before; *school*: still in education the year before; *military service*: doing compulsory military service the year before; *other situation*: all other kinds of non-employment.
[b]   Total recruitment: people who started their current job after January 1 1994; observation in spring.
[c]   In thousands.

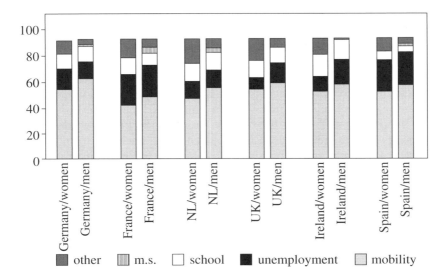

Figure 4.1 Comparison of previous situations of men and women recruited in 1995

The table is to be read in the following way. In Germany, in spring 1995, 5 120 000 people were in a job that they had started after January 1 1994. Of these, 63.3 per cent had been in employment the year before but in another firm, while 15.6 per cent were unemployed, 13 per cent still at school and so on.

Figure 4.1 shows that, in general, men have greater job-to-job mobility than women. In the UK, Ireland and Spain, men are also more likely to enter a new job from unemployment. This rather general pattern is due largely to women's frequent moves between employment and non-participation. Thus women's mobility patterns are more widely spread over the whole range of transitional labour markets and labour market statuses.

The high share of job-to-job mobility within total recruitment indicates that people change jobs frequently. Of course they do so for various reasons. They might find a better position, but job changes are frequently enforced (dismissal, relocation, bad working or living conditions). The balance between voluntary and enforced job changes varies a lot according to period, labour force category and country.

The share of mobility in total recruitment (that is, the proportion of individuals who, in spring 1995, were not working in the same firm as a year before) is highest in Germany (63.3 per cent) and in the UK, Ireland and

Spain (around 60 per cent). In the Netherlands and, most notably, in France, the rates are lower. If gender is taken into account, the ranking remains much the same, in spite of the decreasing importance of mobility within female recruitment because of the numerous transitions women make between employment and non-employment. For example, the share of mobility in total recruitment in Germany and in the Netherlands is much lower for women than for men, while in France and, particularly, in Spain and Ireland, the differences between the sexes are less pronounced.

There is no apparent relationship between a high unemployment rate, or a high renewal rate, and a high share of mobility in total recruitment, as the examples of Germany and Spain show. Germany has the lowest renewal rate and a low unemployment rate, but the highest mobility rate. Spain has a moderate mobility rate, whereas the renewal rate is almost twice that in Germany and unemployment the highest of the countries studied.

The proportion of *school leavers*[4] within recruitment varies considerably from country to country, and seems to be relatively independent of the economic situation and of the general unemployment rate. The lowest rate, around 5 per cent, is found in Spain, while the highest rate is found in Ireland, where school leavers represent more than 17 per cent of 'new workers'. In the other countries studied, the rate is between 12 and 14 per cent. If young men recruited after the end of their military service (in those countries where compulsory service still exists) are included with the school leavers, we find that, in spite of the very different structures, the young beginners' share of total recruitment begins to converge in the various countries at around 15 to 16 per cent, except in the UK (12.7 per cent) and, notably, Spain (6.9 per cent).

Comparison of the recruitment of men and women shows that in, all the countries studied, female school leavers are more likely to be recruited than their male counterparts (on the French case, cf. Audier, 1988). If those finishing military service are included with school leavers, the share of male beginners in total recruitment in Germany, France and the Netherlands becomes higher than that of females and it is only in the UK and in Ireland, where there is no compulsory military service, that young women still outstrip young men.[5]

At this stage, some interesting observations can be made. Whatever the evaluation method used, labour market flows seem to be very high, and young beginners always represent only a small percentage of total annual recruitment. It follows from this that the *short-term* difficulties beginners encounter in entering the labour market cannot be directly caused by a shortage of job opportunities (Bilans formation-emploi, 1983–96). They account for only one out of 20 hires in Spain, and only one out of seven in most of the other countries. Even in Ireland, where the rate is the highest, young labour market entrants account for only one new recruit in six. It is certainly helpful for an improved understanding of how the labour market works to supplement the classical approach based on *stocks*, which analyses the structure of the labour force at a given point in time, with one based on *flows*, which takes account of recruitment (Schömann and Kruppe, 1998).

However, these evaluations have to be interpreted cautiously, since not *all* young people without any work experience prior to recruitment are included in the 'school leavers' or 'military service leavers' categories. Some of them will be in the 'unemployment' or 'other situation' categories, if they have not found a job soon enough. For instance, the previous situation of those school leavers who have not found a job during the year after they left school but do so later on (for instance 16 or 18 months afterwards), is not *school* but *unemployment*. In other cases, young beginners who interrupt their studies for more than a year without looking for a job, or those who only study part-time or who just stay at home, may fall into the 'other situation' category. This category is not in fact clearly defined, and covers at least two kinds of persons: those looking for a job without registering as unemployed, or what is usually understood as inactive persons. The LFS data are not very useful in clarifying this point (Auer, 1998).

Whatever the 'correct method' of evaluation may be, this category of labour market entrants is clearly a very mixed group, and there is some evidence that the major factor to take in account is the educational level, which plays a central role in employers' recruitment strategies.

The Importance of Educational Level in Determining Access to Employment

In this section, we examine the importance in each country of educational level in determining the likelihood of finding employment a few months after leaving school or university, relative to the other categories recruited during the same period (Audier, 1988; OECD, 1998; Schömann, Kruppe and Oschmiansky, 1998). The educational levels used here are those proposed by Eurostat: ISCED 1 for the lowest level, ISCED 3 for the upper secondary school level and ISCED 5 for the higher level. We find that *the educational levels of beginners are completely different in the six countries and that these differences seem to be correlated to background institutional factors.*

A comparison between the level attained by *all* school leavers and that attained *only by those in employment* a few months after they have left school gives some interesting insights, firstly into the sorting process that may take place when young labour market entrants first seek employment, and secondly into the kind of competition they face in doing so. In the UK, for instance, the two populations are very similar. This means that the educational levels of those who are working are not significantly different from those who are not, and that educational level seems not to be a major discriminating factor. Some similarities between both populations can also be found in Spain and Ireland. In Germany and the Netherlands, in contrast, ISCED level 1 is much more representative of the population in employment than of the total flow. This could be interpreted as confirmation of the role of the apprenticeship system. In these two countries, both of which have a highly developed apprenticeship system, labour market entrants leaving the education system probably experience greater difficulty in finding a job than those seeking just an apprenticeship position.

These different rates may be linked to the general level of educational attainment in the population as a whole. *A comparison of total recruitment* reveals pronounced differences between the countries in our sample. The educational level of those recruited is highest in the UK. The situation in Spain is highly polarised. In the Netherlands, Germany and France, the intermediate level of education continues to play an important role.

As Table 4.3 shows, in two countries, Germany and the Netherlands, ISCED 1 accounts for only about 20 per cent of all recruitment. In three other countries, France, Ireland and the UK, the rate is about 30 per cent. In Spain the situation is very different, with more than 60 per cent of recruits having the lowest level of education. On the other hand, in four of the six countries – Germany, France, the Netherlands and Spain – 21 to 24 per cent of all people recruited in 1995 had attained the highest educational level (ISCED 5). In Ireland the percentage is around 30 per cent, while the rate in the UK is much higher, at 36 per cent.

Another way of illustrating the influence of educational level on the likelihood of young beginners finding a job is to evaluate their position at each level. As Figure 4.2 shows, only in Germany and the Netherlands do these labour market entrants occupy a central position in the total recruitment of individuals in category ISCED 1, with 30 per cent to 36 per cent of all recruitment at this level involving young beginners. At the same time, young beginners represent less than 8 per cent in ISCED 3 and less than 12 per cent in ISCED 5. In France and Ireland, in contrast, the highest rate is found in the highest level (ISCED 5): nearly one person out of two recruited at this level is a young beginner, while the rate in ISCED 1 is only around 10 per cent. In the UK, the situation is more balanced.

In Germany, 30.5 per cent of all persons recruited at ISCED 1 level are young beginners, and they account for 8.6 per cent of all recruitment at ISCED 3 level. Young beginners represent, on average, 14 per cent of total recruitment. To sum up, comparisons between young beginners and the

Table 4.3 The educational level of persons recruited in 1995 (comparison between those who were either at school or unemployed in the previous year and the total population recruited)

	Germany			France			NL		
ISCED	School and military service	Unemployment	All recruitment	School and military service	Unemployment	All recruitment	School and military service	Unemployment	All recruitment
1	42.0	17.5	19.2	20.8	37.8	30.8	46.5	25.9	23.0
3	35.5	63.0	57.5	41.6	47.6	46.7	33.7	56.0	54.5
5	20.6	17.4	21.4	37.5	14.6	22.5	19.8	17.9	22.3
?	1.9	2.1	1.9	0.1	0	0	0	0.2	0.2
Total	100	100	100	100	100	100	100	100	100

	UK			Ireland			Spain		
ISCED	School	Unemployment	All recruitment	School	Unemployment	All recruitment	School and military service	Unemployment	All recruitment
1	21.5	54.7	31.3	26.3	60.7	34.7	39.9	34.0	64.3
3	45.4	30.5	32.8	36.1	18.9	36.4	26.8	33.5	17.6
5	33.1	14.8	35.7	37.6	20.4	28.8	33.3	32.2	18.1
?	0	0	0.2	0	0	0.1	0	0.2	0
Total	100	100	100	100	100	100	100	100	100

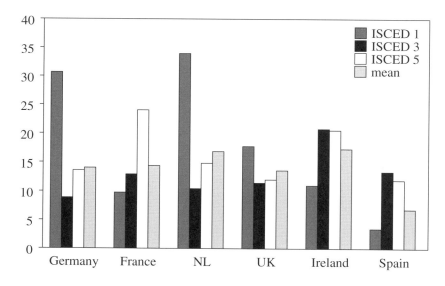

*Figure 4.2   Proportion of beginners in each educational level
            (recruitment 1995)*

other categories of persons recruited during the same period show that education or levels among beginners are much higher than the national average in France, Ireland and, particularly, in Spain, while the opposite is true in Germany and the Netherlands. Educational levels among beginners seems to be closer to the average in the UK.

As we have already suggested, these differences need to be interpreted against the background of national education and training systems. The very particular importance of the lowest educational level in Germany and the Netherlands is directly linked to the apprenticeship system. In these countries, young labour market entrants are recruited at the lowest level and they will obtain their skills, generally ISCED 3, within the firm. Here, therefore, the unemployment rate among the under 25s is very low and the participation rate very high (an apprenticeship is considered as a job), while transition difficulties may occur later on. In France, in contrast, young people enter employment after they have obtained their qualifications within the initial educational or vocational training system. They are, of course, older than their British or Dutch counterparts, and they may experience transition difficulties at this stage of their careers (OECD, 1998).

Thus it is evident that the labour market position of young entrants in the countries under consideration varies considerably. Some of them have already finished their initial education or training when they seek their first jobs, while others have not really finished at all. The institutional link between the education system and the labour market seems to be organized quite differently, and the way this link is institutionalized determines to a large extent the flows at the transition from school to work, as already argued in the previous two chapters of this volume.

4. THE SPECIFIC ROLE OF ECONOMIC SECTORS IN LABOUR MARKET INTEGRATION

In the light of the differences in educational levels between young labour market entrants and other persons recruited at the same time, we further hypothesize that, whatever their initial situation in the labour market, neither category is in direct competition with the other for the same jobs.

One way of testing whether young entrants are in competition with other categories recruited at the same time is to identify those sectors to which young people are typically recruited and those industries in which firms preferred to employ other types of worker, for instance adults with labour force experience (Audier, 1990, 1997). This question, which is linked to that of possible segmentation of the recruitment process, needs to be tackled in two different ways. In the first, an assessment is attempted of the kind of choices made by employers when they recruit, with the aim of ascertaining the proportion of young labour market entrants selected. The second approach is more pragmatic, since it attempts to evaluate the distribution of the jobs found by young people over various areas of economic activity, firstly relative to total recruitment and secondly relative to other labour force categories, for example the unemployed. The data relate to 1995, and the industrial classification used is the NACE nomenclature.

BOX 4.1   THE SHARE OF BEGINNERS IN TOTAL
RECRUITMENT BY SECTOR (NAF
CLASSIFICATION)

Germany > *mean* finance/business (14.9%), public administra-
(14%)* tion/education (18%), health (17.7%)
< *mean* agriculture (8.4%), manufacturing (13.8%)
construction (13.3%), distribution (12.5%), HR
(10.6%), transport and communications (10.7%),
other services (12.2%)

BOX 4.1 (continued)

France
(14.5%)
>*mean* manufacturing (15%), distribution (16.7%), HR (15.4%), finance/business (15.1%), public administration/education (15.5%) <*mean* agriculture (13.5%), construction (12.2%), transport and communications (10.5%), health (13.1%), other services (11.3%)

NL
(15.6%)*
>*mean* distribution (19.5%), HR (24.5%), public administration/education (17.3%)
<*mean* manufacturing (11.8%), construction (7.7%), transport and communications (13.5%), finance/business (12.4%), health (13.5%), other services (14.2%)
=*mean* agriculture (15.3%)

UK
(13.6%)*
>*mean* distribution (19.4%), HR (22.7%), public administration/education (16.2%), other services (16.6%)
<*mean* agriculture (12.4%), manufacturing (9.9%), construction (7.6%), transport and communications (8.3%), finance/business (10.4%), health (9.3%)

Ireland
(17.4%)*
>*mean* distribution (25.9%), HR (24.8%), finance/business (18.1%)
<*mean* construction (11%), transport and communications (7%), public administration/education (13.9%), health (11.1%), other services (14.3%)
=*mean* agriculture (17%), manufacturing (17.6%)

Spain
(6.9%)*
>*mean* distribution (9.1%), public administration/education (9%), health (8%)
<*mean* agriculture (4.7%), construction (4.4%), transport and communications (4.9%), other services (6.3%)
=*mean* manufacturing (3.6%), HR (7%), finance/business (7%)

* The numbers in brackets represent the mean share of young beginners in the sectors listed. For example, in the UK, on average, young beginners account for 13.6 per cent of the total number of persons recruited, but 19.4 per cent in distribution and only 7.6 per cent in construction.

As shown in Box 4.1, the percentage of young beginners is generally much higher than the average in a limited number of economic sectors. In other words, beginners account for a particularly high share of recruitment in public administration/education, the wholesale and retail trade and hotels and catering. The same applies, albeit to a lesser extent, in health and social work. This means that the public administration/education sector is comparatively open to young beginners in Germany, France, Spain and the UK, and also, to some extent, in Ireland. The situation is completely reversed in the Netherlands. Distribution, as well as hotels and catering, are also important economic sectors for the young. In all the countries investigated here, with the exception of Germany, they recruit a relatively high percentage of beginners. These are expanding sectors with plenty of job opportunities; however, the jobs on offer are often unattractive, with difficult working conditions and high turnover rates.

On the other hand, in almost all the countries, those sectors suffering from various degrees of decline and difficulty, such as transport and communications, agriculture and manufacturing, recruit a below-average share of beginners. They tend to recruit either from among the unemployed or, most frequently of course, from those changing jobs.

Thus, as far as the share of young people in total recruitment is concerned, the 'best' sectors in the countries in the sample are public administration/education, health, distribution and hotels/catering, which represent a fairly wide diversity of economic activity. The major contribution to the employment of labour market entrants comes from the tertiary sector. The fact that these different sectors are relatively open to young entrants in no way guarantees that they will find it easy to obtain employment there. It is possible in theory, but the sectors in question will have to be recruiting in substantial numbers if it is to be true in practice.

The distribution of jobs found by new entrants in 1995 shows that the great majority of them were in the tertiary sector. This is the case in Germany (64 per cent), Ireland (71 per cent), France (74 per cent), Spain (74 per cent) and, particularly, the Netherlands (83 per cent) and the UK (82 per cent). A comparison with the distribution of the *total new hires* shows that, in Germany, the patterns of distribution are very similar, with beginners spread over more or less the same areas of economic activity as other recruits. In France, on the other hand, the situation is completely different, with beginners finding employment much more frequently in the tertiary sector, especially in distribution and public administration/education. In the Netherlands, this phenomenon is even more pronounced, with *one beginner in every two* starting work in distribution. The cause of this phenomenon is probably to be found in the rapid development of short-term contracts in specific sectors of the economy (Schömann, Rogowski

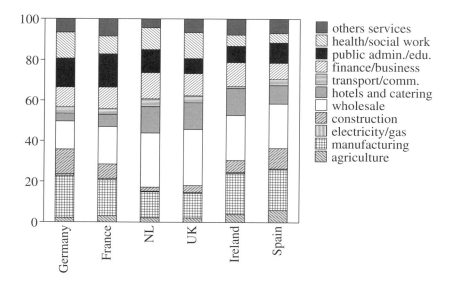

Figure 4.3   The recruitment of school leavers, by section, 1995

and Kruppe, 1998). Distribution is also very significant in the UK, albeit to a lesser extent, since it provides more than 29 per cent of all jobs for beginners.

These results suggest that young labour market entrants are not really in competition with other labour force categories for access to employment. The jobs they take seem to be quite different from those offered to adults coming either from other jobs or from unemployment.

Figure 4.3 and Table 4.4, which is broken down by gender, provide a general overview of the distribution of 'new' jobs found in 1995 by the school leavers of 1994, in comparison with the jobs found by the unemployed, and in comparison with the general situation regarding the whole recruitment (the mean).

5.   ARE YOUNG BEGINNERS COMPETING WITH EACH OTHER?

As we have already seen, young beginners do not seem to be in competition with other labour force categories, since they tend not to find employment in the same areas of economic activity. But are they in competition among themselves? The polarization of their recruitment in areas is as different as distribution and public administration/education suggests that they are,

Table 4.4   Distribution of jobs, by gender

Men	Agriculture	Manufac-turing	Electricity/gas	Con-struction	Distrib-ution	Hotels and catering
Germany						
Unempl.	5.5	26.1	0.8	19.4	11.2	3.9
School + m.s.	2.4	26.5	1.1	19.0	13.0	2.6
Total recruitment	3.3	25.4	0.8	20.5	13.0	3.8
France						
Unempl.	3.5	21.1	0.7	15.1	14.8	5.1
School + m.s.	4.5	22.7	0.6	11.8	19.0	6.2
Total recruitment	4.3	21.1	0.5	14.1	16.4	5.7
NL						
Unempl.	1.7	24.2	0.3	11.5	17.6	6.9
School + m.s.	4.1	16.3	0.6	4.5	20.7	10.8
Total recruitment	4.0	18.7	0.7	10.9	19.5	6.6
UK						
Unempl.	2.8	25.7	0.2	14.3	17.0	5.2
School	2.1	17.0	0.4	5.6	29.2	11.4
Total recruitment	2.6	22.4	0.4	11.0	18.2	6.3
Ireland						
Unempl.	3.8	21.5	0	21.5	8.8	4.2
School	6.6	24.7	0.3	11.0	21.7	9.8
Total recruitment	6.1	22.8	0.3	16.7	13.9	6.3
Spain						
Unempl.	11.0	20.3	0.5	26.9	12.5	7.7
School + m.s.	8.0	25.3	0.1	15.8	20.4	9.0
Total recruitment	10.8	21.2	0.5	24.2	14.3	7.6

Men	Transport/comm.	Finance/business	Public admin./edu.	Health and social work	Other services	All sectors
Germany						
Unempl.	4.7	8.4	10.6	3.5	5.8	100
School + m.s.	3.3	10.3	12.8	5.9	3.1	100
Total recruitment	5.6	9.5	9.7	4.0	4.3	100
France						
Unempl.	6.3	11.9	10.6	4.4	6.6	100
School + m.s.	2.9	13.5	11.1	3.4	4.3	100
Total recruitment	6.2	13.0	9.2	4.2	5.2	100

Table 4.4 (continued)

Men	Transport/ comm.	Finance/ business	Public admin./ edu.	Health and social work	Other services	All sectors
NL						
Unempl.	8.2	12.0	7.9	5.4	4.3	100
School + m.s.	5.2	12.7	11.3	9.0	3.4	100
Total recruitment	6.5	15.3	8.9	5.3	3.6	100
UK						
Unempl.	8.4	11.6	4.2	4.6	6.0	100
School	4.4	12.2	8.5	2.6	6.7	100
Total recruitment	8.5	15.0	6.1	4.0	5.5	100
Ireland						
Unempl.	4.5	6.2	7.3	5.5	16.8	100
School	1.0	11.4	4.8	2.2	6.5	100
Total recruitment	4.2	10.5	6.2	3.9	9.0	100
Spain						
Unempl.	4.4	6.2	5.4	1.1	3.9	100
School + m.s.	2.6	5.7	7.8	1.9	3.4	100
Total recruitment	5.2	5.8	5.3	1.5	3.6	100

Women	Agriculture	Manufac- turing	Electricity/ gas	Con- struction	Distrib- ution	Hotels and catering
Germany						
Unempl.	7.9	13.8	0.3	3.6	17.7	6.7
School	1.4	12.6	0.1	2.6	14.6	5.6
Total recruitment	3.2	15.0	0.3	3.0	18.1	6.7
France						
Unempl.	1.5	12.0	0.3	1.5	16.4	5.1
School	1.6	11.3	0.4	1.0	18.8	5.6
Total recruitment	2.5	12.0	0.2	1.6	16.0	5.2
NL						
Unempl.	1.6	14.1	0.1	1.2	17.7	8.4
School	1.3	9.0	0	1.2	31.6	12.8
Total recruitment	1.8	9.5	0.1	1.2	21.1	8.3
UK						
Unempl.	0.5	12.6	0	1.5	20.9	10.0
School	1.1	8.4	0.1	1.5	26.4	15.0
Total recruitment	0.8	12.0	0.2	1.4	20.8	9.6

Table 4.4 (continued)

Women	Agriculture	Manufac-turing	Electricity/gas	Con-struction	Distrib-ution	Hotels and catering
Ireland						
Unempl.	1.4	22.2	2.6	12.5	10.7	0.7
School	0.1	15.5	1.0	22.7	17.2	17.2
Total recruitment	1.3	16.6	1.3	16.1	13.1	13.1
Spain						
Unempl.	3.7	16.9	0	0.8	18.8	11.6
School	2.5	11.1	0.2	1.4	25.1	9.4
Total recruitment	5.1	15.6	0.1	1.2	20.6	11.3

Women	Transport/comm.	Finance/business	Public admin./edu.	Health and social work	Other services	All sectors
Germany						
Unempl.	2.5	10.2	17.5	11.1	8.6	100
School	3.3	12.1	18.2	20.9	8.5	100
Total recruitment	2.9	11.5	14.2	16.6	8.4	100
France						
Unempl.	2.8	12.2	17.8	14.6	15.9	100
School	3.9	14.9	16.1	14.2	12.0	100
Total recruitment	3.0	13.7	16.1	14.6	15.1	100
NL						
Unempl.	2.4	15.4	9.8	24.3	4.9	100
School	2.8	13.4	9.9	13.4	4.6	100
Total recruitment	2.9	17.3	11.7	20.6	5.4	100
UK						
Unempl.	3.2	12.5	10.8	18.7	9.2	100
School	2.9	10.4	13.2	11.4	10.0	100
Total recruitment	3.3	14.3	12.3	16.9	8.3	100
Ireland						
Unempl.	0.7	10.0	12.9	14.9	12.0	100
School	1.3	12.6	10.2	9.2	9.3	100
Total recruitment	1.4	12.6	13.0	14.6	10.1	100
Spain						
Unempl.	1.9	12.2	11.3	8.1	14.8	100
School	3.4	12.2	12.4	9.2	13.0	100
Total recruitment	2.1	11.5	10.3	8.1	14.1	100

in fact, in separate labour markets defined by educational level. To clarify this question we shall analyse the areas in which beginners find employment, taking individual educational level into account (Audier, 1987).

The main conclusion we draw is that many of those who have only a low level of education (ISCED 1) find employment in distribution or in the hotel and catering industry, and even in manufacturing and construction, while those with higher-level qualifications are more likely to find jobs in the public administration/education or finance sectors, because these are activities that often require people with advanced qualifications. Many examples can be provided, but the extent of the differences varies from country to country. In Spain, for instance, 45 per cent of those recruited with a low educational level are in distribution. This is the case for only 26 per cent of those who possess a middle-level qualification and for 12 per cent of those with a higher-level qualification. On the other hand, 24 per cent of those with a middle-level qualification are recruited into public administration/education, compared with just 4 per cent of those with the lowest educational level.

In Germany, one hire out of five at ISCED 1 enters the construction sector, while recruitment in this sector is almost non-existent at the other levels. It is interesting to note that, in several countries, the main difference between the various sectors of employment is in the middle and the upper levels. This is the case, for instance, in Ireland, where among beginners at ISCED 5, 18 per cent find jobs in finance, public administration or health care and only 17 per cent in distribution or the hotel and catering industry, while at ISCED 1, 52 per cent find employment in distribution or hotels and catering and only 8 per cent in finance, public administration or health care. At ISCED 3, these figures are respectively 46 per cent and 16 per cent. In France, 60 per cent of beginners with the highest level of education are employed in administration, education or health care while 10 per cent of those at level 1 find work in similar sectors (cf. Table 4.5).

The Jobs Found by Young Beginners Generally Offer Fewer Hours than the Standard Working Week

In investigating the quality of the school-to-work transition, it is useful to examine the employment status young beginners acquire when they enter the labour force (Schömann, Rogowski and Kruppe, 1998).

According to the information provided by the LFS, the proportion of beginners who go straight into a permanent job varies considerably in the six countries studied, from a quarter to two-thirds. However, this result is difficult to interpret and must be clarified because, as already explained, the beginners category is a very mixed one. In Germany or in the Netherlands,

Table 4.5   The most important sectors for young labour market entrants, by individual educational level, 1995

Men and women/ ISCED	Manufacturing	Distribution	Hotels and catering	Finance/ business	Public admin./edu.	Health and social work	Other services	All sectors % in line
Germany								
1	21.2	18.4	5.0	5.2	6.3	12.6	31.3	100
3	18.3	12.3	4.5	16.3	15.4	14.5	18.7	100
5	18.1	5.8	0.7	16.5	33.5	11.1	14.3	100
France								
1	19.1	28.4	11.5	3.6	5.3	2.1	30.0	100
3	16.3	21.1	6.8	12.4	8.3	10.1	25.0	100
5	12.0	12.0	2.3	18.6	25.7	13.6	15.8	100
NL								
1	15.6	31.4	15.2	7.4	5.8	11.2	13.4	100
3	10.4	27.7	13.9	14.2	6.3	9.6	17.9	100
5	6.9	15.0	6.9	24.6	19.9	17.8	8.9	100
UK								
1	10.2	41.4	8.3	5.6	4.0	3.2	27.3	100
3	14.1	25.4	13.2	11.7	9.1	7.6	18.9	100
5	14.4	11.7	6.6	17.8	21.5	11.8	16.2	100
Ireland								
1	20.1	31.5	18.0	1.9	2.8	3.3	22.4	100
3	19.4	26.1	16.6	7.9	3.5	5.4	21.1	100
5	21.0	11.1	6.4	23.7	15.5	7.4	14.9	100
Spain								
1	28.2	23.8	11.8	3.1	1.5	0.5	31.1	100
3	13.4	27.8	13.6	6.4	11.2	4.0	23.6	100
5	15.5	16.9	4.5	18.7	17.7	11.0	16.9	100

Example: In the UK, 41.4 per cent of beginners with level 1 educational attainment were recruited into distribution; 13.2 per cent with level 3 went into hotels and catering, and so on.

for instance, beginners often go into apprenticeships. In other countries, this route into the labour market is by no means as common. Other countries have their own particularities. Although a high proportion of young people in France go into 'real' jobs, a small but significant share of beginners join special employment policy programmes on fixed-term contracts, which gives them a particular employment status. These features appear clearly in Table 4.6.

According to these data, it is in the UK that permanent jobs are most frequent. Two-thirds of beginners obtain such positions, the same rate as in the rest of the labour force. At the opposite extreme, the worst situation is in Spain, where a large majority of labour market entrants find themselves on fixed-term contracts. However, even here, young beginners are better off than other people recruited during the same period. It is interesting to note that, in the Netherlands and the UK, the share of new entrants and the previously unemployed being offered permanent jobs is not significantly different, while, in the other countries, beginners seem to fare significantly better than the unemployed.

The relationship between employment status and educational level clarifies several questions. The effects are quite contradictory, depending on the country. In France and Ireland, the share of permanent contracts rises with educational level, both for beginners and the unemployed. In the Netherlands and the UK, on the other hand, exactly the opposite pertains (cf. Table 4.6). It should be remembered that, in these four countries, a high proportion of beginners are concentrated in just a few sectors (the less educated in distribution and hotels and catering). One explanation is that the legal status of their jobs is not the same in the different countries, because of differences in the regulatory and legislative framework governing the labour market. In the UK and the Netherlands, this framework is less influential than in France, where lay-offs are highly regulated and permanent employment contracts offer employees real protection. In other circumstances, or in other legislative contexts, short-term contracts may mean that employees are sure to keep their jobs at least until the end of their contracts. Again, the interpretation must take into account the institutional context.

Only a Small Share of Beginners are Actively Seeking Another Job

Since it is very difficult to interpret employment status in international comparisons, another way of exploring the quality of the jobs that young labour market entrants obtain relative to those obtained by other labour force categories is to ask whether they are looking for another job or not.

A main finding of the ELFS data is that only a very small fraction,

Table 4.6   Employment status of the various categories of recruits, by previous situation, 1995 (per cent)

Previous situation	Permanent contracts	Fixed-term contracts	Self-employment
Germany			
School	26.8	70.6	2.6
Military service	48.4	51.0	0.6
Unemployment	50.7	45.0	4.3
Total recruitment	58.9	34.0	7.1
France			
School	27.2	69.2	3.6
Military service	42.8	54.6	2.6
Unemployment	37.8	56.6	5.6
Total recruitment	46.3	55.0	8.7
NL			
School	52.7	42.0	5.3
Military service	58.2	39.4	2.4
Unemployment	53.9	38.5	7.6
Total recruitment	60.6	30.4	9.0
UK			
School	66.5	30.2	3.3
Military service	—	—	—
Unemployment	66.5	19.9	13.6
Total recruitment	72.3	17.7	10.0
Ireland			
School	55.7	41.9	2.4
Military service	—	—	—
Unemployment	46.7	36.6	6.7
Total recruitment	62.6	27.8	9.6
Spain			
School	8.4	74.0	17.1
Military service	6.9	73.8	19.3
Unemployment	9.3	72.5	8.2
Total recruitment	13.2	76.1	10.7

Note: Survey conducted in spring 1995. These employees stated their current job after 1 January 1994.

Table 4.7   Share of recruits looking for other jobs, 1995

Previous situation	% of employees who declare they are not looking for another job*
Germany	
Mobility	92.3
Unemployment	78.9
School	95.4
Total recruitment	90.6
France	
Mobility	84.2
Unemployment	69.8
School	84.6
Total recruitment	80.0
NL	
Mobility	84.2
Unemployment	73.2
School	92.2
Total recruitment	83.7
UK	
Mobility	88.4
Unemployment	82.6
School	86.9
Total recruitment	87.7
Ireland	
Mobility	87.5
Unemployment	72.2
School	82.3
Total recruitment	83.9
Spain	
Mobility	95.4
Unemployment	90.7
School	93.0
Total recruitment	93.8

Note: * Survey conducted in spring 1995. These employees had obtained their current job after 1 January 1994.

between 10 and 17 per cent, of recent recruits (that is, in our sample, those who had a job in spring 1995 and had been recruited for that job after 1 January 1994) is actively looking for another job.

The lowest shares of school leavers looking for another job are found in Germany, Spain and the Netherlands, while the highest shares are found in the UK, France and Ireland. In any event, in almost all countries, young beginners are less likely than the average to be looking for another job, and significantly less likely than those recruited from unemployment at the same time, as shown in Table 4.7.

6. CONCLUSION

In view of the marked differences in the position of labour market entrants in the various countries, and also the differences between their situation and that of adults recruited during the same period, it seems very difficult to draw general conclusions. However, we can point to some common elements.

Firstly, young entrants always represent a small proportion of total recruitment. Even when unemployment is growing, mobility remains very high, either because people want to improve their situation or because the circumstances force them to change their job. Thus the major problem for young labour market entrants seems to be how to gain access to employment.

The fact that, in all the countries studied, only a very small share of the jobs on offer are open to beginners is further compounded by the tendency for beginners to be concentrated in a limited number of sectors, which are by no means the same as those to which the unemployed, for instance, are recruited. This phenomenon is common to almost all the countries, despite their structural and institutional differences. In addition, not all young beginners end up in the same kind of firms, nor do they occupy similar jobs. Those who have a high level of education will enter highly-skilled jobs in sectors such as public administration/education, where employment contracts and working conditions are still attractive. On the other hand, those with only the basic level of education will tend to find employment in distribution or the hotel and catering industry (except, of course, for those who obtain an apprenticeship). Employers in these sectors usually offer unskilled young workers fixed-term contracts as well as low wages and difficult working conditions (the small number of highly skilled young school leavers entering these sectors are of course not affected in the same way).

As a result, it seems evident, firstly, that young labour market entrants are not really in competition with adult job seekers and, secondly, that in some respects at least they are not in competition with each other either, since they are segmented into labour markets organized by educational level.

This situation raises a number of difficult issues for the young, as well as for society as a whole. The young risk being confined to specific sectors, and this in turn not only makes them vulnerable to cyclical demand variations but also leads to a standardization of their characteristics. Moreover, if the only opportunities open to the less skilled of them as they leave education are in a limited range of activities involving mainly repetitive tasks, they risk being restricted to specific sectors and will find it very difficult to enter other types of jobs and other sectors. This tendency seems to be a handicap in their subsequent careers.

Furthermore, the division between high-skill and low-skill workers, employed in 'good' and 'bad' sectors, may reinforce and even generalize inequalities, to the detriment of relationships within society as a whole. If employers were willing to change their behaviour, even marginally, in order to meet the demand from young people for jobs, or even if recruitment rates rose slightly, young people's situation would improve significantly. The important role played by low-wage industries in the employment of young people of low education attainment, and the relatively fragile status of their jobs, should prompt consideration of ways in which their employment opportunities could be diversified, with a more even distribution over the whole range of jobs. Public policies should help to open up 'closed segments', either through selective measures or by offering specific subsidies, linked to working-time reductions, for example. Such a policy could also help firms to engage in some forward-looking manpower planning. In many firms, the share of employees approaching retirement age is increasing sharply, and employers will face great difficulties if they do not start taking account of this major phenomenon.

NOTES

1. The term 'young beginners' denotes all young persons entering the labour market for the first time, without any previous experience. They have come straight from school or from military service, that is they answer to the question corresponding to their situation during the reference week that they have a job, and that one year before the survey, they have a job and that one year before the survey they were either a student or a conscript.
2. The various national surveys are generally conducted during January, February or March, but they may also be spread over a longer period during the spring months. This is a real difficulty for international comparisons.
3   This methodology is adapted from that used in the employment-training assessments (*bilans formation–emploi*).
4. School leavers are those who had a job in spring 1995 and were at school one year before.
5. Combining school leavers with young people completing their military or community service is not so simple because in some countries, such as France, employers are legally obliged to re-employ the young men who were their employees before their conscription. Thus these young men cannot be considered as beginners. On the other hand, the lengthening of the time spent in the education and training system means that military service has to be done immediately on leaving education or training. In spite of these difficulties, comparisons between countries that have compulsory military service and those that do not can be made by including young people entering the labour market from military service with school leavers.

BIBLIOGRAPHY

Audier, F. (1987), 'Renouvellement des professions et insertion des jeunes', *Revue Formation emploi*, 18, La Documentation Française.

Audier, F. (1988), 'Les recrutements des entreprises depuis 15 ans. La part moins belle aux débutants'. *Economie et Statistiques INSEE*, 216.

Audier, F. (1990), 'Secteurs d'activité économique et emploi des jeunes à la sortie du système éducatif', *Formation Emploi*, 31, La Documentation Française.

Audier, F. (1995), 'Jeunes débutants et marché du travail en France: évolutions et transformations durant la dernière décennie', *Network transitions in youth*, Oostvorne: European Science Foundation.

Audier, F. (1997), 'La Fonction publique: un débouché majeur pour les plus diplomés', *Economie & Statistiques*, 304–305.

Auer, P. (1998), 'Inactivity Rates in European Union', in Peter Auer (ed.), *Employment Policies in Focus. Labour Markets and Labour Market Policy in Europe and Beyond – International Experiences*, Berlin: I.A.S. Institute for Applied Socio-Economics, pp. 266–81.

Bilans formation-emploi (1983–96), *Collections de l'INSEE*, INSEE Résultats.

Economie & Statistiques (1997), 304–305 and (1995) 283–84 focused to transition in youth.

Elbaum, M. and Marchand, O. (1993), 'Emploi et chômage des jeunes dans les pays industrialisés: la spécificité française', *Première synthèses*, 34, DARES.

Estrade, M.A. and Thiesset, C. (1998), 'Des débuts de carrière moins assurés', *INSEE Première*, 598

Fondeur, Y. and Lefresne, F. (1999), 'Les Jeunes et le Marché du Travail', *La Revue de l'IRES*, 31 (3).

Fournié, D. (1994), 'La place des jeunes dans les recrutements', *Economie & Statistiques*, 277–8.

Freysson, L. (1996), 'Potential use of the Community Labour Force Survey in analysis of the young', *Provence Workshop*.

Freysson, L. (1997), 'Labour market exclusion of young people: some illustrations of the situation in the European Union. Network on transition in youth', *Workshop Dublin.*

Gissot, C. and Meron, M. (1996), 'Chômage et emploi en Mars 1996', *INSEE première*, 467.

Goux, D. and Maurin, E. (1996), 'La sécurité de l'emploi, une priorité croissante pour les diplômés', *Economie & Statistiques*, 261.

IRES (1995), 'Comparaison européenne des dispositifs d'insertion professionnelle des jeunes', *La Revue de l'Ires*, 17, particularly F. Lefresne: présentation et synthèse.

OECD (1998), *Perspectives de l'emploi*, Paris.

O'Reilly, J. and Bothfeld, S. (1998), 'Labour Market Transitions and Part-Time Work', in Peter Auer (ed.), *Employment Policies in Focus. Labour Markets and Labour Market Policy in Europe and Beyond – International Experiences*, Berlin: I.A.S. Institute for Applied Socio-Economics, pp.158–71.

Poulet, P. (1996), 'Allongement de la scolarisation et insertion des jeunes: une liaison délicate', *Economie & Statistiques*, 300.

Schömann, K. and Kruppe, Th. (1998), 'The dynamics of Employment in the European Union', in Peter Auer (ed.), *Employment Policies in Focus. Labour Markets and Labour Market Policy in Europe and Beyond – International Experiences*, Berlin: I.A.S. Institute for Applied Socio-Economics, pp. 282–303.

Schömann, K., Blossfeld, H.P. and Hannan, M.T. (1995), 'The segmentation of transitions from school to work in postwar Germany: a dynamic perspective', *Comparative Social Research.*

Schömann, K., Rogowski, R. and Kruppe, Th. (1998), 'Fixed term contracts in the European Union' in Peter Auer (ed.), *Employment Policies in Focus. Labour Markets and Labour Market Policy in Europe and Beyond – International Experiences*, Berlin: I.A.S. Institute for Applied Socio-Economics, pp. 137–57.

Schömann, K., Kruppe, Th. and Oschmiansky, H. (1998), 'Beschäftigungsdynamik und Arbeitslosigkeit in der Europäischen Union', WZB Discussion Paper FSI 98–203, WZB, Berlin.

Shavit, Y. and Müller, W. (1998), 'The Institutional Embeddedness of the Stratification Process: A Comparative Study of Qualifications and Occupations in Thirteen Countries', in Yossi Shavit and Walter Müller (eds), *From School to Work – A Comparative Study of Educational Qualifications and Occupational Destinations*, Oxford: Oxford University Press, pp. 1–48.

Vernières, M. (1997), 'L'insertion professionnelle. Analyse et débats', *Economica*, Paris.

PART II

Evaluation of Training Transitions and
Training Policies

5. Active labour market policies, market orientation and gender: findings for young people in Ireland

Philip J. O'Connell and Frances McGinnity

1. INTRODUCTION

Our focus in this chapter is the transition from unemployment to employment, and the impact of active labour market programmes (ALMPs) on this transition. Such programmes have become the principal policy instruments by which states seek to assist individual transitions into the labour market, so it is vital to assess their equity and efficiency. How effective are these programmes in facilitating the transition back into employment? Do the effects differ for men and women?

With persistent unemployment throughout the advanced industrial countries there has been a marked shift in labour market policies from passive support for unemployed workers to active measures providing training and temporary employment subsidies. This shift in emphasis is reflected in the policy recommendations of the OECD (1990) to shift labour market expenditures from passive to active measures which mobilize labour supply, improve the skills and competencies of the labour force and strengthen the search process in the labour market. In Europe, where labour market problems have been particularly intense and intractable, there has been the additional concern that education and training systems have failed to respond to rapid changes in the technology and organization of production, leading to skill shortages and mismatches, which undermine competitiveness, leading to sluggish growth in both output and employment (European Commission, 1994). In Ireland, which has suffered from mass unemployment for much of the last two decades, labour market policy has closely followed international developments, and Ireland is one of the leading countries in the proportion of national income spent on active measures (OECD, 1997).

In general, women suffer higher rates of unemployment than men.

Average unemployment among women across the OECD countries was 7.7 per cent of the female labour force in 1996, compared to a rate of 6.7 per cent among men, while in the European Union, the female unemployment rate was 13.8 per cent compared to 9.8 per cent among men (OECD, 1997). Ireland differs from this general pattern: in 1996 unemployment among women was just under 10 per cent, substantially lower than the rate of 14.7 per cent among men. Among young people in Ireland, with whom this chapter is concerned, women's unemployment rates are typically 2–3 percentage points lower than those of men. For example in 1996, 18.6 per cent of female labour force participants under the age of 25 were unemployed, compared with 21.8 per cent of young men. Some caution should be exercised, however, in interpreting these figures. O'Connell and McGinnity (1997a) argue that unemployment among women is more likely to be underestimated than that among men, largely owing to gender differences in self-reporting of unemployment versus withdrawal from the labour force to engage in domestic work.

Cross-national variation in gender differences in unemployment rates notwithstanding, it is of some importance to assess the extent to which active labour market policies mitigate this gender-based inequality in the labour market. This chapter focuses on gender differences in the impact of active labour market policies on the job prospects of their participants. We are thus interested both in whether men and women benefit equally from participation in ALMPs and in the differential effects of different types of programme by gender.

The theoretical rationale for the chapter draws on earlier work which distinguishes between broad types of ALMP, based on a fourfold distinction between (1) supply (training) versus demand (temporary employment) measures; and (2) between programmes characterized by strong versus weak linkages to the open labour market (O'Connell and McGinnity, 1997a, 1997b). These two distinctions give rise to the fourfold typology of active labour market programmes outlined in Figure 5.1.

General training includes a range of measures to provide basic or foundation-level training in general skills. Most of the programmes in this category are designed for those with poor educational qualifications experiencing difficulties in the labour market. This group also includes second-chance education programmes, training courses designed for women seeking to return to the labour market, and community training programmes, intended to develop community resources and responses to unemployment.

Specific skills courses provide training designed to meet skill needs in local labour markets. The distinction between general and specific skills training is not simply a question of the level of training, although the latter

Labour market leverage	Market orientation	
	Weak	Strong
Supply – training	General training	Specific skills training
Demand – employment	Direct employment schemes	Employment subsidies

Figure 5.1   A typology of active labour market programmes

may often be at a more advanced level than the former. Specific skills training can cover a wide range of skill levels. In the Irish case, for example, the category includes courses in retail sales as well as advanced courses in computer-aided engineering. The common characteristic of these training courses is that they are designed to meet specific skill needs in particular occupations and industries.[1]

Direct employment schemes provide subsidized temporary employment in the public or voluntary sectors. In this sense, they are variants of the conventional public works programmes. Most work in this type of programme is of a nature which would not be commercially viable: for example, environmental improvement or the provision of community-based childcare. Employment subsidies provide subsidies to the recruitment or self-employment of unemployed workers in the private sector. Typically they are aimed at those who would otherwise be hard to place in employment, such as the long-term unemployed.

O'Connell and McGinnity (1997a, 1997b) test the hypothesis that programmes with a strong orientation to the open labour market are more likely to enhance the employment prospects of participants than programmes with weak market linkages. Thus skills training programmes should have a greater positive impact on subsequent employment to the extent that they provide participants with skills that meet identified needs

of employers. Similarly, employment subsidies are designed to place participants in real jobs in the marketplace, with the result that the work experience and skills learned on the job are likely to be closer to those in demand
in the labour market than work experience or skills learned while participating in direct employment schemes on projects which, by their nature,
are not viable in the market. The findings, based on a follow-up survey
of young programme participants and a comparison group of non-
participants, provide strong support for the importance of market orientation: programmes with strong linkages to the labour market were found
both to enhance the employment prospects of their participants and to
increase their employment duration and earnings from employment, even
when account was taken of relevant individual characteristics such as education and previous labour market experience.

The principal focus of this earlier work was the relative impact of programmes. Gender was included in the analysis as a control variable, and
while gender was not found to influence post-programme job placement,
women had significantly shorter employment duration and lower wages
than men (O'Connell and McGinnity, 1997b). The earlier work does not,
therefore, allow us to examine the extent to which different types of ALMP
might have differential effects by gender. In this chapter we attempt to
bridge this important gap in our knowledge by directly comparing the
impact of programme participation for men's and women's subsequent
employment and earnings.

The empirical literature on gender differences in the impact of ALMPs
is quite limited and inconclusive, with some studies finding that women
tend to benefit more than men in terms of subsequent employment chances
(Tricam, 1993) or earnings (Bloom, 1994) and others finding the reverse
(Payne *et al.*, 1996; Jacobson *et al.*, 1994). Payne (1991), in her analysis of
the Training Opportunities Programme in Britain, finds that women found
work more quickly than men and had a better chance of finding work that
made direct use of the skills for which they had been trained. Given that
employers invest much less in training female than male employees, she
argues for investment in training for women prior to entry to work in order
to counteract this unequal access to training at work (Payne, 1991, p. 144).
Fay (1996), in his review of the empirical evaluation literature on the effects
of ALMPs, concludes that women can benefit from all areas of intervention, but particularly from classroom training, wage subsidies and job-
search assistance. This conclusion is more a judgment on the effectiveness
of ALMPs than an assessment of the relative gains to women compared to
men, and it is based on a survey of studies rather than on a direct comparison of programme outcomes. We have argued elsewhere that one of the
methodological weaknesses of the existing empirical literature is that most

assessments of the impact of ALMPs are based on single programme evaluations, a research design which precludes the analyst from comparing the effects of different types of programmes within the scope of a single study (O'Connell and McGinnity, 1997a). One of the principal strengths of the data set upon which the present study is based is that it is derived from a survey of participants in a comprehensive range of programmes, representing virtually all of the main education and training programmes operative in Ireland in 1992 and catering to a wide diversity of target groups. This provides us with an opportunity to compare directly the effectiveness of different types of programmes separately for men and women.

2. THE DATA

The post-programme follow-up survey of participants was commissioned by the Department of Enterprise and Employment and the Commission of the European Union with the objective of assessing the impact of active labour market programmes on their participants. The sample of 4654 programme participants was drawn from administrative records of the population of almost 20000 individuals who left programmes during the target period in 1992. The sample was stratified by programme and target group to allow comparison between 17 different programmes and it included both those who completed programmes and drop-outs who left programmes prior to their scheduled completion date. Fieldwork was conducted between April and September 1994 by face-to-face interview. A total of 3267 interviews were completed, representing a response rate of about 70 per cent.

The present analysis is based on a subset of the original data set consisting of young programme participants and a comparison group of non-participants. The comparison group sample of 600 young people was drawn from two cohorts of the Irish annual survey of school leavers who were reinterviewed in summer 1994 to collect a record of labour market and training experiences over the entire period since they left school. From this sample were selected 246 individuals who were unemployed in July 1992, one month after the last of them would have left school, and who had never participated in any state-sponsored labour market programme. This constitutes the 'risk set' among the comparison group, comparable with programme participants, all of whom were at risk of unemployment immediately after leaving their programmes. Virtually all of the school leaver sample were aged under 23 years, so the analysis in this paper is confined to a comparison of 1296 young programme participants (all aged under 23) with the 246 non-participants in the risk set.[2]

3. THE EFFECTS OF PROGRAMME PARTICIPATION

The Probability of Employment

Table 5.1 presents the results of logistic regression analyses of the log-odds of obtaining a job, distinguishing four ALMP programme types and controlling for individual characteristics and labour market experience; the programme reference category is non-participants.

Equation (1) includes both men and women and shows that participants in both of the market-oriented programme types – specific skills training and employment subsidies – had a positive and significant effect on the employment probabilities of their participants 18 months after leaving the programme. The effects of participating in programmes with weak market linkages – general training and direct employment schemes – were negative but not statistically significant. The effects of the control variables in the model are largely as might be expected from conventional understandings of labour market processes. Age had a weak positive but non-significant effect on employment probability. Both of the educational attainment variables – completion of lower secondary and completion of upper secondary school (including third-level attendance) – had positive and significant effects compared with those with no qualifications (the reference category). Duration of unemployment prior to programme participation (or before July 1992 in the case of non-participants) had a negative impact on subsequent employment probabilities. Dropping out of a programme to take a job continued to have a positive impact on employment 18 months later, while dropping out for other reasons had a negative effect.

Gender had no significant impact on subsequent employment probabilities. This, however, tells us little about the relative effectiveness of programmes by gender. Equation (2) adds a series of interaction terms for women with each of the independent variables in equation (1). In effect this is equivalent to estimating separate equations for men and women, but it has the advantage of allowing us to test for the significance of differences in the effects for men and women. For the female interaction terms, if the coefficient is significantly different from zero, then the effect of the variable among women differs from that among men. First, the model shows that the superiority of market-oriented programmes is maintained for both genders, although the statistical significance of the coefficients for both skills training and employment subsidies falls somewhat. Second, most of the female interaction terms are non-significant, suggesting that, in general, the pattern of effects on employment chances is remarkably similar among young men and women. This applies not only to the programme participation variables

Table 5.1 Logistic regression of the log-odds of obtaining a job, 18 months post-programme

Equation:	(1) All		(2) Interaction model			
			Men		Female interactions	
	Coefficient	Standard error	Coefficient	Standard error	Coefficient	Standard error
Programmes						
General training	−0.11	0.18	−0.06	0.24	−0.13	0.36
Specific skills	0.65***	0.175	0.54*	0.23	0.30	0.36
Employment subsidies	0.85***	0.254	0.78*	0.33	0.12	0.53
Direct employment schemes	−0.01	0.226	−0.75	0.42	1.02*	0.51
Control variables						
Age	0.09*	0.042	0.13	0.06	−0.08	0.09
Lower secondary	0.58***	0.181	0.64**	0.24	−0.28	0.37
Upper secondary +	1.32***	0.199	1.08****	0.28	0.46	0.40
Unemployment duration	−0.04***	0.01	−0.05***	0.01	0.03	0.02
Dropout to job	1.04***	0.25	0.80**	0.29	0.73	0.59
Dropout – other	−0.75**	0.229	−0.76*	0.29	0.08	0.48
Female	−0.03	0.118				
Constant	−2.56***	0.74	−3.21**	0.97	1.18	1.51
-2 Log-likelihood	1824.56		1807.85			
Chi squared	242.34		259.05			
No. of cases	1703		1703			

Note: *P<0.05, **P<0.01, ***P<0.001.

but also to the effects of other personal characteristics, including educational attainment, age and duration of unemployment. The only significant interaction term is the female*direct employment schemes term, indicating significant gender differences in the employment effects of these schemes. Among men, participation has a negative effect, marginally significant (at $P < 0.10$). Among women, the effect is positive and significant.

Table 5.2   Measures of programme effectiveness: predicted probabilities of employment, 18 months post-programme

	Men		Women	
	Employment rate	Difference	Employment rate	Difference
Comparison group	0.25	—	0.25	—
Difference				
General training	0.25	0.0	0.25	0.0
Specific skills training	0.36	+0.11	0.36	+0.11
Employment subsidies	0.42	+0.17	0.42	+0.17
Direct employment schemes	0.14	−0.11	0.30	+0.05
Completed secondary education	0.50	+0.25	0.50	+0.25
Unemployed 18 months	0.15	−0.10	0.15	−0.10

Table 5.2 compares predicted placement rates in employment for the four programme types and the non-participant comparison group derived from the multivariate logistic model reported in Table 5.1. The table thus 'translates' the coefficients in equation (2) into changes in the probability of employment associated with programme participation. The predicated probabilities shown in the first row relate to an 18-year-old individual who had been unemployed for four months and had not participated in a programme: about one-quarter of the control group with these characteristics were at work 18 months after the target/programme-exit period. There are no gender differences in the employment chances of the control group once the other variables in the model are controlled for. Participation in general training programmes had no discernible impact on employment chances 18 months later. Participation in skills training increased the probability of employment to 0.36, a substantial net impact of 11 percentage points. The net impact of participating in a wage-subsidy scheme was even greater at 17 percentage points. The employment chances of men who participated in a direct employment scheme fell 14 per cent, a substantial net decline of 11 percentage points. Among women, on the other hand, participation in

direct employment schemes increased their employment chances by 5 percentage points compared to non-participants.

These differential effects of direct employment schemes may be due to gender segregation in the labour market. Most direct employment schemes are in the voluntary and community sector, and it may be that the nature of work experience on such schemes may be of greater relevance (or considered by employers to be so) in the services sector, particularly sales and personal services, where women are more likely to be employed than men. Nevertheless, the findings suggest that young men's employment chances are diminished rather than improved by participation in direct employment schemes, and it is possible that participation in such programmes may have a stigmatizing effect on young men.

We can gauge the relative impact of programme participation by comparing the effects of programmes with other personal characteristics. The final two rows of Table 5.2 show the employment effects of completing secondary education and of having been unemployed for a duration of 18 months. Completion of the senior cycle of secondary school doubled the probability of employment, from 0.25 to 0.50, compared with an individual with no qualifications. Staying on at school has a substantially greater impact on young people's employment chances than participating in an active labour market programme, and this effect is similar for both men and women. On the other hand, having been unemployed for 18 months reduced the probability of employment 18 months later by 10 percentage points, irrespective of programme participation and controlling for the effects of other variables.

Employment Duration and Earnings

Up to this point, we have focused on the chances of being at work at particular points in time. Dolton *et al.* (1994) argue that measuring the probability of employment at a single point in time does not preclude the possibility of differing effects at other post-programme durations. Korpi (1994) argues that employment instability is associated with precarious jobs in the secondary labour market – the labour market segment for which many young participants in active labour market programmes are destined – and he finds that programme participation increases the duration of subsequent employment. We are, moreover, interested in aspects of participants' post-programme labour market experience other than employment chances, and we introduce two additional measures designed as proxy measures to capture the quality of that experience. The first of these measures – the proportion of time at work – is the proportion of time elapsed between leaving a programme and being interviewed for the survey (about

20–24 months) that was spent in employment (that is, number of months in all post-programme jobs, divided by the number of months elapsed since leaving a programme). We know that some participants may have obtained a job after leaving a programme but lost it again after a short period, while others may have obtained a job and retained it throughout the observed post-programme period. Our measure of the proportion of post-programme time in employment is designed to capture such important differences in the stability of post-programme employment.

Second, we expect substantial variation in the quality of jobs obtained and take account of this variation by measuring total income from each job held during the post-programme period, again standardized by the number of months elapsed between leaving a programme and being interviewed for the survey (that is, monthly income multiplied by duration of job(s), divided by number of months elapsed after leaving a programme). As about 40 per cent of programme participants did not get any job after leaving their programme, both proportion of time employed and income from employment are left-censored: that is, with zero values for those unemployed but variation in the remaining cases. For this reason, logistic regression analysis is inappropriate and we use a Tobit model to estimate the parameters of the models of both proportion of time in employment (Table 5.3) and income from employment (Table 5.4). The independent variables used in this model are the same as those used in the analysis of employment probabilities above.

The results for proportion of time employed are presented in Table 5.3. Equation (3) shows the model for men and women combined. Compared with non-participants, participation in any programme had a positive and significant effect on the proportion of time in employment, although the effect of general training, while positive, was of only marginal significance. This was mainly due to the fact that the rate of employment of the comparison group increased gradually over the first 15 months of the 'post-programme' period, while that for programme participants was fairly stable throughout the period. The effect of participation in either skills training or employment subsidies was, however, substantially greater than that of either of the programmes with weak market linkages.

The results of the interaction model suggest some differences in programme effects between men and women. First, the positive significant effect of the female*direct employment schemes in equation (4) confirms that women benefited from participation in direct employment schemes. Men did not, so the weak positive effect of direct employment schemes in the combined equation (3) conceals an important gender difference in the impact of this programme on subsequent stability of employment. This is an effect which has important implications for policy, since a substantial

Table 5.3 Tobit estimations of post-programme employment duration

| Equation: | (3) All | | (4) Interaction model | | | |
| | | | Men | | Female interactions | |
	Coefficient	Standard error	Coefficient	Standard error	Coefficient	Standard error
Programmes						
General training	0.06	0.03	−0.02	0.05	0.09	0.07
Specific skills	0.26***	0.04	0.19***	0.05	0.16*	0.07
Employment subsidies	0.37***	0.05	0.32***	0.06	0.11	0.11
Direct employment schemes	0.12*	0.05	−0.08	0.08	0.29**	0.10
Control variables						
Age	0.02*	0.01	0.03**	0.01	−0.02	0.02
Lower secondary	0.18***	0.04	0.21***	0.04	−0.12	0.07
Upper secondary +	0.34***	0.04	0.26***	0.05	0.16*	0.08
Unemployment duration	−0.01***	0.001	−0.01***	0.02	0.01*	0.003
Dropout to job	0.03***	0.05	0.29**	0.05	0.01	0.10
Dropout – other	−0.28***	0.05	−0.27*	0.06	0.01	0.10
Female	−0.05*	0.02				
Constant	−0.26	0.14	−0.42*	0.19	0.15	0.29
Sigma	0.51	0.01	0.04	0.01		
-2 Log-likelihood	2327.2		2243.6			
No. of cases	1710		1710			

Note: *P<0.05, **P<0.01, ***P<0.001.

majority of participants in programmes of this type in Ireland (mainly Community Employment) are long-term unemployed males. Second, the effect of specific skills training programmes, positive for men, is even stronger among women.

Other effects are as expected, and similar to the pattern of effects found for employment probability reported in Table 5.1, although in relation to employment duration there are some interesting gender differences. Educational attainment has a positive significant effect, and the effect increases with level of education. Moreover, young women who have completed upper secondary education experience greater post-programme employment stability than do their male counterparts. Previous unemployment had a negative impact on men's employment duration, but the positive coefficient for women – about half the size of the coefficient for men – suggests that they suffered less than men from previous unemployment duration. Dropping out of a programme for reasons other than taking a job had negative effects on employment duration for both men and women equally, while dropping out of a programme to take up a job had a positive effect.

Table 5.4 reports the Tobit estimations of income from employment averaged over the post-programme period. In general, the pattern of effects is very similar to that in respect of aggregate duration of employment. Women tend to derive higher income returns from participation in specific skills training than men. While the effect of participation in direct employment schemes is negative, although not significant, on men's wages, the effect for women is positive and significant.

The income returns to educational attainment were steeper among women than among men, with women who completed upper secondary or attended third-level education experiencing earnings gains and women with no qualifications experiencing an income loss, even compared with their male counterparts. These findings are consistent with the gender differences in returns to educational attainment found in other studies of Irish data (OECD, 1998). Duration of previous unemployment significantly reduced male incomes but had no effect on women's incomes.

Our estimations confirm our general thesis that market-oriented programmes are of greater benefit to their participants than programmes with weak market linkages, but they also suggest some gender differences in the impact of ALMPs. The clearest differences occur in respect of direct employment schemes. Participation in such schemes had no impact on young men's employment chances, but they did increase women's employment probability. Direct employment schemes had negative, although non-significant, effects on both employment duration and earnings from employment among men, but they significantly increased both employment duration and earnings

Table 5.4 Tobit estimations of post-programme earnings from employment

Equation:	(5) All		(6) Interaction model			
			Men		Female interactions	
	Coefficient	Standard error	Coefficient	Standard error	Coefficient	Standard error
Programmes						
General training	0.21	0.96	0.03	0.29	0.33	0.41
Specific skills	1.20***	0.20	0.88**	0.23	0.78*	0.41
Employment subsidies	1.60***	0.29	1.30***	0.37	0.61	0.60
Direct employment schemes	0.38	0.27	−0.58	0.47	1.43**	0.58
Control variables						
Age	0.05	0.05	0.14*	0.06	−0.14	0.10
Lower secondary	0.20***	0.20	1.31***	0.26	−0.81*	0.40
Upper secondary +	1.95***	0.22	1.50***	0.31	0.83*	0.44
Unemployment duration	−0.06***	0.01	−0.08***	0.01	0.06**	0.02
Dropout to job	1.66***	0.27	1.62***	0.31	0.04	0.59
Dropout – other	−1.50**	0.25	−1.28***	0.31	−0.35	0.50
Female	−0.39*	0.13				
Constant	−0.54	0.83	−1.58	1.08	1.35	1.66
Sigma	2.42***	0.06	2.37***	0.07		
-2 Log-likelihood	5744.4		5704.2			
No. of cases	1556		1556			

Note: *P<0.05, **P<0.01, ***P<0.001.

among women. While there were no gender differences in the impact of specific skills training programmes on employment chances, such training schemes did lead to longer duration of employment and higher earnings from employment among women than among men.

4.   WOMEN AND ACCESS TO ACTIVE LABOUR MARKET PROGRAMMES

Having shown that some programmes are of greater benefit to their participants than others, it is useful to consider whether young men and women have equal access to the more effective programmes. Given the nature of our data, which are based on a follow-up survey of programme participants and a comparison group of non-participants drawn from a separate but nationally representative sample of young people, we are unable directly to address the question of unequal access to programmes for the aggregate population.[3] However, we can look at the way women are distributed across the programmes once the initial selection process determining who obtains a place in any programme has occurred. We can thus examine the extent to which young women who do gain access to ALMPs in Ireland have equality of access to the more effective types of programmes.

Table 5.5 shows the numbers and proportion in each programme type and the comparison group by gender. These data have been weighted to be representative of the total population of young people who left programmes during the sampling period April–July 1992. From the first column we see that, of all 1296 participants under 23, the majority participated in training, either general training or specific skills training, with much fewer in temporary employment measures. However, when we distinguish between men and women the pattern looks different. While the largest proportion of both men and women participate in general training,

Table 5.5   Programme participants and non-participants, by gender

	All		Men		Women		Per cent
	(no.)	%	(no.)	%	(no.)	%	female
General training	551	42.5	318	43.8	233	40.8	42.4
Specific skills training	466	35.9	287	39.6	179	31.3	38.4
Employment subsidies	115	8.9	76	10.5	39	6.9	34.0
Direct emp. schemes	164	12.7	44	6.1	120	21.0	73.1
All participants under 23	1296	100.0	725	100.0	571	100.0	44.1
Non-participants	246		128		118		48.0

a greater proportion of men participate in specific skills training. Women are underrepresented on employment subsidy schemes and substantially overrepresented on direct employment schemes: 21 per cent of women participate in the latter, compared to less than 13 per cent of men. Women are thus underrepresented on the more effective market-oriented programmes: about 38 per cent of women participated in either specific skills training or employment subsidy schemes, compared to 50 per cent of men.

However, within the less effective programmes – those with weak market linkages – there is a stronger tendency for women to participate in direct employment schemes, which we have shown to have beneficial effects on women's transition to work but not on men's. We have also shown, however, that these positive effects of direct employment schemes are weaker than those of the market-oriented programmes – specific skills training and employment subsidy schemes. These findings are consistent with the argument advanced by Rubery *et al.*: 'While it is by no means the case that women are always underrepresented in active labour market policies, there does seem to be some consensus that, where schemes are effective at integration, underrepresentation is more likely' (Rubery *et al.*, 1998, p. 185).

5. CONCLUSIONS

Given that women generally suffer higher rates of unemployment than men, this chapter is motivated by a concern to ascertain which types of ALMP are more effective in enhancing post-programme employment prospects and earnings of men and women and whether there are gender differences in the impact of different types of programme.

The analysis draws on the typology of ALMPs developed by O'Connell and McGinnity (1997a), which distinguishes between training and employment programmes on the basis of the strength of their orientation to the labour market. That approach argues that programmes characterized by strong linkages to the open labour market confer greater benefits on their participants than those with weak market linkages.

To investigate gender differences in the impact of different types of ALMP we analysed the 1992 post-programme follow-up survey of programme participants in Ireland, estimating separate models for men and women. Our findings provide strong support for the general theory of the importance of market orientation: for both men and women, participation in market-oriented programmes leads to higher chances of employment 18 months after leaving a programme, and increases both aggregate employment duration and earnings from employment averaged over a post-programme period extending from 18 to about 24 months. We also found gender differences in programme impact. First, the effects of specific skills training were stronger among women than men for two of our three dependent variables: employment duration and earnings from employment, but not in respect of employment chances. Second, while direct employment schemes had no discernible impact on employment chances, participation in such schemes had positive and significant effects on both employment duration and earnings of women, but not among men. This finding has important policy implications, not least because a substantial majority of participants in programmes of this type in Ireland (Community Employment, the largest single ALMP in Ireland) are long-term unemployed men.

Other variables in our models, introduced to control for the effects of individual characteristics and labour market experience, also show interesting patterns of variation by gender. In general, the returns to education – in terms of employment chances and duration, as well as earnings – are higher among women than among men. Men appear to suffer more than women in terms of post-programme outcomes from poor previous labour market experience, as measured by the duration of previous unemployment.

Active labour market programmes represent important interventions by which states seek to help individuals to make the transition from unemployment to employment. This chapter has demonstrated, first, that market-oriented programmes are more effective in assisting that transition and in improving employment stability and earnings than programmes with weak market linkages and, second, that women tend to benefit more than men from participation in both specific skills training and direct employment schemes. We acknowledge, however, that our findings relate to a sample of young people aged under 23. It is likely, however, that gender differences in labour market outcomes are more pronounced among older age groups. Rubery *et al.* (1998) argue that gender differences in both unemployment and non-employment increase with age. Given age and gender-related patterns in unemployment and non-employment, it is entirely possible that the gender differences we have found among young people in Ireland may not be simply generalizable to older age groups and to other countries; this caveat may be particularly pertinent to older women seeking to return to the world of work after an extended interruption of labour force participation. These considerations suggest that further empirical research is warranted into the relative effectiveness of programmes among older age groups, covering not only the transition from unemployment to employment, but also that from outside the labour force to work.

NOTES

1. Our distinction between general and specific skills training measures for the unemployed should not be confused with Becker's (1975) distinction. Becker's concept of specific training, usually applied to the training of employed workers, refers to training that is specific to a single employer, while his concept of general skills refers to broad skills which are portable between different employers. Thus both of our training categories would be included within Becker's category of general training.
2. For a more detailed description of the sample and data collection, see O'Connell and McGinnity (1997a).
3. We noted above the tendency for official statistics to underestimate women's unemployment in Ireland. Cousins (1996), in his analysis of women's access to employment and training schemes in Ireland, argues that the Live Register is a poor basis for establishing eligibility for access to programmes as it tends to undercount women's unemployment. Without a clearly defined population of female unemployed it is difficult to estimate women's access to labour market programmes.

BIBLIOGRAPHY

Becker, H. (1975), *Human Capital*, New York: Columbia University Press.

Bloom, H.S. (1994), *The National JTPA Study: Overview of Impacts, Benefits and Costs of Title II-A*, Bethesda, MD: Abt Associates

Cousins, M. (1996), *Pathways to Employment for Women Returning to Paid Work*, Dublin: Employment Equality Agency.

Dolton, P., Makepiece, G. and Treble, J. (1994), 'The Youth Training Scheme and the School-to-Work Transition', *Oxford Economic Papers*, 46, 629–57.

European Commission (1994), 'Growth, Competitiveness, Employment: The Challenges and Ways Forward into the 21st Century', White Paper, European Commission, Luxembourg.

Fay, R. (1996), 'Enhancing the Effectiveness of Active Labour Market Policies', *Evidence from Programme Evaluations in OECD Countries*, Paris: OECD.

Jacobson, L.S., Lalonde, R.J., Sullivan, D.G. and Bednarzik, R. (1994), 'The Returns from Classroom Training for Displaced Workers', mimeo.

Korpi, T. (1994), 'Employment Stability following Unemployment: Evidence of the Effect of Manpower Programmes among Youth', *Escaping Unemployment: Studies in the Individual Consequences of Unemployment and Labour Market Policy*, Stockholm: Swedish Institute for Social Research.

O'Connell, P.J. and McGinnity, F. (1997a), *Working Schemes: Active Labour Market Policies in Ireland*, Aldershot: Ashgate.

O'Connell, P.J. and McGinnity, F. (1997b), 'What Works, Who Works? The Employment and Earnings Effects of Active Labour Market Programmes among Young People in Ireland', *Work, Employment and Society*, 11(4).

OECD (1980), *Human Capital Investment Report*, Paris: OECD

OECD (1990), *Labour Market Policies for the Nineties*, Paris: OECD.

OECD (1997), *Employment Outlook*, July, Paris: OECD.

OECD (1998) *Human Capital Investment, An International Comparison*, Paris: OECD.

Payne, J. (1991) *Women, Training and the Skills Shortage. The Case for Public Investment*, London: Policy Studies Institute.

Payne, J., Lissenburgh, S., White, M. and Payne, C. (1996), 'Employment Training and Employment Action: An Evaluation by the Matched Comparison Method', *Department for Education and Employment Research Series No. 74*, Department for Education and Employment, Sheffield.

Rubery, J., Smith, M., Fagan, C. and Grimshaw, D. (1998) *Women and European Employment*, London: Routledge.

Trican Consulting Group (1993), 'Evaluation of the Severely Employment Disadvantaged (SED) Option of the Job Entry Programme', Programme Evaluation Branch, Strategic Policy and Planning, Employment and Immigration Canada, January.

6. Training for the unemployed in the Netherlands: what do we know after more than 50 evaluation studies?

Jaap de Koning

1. INTRODUCTION

This chapter reviews the evaluation studies carried out in the Netherlands since the mid-1980s through to the 1990s, with respect to training policy for the unemployed. At the time of the study, the Dutch situation was such that the Public Employment Service (PES) had a number of, partly overlapping, measures for training unemployed persons, with the overlaps applying both to the characteristics of the trainees and to the fields of training.[1] A considerable part of the training is carried out directly by the PES, although training is also contracted out to state schools and private training institutions. Since the PES became a decentralized organization in 1991, the regional boards of the PES have been able largely to determine their own policy and strategy with respect to training unemployed persons. As a result, many regional evaluation studies have been carried out to underpin the training policies of the regional boards. However, a number of studies have also been carried out at national level. But what do all these studies tell us about training for the unemployed? Can we observe a general pattern in the results of the various studies? Does training 'work'? Answering this type of question is the purpose of this chapter.

Although the focus is on the Netherlands, the aim is to provide a general framework for the evaluation of training for the unemployed. As indicators from more than 50 studies are used for the secondary analysis, this method could also be applied to training studies in other countries or for cross-country studies.

Answering a question such as 'does training work?' presupposes that we know what purposes training of unemployed people serves. When can training policy be said to be successful? It is when the available training budget is spent so that (a) mismatch between labour supply and demand is diminished or prevented, and (b) unequal opportunities among the suppliers of labour are diminished or prevented. Mismatch occurs when unemployment and unfilled demand coexist because job seekers have qualifications that do not fit job requirements. Training is an obvious means in this case to remove imbalances. Unequal opportunities exist if some people have a poorer chance of finding a job at the current wage rate or even below that wage rate than others. These unequal opportunities may arise out of too low a productivity level due to lack of formal education (the unskilled) or lack of experience (young people, migrants) or loss of human capital (women having been out of the labour market for a long time or long-term unemployed persons). Under these conditions training may be used to make the persons involved employable again.

Now the fact that training is useful for employers and unemployed persons does not necessarily imply that government money should be spent on it. We have first to ask why it could not be arranged by the employers and the unemployed persons involved; if the training is beneficial to the employer or the unemployed person, or to both, why would they not want to invest in training themselves? There are a number of reasons. First, the return to the unemployed person will be uncertain. He has no guarantee of finding a job and, even if he does, the initial pay may be relatively low. If he is risk-averse, he might not engage in training, even if there is a positive expected return on training (Kodde, 1987; Ritzen, 1989). Another difficulty is that training costs are high, implying that most people would have to borrow money. However, it is hard to imagine that banks would lend to an unemployed person. Finally, for some people, private returns may be negative (or too small), but the social returns may be positive. Without training the unemployed persons involved may remain unemployed, society having to pay an unemployment benefit.

If unemployed persons are unable to invest in training, employers may take over responsibility. However, in the case of general training,[2] the poaching practices of some firms may cause others to refrain from investing. If one company invests, another company may have the benefits. Only in the case of firm-specific training will this not apply. However, in that case, employers may be reluctant to hire certain categories of unemployed persons. Of course, this problem also applies to general training. Employers may fear that unemployed persons do not meet minimum standards of motivation and ability. The simple fact that people are unemployed is often interpreted by employers as an indication of such inadequacies. Both statistical and racial discrimination occur in practice. If the unemployed person is trained before applying to the employer or if the employer gets a training subsidy, then he/she might be persuaded to hire the unemployed person involved. Thus training can play a role in creating more equal opportunities.

But even if employers and/or unemployed persons were inclined to invest in training, it would still be questionable whether an adequate supply of training courses would exist. This applies mainly to the type of training for which major investment in equipment is necessary; that is, technical training. What we observe is that the demand for training in technical professions is relatively specialized, applies to relatively small numbers, is subject to business cycle fluctuations and is very costly. Supplying technical training on a commercial basis may be a very uncertain activity.

So we can conclude that there is some point in the government (or an organization such as the PES acting on behalf of the government) subsidizing training. Otherwise, underinvestment may occur and mismatch and unequal opportunities may persist. Sometimes subsidizing training to prevent or diminish mismatch may go hand in hand with creating more equal opportunities. That is the case when someone without any prospects of finding a job is trained (and placed) in an occupation in which shortages exist. Training may also be subsidized with the sole purpose of creating more equal opportunities or preventing/diminishing mismatch. There may even be a tension between the two objectives.[3]

If subsidizing training is considered useful, the next question is what is the best way to do it. There are basically three ways in which the government can stimulate training. First, it can subsidize institutions that train unemployed persons. The most far-reaching option is to have training carried out by a government organization or an organization that is completely subsidized by the government. Second, it can refund the training costs for individual trainees to the trainees or the training institutions involved. And, third, it can pay companies to provide the training and these in turn can decide either to do the training in-house or to 'outsource' it. All these variants exist in practice. From an economic point of view, subsidizing training schools makes sense only if state schools and the private sector are not able to offer the training, even if the government is paying for a number of trainees.[4] If an adequate supply exists, it is probably better to use it, rather than creating new training institutions. In that case the government could pay for the training. If companies are willing to train unemployed people, this may also be a good option, particularly as the trainee will often be hired by the company offering the training. Giving the subsidy directly to the trainee will usually require guidance by the employment service. Most trainees will not have the necessary knowledge and information to decide for themselves what type of training to follow.

So far, we have discussed the effectiveness of training. Efficiency is, of course, also an important criterion. Some of the points discussed in the former paragraph are related to efficiency, for instance the question of whether the government should have training centres of its own. Other questions relating to efficiency include the following. Are the effects of training achieved at the lowest possible costs? Where training schools are receiving subsidies are they being run in the most efficient way? And where external agencies (schools for initial vocational education, commercial schools, companies, and so on) are being paid to carry out the training, could others provide the same quality at a lower price than the agencies engaged?

In section 2, we elaborate on the questions which in our opinion should be answered in an evaluation of training policy. Most of these questions are quite difficult to answer. Even answering the basic question of whether trainees benefit from the training raises serious methodological problems. In many important respects watertight methods simply do not exist. Section 3 then reviews the 50 or more Dutch evaluation studies that were carried out between 1985 and 1994. This review is used to construct a data file which can be used, for instance, to analyse whether placement results depend on the type of training instrument when we correct for the composition of the trainee population. In most studies, only gross effects are dealt with, but in a few studies a (non-experimental) comparison group methodology is used that enables us to draw conclusions about the net placement effects. We not only focus on effects but also pay attention to costs. In section 4 the results obtained for the Dutch situation will be compared with results obtained in other countries. Some concluding remarks are given in the final section, section 5.

2.   THE EVALUATION METHOD

The various evaluation aspects may be classified under the following headings:

- reach,
- anticipated effects,
- side-effects,
- costs,
- implementation and control.

By *reach* we mean gross effect, that is the number of trainees relative to the number of unemployed persons in need of training (reach of supply) and employers applying to participate in the training (reach of demand). This measure indicates to what extent the training needs of both unemployed persons and employers are being fulfilled. The relevant factors here are not only the extent to which training needs are being fulfilled but also the representation of specific groups of unemployed persons and companies having vacancies. Questions related to reach include whether regional training capacity is sufficient to fulfil training needs and to what extent different training measures overlap.

Anticipated effects relate to the extent to which training helps to remove imbalances and create more equal opportunities in the labour market. If an unemployed person applies for training or if an employer wants an unemployed person to be trained before hiring him, this, of course, does not mean that training has a real or net effect. A trainee may have found a job if not trained and a vacancy may have been filled without somebody being trained. In other words, there could be an element of dead weight involved. Gross effect corrected for dead weight is net or real effect. Net supply effectiveness is defined as the net effect of training on the labour-market position of the trainees; net demand effectiveness refers to the net effect on the filling of vacancies.

The simple question of whether an unemployed person is better off after being trained is very difficult to answer. Many social scientists claim that experiments constitute a watertight method to detect the net effects of training and other measures. Taking a random sample of potential participants, assigning individuals to training and non-training randomly and monitoring the trainees and the non-trainees for some time seems to remove any doubts about the validity of the results. Burtless (1993) is a strong advocate of the experimental method. His criticism of the non-experimental control group approach is convincing. In the latter approach, selectivity cannot be avoided and complicated methods have to be used to correct for selectivity bias, making the results depend strongly on the model and the method used. However, the fact that the non-experimental method is not watertight does not imply that the experimental method can be so considered. In fact, Heckman and Smith (1993) list a whole range of disadvantages of the experimental approach. The most important is that an experiment carried out with a scheme is never equal to its generic application. For one thing, people who would join a general scheme may well refuse to function as guinea pigs. For another, in an experiment the participants are chosen at random, whereas in practice implementing institutions consciously select certain groups. Furthermore, the behaviour of both participants and programme officials may be different in an experiment from what it would be in 'real life'. So, even if experiments gave watertight results, generalization to practice would still be questionable.[5]

On the whole, we support Heckman and Smith's opinion that the experimental approach is not a panacea for evaluation research. Nevertheless, experiments can fulfil an important function in the design of new policy, because they can give a good indication of the potential effects of a scheme.

Once a measure has been enacted, its real effects will depend in part on its implementation, which may differ from that of the experiment.

A weakness of the control group approach, whether experimental or non-experimental, is that it assumes that improving the opportunities of the trainees will not affect the chances of the members of the control group. That may not be true, in particular when a scheme is applied to a large percentage of the target group. In those cases measurement on the group level is appropriate. This also applies when the effects of training on market efficiency are to be measured. Improving the chances of trainees may diminish the chances of non-trainees and easing the recruitment problems of some employers may increase the recruitment problems of other employers. In other words, displacement may imply that the overall results for the labour market are less impressive than they might appear on first sight. Other *side-effects* can be beneficial to the economy. If displacement does not occur, or not to the extent of wiping out the net effects, unemployment and/or unfilled demand may go down, which would be beneficial both socially and economically.[6] Income and productivity may increase and expenditure on social benefits may decrease. In order to measure the possible impact of training on the overall performance of the labour market, methods such as unemployment/vacancy analysis may be used (de Grip, 1987; OECD, 1993).

It may seem strange to consider the effects of training on productivity, income and total employment as side-effects. However, these effects are not those that the government is aiming at when it organizes and subsidizes training for the unemployed. Removing and preventing mismatch and promoting more equal opportunities are its two central objectives.

Effectiveness should be assessed against *costs*. The phrase, 'costs of training', can mean different things. From the viewpoint of the PES it refers to the costs the service itself incurs, that is, the training subsidy, and time spent by government officials in planning training, selecting trainees, monitoring training results and so on.

From a societal point of view, a different concept of costs applies, however. For instance, if training is carried out by regular schools the subsidy will usually cover only part of the costs, the Ministry of Education paying the remainder.

Implementation and control are relevant to each of the former criteria. With respect to reach, the first question is how the training capacity can be guaranteed to meet training needs. Is a planning method operational? Are training institutions given incentives to adjust their capacity to training demand? In this context, the 'make or buy' question is also vitally important. Having your own training schools may reduce the likelihood of a training supply shortage, but perhaps only at considerable cost.

Reach, of course, also refers to the selection of trainees and the types of training, which may, indeed should, be closely linked to the planning of training.

The net effects of training will be determined by selection (characteristics of trainees and type of training), quality and field of training, training results and counselling activities after training completion. Training results will probably depend on selection and training quality. Quality will depend on duration, quality of teaching and curriculum, and will be closely related to the type of training. The effectiveness of training in a certain case is not the only relevant consideration. It is also necessary to ascertain whether the effect would have been bigger if another type of training and/or another training measure had been applied.[7] In order to be effective, the time lag between the emergence of a training need and the 'delivery' of a trained person should be as short as possible. Duration of courses, the number of inflow opportunities and the ability to develop new forms of training will determine the term of delivery.

Employment offices play a role in both selection and placement. Therefore, if training is not successful, the training agency involved may not be to blame, or only partly to blame. Side-effects depend strongly on selection. If people with very few opportunities are selected for training in occupations in which shortages exist, displacement is not likely to occur. Costs depend very strongly on reach and therefore on all the aspects of implementation determining reach. If one corrects for dropout rates, costs will also be related to training quality. The utilization rate of training capacity is an important determining factor for training costs. Adjusting capacity to training needs is one way to avoid underutilization, but diminishing absence rates and avoiding long time lags between one person completing training and the next one starting are also important.

Table 6.1 lists the criteria for evaluating training policy. The result of an actual evaluation will be a list of scores on the various criteria, a relation between results and implementation and suggestions for improvement. It will be impossible to derive an overall score on the basis of the scores on the various criteria, because some indicators are qualitative in nature and cannot be put in financial terms (or only in a rather artificial way).[8] However, in principle, most effects and their mutual dependencies could be analysed within the framework of a macroeconometric model. But this goes far beyond the scope of this chapter.

Table 6.1 may imply that the training process and therefore the training results can be controlled completely. However, the labour market situation will have strong effects on the results. This is particularly true for gross placement results. When the labour market is tight, job seekers easily find jobs and trainees will also benefit. The net increase in placement probability will

Table 6.1   Criteria for evaluating training policy

Criterion	Description	Implementation and control aspects
Reach	– extent to which training needs of supply are being met – same for demand – representation of target groups among trainees – representation of specific types of vacancies (demand characteristics) among the vacancies filled by trainees – ratio between training volume and training capacity – overlaps between training measures	– planning – budgeting system – 'make or buy' decisions – selection of trainees, types of training and training measures
Envisaged effects	– extent to which mismatch is prevented/diminished – extent to which opportunities have become more equal	– selection – training results – training quality – term of delivery – placement
Side-effects	– displacement – diminishing expenditure on unemployment benefits – higher output/ productivity/income	– selection – training quality – placement
Costs	– costs per trainee – same corrected for dropout – costs per hour	– same aspects as reach – training quality – utilization of training capacity

be less sensitive to labour market tightness, but we cannot a priori exclude the possibility that net effects are also affected by it. Side-effects will almost certainly be affected. When unemployment is high and unfilled demand is low, training will hardly add to total employment, implying that displacement is inevitable.

Still another criterion has perhaps to be added, namely the *uniqueness* of an instrument. This represents the extent to which an instrument supplies a unique training for a given target group. The main question is whether the need for education of (specific groups of) unemployed persons could be provided for in another way. Not only factual but also potential alternatives are relevant.

Even when instruments address different groups of unemployed as well as different vacancies, a comparison can be useful. An example may illustrate this. The centre for basic training (CBB; for a description see the next section) is concerned with the 'more difficult' groups, implying that (gross) placement results are relatively poor. Therefore, CBB will have a low score on (gross) placement results. However, if CBB really addresses 'difficult' groups it should show a higher share of these groups in its population of students than other instruments. CBB would, then, have a good score on 'reach'. Thus less satisfactory results in some aspects might be permissible, provided there is compensation on other points (such as reach). The final overall judgment depends also on the weights allotted to the different criteria, and they are a matter of policy.

3. A REVIEW OF DUTCH EVALUATION STUDIES

A Brief Description of the Dutch System

In the period under consideration, training for the unemployed was largely the responsibility of the Public Employment Service. Recently, the picture has changed considerably. The responsibility for subsidizing training for the unemployed has been transferred from the PES to the organizations that deal with unemployment compensation and social assistance. A large part of the PES is in the process of being privatized. However, for the period under consideration (1985–94) it is fair to say that training for the unemployed was largely organized by the PES.

Until 1991, the PES was a Directorate General of the Ministry of Social Affairs and Employment, but in 1991 it became an independent organization. However, funding was still provided by the ministry. During the 1991–94 period, an increasing share of the funds made available for training and other policies originated in the European Social Fund.

The following training instruments were used by the PES:

- centres for adult vocational training which were part of the PES (CV in Dutch);
- centres for basic training (CBB in Dutch);

- centres for vocational training for women ('Vrouwenvakschool' (VVS) in Dutch);
- a subsidy scheme for training which was also open to regular schools and private training agencies (KRS in Dutch);
- a scheme for adult apprenticeship training (PBVE in Dutch).

The centres for adult vocational training were founded at the end of the Second World War, when the country had to be rebuilt and there was a shortage of construction workers. After some years, courses in metal working were included. It was not until the 1980s that courses in administrative skills were introduced. Some of the centres specialize in technical or administrative training; others cover both. The training contents resemble apprenticeship training, although a person has to take further training once in employment in order to obtain the apprenticeship diploma. A strong point of the centres is that people can enrol at various points of time during the year. Another strength of the technical centres is that, for many fields of technical training, they are the only option for unemployed people. It is probable that the centres will be privatized in the near future. Centres which provide both technical and administrative training are denoted by the abbreviation CV, specialized technical centres by CVT and specialized administrative ones by CVA.

The basic training centres and the vocational training centres for women were not part of the PES, but they were financially completely dependent on the PES. The basic training centres fell within the scope of the Ministry for Health and Well-being. During the period in question here, they helped immigrants to integrate into Dutch society. Although ethnic minorities still form a large share of the trainees, the centres are now also open to other groups with a weak labour-market position. Furthermore, the centres have become more oriented to labour market integration. Training is basic, that is it:

- provides general information about the labour market;
- provides general (Dutch) language and mathematical skills, as well as social skills;
- provides basic pre-qualification vocational skills.

It was hoped that, having followed basic training at the CBB, trainees would enter vocational training, but this has not happened very often in practice.

The main purpose of the vocational training centres for women is to provide training in non-traditional fields, particularly information and communication technology, for women re-entering the labour market. However, more traditional office and secretarial courses are also provided.

Although existing courses are also open to women, it may be difficult for them to cope with the male-dominated environment. VVS courses are at the secondary or even upper secondary level, that is higher than those provided in the vocational training centres. Training duration is also longer.

Both the basic training centres and the vocational training centres for women suffered from the cuts in the PES budget and a number of them did not survive. Most of the remaining CBBs have become part of the regional education centres. The remaining centres for women will most likely be privatized.

The general training subsidy scheme allowed employment offices to subsidize training for unemployed persons. Both field and duration of training varied considerably. The training subsidized under this scheme was carried out by different types of training institutions. The vocational schools mentioned above also provided some of the training under this scheme. These centres, regular schools and commercial training agencies each accounted for one-third of training expenditure in this scheme (Zandvliet, 1991). A similar scheme to the general subsidy scheme still exists, although nowadays the organizations responsible for unemployment compensation and social assistance manage it.

Finally, we come to a training instrument that no longer exists: apprenticeship training for adult unemployed persons (the so-called PBVE measure). This was a joint initiative of the PES and the Ministry of Education. It has already been noted that, although the training provided by adult vocational training centres resembles apprenticeship training, trainees cannot obtain the official diploma unless they continue training after finding a job. The apprenticeship training scheme was intended to provide the opportunity for unemployed people to obtain this diploma. However, many trainees lacked the basic knowledge to enrol in an apprentice relationship with an employer. Although the scheme included prequalification training in an attempt to resolve this problem, it was not successful for most trainees. In most cases only regular schools were involved, although the centres discussed earlier played some role in it. PBVE training covered a broad range of occupations. When the Ministry of Education stopped subsidizing the scheme it was terminated, although some PES regional boards continued the scheme on a smaller scale.

Table 6.2 summarizes the main characteristics of the various instruments. The list of training instruments in the table is not complete. Examples of other training measures include a subsidy scheme for computer courses and so-called 'applications clubs'. These instruments will be included under 'other' instruments in this chapter. 'Normal' apprenticeship training is not covered in this study, because 'normal' apprentices usually have a regular job.

Table 6.2 Dutch instruments for training the unemployed

	Nature of the measure	Profile of the trainees	Level of training	Duration of training	Fields of training	Current situation
Vocational training centres	Training centres which were part of the PES organization	Unemployed persons	A number of modules of the official apprenticeship training	One year (in practice often shorter)	Technical occupations (CVT) Administrative occupations (CVA)	Will most probably be privatized
Basic training centres	Training centres outside the PES organization, but heavily dependent on the PES financially	Long-term unemployed Low-skilled Ethnic minorities	Pre-qualification	One year (in practice often shorter)	Very diverse	Some of the centres disappeared owing to cuts in the PES budget; most of the remaining ones have become part of the regional education centres
Vocational training centres for women	Training centres outside the PES organization, but heavily dependent on the PES financially	Women wanting to re-enter the labour market Women from minority groups	Secondary and upper secondary level	Two years	Information and Communication Technology Administrative occupations	Some centres disappeared owing to cuts in the PES budget. The remaining ones will probably be privatized.

General subsidy scheme for the training of unemployed people	Umbrella measure by which the PES subsidizes training carried out by schools, private agencies, companies and the centres mentioned in the previous rows	Unemployed persons	Varies considerably	Mostly relatively short	Very diverse	Still exists in more or less the same form, but is now coming under the responsibility of the organizations for unemployment compensation and social assistance
Apprenticeship training for the adult unemployed	Theory component provided by schools, practical component by companies (in principle)	Low-skilled unemployed persons	Apprenticeship training	Two years (in practice often shorter)	A broad range of occupations	No longer exists

The Data[9]

Between 1985 and 1994, some 52 evaluation studies relating to training for the unemployed were carried out in the Netherlands.[10] Although the studies differ in scope, the definitions used in the various studies were, fortunately, very similar, since most studies based their questionnaires on the early studies. A number of indicators were recorded in almost all the studies and we were therefore able to construct a data file in which the evaluation studies are treated as observations. Each observation consists of a record with the following data:

- the type of training measure/instrument,
- the share of women and of ethnic minorities among the trainees,
- the dropout rate,
- the placement rate,
- the average length of time between the completion of training and the survey in which placement was measured, the net placement rate as measured by participants' opinions.

Where studies covered more than one training instrument, a record was made for each instrument separately and they were treated as different observations. Thus the total number of 'observations' equals 112. However, not every record is complete. For some studies the share of ethnic minorities is lacking, for instance.

It was important that, for each study, we knew how much time elapsed between the completion of the training and the moment the participants were surveyed, since placement rates will obviously be relatively low if former participants are surveyed shortly after completion of the training.

On the basis of this data set we can, for instance, analyse to what extent the placement rate depends on the type of instrument and the characteristics of the participants, using regression analysis. The studies involved refer to different periods with different labour market situations. Obviously, the variance in placement rates is partly caused by changing labour market conditions. For this reason, the unemployment rate in the region (or the country when the study is a national one) at the time to which the study refers is added to the record. We also added the average length of time between the completion of training and the survey date.

Some aspects relevant to training cannot be analysed in this way, because they were addressed only in a limited number of studies. This is the case for net effects measured on the basis of the control group approach and costs. We simply give a description of the main results from the studies which do treat these aspects.

Results

Reach viewed from the supply side

Table 6.3 contains information on the total number of unemployed trainees and their distributions over the various instruments. Up to 1993 we have information about the number of participants for each training instrument. For 1994 only estimates are available. The definitions underlying the figures are not always that clear. Normally, however, they refer to new trainees. The figures show that the total number of trainees rose from slightly more than 40 000 to more than 130 000 in 1993. There was a sharp decline in 1994 due to a budget cut for the PES. The figures for the vocational training centres for women is included in the figures for the general training scheme. Moreover, the figures for the latter scheme include cases in which the other centres provided the training. This applies to the adult apprenticeship training scheme too.

These figures mean very little unless they are compared with the number of unemployed. The total number of trainees as a share of the unemployed population is added to Table 6.3. From the figures we can conclude that a considerable proportion of the unemployed was trained during the years before 1994. In 1992 this proportion reaches its maximum of almost one-third of the stock of unemployed. In 1994 the number of trainees had dropped to no more than 12.5 per cent of the stock of unemployed, which is almost as low as at the start of the period (8.4 per cent). One could argue that it is wrong to compare the number of trainees, which is a flow variable, with the stock of unemployment. We should take the stock at the beginning of the year and add the total inflow into unemployment during the year. However, a considerable proportion of the people flowing into unemployment flows out again after only a short while. It is not likely that this group will engage in training. Therefore we should probably exclude people with an unemployment duration of less than, say, three months. Unfortunately, information on unemployment flows is not available. However, the stock of unemployment is probably a better figure with which to compare trainee participation than the sum total of this stock and the inflow.[11]

There are no administrative data on the composition of the trainee groups. On the basis of the information in the training studies we can only give a qualitative impression of the characteristics of the trainees for the different instruments (see Table 6.4). Clearly, unskilled persons are under-represented in most instruments, although they are probably most in need of training. On the whole women are overrepresented. However, one should take into consideration that the participation rate of women in the Netherlands is relatively low. For most training instruments, women are eligible even when they are not officially unemployed (provided that they do not have a paid job, of course).

Table 6.3   Number of participants in the various training schemes for the unemployed, 1985–94 (*1000 persons)

	1985	1986	1987	1988	1989	1990	1991	1992	1993	1994[a]
Vocational training centres	6.9	10.5	11.9	12.1	12.6	16.1	16.2	16.2	16.9	16.0
Basic training centres	3.0	3.2	3.4	3.8	4.0	4.2	4.2	4.2	5.0	6.0
General training scheme, including the vocational training centres for women	25.7	28.7	58.5	59.0	62.3	71.0	78.2	81.3	80.5	46.5
Adult apprenticeship training	7.3	3.2	10.8	16.5	18.1	18.7	16.8	21.4	20.5	—
Other	—	4.6	6.6	4.5	5.6	6.3	7.6	9.6	10.1	10.0
Total number of trainees	42.9	50.0	91.2	99.9	102.6	116.3	123.0	132.7	133.0	68.5
As a percentage of unemployment[b]	8.4	10.5	18.8	20.4	22.7	27.8	30.1	32.3	27.7	12.5
As a percentage of vacancies[c]	79.5	97.6	129.2	154.9	110.9	111.1	142.2	228.0	397.0	173.9

Notes:
[a] Estimates.
[b] Registered unemployment as measured by CBS since 1987.
[c] Since 1989, September figures; before 1989, January figures.

Source: Public Employment Service.

Table 6.4   *Qualitative impression of the composition of the participant groups of the various instruments, compared with their share in unemployment*

	Women	Ethnic minorities	40 years or older	Low-skilled	Unemployed for more than 1 year
Vocational training centre: technical training	−	0	−	0	0
Vocational training centre: administrative training	+	−	0	−	0
Basic training centre	0	+	−	0	0
Vocational training centre for women	+	0	+	−	0
General training scheme	+	0	+	−	0
Adult apprenticeship training	+	+	0	−	0
Other	+	+	0	−	−
Total	+	0	0	−	0

Note: '0' means no significant difference, '+' means significantly higher and '−' means significantly lower.

Source: Dutch training studies.

Ethnic minorities, people unemployed for more than one year and people older than 40 years, all of them vulnerable groups, are represented more or less proportionately to their shares in the unemployed population. However, proportional representation may not be good enough. Moreover, ethnic minorities engage mainly in pre-qualifying training which is often not followed by qualifying training. In order to improve the labour market position of these groups they should probably be overrepresented. However, from the policy maker's point of view (as already noted above), the proportions of the various target groups should not depend on priorities only, but also on effectiveness and costs.

So far we have not looked at training from a longitudinal perspective. However, people may follow a number of courses successively. We have already pointed to pre-qualifying courses which could (or perhaps should) be followed by qualifying training. However, some people could, in theory, move from one course to another and stay unemployed all the time. There could be two reasons for this. First, people may engage in training in order to evade the obligation to apply for jobs. In the second place it may not be that easy for the authorities to find enough trainees. Consequently, selection criteria may be loosened up. This may appear to be a cynical interpretation, but it is by no means entirely implausible. We return to this point in the section on implementation.

Unemployed people permanently registered on training courses without making much progress in terms of employability are called 'training nomads'. The question, of course, is whether they constitute a large group among the trainees. In a study for the employment board in the city of Utrecht (De Koning, Zandvliet, Bokhoven and Olieman, 1993) it was found that fewer than 8 per cent of trainees are nomads. A similar figure (7 per cent) was found for the Drechtsteden region (De Koning, Zandvliet and Bokhoven, 1993).

Completion rates

Training is said to be completed when the trainee has completed the training course. In most cases, training courses for the unemployed do not result in a formal diploma. So passing exams cannot be used as a criterion. In the case of pre-qualification training, interpretation of the completion rate is not always straightforward. In some cases, the first phase of pre-qualification training closely resembles assessment. When a trainee quits training after the assessment period there is not necessarily anything wrong. Secondly, many trainees quit training because they find a job. When this happens, particularly in the last phase of the training, it might be considered a 'good' outcome.

In Table 6.5, sample means and standard deviations of the proportion of the trainees completing the training are given for each training instrument.

Table 6.5   Results for the completion percentage: mean, standard deviation and number of cases

	Mean completion percentage	Standard deviation	Number of cases
CBB	60	11	12
CV	83	9	5
CVA	84	4	9
CVT	70	11	11
KRS	79	13	21
PBVE	70	13	11
VVS	92	10	5
Other	75	22	8
Total	75	16	82

Source: Dutch training studies.

Information on the completion percentage is available for 82 cases. The unweighted sample mean of this variable is 75 per cent; that is, on average, three-quarters of trainees complete the training. The vocational training centre for women has the highest score (mean of 92 per cent), basic training the lowest score (mean of 60 per cent). However, as already noted above, low completion rates may not mean much in the case of basic training. Furthermore, differences in completion rate between instruments may partly reflect differences in the composition of their trainee population. Information is available on only two characteristics of the trainees, namely gender and ethnic origin.

The reasons for dropout have been investigated in a limited number of studies. It appears that some of the trainees quit training because they find a job. Zandvliet and van Bokhoven (1994) find that 15 per cent of the trainees that did not complete the training quit because they found a job. Their study for the Friesland region covers seven cases. De Koning and Van Nes (1989) find a figure of 40 per cent in their national evaluation of the KRS.

Table 6.6 shows the results of an equation in which the completion rate is explained by:

- the composition of the participant group;
- the type of training instrument;
- the unemployment rate;
- a time trend starting from 1985.

It is evident that the completion rate may depend on the composition of the participant group and on the type of instrument. But why did we include the unemployment rate? High unemployment rates may demotivate trainees, because of poor job prospects. On the other hand, it could also be argued that high unemployment motivates trainees, because their chances in the labour market will improve when trained. Furthermore, in conditions of high unemployment, it is less likely that trainees will find a job during training. Unemployment, then, could influence success rates, although it is theoretically unclear in which direction. In the regression equation, the sign of the unemployment variable is positive, but not significant.

The table contains the results of two regressions, one including the share of women in the trainee group as an explanatory variable and the other not. Inclusion of this variable has a tremendous effect on the explanatory power of the equation (the R-square increases from 0.32 to 0.50). Thus we are inclined to conclude that the good performance of the administrative centre for adult vocational training (CVA) and the vocational training centre for women (VVS) is due to the fact that women form a large part of the trainee group (in the case of the VVS even 100 per cent). CV/CVT and

Table 6.6   Equation for the completion rate (t-values in brackets)

Variable	Equation 1	Equation 2
CV/CVT	24.7 (4.0)	11.4 (1.8)
CVA/VVS	9.09 (1.3)	24.7 (3.6)
KRS	15.9 (3.0)	19.7 (3.3)
PBVE	−0.649 (−0.11)	10.4 (1.8)
CBB	Reference instrument	Reference instrument
Other training measures	7.87 (1.2)	16.3 (2.1)
Percentage share of women among the trainees	0.461 (4.2)	−
Percentage share of ethnic minorities among the trainees	−0.081 (−0.77)	−0.185 (−1.5)
Percentage share of 15–24-year-olds among the trainees	−0.193 (−0.50)	−0.306 (−0.7)
Time trend	0.455 (0.39)	0.671 (0.5)
Unemployment rate	1.51 (1.3)	0.944 (0.7)
Constant	34.3 (2.5)	61.9 (4.4)
Adjusted R^2	0.50	0.32
Number of observations	56	56

Source: Dutch training studies.

KRS outperform the other training measures in terms of completion rate when the share of women in the trainee group is included in the equation. CVA/VVS and 'other' measures occupy an intermediate position. CBB and PBVE are the worst performers in terms of completion rate. When CV and CVT are included separately the coefficients appear to be similar in size. Furthermore, CV and CVT training largely overlap. The same is true for CVA and VVS.

Other characteristics of the trainee group (age and ethnic origin) do not have a significant influence on the completion rate. The share of unskilled workers is not included in the equations presented in Table 6.6 because inclusion of this variable reduces the number of observations considerably. However, when it was included it proved to be insignificant. Finally, there is no indication of a structural change in the completion rate over time.

In the equations presented in Table 6.6 we tried to make the various instruments comparable by correcting for differences in the composition of the trainee group. However, it should be remembered that people are not assigned randomly to the instruments. It is possible that unobserved characteristics of the trainees influence both the selection for a specific training measure and the training outcomes.

Gross placement rates

In 95 of the cases we know how many people have found a job after training. On average this is measured about six months after leaving training. The (unweighted) mean placement rate is 60 per cent (see Table 6.7), including trainees who did not finish the training. Basic training and adult apprenticeship training have relatively low placement scores, in part due to the fact that a number of trainees move to other forms of training after a course in basic training or adult apprenticeship training. But there is evidence (de Koning, Zandvliet and Bokhoven, 1993) that most of these people change from one pre-qualification course to another. In those cases, the transition from one course to another cannot be seen as a positive result. This may seem strange in the case of the adult apprenticeship training scheme, but it should be noted that many trainees on this scheme need a pre-qualification course before they can enter vocational training.

Table 6.7   Results for the placement percentage: mean, standard deviation and number of cases

	Mean placement percentage	Standard deviation	Number of cases
CBB	49	16	14
CV	80	6	6
CVA	61	14	10
CVT	68	8	14
KRS	67	14	21
PBVE	47	18	13
VVS	69	11	7
Other	46	25	10
Total	60	25	95

Source: Dutch training studies.

Table 6.8 gives the result for the equation explaining the gross placement rate after training. The same variables are included as in the success rate equation. Two variables are added, namely the time expired on average between the outflow from training and the survey date and the completion rate.

From Table 6.8 we conclude that the shares of young people and of

Table 6.8   Equation for the placement rate (t-values in brackets)

Variable	Equation 1	Equation 2
CV/CVT	19.0 (2.7)	20.4 (4.0)
CVA/VVS	8.55 (1.3)	7.92 (1.3)
KRS	11.0 (2.0)	11.3 (2.1)
PBVE	−0.631 (−0.11)	−1.22 (−0.24)
CBB	Reference instrument	Reference instrument
Other training measures	−8.03 (−1.2)	−8.21 (−1.3)
Percentage share of women among the trainees	−0.038 (−0.29)	−
Percentage share of ethnic minorities among the trainees	−0.238 (−2.2)	−0.235 (−2.3)
Percentage share of 15–24-year-olds among the trainees	−0.743 (−1.9)	−0.75 (−2.0)
Time trend from 1990 on	−2.05 (−1.3)	−2.02 (−1.3)
Unemployment rate	0.227 (0.2)	0.341 (0.28)
Length of period between outflow from training and survey date	0.968 (4.4)	0.989 (4.8)
Constant	38.9 (3.2)	37.8 (3.3)
Adjusted R^2	0.71	0.71
Number of observations	54	54

Source: Dutch training studies.

ethnic minorities have a negative impact on the placement rate. For this equation also, the number of observations is reduced considerably when the share of the low-skilled among the trainees is taken into account. However, when it is included in the equation it appears to be insignificant.

The placement rate is also found to be proportionally higher the longer the period between the outflow from training and the survey date. There is only weak evidence of a structural change in the placement rate over time. Surprisingly, the unemployment rate is not significant.

With respect to the various measures, a similar order emerges to that in Table 6.6: CV/CVT performs best, followed by KRS and CVA/VVS. CBB and PBVE show much weaker results. Other measures perform even worse. Here again the reader should be warned that the relative performance of the various measures in Table 6.8 may partly reflect unobserved characteristics of the trainees.

Net placement results

Gross placement results may not mean that much, because trainees might well have found a job when not trained. Gross placement rates have to be corrected for so-called 'dead weight' in order to estimate net placement rates or net effectiveness. Many of the training studies deal with this issue by asking people whether training had improved their chances of finding a job. This is then taken as an indication of net effectiveness. Although we used this device in several studies, we do not trust the figures resulting from this method and we will not present them in this chapter.

However, some studies use the quasi-experimental control group method to measure net effects on placement. In Table 6.9 an overview is given of the studies concerned. For each study, the table provides the following information: (a) the period to which the results refer, (b) the training instrument dealt with in the study, (c) the region to which the study refers, and (d) the main results.

Three out of four of the studies show a relatively large net effect of training on the placement rate: a doubling or almost a doubling of the

Table 6.9   Overview of Dutch studies based on the non-experimental control group approach

	Reference period	Training instrument	Region	Main results
De Koning *et al.* (1987, 1988)	1986–7	Centre for vocational training	National	Small positive effect on re-employment probability
De Koning and Van Nes (1990)	1988–9	Centre for basic training	National	Doubling of re-employment probability
De Koning, Zandvliet, Bokhoven and Olieman (1993)	1991–3	Most training instruments	Regional board for West Utrecht	Almost doubling of re-employment probability
Bavinck and Van der Burgh (1994)	1992–4	Centre for vocational training General training scheme Job application training	Regional board for Noord-en Midden Limburg	Almost doubling of re-employment probability

placement probability (see Table 6.9). In a somewhat older study a small net increase in placement probability was found. There are two explanations for this discrepancy. First, the control group was selected in a different way, since the trainees were compared with people who became unemployed at the time the trainees left training and went looking for a job. In the other studies, the control group was selected from the people who were unemployed at the time the trainees were selected for training. The second explanation is that, at the time the older study was carried out, the centre for vocational training recruited its trainees mainly from the ranks of young people of Dutch origin with short unemployment duration, that is, individuals with relatively high job entry chances. This changed subsequently. The share of groups with a lower profile in the labour market, such as the long-term unemployment and ethnic minorities, increased.

De Koning and Van Nes (1990) and Bavinck and Van der Burgh (1994) also present results for subgroups among the participants. In both cases, net placement results for long-term unemployed trainees appear to lie considerably above average. In particular, those people who had been out of work for more than six years were found to have virtually no chance of getting a job without being trained. And, even though the placement rate when trained is relatively low among the long-term unemployed, it is much higher than for the long-term unemployed in the control group.

A weakness of all these studies is that no attempt is made to correct for selectivity bias.

Side-effects
Supposing that training has a positive effect on the re-employment probability of the trainees, the initial effect could be merely distributive. This is the case when total employment remains the same and the positive effects for the trainees imply that other job seekers remain unemployed. This is not necessarily a negative outcome if the trainees would otherwise have had few chances of obtaining employment and if they were displacing people with good opportunities who have only to wait a little longer for a job. However, when an unemployed person is trained in an occupation for which a shortage exists, then total employment could increase. In assessing the effect on total employment we should also take into account that training involves costs, which could have been spent in an alternative way. The alternative option (for instance a wage subsidy) may also have had positive effects on employment. However, it must be acknowledged that our knowledge about side-effects is very incomplete.

Examples of studies assessing the effects of training on the mismatch between demand and supply have been scarce in the Netherlands. De Grip

(1987) found a negative effect of CV training on mismatch in the construction sector using u/v analysis (where u and v denote unemployment and vacancies respectively), but the effect was hardly significant. In a more recent study, De Koning *et al.* (1995) failed to find a significant effect of employment and training policy on the total number of people finding a job. De Koning and Arents (2001) repeated this analysis for two duration classes: the short-term unemployed and the long-term unemployed. They found a small impact on short-term unemployment, but no significant effect on long-term unemployment. In these studies, employment and training policy as a whole is taken as a policy indicator. The results for training alone could be different, therefore.

However, even when the initial effect of training is merely redistributive in the short term, there might be some effect on total employment in the long run. This is the case when training makes totally unemployable unemployed persons attractive for employers again, thereby increasing the total effective supply of labour, which in turn will have a downward effect on wages and a positive effect on employment. In other words, training may (just like employment policies) diminish the hysteresis effect (Layard *et al.*, 1991). However, nothing is known about this possible effect for the Netherlands. There is only circumstantial evidence. Using a VAR (vector autoregression) approach, Broersma *et al.* (1997) found that a 1 per cent increase in the actual labour supply leads in the long term to a 0.8 to 0.9 per cent increase in employment. That would mean that it pays to reintegrate long-term unemployed individuals who quit job search and no longer receive job offers from employers (and thus no longer belong to the actual labour supply). However, only a minority of the trainees belong to this category.[12]

The same is true for a possible productivity effect of training. Several evaluation studies show that many trainees find a job whose content does not match that of the training programme. This finding might indicate that often the positive placement effect is a signalling effect. It is not the contents of the training that matters to employers, but the fact that the trainee has the ability and the motivation to complete a training course.[13] Under these conditions it would be implausible for the training of unemployed persons to have a large productivity effect.

Costs

The costs of training consist of the direct costs borne by the training agencies involved and the indirect costs associated with the design and implementation of training policy. In addition to the staff of the training centres directly managed by the Public Employment Service, policy advisors and counsellors also spend time on training policy. Little is known about the indirect costs, however, so that we can only present information about the direct costs. Even here, however, there are no precise data. In particular, there is an absence of good data on capital costs. Depreciation is taken as an approximation in most cases. Training duration varies between the instruments, which partly explains the differences in costs between them. It might be helpful, therefore, to look at training costs per hour. It is also possible to correct for differences in completion rates and placement rates. In that case total (direct) training costs would be divided, not by the total number of trainees, but by the total number of trainees who completed training or the total number who found a job after training.

De Koning, Zandvliet and Knol (1993) tried to estimate the costs of a training place, that is the costs of training one person for one year, for the adult vocational training centre, the basic training centre and the vocational training centre for women. For adult apprenticeship training, only rough estimates are available, assuming that the costs of the theory component are similar to the costs of initial vocational education. For the general training scheme and adult apprenticeship training, less information is available and even that information which is available is less reliable. The average costs per trainee vary between 3500 and 8500 euros among the various training measures. The vocational training centre for women and adult apprenticeship training are the most expensive training instruments on the basis of average training costs. There is only limited information available about the cost of training courses in various fields. However, the information we have for one region (Friesland) indicates that the differences are considerable. Some technical courses costs more than 30000 euros, while, for instance, a course in word-processing costs only a few thousand euros.

4.   COMPARING THE RESULTS WITH NON-DUTCH STUDIES

How do the outcomes compare with the results found in non-Dutch studies? This is difficult to say. Most studies published in international journals concentrate on assessing the net effects of training for the unemployed on placement and income and do not cover other aspects such as reach, completion rates, implementation aspects and costs. National studies may exist which include these kinds of issues. Indeed, most of the studies covered in this chapter are available in Dutch only. We hope that researchers in other countries will be encouraged to come up with similar information.

For the time being, therefore, a comparison with non-Dutch studies can be made only with respect to placement effects. In making this comparison it is important to note that many evaluation studies concentrate on income effects. This is particularly true of American studies. The income effects of training for the unemployed have hardly received any attention in Dutch evaluation studies, which deal only with the impact of training on the likelihood of re-employment. And the two effects will not always point in the same direction. In the Dutch situation, accepting a job often does not imply a significant increase in net income for an unemployed person. This is particularly true for the low-paid segment, where net benefits and net income levels do not differ much.

Several attempts have already been made to review the literature on the evaluation of training schemes for the unemployed. The most recent review is, to the best of our knowledge, that conducted by Fay (1996). From this article one would be inclined to conclude that, although these evaluation studies show a variety of outcomes, the overall picture is quite pessimistic. It is certainly not possible to conclude from the existing literature that training has a strong impact on the probability of re-employment for unemployed people. According to Fay, most studies only measure short-term effects and may therefore underestimate the long-term effects, assuming that these are more positive. However, the long-term effects of training are difficult to trace as many other things will happen to a person that will also influence his or her labour market history.

However, the negative picture of the effects of training is based to a large extent on experimental studies in the United States. In most cases, experiments with training measures for the unemployed have produced insignificant or even negative results. Until recently, most researchers were of the opinion that experiments are the only reliable method of evaluating labour-market policies. The experiments that have actually been carried out were taken more or less as 'the truth about training'. As Lynch (1997) has pointed out recently, this view is challenged by Heckman and Smith (1997). Their recent work has shown that many problems, such as attrition, occur in experimental studies that are not dealt with correctly. Re-examining these studies, Heckman and Smith conclude that the net results are much more positive when these problems are handled in a more satisfactory way. Thus we tend to conclude that the relatively small, but positive, net placement effects found in Dutch evaluation may really mean something.

5. CONCLUSION AND FINAL REMARKS

Table 6.10 provides a summary of all training instruments for the unemployed. It is clear that training is an important instrument. In some years,

Table 6.10   Summary of results for all training instruments for the unemployed taken together, 1985–94

Reach: quantitative	The number of participants as a percentage of the stock of unemployment on a yearly basis varies between 8 and 33 per cent
Reach: qualitative	Overrepresentation of women Underrepresentation of the low-skilled
Completion rate	Approximately 75 per cent
Gross placement rate	Approximately 60 per cent measured 6 to 9 months after training completion
Net effectiveness: participants	10 to 50 per cent for the participants who did find a job after finishing training
Net effectiveness: reduction of mismatch	Hardly relevant in the period under consideration Perhaps important on some specific (technical) segments of the labour market
Macro effects	Only indirect evidence of positive effects on total employment
Average costs per trainee	Approximately 5000 euros

the number of participants amounted to one-third of the total stock of unemployed. A weak element in the application of training for the unemployed is that the low-skilled are underrepresented. Most likely these are precisely the people who need training most. Approximately 75 per cent of the participants complete the training. However, a considerable number of the dropouts attend a large part of the training and some of them may still find a job as a result of the training. Approximately 60 per cent of the trainees find a job within a period of six to nine months after finishing the training. But not more than 50 per cent of them, and perhaps as few as 10 per cent, find a job as a result of the training. For the long-term unemployed, 50 per cent or more is not improbable. This suggests that the total impact is rather poor. However, it should be borne in mind that the average costs of training are relatively low (approximately 5000 euros). An unemployed person receiving benefit costs society tens of thousands of euros for each year of inactivity. Thus, even when the net effect of training is relatively small, the financial returns may still be positive for society as a whole. To make that point clear, let us assume that net effectiveness is only 33.3 per cent (which is approximately the mean value of the interval given in Table 6.10 for net effectiveness for participants). Thus if five persons are trained, only one of them finds a job thanks to the training (given the fact that 60 per cent of the trainees find a job). The cost of training five persons amounts to 25 000 euros, which is somewhat lower than the average unemployment benefit of a person over a period of two years. Furthermore, it should be borne in mind that the benefits for society will be higher than a reduction in unemployment benefit expenditure, since (a) value added produced by the trainee may exceed the reduction in unemployment benefits; (b) some benefits (but probably not much in the period under consideration) will occur as a result of a reduction in mismatch; and (c) training may have some non-market benefits. Thus the returns to training for society as a whole seem to be positive when people who would have stayed unemployed for a long time if not trained are reintegrated, even though net effectiveness is relatively low.

We do not know very much about the macroeconomic impact of training for the unemployed. In the period under consideration, the effect of training on mismatch was small, perhaps with the exception of some highly specialized (technical) segments of the labour market. There might have been a positive long-term effect on aggregate employment to the extent that unemployed people who were virtually out of the labour market were made employable again.

There is also a serious lack of information about the role of implementation. For instance, how and to what extent the authorities control the inflow of trainees will probably have a big impact on the results.

Table 6.11 shows the relative performance of the various instruments on the basis of the results of the previous sections for four criteria: reach with respect to disadvantaged groups, completion rate, placement rate and average costs per trainee. The general training scheme appears to have the best performance; adult apprenticeship training and the basic training centre have the worst performance. The vocational training centre for women and the centre for adult vocational training (both technical and administrative) hold intermediate positions. Of these three instruments, the centre for technical adult vocational training is performing slightly better than the other two. The reader should note that we tried to make the various instruments as comparable as possible. The completion rate was corrected for differences in the composition of the trainee group. The share of women in the trainee group appears to have a strong positive impact on the training results. The same applies to the placement rate. The shares of young people and ethnic minorities appear to have a negative effect on the placement rate.

Table 6.11   Relative performance of the various training instruments

	Reach of disadvantaged groups	Completion rate	Placement rate	Costs per trainee
Technical centre for adult vocational training	−/0	+	+	−
Administrative centre for adult vocational training	−/0	0	0	0/+
Basic training centre	0	−	−	0/+
Vocational training centre for women	0/+	0	0	−
General training scheme	0/+	0/+	0/+	+
Adult vocational training	0/+	−	−	−

Note: '+' = better than average, '−' = worse than average and '0' average.

A number of remarks should be added to the results shown in Table 6.11. First of all, one strength of the centres for adult vocational training is that people can enrol at various times during the year. Of the other instruments, only the general training scheme has a similar degree of flexibility in so far as private training agencies (and of course centres for adult vocational training) provide the training. Furthermore, in many fields of technical training the technical centres for adult vocational training are the only option for unemployed people. In that sense, they are unique. This is not at all the case with the administrative centres. Similar administrative courses are offered by private training institutions, and there seems to be no clear rationale for the existence of the administrative centres. The same applies to the centres for female vocational training as far as the administrative courses are concerned. However, the courses in non-traditional fields of training do have an added value and, moreover, perform quite well (although they are expensive).

It is interesting to see that the general training scheme, a relatively cheap instrument which makes use of a variety of training institutions (schools, private agencies, companies and the centres financed by the PES), performs better than the other instruments (with the exception of the female vocational centre, which is in any case much more expensive). In addition to the general training scheme, the technical centres for adult vocational training are valuable in so far as they offer training opportunities for unemployed persons for which no alternatives exist. This is also true of the vocational training centre for women. The administrative centres for adult vocational training do not, in our view, have any 'value added'. Administrative training is strongly overrepresented compared to the share of administrative vacancies in total vacancies. Moreover, there is an ample supply of courses in administrative training offered by private training institutions. Basic training is extremely important, but the general training scheme offers enough opportunities through state schools and private training institutions. The added value of the basic training centre is doubtful. The scheme for adult apprenticeship training no longer exists. In principle, it is an attractive idea to give the adult unemployed an opportunity to learn a new trade and acquire an official diploma. Perhaps it should be tried again in a different form.

Our overall conclusion is that the effect of training of the unemployed is relatively small in terms of unemployment reduction. When 100 000 unemployed persons are trained, perhaps 20 000 of them find a job as a direct result of the training. During the period under consideration, unemployment fluctuated around 500 000, according to official figures, and more than a million when hidden unemployment is also taken into account. But although the effect on total unemployment is small, the returns to training are likely to be positive for society as a whole when savings on unemployment benefits are taken into account.

The results could be improved by concentrating training on two targets: reintegrating unemployed persons with limited prospects in the labour market, and reducing mismatch. In the present situation these targets can be combined, because the success of the favourable labour-market situation in the Netherlands means that employers are finding it difficult to fill vacancies, while inactivity rates are still high among a number of population groups.

It is difficult to compare the results for the Netherlands with the results found in the non-Dutch literature, most of which concentrates on measuring the net effects of training for the participants. Even these estimated effects are difficult to compare because information about the characteristics of the trainees and the training is lacking. However, the conclusion on the basis of Dutch training studies that the net effect of training on the transition from unemployment to employment is positive but relatively small is not out of tune with non-Dutch studies.

Finally, it is important to note that detailed information about the performance of training instruments is not sufficient for the optimal design of active labour-market policy. Similar information for other types of measure, such as placement and wage subsidy schemes, would be needed. This is a matter for further research. The same applies to the inclusion of non-Dutch studies in the data set, which will perhaps enable us to carry out a secondary analysis of the net effects of training.

NOTES

1. Recently, the organization of active labour market policy in the Netherlands has changed considerably. As a result, a large part of the PES, including its training centres, is in the process of being privatized. In 2001 this process will be finalized.
2. General training is defined here (Becker, 1964) as training which produces knowledge that can be used in a number of firms. One of the problems may be that individuals (and companies) are uncertain about the general character of training and therefore uncertain about the potential benefits outside a given firm.
3. However, even when training has the sole purpose of creating equal opportunities, it may have some positive economic side-effects in the long term. If the people involved were no longer receiving job offers from employers and training leads to renewed job offers, the effective labour supply will increase. This may affect wage formation and have positive effects on employment. This is basically the mechanism described by Layard, Nickell and Jackman (1991).
4. Or if one school is in a monopoly position.
5. An often heard objection against experiments is that it is unethical to exclude people (the control group) from participating in a measure that may improve their situation. However, this criticism does not seem convincing to us. If experiments were watertight then, on the basis of the outcomes, the large-scale implementation of ineffective measures could be avoided. And if a measure proves effective, the control group members can still participate.
6. Under those circumstances it may even be worthwile to train a person with relatively good job prospects, supposing that the training enables this person to find a more qualified job. This then would leave more vacancies open to filling by people with low job chances.
7. Also relevant is, of course whether training is the right option. For instance, a placement subsidy might have been more cost-effective.
8. Multi-criteria methods could be applied. These methods presuppose the involvement of policy-makers which is not very realistic in practice, however. They would have to attach the weights to the criteria, but they may be dissatisfied with the overall results. Therefore, they will be hesitant to make their preferences explicit.
9. The author is grateful to Edwin van Bokhoven, who compiled the data from more than 50 studies and carried out analyses in De Koning *et al* (1995). Thanks are also due to Frank Huitema for carrying out the regression analyses for this chapter.
10. Most of the studies are not included in the list of references since they are available in Dutch only. Only studies referred to in the texts are included.
11. Let us assume that the expected unemployment duration is one year. If the unemployment duration follows an exponential distribution and the inflow into unemployment is constant over time then, assuming that each unemployed person becomes eligible for training after three months, the total number of people eligible for training during a year is equal to 1.32 times the stock of unemployed.
12. The share of long-term unemployed persons among the trainees is approximately the same as their share in total unemployment. That means that about one-third of the trainees have been unemployed for two years or more when they enter training. Note that this figure is based on a very limited number of cases.
13. The signalling theory is well-known from the economics of education (Spence, 1993).

BIBLIOGRAPHY

Bavinck, S. and van der Burgh, Y. (1994), 'Effectiviteit van het scholingsinstrumentarium', Onderzoek naar Centrum Vakopleiding, KRA, KRA-WER en Sollicitatieclub in de regio Noord- en Midden-Limburg, Research voor Beleid, Leiden.

Becker, G.S. (1964), *Human Capital*, New York.

Broersma, L., Koeman, J. and Teulings, C.N. (1997), 'Arbeidsaanbod en werkgelegenheid', *Economische Statistische Berichten*, 82(4127), 836–40.

Burtless, G. (1993), 'The Case for Social Experiments', in Danish Ministry of Labour (ed.), *Measuring Labour Market Measures*, Copenhagen.

Fay R.G. (1996), 'Enhancing the effectiveness of active labour market policies: evidence from program evaluations in OECD countries', OECD Labour Market and Social Policy Occasional Papers no. 18, Paris.

Grip, A. de (1987), 'Onderwijs en arbeidsmarkt: scholingsdiscrepanties', dissertation.

Heckman, J.J. and Smith, J.A. (1993), 'Assessing the Case for Randomized Evaluation of Social Programs' in Danish Ministry of Labour (ed.), *Measuring Labour Market Measures*, Copenhagen.

Heckman J.J. and Smith, J.A. (1997), 'The sensitivity of experimental impact estimates: evidence from the national JTPA study', NBER working paper #6105.

Kodde, D.A. (1987), 'Uncertainty and the Demand for Education', *The Review of Economics and Statistics*, 68(3).

Koning, J. de and Arents, M. (2001), 'The Impact of Active Labour Market Policy on Job Hirings and Unemployment in the Netherlands', in J. de Koning and H. Mosley (eds), *Labour Market Policy and Unemployment: Impact and Process Evaluations in Selected European Countries*, Cheltenham, UK and Northampton, MA, USA: Edward Elgar.

Koning, J. de and van Nes, P.J. (1989), 'Landelijke evaluatie Kaderregeling Scholing', OAV-rapport 90-05, Ministerie van Sociale Zaken en Werkgelegenheid, D.G. ARBVO, Sector Onderzoek Arbeidsmarktvraagstukken, Rijswijk:

Koning, J. de and van Nes, P.J. (1990), 'Evaluatie van het CBB: Bereik en plaatsingseffecten', OAV-rapport 90-11, Centraal Bureau voor de Arbeidsvoorziening, Rijswijk.

Koning, J. de, Koss, M. and Verkaik, A. (1987), *De arbeidsmarkteffecten van het centrum voor (administratieve) vakopleiding van volwassenen. Eerste deelrapport,* The Hague: Ministerie van Sociale Zaken en Werkgelegenheid.

Koning, J. de, Koss, M. and Verkaik, A. (1988), *De arbeidsmarkteffecten van het centrum voor (administratieve) vakopleiding van volwassenen, Tweede Deelrapport,* The Hague: Ministerie van Sociale Zaken en Werkgelegenheid.

Koning, J. de, Zandvliet, C.Th. and van Bokhoven, E.F. (1993), 'Effectiviteit scholing in de RBA-regio Drechtsteden', Rotterdam: Nederlands Economisch Instituut.

Koning, J. de, Zandvliet, C.Th. and Knol, H.W. (1993), *Kosten-baten van het Centrum Vak-opleiding, het CBB en de Vrouwenvakschool*, Rotterdam: Nederlands Economisch Instituut.

Koning, J. de, Zandvliet, C.Th., van Bokhoven, E.F. and Olieman, R. (1993), 'Effectiviteit scholing in de RBA-regio West-Utrecht', OAV-werkdocument 94-03, Centraal Bureau voor de Arbeidsvoorziening, Rijswijk.

Koning J. de, Donker van Heel, P.A., Gelderblom, A., van Nes, P.J. and Zandvliet, C.Th. (1995), *Arbeidsvoorziening in perspectief. Evaluatie Arbeidsvoorzieningswet 1991–1994, Deelonderzoek B: resultaten en kosten* (E2455), The Hague: Ministerie van Sociale Zaken en Werkgelegenheid.

Layard, R., Nickell, S. and Jackman, R. (1991), *Unemployment, Macroeconomic Performance and the Labour Market*, Oxford: Oxford University Press.

Lynch, L.L. (1997), 'Do Investments in Education and Training Matter?', paper for the 9th annual Conference of the European Association of Labour Economists, Aarhus, Denmark, 25–28 September.

OECD (1993), *Employment Outlook*, Paris: OECD.

Ritzen, J.J.M (1980), 'Market Failure for General Training and Remedies', paper for the Robert M. La Follette Symposium on Market Failure for Training.

Spence, M.A. (1973), 'Job Market Signalling', *Quarterly Journal of Economics*, 87, 355–75.

Zandvliet C.Th. (1991), *Gebruik van het reguliere onderwijs in de KRS*, Rotterdam: Nederlands Economisch Instituut.

Zandvliet C.Th. and van Bokhoven, E.F. (1994), *Rendement scholing in Friesland*, Rotterdam: Nederlands Economisch Instituut.

7. A long-term perspective on the effects of training in Germany

Klaus Schömann and Rolf Becker

1. INTRODUCTION

This chapter complements the two previous country-specific analyses of training systems and specific training measures with a thorough analysis of training, general education, skill levels and gender bias in Germany. Like the other country-specific analyses of the transitional labour market of education and training, this chapter is based on micro-level estimates of training participation, training effects and employment/unemployment transitions combined with training. We adopt a long-term approach to the evaluation of training effects which allows a more comprehensive assessment of the costs and benefits of the public funds explicitly devoted to further training in Germany.

Since the main findings of earlier studies have already been discussed in the previous two chapters, our discussion of these findings in section 2 below will be confined to evidence from Germany. In section 3, we derive hypotheses based on the theory of transitions over the lifetime and transitional labour markets as well as hypotheses based on human capital, insider–outsider and segmentation theory. Particular emphasis is placed on deriving testable hypotheses on labour market transitions related to education and further training.

Section 4 briefly describes the data used in the analysis and an innovative method of dealing with selection processes in evaluations of training measures. In section 5, we present empirical analyses of training transitions related to wage growth within jobs in West Germany. These analyses are based on life history data. In section 6, we discuss the hypothesis that further training can work as employment insurance if it takes place on the job. On the basis of German socioeconomic panel data, we also analyse the employment prospects of the unemployed receiving training in East Germany. Section 7, finally, will assess the hypotheses in the light of the empirical evidence for Germany. Additionally, we will make some recommendations on fostering training-related transitions over the lifetime and outline some institutional keys to developing the transitional labour market of education/training and employment in Germany.

2. THE LINK BETWEEN TRAINING EFFICIENCY AND SELECTIVITY IN GERMANY

As the previous two chapters showed for the Netherlands and Ireland, there is ample evidence in Germany as well of a causal relationship between education, further education and higher earnings (Becker and Schömann, 1996; Schömann and Becker, 1998). The significance of initial and further vocational training, as well as of labour market experience, for higher earnings has been confirmed by numerous studies on wages and earnings in West and East Germany[1] (Pfeiffer and Pohlmeier, 1998). Becker (1991) shows that, for West German men and women in three birth cohorts during the period from 1950 to 1983, participation in further education and, in particular, the acquisition of additional formal qualifications, leads to career advancement and increased earnings. Further education and training also increases company loyalty and labour market flexibility so that more secure and higher incomes can be achieved in the course of a career. A study carried out by Pannenberg (1995) also verifies the positive earning effects of further vocational training in Germany for the period 1986 to 1991.

For the period 1990 to 1992, Pannenberg and Helberger (1997) show that further training and retraining schemes have a positive effect on the earnings of East German participants, although this finding must be interpreted with caution because it is based on gross monthly wages (cf. Petersen, 1989; Schömann, 1994). Mobile participants, in particular, were able to achieve increased earnings (Pannenberg, 1995). A study by Hübler on East Germany (1998) reveals that firm-based training has a particularly positive income effect, whereas measures funded under the provisions of the Employment Promotion Law (Arbeitsförderungsgesetz or AFG, now known as SGB III or Social Code III) tend to lead to a decrease in earnings. According to Hübler (1998), the decrease in income following off-the-job training is due to the deskilling or stigmatizing effect of participation in public training measures. However, if the selectivity effect is taken into account, the income effect of on-the-job training diminishes, while the earnings decrease following external training remains significant (Hübler, 1998, p. 119).

However, the influence of further education and training would be underestimated if account were taken solely of the actual earnings of employees in the primary labour market. In many cases, workers' earning potential also depends on continuity of unemployment, avoidance of unemployment or, in the event of job loss, the ability to find a new job without great delay. Publicly funded further training schemes were set up in the wake of structural change in Eastern Germany as educational and labour policy instruments designed to offer continuous and stable employment conditions, to avoid chronic mass unemployment and to help reintegrate the unemployed.

Experience in West Germany has shown that further vocational training can be successful in this context. Hujer *et al.* (1998) showed that, for West Germany between 1986 and 1993, participants in training courses for the unemployed had a better chance of finding a job than non-participants, although this short-term effect tends to weaken the longer the spell of unemployment lasts. On the other hand, state-funded training measures aimed at reintegrating unemployed and handicapped people into the labour market proved less effective (Becker, 1991). In East Germany however, lengthy training measures in particular led to increased re-employment (Pannenberg, 1995; Pannenberg and Helberger, 1997). Re-employment obviously depends on the quality of the training programmes as well as on the actual increase in current market human capital. Thus on-the-job training measures in East Germany tend to increase job security for workers, while schemes provided under the provisions of the Employment Promotion Law do not have the expected positive effects (Hübler, 1998). However, differentiation by gender shows that the employment effects of on-the-job further training courses are significant for males but not for females (Hübler, 1997).

This partial finding shows that we need to differentiate between the effects of training on men and those on women. Differences are often due to the limited number of cases available in analyses or evaluation studies. Differences in men's and women's life cycles, gender-specific differences in occupational field and earnings potential, as well as gender-differentiated selection and segregation processes in the labour and further training markets, necessitate separate analyses for men and women. For this reason, the impact of further training on the earning potentials of men and women in Eastern and Western Germany is examined in this chapter (cf. Schömann and Becker, 1995, 1998; Becker and Schömann, 1996).

We shall test the hypothesis that the gender-specific causal effect of further education and training on earnings and job security has to be understood against the background of unequal opportunities for women and men to participate in further training. This gender-specific selection for further training plays an important role in reproducing inequality in employment opportunities and earnings, much to women's disadvantage.

Thus women often have a lower propensity to participate in further training because of difficulties in balancing family and career (lower self-selection). Furthermore, they are mainly employed in sectors offering fewer opportunities for career advancement and further training. In addition to career segregation, discriminatory practices on the part of employers or training institutes in the selection of participants also reinforce the inequalities in access to further vocational training (lower external selection). If participation in further training leads to an increase in earnings, or at least to job security, part of the wage differentials between men and women can be traced back to gender-specific selectivity in career and training opportunities.

Gender-specific differences in training opportunities can also be observed in Eastern Germany in the case of state-funded further training programmes oriented towards specific target groups. Thus more women than men joined schemes of comparably lesser value (Behringer, 1995) or training programmes holding out little prospect of improved job and earning opportunities. Social inequalities in further training opportunities and gender differences, among other things, can result in relatively low career continuity and high risks of unemployment for East German women. The unemployment rate for women in Eastern Germany was twice as high as for men in 1995 and higher than for men until the end of 1997. Women also tended to become unemployed and remain so longer than East German men.

3. HYPOTHESES ON TRAINING TRANSITIONS OVER THE LIFE COURSE

Following on from the discussion of human capital theory in a previous publication (Schömann and Becker, 1995), we have derived three major hypotheses from the Mincer-type mathematical formulation of human capital theory in respect of participation in and returns to further training.

The first is that off-the-job continuing training will lead to a considerable loss of earnings. These forgone earnings will need to be compensated by higher wages, wage progression or longer employment spells after participation in further training. If this investment rationale is not borne out, participation in further training is likely to decline later in life or among younger cohorts of school leavers. Since the returns to further training are accumulated over shorter periods than those to initial education, most labour economists propose higher investment in initial education as the single best solution to investment in education. With growing uncertainty about the returns to investment in higher education, a more sequential approach to such investment among individuals, households or families might be indicated. An approach of this kind, involving repeated spells of further training, can avoid the considerable sunk costs associated with ill-informed choices made early on in life. Suboptimal investment in human capital may also be due to household budget restrictions or social background, as discussed in Chapter 3 of the present volume.

Secondly, to adopt a more dynamic perspective on adaptive expectations, we hypothesize that a person with high wage growth in previous jobs is likely to continue to invest in human capital in order to avoid the anticipated levelling-off of wage growth in later years.

The third hypothesis is that persons with low initial investment in human capital face a levelling-off of their wage growth early on in their working lives; this constitutes a great incentive to participate in further training early on in their working lives.

In most analyses and discussions of human capital theory and further training issues, the importance of being able to recover investment costs over a relatively short period is advanced as an explanation for low training rates among older employees in particular.

In insider–outsider theory, the rigid division of the workforce into insiders, largely unionized, and outsiders, with no bargaining power, allows us to apply this theoretical framework to participation in further training (Lindbeck and Snower, 1989). Higher trade union bargaining power will lead to higher training participation among insiders. Thus an accumulation of higher earnings and higher training participation among insiders is likely to enhance insiders' income and employment opportunities to the detriment of those of outsiders. This will lead to persistent market failure in training and give rise to market intervention in the form of legislation on access to further training or subsidies intended to stimulate participation in further training, for example by offering training vouchers to outsiders (Snower and Booth, 1996).

The hypothesis derived from segmentation theory leads us to expect persistent inequality of access to training. Primary segment employees, those in large manufacturing firms, have privileged access to training. Employees in smaller firms or in less productive segments of the economy experience greater difficulty in gaining access to training, and rates of return to training are lower. Initial training is a major source of segmentation, and further training (largely off-the-job and publicly financed) is seen as a potential remedy for rigid segmentation. National education systems in which vocational training plays an important part in the compulsory education system are regarded as having higher levels of segmentation, because trainees tend to be recruited at an early stage in their careers. In such systems, further training becomes an important tool for breaking down barriers within a segmented labour force.

The theory of transitions over the lifecourse (see Chapter 2) and its application to the transitional labour market of education and employment, considers the processes of educational attainment and achievement in the labour market as linked processes. The coupling of the two spheres can be deliberately influenced through institutional design. Transitional labour market theory (Schmid, 1998) proposes four criteria against which to check the institutional features of transitional labour markets: (1) empowerment of individuals to manage critical life events, (2) cooperation between public and private actors, (3) dynamic efficiency through more active labour market policies, and (4) sustainability over the lifetime through career trajectories leading to integration rather than social exclusion.

On the basis of transition theory, we assume that educational attainment and progress in the labour market are two independent processes and that the link between them can be modelled in accordance with theoretical considerations. If there is no specifically designed link between the subsystems, each process will evolve largely independently of the other. For example, the education system might deal primarily with education for civil society, whereas the economic system governing the labour market might stress market principles. Clearly, therefore, difficulties in effecting the transition from one societal subsystem to the other would be inherent to such an institutional set-up.

National, regional or sectoral differences can be modelled by choosing different 'coefficients of coupling' for the two processes. The feedback structure between the two processes of education and earnings attainment might be unidirectional, from education to the labour market, as is assumed in human capital theory, or bidirectional. A bidirectional feedback structure between early labour market experience and the qualification attainment process allows for an early return to full-time schooling or other forms of further training. This makes possible more accurate modelling of the process of lifelong learning and of the employment trajectories running parallel to it.

Taking as a starting point the theory of transitions over the lifetime and transitional labour markets outlined in greater detail in Chapter 2 of this volume, this chapter will use German data to test hypotheses 7 and 8. In brief, the first of these hypotheses states that *higher levels of education will lead to higher levels of productivity and earnings only if there is a well-established link between learning, not just initial full-time education, and the labour market.* The sudden cut in the institutional link between the education system and the meritocratic allocation of jobs in East Germany in the wake of German unification reflects a sudden change in the institutional link between education and the labour market.

Thus a regionally specific variant of hypothesis 7 (see Chapter 2 for more details) might run as follows. In Eastern Germany, the link between educational qualifications and productivity is expected to be weaker. Similarly, higher levels of education are less likely than in Western Germany to be associated with longer periods of labour force participation (hypothesis 8 in Chapter 2), since the previous institutional link in Eastern Germany – meritocracy – has been replaced by one based on the principles of the market economy, in which observed or expected productivity potential is rewarded.

4. DATA, METHODS AND THE PROCESS OF SOCIAL SELECTIVITY

We use retrospective life history data for Western Germany and panel data for Eastern Germany in order to ascertain empirically whether and to what extent participation in further education and training can lead to improved job and earning opportunities. In order to monitor the selective influence of further training on wage increases for men and women in Western Germany and on the risk of unemployment and the chances of re-employment for men and women in Eastern Germany, we will take into account the complete career prior to participation when making the dynamic estimates. This will help to monitor the structure and dynamism of the selection processes governing access to training, which will have effects on income progression and job opportunities (Lillard, 1993; Stolzenberg and Relles, 1990). This is necessary because further training opportunities are systematically allocated in a socially selective manner. If the selection mechanism is not taken into account, any findings on the influence of further training on earnings and career progression will not be interpretable because of selection bias (Heckman, 1979; Heckman and Smith, 1996).

We are using as our database event history-oriented longitudinal data from a German life history study (GLHS) carried out by the Max Planck Institute for Human Development and Education, Berlin (Mayer, 1991). This gives us detailed information on 2171 West German men and women over the period 1950 to 1993, which will provide an empirically grounded explanation of the causal effects of further training on earnings. We are also utilizing longitudinal data from the German socioeconomic panel (GSOEP) in order to investigate the labour market situation of 1507 men and 1568 women in Eastern Germany from the end of 1989 to the spring of 1993, taking special account of further vocational training measures (Rendtel, 1995). The panel data will be converted to event history-oriented longitudinal data by means of the episode splitting procedure. In this way, processes at work in career trajectories and training opportunity mechanisms can be closely inspected on a monthly basis (see Schömann *et al.*, 1997). These data will also enable us to differentiate between the various forms of further training, such as retraining, job introductory or updating training and training for the purposes of career advancement. Further differentiations can be made between full- and part-time training and between in-firm and externally provided training.

When assessing the effectiveness of further training, methodological problems arise when the survey data used do not permit a coincidental division of test and control groups (Heckman and Smith, 1996). On the other hand, multi-level assessment and decision-making processes for selecting candidates cannot be simulated with experimental data. Furthermore, when evaluating further training programmes, the 'problem of causal inference' (Holland, 1986) arises, which means that one person cannot be observed simultaneously as both participant and non-participant. The question of the effect participation in a further training programme, for example, has on an individual in comparison with a person who does not participate cannot be immediately answered. It is impossible to say what the individual would have experienced if he/she had not participated. Consequently, the advantages of further training cannot be assessed by comparing participation with non-participation.

Assuming a result variant Y_t, which stands for an individual's participation at a certain period t Y_{1t} and for a non-participant Y_{0t}, then the interesting potential (advantageous) effect $\Delta_t = Y_{1t} - Y_{0t}$ cannot be determined. Assessment problems such as the above also occur, owing to lack of information, when investigating participation likelihood $Pr(D = 1 | c_{it})$ (whereby $D = 1$ event for participation and $c_{it} =$ explanatory variables). Owing to the 'selection bias' in the distribution of further training effects the following is valid:

$$E(\Delta | D = 1, c_{it}) \neq E(Y_{it} | D = 1, c_{it}) - E(Y_{0t} | D = 0, c_{it}),$$

that is, the expected average further training effect is not equal to the difference between the result variants for participation and non-participation.

Furthermore, consideration must be given to the fact that, if true experimental data are not available for assessing further training, any estimates produced will be biased if the selection processes and selectivity in access to training are not explicitly monitored. Thus it is not permissible naively to include non-participants in the control group without monitoring selectivity in further training (Fitzenberger and Prey, 1998, p. 45). Workers take part in further training in the hope of achieving increases in earnings. More highly qualified workers have a better chance of receiving further training, either because they have already acquired characteristics such as productivity and motivation that are much sought-after in the labour market or because such characteristics are imputed to them. They would, in any case, be able to achieve increased earnings whether or not they received any further training. It thus remains unclear whether increased earnings are causally related to formal initial training, to skills learned through work experience or to additional skills acquired through further training measures (Lechner, 1998).

On the other hand, it cannot be ignored that certain occupational groups are exposed to an accumulation of unemployment risks which cannot be countered by further training programmes. Thus retraining measures in Eastern Germany, for example, are often labelled 'unsuccessful' (Behringer, 1995, p. 42) because the employment prospects of participants in these programmes were weaker from the very outset.

The related evaluation problem can be solved by monitoring social selectivity prior to participation in such schemes (Becker and Schömann, 1996; Schömann and Becker, 1995; Heckman and Smith, 1996). However, it has also become clear that the inclusion in a multivariate model of a dummy variable indicating whether or not an individual has participated in a further training scheme is an inadequate solution because it gives rise to considerable statistical problems caused by selectivity bias (Maddala, 1978, p. 426). A number of procedures, of varying efficiency, are now available for solving the selectivity and evaluation problems described above (Heckman and Smith, 1996; Lechner, 1998; Fitzenberger and Prey, 1998).

It can be concluded from these studies that there is no single ideal solution, but that several different procedures are justifiable. The solution to the selection bias problem is to be found beyond the formal statistics. Since the selection process is more a theoretical than a statistical problem, the selection process must be modelled in a theoretically appropriate manner. Although it is accurate to say that 'without sufficient knowledge of the manner in which individuals are selected for a training programme, it is impossible adequately to quantify the effects' (Lechner, 1998, p. 21), in many cases little is known about these selection processes and they cannot be properly tested statistically owing to a lack of information.

For theoretical and pragmatic reasons, we prefer the procedure for controlling sample bias suggested by Heckmann (1979). The first stage of an investigation into the advantages of further education and training (such as the effect of training on income and job security) consists of an evaluation of the selection process. The estimation results for the distribution of further training opportunities are used in the second stage as an instrumental variable to assess the beneficial functions, for example in the model for evaluating income increases.

We apply a modified element of the Heckman procedure for income estimates. It is based on a proposal by Lillard (1993) for analysing simultaneous, mutually influential processes over the lifetime. According to Lillard, it would be desirable to use a more consistent indicator giving a broader testimony than a dummy variant. In this way, structurally-induced selection or self or external selection for transitions to further training could be included, and more information could be provided on the dynamics of these processes. Furthermore, this indicator for developments in earnings or employment should include previous processes, thereby portraying training participation, career development and earnings progression (ibid.).

The indicator value we propose for further training participation is based on dynamic evaluations of training transitions for each individual (Schömann and Becker, 1995). The indicator value is the absolute degree of the dependent variant of the semi-parametric Cox model and thus the transitional rate for further training. The Cox proportional hazard model has the following general structure:

$$r(t\,|\,x) = r_0 + \exp(\mathbf{x}'\beta). \qquad (7.1)$$

The complete modelling for men and women can be seen in Table 7A.1.[2] Through this procedure, the actual selection mechanism governing the entire training transition process in the career to date is directly included in the model evaluations. Moreover, account is taken not only of the social selection process (in this case, the socially structured unequal and intermittent distribution of further training opportunities over the lifetime) but also of the fact that individuals make decisions at certain stages that will have an effect on later events or decisions in their lives. Thus a person's decision to take advantage of further training opportunities can be influenced by the probability of future income increases, which may or may not make further training worthwhile.

This form of simultaneity in both training and earnings progression is based on the probability of events in a process being dependent on the (logarithmic) hazard rates or prior events in another related process (Lillard, 1993, pp. 189, 195). In order to investigate the endogeneity of these processes the explanatory variable 'vocational further training' is entered in the other model calculations as a logarithmic hazard rate (ibid., pp. 191–5).

We evaluate further training in East Germany in a similar manner (see also Schömann *et al.*, 1997; Becker, 1999). In the first stage, the transition rate for participation is calculated using an exponential model – a parametric procedure for event analysis:

$$r(t|x_1, x_2(t)) = \exp(\beta_0 + \beta_1 x_1 + \beta_2 x_2(t) + \beta_n \lambda), \qquad (7.2)$$

in which x_1 represents time constants and $x_2(t)$ covariants that change over time, while λ corrects the random sample selectivity for panel mortality.[3] The result of this calculation, the logarithmic hazard rate for transition to further training, is then entered as an instrumental variant $FT_{\lambda(t)}$ for training participation in the multivariant evaluations of job security for workers and re-employment for jobless people in Eastern Germany. The results of the evaluation according to equation 7.2 can be found in Table 7A.2.[4]

5.   FURTHER TRAINING AND CHANGES IN EARNINGS IN WEST GERMANY

In this section, we report, firstly, our results on earnings increases at job changes and, secondly, the results of wage progression when a person remains in the same job. Since we have reported previously (Schömann, 1994) on the results without taking account of the parallel process of further training, we will focus here on the effects of further training on wages. Earnings increase in relation to job mobility within and between companies.

Table 7.1 illustrates the empirical findings for wage increases for men and women who changed jobs either within their company or to a new employer. The dependent variable is the logarithm of the relation of first earnings in job $N+1$ to the last wage in the previous job N. The estimate equation is:

$$ln(E_{n+1}/E_n) = \beta' x + \beta' FT_{\lambda(t)} + \tau \lambda + u, \qquad (7.3)$$

in which x represents the covariant vector containing features of the individual person and of both jobs, $FT_{\lambda(t)}$ is participation in further training (that is, the result of equation 7.1), λ represents the estimated probability that both incomes have been recorded and u is a residual quantity.

Positive further training effects leading to higher wages are recorded for men but not for women changing jobs within their company. This underlines the relationship between further training and upward career mobility for men (Becker, 1991). The lack of comparable effects for women is an important factor in explaining the differences in earnings between men and women. A bias against women in access to further education and training also leads to lower income growth and to increased wage discrimination.

On the other hand, however, when women change to a new employer, further education and training has positive effects on wage increases. Thus

Table 7.1   Estimates of models of determinants of ratios of starting wage rate in destination job to final wage in origin job in West Germany (standard error of β coefficient in brackets)

	Between firms, women	Within firms, men
Constant	0.9253	−0.8844*
	(0.5660)	(0.4351)
Individual's characteristics		
Age (in years)	−0.0165**	0.0017
	(0.0064)	(0.0103)
Education		
(schooling/training in years)	0.0837*	−0.0210
	(0.0354)	(0.0295)
Education/trend	0.0024	−0.0007
	(0.0013)	(0.0013)
Labour force experience (in		
months)	0.0065	0.0027
	(0.0068)	(0.0054)
First job	0.2097***	0.1024
	(0.0560)	(0.0532)
Duration of original job		
(in months)	0.0134	−0.0032
	(0.0079)	(0.0067)
Duration of job interruption		
(in months)	0.0189**	
	(0.0067)	
Part-time job	0.0278	
	(0.0948)	
Family status		
(Married versus non-married		
individuals)	−0.1901	
	(0.2042)	
Further education and training (FT)		
Further training $FT_{\lambda(t)}$	0.1430*	0.1923**
	(0.0599)	(0.0653)
Further training $FT_{\lambda(t)} \cdot$ trend	−0.0053*	−0.0069*
	(0.0026)	(0.0031)
Labour market segmentation		
Public sector (job N)	0.0975	−0.0220
	(0.0805)	(0.0769)
Public sector (job N + 1)	0.0774	
	(0.0647)	
Large firm (job N)	0.2717**	−0.0644
	(0.0927)	(0.0928)

Table 7.1 (continued)

	Between firms, women	Within firms, men
Large firm (job N + 1)	0.1213	
	(0.0639)	
Skilled job (job N)	0.1186	0.1217
	(0.0684)	(0.0928)
Skilled job (job N + 1)	0.1876**	−0.0809
	(0.0687)	(0.0837)
Large firm · Skilled job (job N)	0.1469	−0.1197
	(0.1023)	(0.1133)
Large firm · Skilled job (job N + 1)	0.0679	0.1430
	(0.0912)	(0.0750)
Economic development		
Trend (years since 1950)	0.0111	0.0392*
	(0.0221)	(0.0165)
Unemployment rate	0.0088	−0.0063
	(0.0051)	(0.0047)
Change in GNP (%)	0.0004	0.0039
	(0.0073)	(0.0063)
Sample selection bias		
Probability of inclusion λ	0.5552	0.9504
	(0.4699)	(0.7903)
Number of cases	898	355
R^2	0.1007	0.1314

Note: *p ≤ 0.05; ** p ≤ 0.01; *** p ≤ 0.001.

Source: German life history study (Max-Planck-Institute for Human Development and Education, Berlin); own calculations.

further training efforts seem 'worthwhile' for women only when they change both job and employer. A more positive interpretation would be that, after training, women are able to react more flexibly to job offers with correspondingly better wages. Since training returns for men and women alike fall to the previous level of training when they change employers, women who participate in further training are better able to compensate for these losses than those who do not. Detailed analyses do not reveal any significant differences between the individual types of further education and training, although promotion-oriented and directly job-related courses predominate.

The interaction term 'further training $FT_{\lambda(t)}$ trend' with a negative sign, which is significant for internal job changes and changes to a new employer when used to monitor initial training, shows that these returns to further education decreased for both men and women during the period up to 1983. Pannenberg (1995) also showed positive effects for further education during the period 1986 to 1991. Investments in further education are still worthwhile despite declining returns to education.

Additional estimates showed that the existence of more data on full-and part-time courses or on-the-job or off-the-job courses does not greatly enhance the explanation of changes in earnings for men and women. However, if men can prove that they have gained additional qualifications through further education, they are in a position to achieve further increased earnings. This is not very surprising, since it is to be expected that further education certification plays a more important role when changing to a new employer than when moving to a new job within the old company. On the other hand, more market-oriented further training (such as qualifications required for promotion, courses aimed at specific occupational skills, master craftsman training or retraining schemes) is rewarded differently, and the market value is more likely to be realized, or realized more quickly, through job mobility than by queueing for a higher position in the same firm.

Furthermore, these analyses show that the increased provision of further education and training since 1970 has not changed existing gender-related wage inequality in West Germany, but has tended rather to reproduce the inequality between the educationally privileged and the less well qualified. Since the effects of further training are stronger for men than for women, and this is also the case when monitoring decreasing further education yields, it may be assumed that for career mobility it has proved more 'worthwhile' for men than for women.

Further Education and Wage Growth in the Same Job

We use a stochastic differential equation to assess the effects of further education on wages when the person remains in the same job. This model, which measures changes in earnings over a continuous period, is based on the following equation (Schömann, 1994, pp. 88–9):

$$\log(E_t/E_0)/\sqrt{t} = a\sqrt{t} + \beta' x_0 \sqrt{t} + \beta' FT_{\lambda(t)} \sqrt{t} + \tfrac{1}{2}\tau t^{3/2} + \varepsilon(t)/\sqrt{t}, \quad (7.4)$$

in which x_0 represents the independent variant, $FT_{\lambda(t)}$ the hazard rate for the limited probability of participation in further training (see equation 7.1) and t monitors the time.

In accordance with human capital theory, educational level adds a favourable effect to the growth rate for wages when the individual remains in the same job (see Table 7.2). Wages for men with the highest level of education are almost four times as high as for those with the lowest level. If we compare the educational effect with the influence of a prior further training course on wage rates for the same job, we find, surprisingly, that further training is not as significant for men as is often maintained. In this case, formal education before job commencement has more positive results than additional further training. Moreover, neither differentiation between full- and part-time courses nor monitoring of further training experience offers substantial explanations for males. Thus financial gains from further training for men are related to a job change within the company or a move up the company hierarchy. Further education without accompanying career mobility was not in itself worthwhile for men during the period 1950 to 1983.

Table 7.2 *Estimates of stochastic differential equation model of wage rate growth within jobs in West Germany (standard error of β coefficient in brackets)*

	Women	Women	Men	Men
Initial growth rate ($\sqrt{}$duration)	0.0337	0.0376	0.0705**	0.0706**
	(0.0478)	(0.0478)	(0.0224)	(0.0226)
Rate of decline (duration$^{3/2}$)	−0.0017**	−0.0017**	−0.0009**	−0.0009**
	(0.0006)	(0.0006)	(0.0003)	(0.0003)
Individual's characteristics +				
Age (in years)	−0.0001	−0.0001	−0.0015	−0.0014
	(0.0010)	(0.0010)	(0.0008)	(0.0008)
Education (schooling/training in years)	−0.0005	−0.0004	0.0038***	0.0033**
	(0.0014)	(0.0015)	(0.0011)	(0.0012)
Labour force experience (in months)	−0.0012	−0.0014	−0.0014	0.0012
	(0.0010)	(0.0010)	(0.0008)	(0.0009)
First job	0.0394***	0.0412***	0.0561***	0.0563***
	(0.0082)	(0.0082)	(0.0080)	(0.0080)
First job, duration$^{3/2}$	−0.0021**	−0.0021**	−0.0020***	−0.0021***
	(0.0007)	(0.0007)	(0.0005)	(0.0005)
Part-time job	−0.0119*	−0.0117*	−0.0119	−0.0122
	(0.0058)	(0.0058)	(0.0157)	(0.0157)
Family status (married versus non-married)	−0.0274	−0.0273	−0.0012	−0.0007
	(0.0148)	(0.0148)	(0.0139)	(0.0139)
Further education and training (FT) +				
Further training $FT_{\lambda(t)}$	0.0104**	0.0109***	−0.0037	−0.0033
	(0.0032)	(0.0032)	(0.0035)	(0.0036)

Table 7.2 (continued)

	Women	Women	Men	Men
Further education $FT_{\lambda(t)}$ · trend	−0.00006*	−0.00006*	−0.00003	−0.00004
	(0.00003)	(0.00003)	(0.00002)	(0.00003)
Duration of participation in FT				
(in months)		0.0002		−0.00004
		(0.0007)		(0.0003)
Duration of previous				
participation in FT (in months)		0.0007*		0.0001
		(0.0003)		(0.0001)
Economic development +				
Trend (years since 1950)	−0.0014*	−0.0014*	−0.0013*	−0.0013*
	(0.0007)	(0.0007)	(0.0005)	(0.0005)
Unemployment rate	−0.0015*	−0.0016*	−0.0007	−0.0007
	(0.0007)	(0.0007)	(0.0005)	(0.0005)
Change in GNP %	−0.0011	−0.0010	−0.0004	−0.0004
	(0.0007)	(0.0007)	(0.0006)	(0.0006)
Sample selection bias				
Probability of inclusion λ	0.0093	0.0080	0.0445***	0.0448***
	(0.0351)	(0.0351)	(0.0080)	(0.0081)
Number of cases	1599	1599	2182	2182
R^2	0.2791	0.2826	0.2232	0.2234

Note: *p $\leq$ 0.05; ** p $\leq$ 0.01; *** p $\leq$ 0.001; + all variable multiplied with $\sqrt{\text{duration}}$.

Source: German life history study (Max-Planck-Institute for Human Development and Education, Berlin); own calculations.

The effect for women is clear. Further education and training contributes to higher earnings in the same job. It is very important that women take part continuously in further training. These continual investments in human capital will be rewarded appropriately. As in the previous case of mobility within the same firm and a move to a new employer, monitoring the various forms of further training does not offer any additional explanation (Becker and Schömann, 1996). The interaction term for further vocational training and time trend shows that the yields for further training have decreased since 1950. Comparison of the absolute degrees of the further training variants leads unequivocally to the conclusion that further training is worthwhile for women who remain in the same job. Greater wage increases for women depend on their opportunities to participate in further training. Unequal access opportunities among women can, therefore, partially explain the gender pay gap.

6. FURTHER TRAINING AND EMPLOYMENT OPPORTUNITIES IN EAST GERMANY

The longitudinal information in the GSOEP for East Germany allows us to reconstruct selection processes in further training and their consequences for individual career trajectories. We discuss first the results of the analysis of training and its role in providing 'employment insurance' or at least in enhancing job security. The second part examines the much-debated use of publicly funded further training to enhance the employment prospects of the unemployed.

The Role of Further Training in Improving Job Security

Both the dynamics of further training effects over the course of a career and the causal effect of further education on permanent employment can be analysed only by using longitudinal data (Blossfeld and Rohwer, 1995). Thus, in event analysis, dynamic estimation procedures are used to ascertain whether further education and training can influence job security or help avoid unemployment during the East German transformation process. The distribution of the time periods in which further training participants become unemployed in comparison to non-participants is estimated using the following exponential model. The hazard rates determined according to equation (7.2) are entered in the model estimate as independent instrumental variants for participation in further education. In other words, the results of equation (7.2) are integrated into equation (7.5) for the transition from employment to unemployment:

$$r(t|x_1, x_2(t)) = \exp(\beta_0 + \beta_1 x_1 + \beta_2 x_2(t) + \beta_{n-1} FT_{\lambda(t)kn-1}(t) + \beta_n \lambda), \quad (7.5)$$

in which $FT_{\lambda(t)}$ represents the logarithm for the hazard rate for participation in education after 1989.

As expected, East Germans with a higher level of formal education stand less of a risk of becoming unemployed than those with poorer education (see Table 7.3). When initial education is supplemented by further training, the risk of unemployment decreases. Monitoring the social selectivity of further training opportunities shows empirically that, for the period December 1989 to April 1993, participants became unemployed less often than non-participants (see Pannenberg, 1995). Accordingly, further vocational training also has positive wage effects in Eastern Germany once earning opportunities are no longer given greater importance than job security (Pannenberg and Helberger, 1997).

However, this is more valid for men than for women when the strength of the effects is borne in mind. There is no great difference in the further

Table 7.3   Estimates of determinants of transition into unemployment in East Germany, 1989–93 (exponential model including episode splitting; standard error of β coefficient in brackets)

	Women	Women	Women	Men	Men	Men
Constant	−4.1314*	−4.2398*	−4.2928*	−6.1428*	−6.1200*	−6.1510*
	(0.9505)	(0.9485)	(0.9495)	(1.1652)	(1.1654)	(1.1655)
Full-time job+	−2.1212*	−2.1000*	−2.0956*	−1.6220*	−1.6165*	−1.6014*
	(0.0913)	(0.0915)	(0.0914)	(0.1178)	(0.1181)	(0.1179)
Part-time job+	−1.5922*	−1.5841*	−1.5857*	0.2827	0.2414	0.2885
	(0.1178)	(0.1177)	(0.1177)	(0.2242)	(0.2248)	(0.2243)
Education + (schooling/training in years)	−0.0702*	−0.0585*	−0.0561*	−0.0748*	−0.0711*	−0.0714*
	(0.0272)	(0.0274)	(0.0274)	(0.0209)	(0.0212)	(0.0213)
Cohort 1935–39 (versus cohort 1930–34)	0.5474	0.5430	0.5418	−0.3996	−0.4116	−0.4125
	(0.3963)	(0.3961)	(0.3961)	(0.2509)	(0.2510)	(0.2510)
Cohort 1940–44	0.6596*	0.6477	0.6468	−0.2032	−0.2107	−0.2467
	(0.3942)	(0.3938)	(0.3938)	(0.2369)	(0.2370)	(0.2374)
Cohort 1945–49	0.8144*	0.8079*	0.8142*	−0.0131	−0.0209	−0.0217
	(0.3966)	(0.3963)	(0.3963)	(0.2357)	(0.2357)	(0.2361)
Cohort 1950–54	0.9266*	0.9173*	0.9242*	−0.1672	−0.1805	−0.2076
	(0.3867)	(0.3863)	(0.3863)	(0.2357)	(0.2358)	(0.2363)
Cohort 1955–59	0.9299*	0.8967*	0.8962*	0.0526	0.0348	0.0390
	(0.3906)	(0.3904)	(0.3904)	(0.2237)	(0.2238)	(0.2239)
Cohort 1960–64	0.7869*	0.7540	0.7578	−0.1763	−0.1958	−0.1989
	(0.3923)	(0.3922)	(0.3921)	(0.2356)	(0.2357)	(0.2358)
Cohort 1965–69	1.1941*	1.1507*	1.1529*	−0.0799	−0.1005	−0.0973
	(0.3882)	(0.3882)	(0.3881)	(0.2536)	(0.2538)	(0.2538)

Cohort 1970–74	1.1811*	1.1516*	1.1542*	0.9322*	0.9109*	0.8919*
	(0.4003)	(0.4001)	(0.4001)	(0.2434)	(0.2436)	(0.2441)
Trend + (months since November 1989)	0.0351*	0.0379*	0.0385*	0.0348*	0.0357*	0.0357*
	(0.0050)	(0.0051)	(0.0050)	(0.0062)	(0.0063)	(0.0063)
Further training +						
Further training FT$_{A(t)}$	−0.1945*	−0.1855*	−0.1884*	−0.4674*	−0.4582*	−0.4621*
	(0.0970)	(0.0967)	(0.0968)	(0.1385)	(0.1384)	(0.1383)
Participation during regular working time		−0.6740*			−0.5100*	
		(0.2389)			(0.2109)	
Participation outside regular working time		−0.2989			0.2430	
		(0.1795)			(0.2048)	
Full-time course			−0.3613			0.4057*
			(0.2437)			(0.1856)
Part-time course			−0.6329*			−0.6650*
			(0.1947)			(0.2397)
Correspondence course			−0.6067			
			(1.0046)			
Number of episodes	43 584	43 584	43 584	49 763	49 763	49 763
Number of events	660	660	660	505	505	505
χ²	587.80	599.22	601.89	296.65	305.45	311.69
Degree of freedom	13	15	16	13	15	15

Note: *p ≤ 0.05; + time-dependent covariates.

Source: German Socio-Economic Panel (DIW, Berlin); own calculations.

training rates for men and women, with approximately 42 per cent of women and 45 per cent of men taking part in training between November 1989 and April 1993 (although the possibility of compound counts due to the GSOEP questionnaire cannot be eliminated). However, bearing in mind the differences in the effects on job security, there are signs that further education is more worthwhile for men than it is for women. East German women must invest much more in further training in order to achieve the same yields as men. On the other hand, the inequality of unemployment risks for educationally privileged workers and those with lower qualifications increases, particularly for men. Socially selective opportunities for further training leads rather to a polarization of employment prospects for both men and women, with the latter also being at greater risk of unemployment.

If further training participation during working hours is differentiated from that outside working hours and it is assumed that this will show differences between on-the-job and off-the job training, the result is that only on-the-job training is successful in reducing existing risks of unemployment. This fits with Hübler's findings (1998), which show that in-firm training in particular leads to heightened job security, while publicly funded measures do not result in the expected positive increases in job security and wage growth. Differentiation between full-time and part-time participation shows that those taking part in part-time measures (job introduction, skills upgrading or career advancement courses) were less likely to become unemployed than either non-participants or participants in full-time training schemes.

However, we found that men who take full-time courses have a much higher risk of unemployment than non-participants or those on part-time courses. Detailed analyses showed that men were mainly involved in retraining measures (Schömann *et al.*, 1997). This form of further training obviously results in stigmatization (Becker, 1999) and deskilling for the participants (Hübler, 1998, p.119), leading to an increased risk of becoming unemployed in the near future. When the yields from on-the-job and part-time training are compared, the gender-related differences are reduced. This finding again proves that evaluations of further training have to differentiate not only between the sexes but also among the individual forms of training, as well as among the locations at which it is provided and the providing bodies.

Further Training Designed to Help Unemployed Jobseekers

Once again, an exponential model is used to evaluate the length of time until re-employment. In order to reach the parametric evaluation, the result from equation (7.2) is again entered into equation (7.6) as follows (compare Table 7.4 for estimation results):

Table 7.4   Estimates of effects of further education on re-employment of
            unemployed men and women in East Germany, 1989–93
            (exponential model including episode splitting; standard error of
            β coefficient in brackets)

	Women	Men	Men	Men
Constant	−3.3808**	−3.0883**	−3.0638**	−3.0370**
	(1.1580)	(1.0209)	(1.0206)	(1.0252)
Education + (schooling/	0.0965***	0.0219	0.0146	0.0146
training in years)	(0.0292)	(0.0303)	(0.0306)	(0.0307)
Cohort 1935–39 (versus	0.5714	1.6740**	1.6692**	1.6351**
cohort 1930–34)	(0.7603)	(0.5613)	(0.5614)	(0.5616)
Cohort 1940–44	1.7549*	2.4011***	2.3744***	2.3860***
	(0.7310)	(0.5255)	(0.5259)	(0.5259)
Cohort 1945–49	1.4563*	2.3004***	2.3063***	2.2967***
	(0.7383)	(0.5260)	(0.5259)	(0.5260)
Cohort 1950–54	1.3988	2.1822***	2.1797***	2.1640***
	(0.7277)	(0.5230)	(0.5232)	(0.5232)
Cohort 1955–59	1.1858	2.2064***	2.1722***	2.1533***
	(0.7273)	(0.5164)	(0.5169)	(0.5171)
Cohort 1960–64	1.1088	2.1723***	2.1574***	2.1199***
	(0.7277)	(0.5235)	(0.5236)	(0.5241)
Cohort 1965–69	1.3610	2.2945***	2.2937***	2.2954***
	(0.7294)	(0.5261)	(0.5265)	(0.5261)
Cohort 1970–74	1.3813	1.7927***	1.7585***	1.7290***
	(0.7396)	(0.5334)	(0.5338)	(0.5342)
Trend + (months since	−0.0360***	−0.0167**	−0.0191**	−0.0185**
November 1989)	(0.0066)	(0.0064)	(0.0065)	(0.0065)
Further training and programme characteristics +				
Further training $FT_{\lambda(t)}$	0.1106	0.1672	0.1623	0.1612
	(0.0992)	(0.1109)	(0.1106)	(0.1113)
Full-time course			0.2642	
			(0.2114)	
Part-time course			0.4601	
			(0.2684)	
Participation during				0.1612
regular working time				(0.1113)
Participation outside				0.5286**
regular working time				(0.2027)
Previous unemployment +				
Unemployment	0.0133	−0.0279	−0.0428	−0.0375
risk $UR_{\lambda(t)}$	(0.0277)	(0.0489)	(0.0496)	(0.0497)

Table 7.4 (continued)

	Women	Men	Men	Men
Duration of	−0.0349***	−0.0593***	−0.0581***	−0.0593***
unemployment	(0.0109)	(0.0116)	(0.0116)	(0.0116)
Number of episodes	5370	2822	2822	2822
Number of events	362	328	328	328
χ^2	126.00	123.33	127.05	129.68
Degree of freedom	13	13	15	15

Note: *p≤0.05; ** p≤0.01; *** p≤0.001; + time-dependent covariates.
Source: German Socio-Economic Panel (DIW, Berlin); own calculations.

$$r(t|x_1, x_2(t)) = \exp(\beta_0 + \beta_1 x_1 + \beta_2 x_2(t) + \beta_{n-1} FT_{\lambda(t)}(t) + \beta_n UR_{\lambda(t)}), \ (7.6)$$

where $UR_{\lambda(t)}$ represents the logarithm for the hazard rate for the socially selected unemployment risk, whose value is based on the estimates produced by equation (7.5), and participation in further education is monitored by $FT_{\lambda(t)}(t)$ (see equation (7.2)).

It must be noted that unemployed women are able to mobilize the education they have acquired in order to exit from unemployment, while for men the level of education does not influence the length of the unemployment spell. Further vocational training does not have a significant influence on the chances of re-employment either. Differentiating between men's participation in full-time and part-time training measures does not reveal any marked further training effects (cf. Hübler, 1998).

Differentiating between further training taking place during and that taking place outside working hours reveals, in the case of men, that those taking part in courses outside working hours found employment sooner than other participants or non-participants. This result can be seen as an indicator that state-funded, target group-oriented courses have played a role in reintegrating unemployed males. Seen in this light, these measures can be said to have been successful in integrating the unemployed into the primary labour market, while in-firm courses have been successful in reducing the risk of unemployment.

The question as to why target group-oriented schemes have not had such an effect in the case of women remains to be answered. In view of the higher risk of unemployment and the lower likelihood of a return to employment for women in Eastern Germany, it can be assumed that employers adopt stigmatization and discrimination strategies. Thus, despite further training and a high degree of career orientation, women are far more disadvantaged than males in respect of wage progression. Spells of unemployment and other cessation processes often force them ultimately from the labour market (Becker, 1999). In this context, the transit and alleviation functions of further training are successful primarily for men.

As far as continuity and security of job opportunities and the related earning capacity are concerned, the main effect of further training in Eastern Germany is limited to a reduction in the risk of unemployment. Individuals who become unemployed even after further training are not protected from long-term unemployment by their participation in such training. This is also confirmed by our results: the longer a person remains unemployed, the less chance he or she has of finding a new job (see also Pannenberg and Helberger, 1997). This reduction in employment prospects with increasing duration of unemployment is far more marked in Eastern than in Western Germany (Hujer *et al.*, 1998).

7.   CONCLUSION

The aim of this chapter has been to investigate the causal link between further training, on the one hand, and wages and employment transitions, on the other, for men and women in Eastern and Western Germany. Special attention has been paid both theoretically and methodologically to social selectivity in respect of, firstly, access to further training and, secondly, labour market processes. We have focused particularly on the link between these processes and those changes, such as policy interventions, that have sought to restructure that link. We have used life history (GLHS) data on further training and wage rates in the case of Western Germany and socio-economic panel data (GSOEP) on job security and re-employment in that of Eastern Germany. We will now discuss the hypotheses outlined in section 3 of this chapter in the light of the empirical evidence presented thereafter.

The first hypothesis based on human capital theory states that high forgone earnings in later stages of life make participation in further training less likely; training will take place only if there is a high probability that the earnings forgone can be recouped subsequently through higher earnings. The evidence for Germany confirmed the education and age selectivity of further training rather than a strict investment rationale for participation. Young, highly educated men will find that their investment rationale yields the expected pay-off mainly through upward job mobility within the same firm or a move to a better-paid job with another employer.

Despite lower forgone earnings, the reluctance of less well-educated employees to participate in further training is most likely due to the fact that training investments do not pay back the initial investment, or to negative experiences during previous periods of education or training. Over the lifetime, earnings differentials between these two groups are likely to grow if the link between education and the labour market is based solely on the investment aspect.

Career trajectories for West German women are apparently still hampered by unequal access to further training. Only in a few cases is women's participation in training rewarded by the current employer, and even this applies mainly to employees who remain with the same firm for long periods. If women want to capitalize on further training investment, they need to have longer service with the same employer if they are to be selected for training and achieve a steeper earnings profile. For women, job mobility is a less attractive means of career advancement because of the organizational impediments to such mobility created by the German welfare state, which remains oriented largely to the single male breadwinner model of the family. The corresponding institutional arrangements make it difficult for most women, particularly those with dependent children or other caring responsibilities, to put into practice a long-term investment strategy. Public policies intended to address this deficiency need to do more than just introduce an equal pay policy. A broader institutional restructuring of the link between learning, labour market dynamics and household activities is indicated.

The second hypothesis, which added an adaptive expectations perspective to human capital theory, is confirmed: individuals who are already well paid and enjoy high early-career wage growth consider additional investment in further training to be a promising investment strategy and are able to capitalize on this additional investment, albeit mainly through job mobility. The narrowness of the pay bands laid down in collective agreements for the various qualificational levels apparently allows little scope for accelerated progression through the ranks within the same firm, giving rise to inter-firm mobility.

Adaptive expectations in combination with human capital investment does not encourage individuals with low wage-growth profiles to invest in continuing training. Hypothesis three (see section 3 above) is therefore rejected. Low returns to training in the labour market for lower levels of qualification also have an influence on expected returns to training, thereby contributing to a widening of the qualification and skill gap between high- and low-skill workers over the lifetime. Promising escape routes out of this adaptive expectations trap might be offered by well-constructed learning paths combined with work experience, leading possibly to business start-ups. The career path from apprenticeship to a master craftsman's qualification in Germany offers a potential route of this kind, but here again high levels of selectivity act against more widespread use of such career paths, in which learning and working are combined.

The polarization hypothesis derived from insider–outsider theory finds some support in our empirical evidence from Germany. Persons who can reasonably be identified as insiders, that is workers in highly unionized sectors with comparably high wage increases and a lower risk of unemployment, tend to enjoy greater access to further training, frequently during working hours. Power in wage bargaining seems to spread to bargaining on training during working time, with lower wage increases being traded for increased training provision for insiders.

In the absence of an agreement on training, access to training acts as a substitute for higher wage increases, which goes some way towards explaining the weak link between further training and subsequent pay. On the other hand, the use of training as a preventive strategy against the risk of unemployment has not played an important part in collective agreements in Germany. In retrospect, this represents a missed opportunity and a huge potential sphere for future union activity and bargaining.

The same conclusion can be derived from segmentation theory, which suggests the existence of persistent inequality of access to training. Our evidence for Germany suggests that public policy can properly play a role in correcting market failure and persistent segmentation. Our evidence on the working of the Employment Promotion Act during the late 1960s and on subsequent reforms shows that public measures need close monitoring in order to avoid a 'creaming' or selection effect. Similarly, in Eastern Germany, the post-unification expansion of further training was largely unsuccessful in returning people to employment, at least in the relatively short term, since macroeconomic conditions remained difficult and overall job growth was low.

Finally, hypotheses 7 and 8 derived from the theory of transitions over the lifetime outlined in Chapter 2 receive some support from the evidence presented in this chapter. The institutional link between initial full-time education and the labour market operates quite well in terms of low levels of unemployment and earnings which correspond to levels of qualifications. In the case of further education and training, there is only a loose link between learning and labour market rewards in both Eastern and Western Germany. Because of the high degree of education selectivity in further training, the process of lifelong learning is still rather detached from labour market dynamics and breaks down almost completely after the age of 40–45 years for both men and women.

The importance of the German apprenticeship system in sustaining the link between education, training and the labour market is widely recognized. However, after this initial intensive phase of interaction between learning and working, the feedback between the two spheres seems to weaken at about age 30 for those in work, to say nothing of the unemployed and those engaged in unpaid household activities. Probably as a consequence of a rather short-sighted view of the labour market potential and likely returns to human capital for people in middle age, past earnings and experience do not lead to renewed learning among broad sections of the German population. In view of the blistering pace of technological change in recent years, however, this would seem to be a risky strategy for competing in world markets, and brings with it a high risk of social exclusion for groups in society that are disadvantaged or reluctant to develop their own potential for learning and working.

In Eastern Germany, further training reduced the risk of unemployment for women. For men, this is true only of longer and relatively costly retraining courses. The regulative concept of transitional labour markets, in which a system of employment insurance independent of the current employer is built up by establishing a continuous link between learning and working (including unpaid work in the household), might be an interesting policy option. Additionally, our results point to an accumulation of labour market disadvantages among a specific group of men, particularly those in need of more than a short retraining course to make themselves employable again or to acquire marketable skills. These accumulated disadvantages lead to increased polarization within the labour force.

The transitional labour market of learning and working functions quite well in Germany at first entry into the labour market, despite relatively constant occupational segregation and persistent wage differentials between women and men. The almost non-existent link between learning and working after some ten years of participation in the labour market raises a rather urgent concern about the institutional redesign of this link. Some industry-level agreements between the social partners have been concluded recently in Germany, and some regional initiatives have been launched, but a more vigorous drive to forge robust links between learning and working is needed in order to increase the level of social integration in the country at large.

NOTES

1. The main significance of further vocational education and training for job and earning opportunities cannot be measured solely in terms of workers' further training behaviour, but we must also take account of its value for their careers. Personal careers and advancement are becoming increasingly linked, with general education and initial training continuing to play a critical role in job and further training opportunities. Further education

and training is not only very important for career orientation but also for gaining additional qualifications which are important in specialist, cross-occupational and extrafunctional senses. Thus, along with formal job-related proficiency, informal personal and social skills are becoming increasingly important – all the more so as competition for scarce goods and positions becomes ever more intense in a tight labour market (cf. Pfeiffer, 1998).

2. The following factors are of the utmost importance in determining the chances of selection for further training: age through birth cohorts, education level already attained, employment in the public sector and in specialist and occupation-specific labour markets in the private sector, previous career trajectory and the improved provision of further education and training after the introduction of the Employment Promotion Law in 1969. A more polarized tendency towards further training participation in the form of a continual accumulation of training can be observed in certain groups of workers for the period 1990 to 1993.

3. In 1993, when the fourth wave of the socioeconomic panel was carried out for Eastern Germany, an investigation into further vocational education and training was also conducted, producing very detailed information for the period 1990 to 1993. This gave a selective random check in regard to training, since only employed persons who had taken part in at least one of these waves were surveyed. The correction of this random sample selectivity comes from the reciprocal value of the projection factor for the first panel participation and the multiplication of the probability of remaining for future questionnaires (Schömann et al., 1997). Because of the variable in this factor, the logarithm is calculated so that $\lambda = \log((1/\text{projection factor})$ probability of remaining).

4. In actual fact, the opportunities for further training and education were highly selective in East Germany from the end of 1989 up to the spring of 1993 (see Table 7A.2). Besides formal education and vocational training, the most decisive factor, especially for women, was direct connections to the primary labour market. Despite the increasing provision of further training schemes, opportunities for older women deteriorated continuously up to the end of 1992. Furthermore, selectivity of education and training opportunities by employment and job characteristics can be observed. Continuity of permanent employment, a job commensurate with qualifications, good working conditions and a privileged career position are all signals and mechanisms which reinforce social inequality in access to further education and training. All in all, the significance of both self-selection and external selection along with the related termination processes became evident. This intensifies the exclusion of those members of the working population who have lost their positions in the labour market as a result of the changes.

BIBLIOGRAPHY

Becker, Rolf (1991), 'Berufliche Weiterbildung und Berufsverlauf. Eine Längsschnittuntersuchung von drei Geburtskohorten', *Mitteilungen aus der Arbeitsmarkt- und Berufsforschung*, 24, 351–64.

Becker, Rolf (1993), 'Zur Bedeutung der beruflichen Weiterbildung für den Berufsverlauf. Eine empirische Längsschnittuntersuchung über Weiterbildungs- und Berufschancen', in Arthur Meier und Ursula Rabe-Kleberg (eds), *Weiterbildung, Lebenslauf, sozialer Wandel*, Neuwied: Luchterhand, pp. 61–86.

Becker, Rolf (1999), 'Berufliche Weiterbildung und Arbeitsmarktchancen im gesellschaftlichen Umbruch', in Felix Büchel, Martin Diewald, Peter Krause, Antje Mertens und Heike Solga (eds), *Zwischen drinnen und draußen – Soziale Ausgrenzung am deutschen Arbeitsmarkt*, Opladen: Leske and Budrich, pp. 95–106.

Becker, Rolf and Schömann, Klaus (1996), 'Berufliche Weiterbildung und Einkommensdynamik. Eine Längsschnittstudie mit besonderer Berücksichtigung von Selektionsprozessen', *Kölner Zeitschrift für Soziologie und Sozialpsychologie*, 48(3), 426–61.

Behringer, Friederike (1995), 'Weiterbildung in Ost- und Westdeutschland', *Vierteljahreshefte zur Wirtschaftsforschung*, 64, 26–50.

Blaschke, Dieter and Nagel, Elisabeth (1995), 'Beschäftigungssituation von Teilnehmern an AFG-finanzierter beruflicher Weiterbildung', *Mitteilungen aus der Arbeitsmarkt- und Berufsforschung*, 28, 195–215.

Blossfeld, Hans-Peter and Rohwer, Götz (1995), *Techniques of Event History Modeling – New Approaches to Causal Analysis*, Mawah, NJ: Erlbaum.

Fitzenberger, Bernd and Prey, Hedwig (1998), 'Beschäftigungs- und Verdienstwirkungen von Weiterbildungsmaßnahmen im ostdeutschen Transformationsprozeß', Eine Methodenkritik', in Friedhelm Pfeiffer und Winfried Pohlmeier (eds), *Qualifikation, Weiterbildung und Arbeitsmarkterfolg*, Baden-Baden: Nomos, pp. 39–96.

Heckman, James J. (1979), 'Sample Selection Bias as a Specification Error', *Econometrica*, 47, 153–61.

Heckman, James J. and Smith, Jeffrey (1996), 'Experimental and Nonexperimental Evaluation', in Günther Schmid, Jacqueline O'Reilly und Klaus Schömann (eds), *International Handbook of Labour Market Policy and Evaluation*, Cheltenham, UK and Brookfield, US: Edward Elgar, pp. 34–76.

Holland, Paul W. (1986), 'Statistics and Causal Inference', *Journal of the American Statistical Association*, 81, 945–70.

Hübler, Olaf (1997), 'Evaluation beschäftigungspolitischer Maßnahmen in Ostdeutschland', *Jahrbücher für Nationalökonomie und Statistik*, 216, 21–44.

Hübler, Olaf (1998), 'Berufliche Weiterbildung und Umschulung in Ostdeutschland – Erfahrungen und Perspektiven', in Friedhelm Pfeiffer und Winfried Pohlmeier (eds), *Qualifikation, Weiterbildung und Arbeitsmarkterfolg*, Baden-Baden, Nomos, pp. 97–132.

Hujer, Reinhard, Maurer, Kai-Oliver and Wellner, Marc (1998), 'Kurz- und langfristige Effekte von Weiterbildungsmaßnahmen auf die Arbeitslosigkeitsdauer in Westdeutschland', in Friedhelm Pfeiffer and Winfried Pohlmeier (eds), *Qualifikation, Weiterbildung und Arbeitsmarkterfolg*, Baden-Baden: Nomos, pp. 197–222.

Lechner, Michael (1998), 'Mikroökonomische Evaluationsstudien, Anmerkungen zu Theorie und Praxis', in Friedhelm Pfeiffer und Winfried Pohlmeier (eds), *Qualifikation, Weiterbildung und Arbeitsmarkterfolg*, Baden-Baden, Nomos, pp. 13–38.

Lillard, Lee (1993), 'Simultaneous equations for hazards. Marriage duration and fertility timing', *Journal of Econometrics*, 56, 189–217.

Lindbeck, Assar and Snower, Dennis J. (1989), *The insider–outsider theory of employment and unemployment*, Cambridge, MA: MIT Press.

Maddala, Gangadharrao S. (1978), 'Selectivity problems in longitudinal data', *Annales De L'Insee*, 30–31, 423–50.

Mayer, Karl Ulrich (1991), 'Lebensverlauf und Bildung, Ergebnisse aus dem Forschungsprojekt "Lebensverläufe und gesellschaftlicher Wandel" des Max-Planck-Instituts für Bildungsforschung', *Unterrichtswissenschaft*, 19, 313–32.

Pannenberg, Markus (1995), *Weiterbildungsaktivitäten und Erwerbsbiographie*, Frankfurt am Main: Campus.

Pannenberg, Markus (1998), 'Weiterbildung, Betriebszugehörigkeit und Löhne, Ökonomische Effekte des "timings" von Investitionen in die berufliche Weiterbildung', in Friedhelm Pfeiffer and Winfried Pohlmeier (eds), *Qualifikation, Weiterbildung und Arbeitsmarkterfolg*, Baden-Baden: Nomos, pp. 257–78.

Pannenberg, Markus and Helberger, Christof (1997), 'Kurzfristige Auswirkungen staatlicher Qualifizierungsmaßnahmen in Ostdeutschland, Das Beispiel Fortbildung und Umschulung', in Dieter Timmermann (eds), *Bildung und Arbeit in Ostdeutschland*, Berlin: Duncker & Humblot, pp. 77–97.

Petersen, Trond (1989), 'The Earning Function in Sociological Studies of Earnings Inequality, Functional Form and Hours Worked', *Research in Social Stratification and Mobility*, 8, 221–50.

Pfeiffer, Friedhelm (1998), 'Eine vergleichende Analyse der Bedeutung von Ausbildung, Fortbildung und nicht formalem Lernen im Arbeitsleben', in Friedhelm Pfeiffer and Winfried Pohlmeier (ed.), *Qualifikation, Weiterbildung und Arbeitsmarkterfolg*, Baden-Baden: Nomos, pp. 155–96.

Pfeiffer, Friedhelm and Pohlmeier, Winfried (eds) (1998), *Qualifikation, Weiterbildung und Arbeitsmarkterfolg, Schriftenreihe des ZEW*, vol. 31, Baden-Baden: Nomos.

Rendtel, Ulrich (1995), *Panelausfälle und Panelrepräsentativität*, Frankfurt am Main: Campus.

Schömann, Klaus (1994), *The Dynamics of Labor Earnings over the Life Course. A Comparative and Longitudinal Analysis of Germany and Poland*, Max-Planck-Institut für Bildungsforschung, Berlin: edition sigma.

Schömann, Klaus (1996), 'Longitudinal Designs in Evaluation Studies', in Günther Schmid, Jacqueline O'Reilly and Klaus Schömann (eds), *International Handbook of Labour Market Policy and Evaluation*, Cheltenham, UK and Brookfield, US: Edward Elgar, pp. 115–37.

Schömann, Klaus and Becker, Rolf (1995), 'Participation in Further Education over the Life Course', *European Sociological Review*, 11, 187–208.

Schömann, Klaus and Becker, Rolf (1998), 'Selektivität in der beruflichen Weiterbildung und Einkommensverläufe', in Friedhelm Pfeiffer und Winfried Pohlmeier (eds), *Qualifikation, Weiterbildung und Arbeitsmarkterfolg*, Baden-Baden: Nomos, pp. 279–310.

Schömann, Klaus, Becker, Rolf and Zühlke, Sylvia (1997), 'Further Education and Occupational Careers in East Germany, a Longitudinal Study on Participation in Further Education and its Impact on Employment Prospects', in Thomas Dunn and Johannes Schwarze (eds), *Proceedings of the 1996 International Conference of German Socio-Economic Panel Study User*, Vierteljahreshefte zur Wirtschaftsforschung, 66, 187–96.

Schmid, Günther (1998), 'Transitional Labour Markets, A New European Employment Strategy', *WZB Discussion Paper*, FS I 98-206, Berlin.

Snower, Dennis and Booth, Alison L. (1996), 'Conclusions, government policy to promote the acquisition of skills', in Alison L. Booth and Dennis J. Snower (eds), *Acquiring Skills. Market Failures, Their Symptoms and Policy Responses*, Cambridge: Cambridge University Press, pp. 337–49.

Stolzenberg, Ross M. and Relles, Daniel A. (1990), 'Theory Testing in a World of Constrained Research Design', *Sociological Methods and Research*, 18, 394–415.

APPENDIX

Table 7A.1 *Partial-likelihood estimates of effects of independent variables on the likelihood of participation in further training in West Germany (standard error of β coefficient in brackets)*

	Women	Men
Individual's characteristics		
Cohort 1939–41 (versus cohort 1929–31)	0.4791	0.2071
	(0.2833)	(0.1331)
Cohort 1949–51	1.169***	0.6321***
	(0.3208)	(0.1897)
Family status (married versus non-married individuals)	0.9113***	
	(0.3385)	
Education (schooling/training in years)	0.2005***	0.1012***
	(0.0347)	(0.0212)
Net hourly wage (in Deutsche Marks)	0.0109	−0.0708
	(0.1295)	(0.0843)
Labour force experience (in months)	−0.0004	−0.0034**
	(0.0016)	(0.0010)
Job duration in same firm (in months)	0.0006	0.0032*
	(0.0041)	(0.0014)
Labour market structures		
Public sector (versus secondary labour markets in small firms)	0.9960***	0.4888**
	(0.3090)	(0.1983)
Secondary labour markets in large firms	0.1213	0.0905
	(0.4177)	(0.2465)
Primary labour market in small firms	0.8020**	0.3199
	(0.3047)	(0.1971)
Primary labour market in large firms	0.9932***	0.4471*
	(0.3358)	(0.1983)
Characteristics of occupational history		
Part-time job	−0.1895	
	(0.2214)	
Unemployment	0.3349	0.0740
	(0.5989)	(0.2965)
Voluntarily job interruption	0.0461	−0.8928*
	(0.2444)	(0.4124)

Table 7A.1 (continued)

	Women	Men
Period 1969–74 (versus period before promulgation of Employment Promotion Act (AFG))	0.1504 (0.2932)	0.7240*** (0.1886)
Period after 1974	0.0187 (0.2776)	0.1095 (0.1826)
Number of episodes	1 767	2 554
Number of events	160	419
Chi^2	233.55	156.5
Degree of freedom	16	14

Note: *p ≤ 0.05; ** p ≤ 0.01; *** p ≤ 0.001
Source: German life history study (Max-Planck-Institute for Human Development and Education, Berlin); own calculations.

Table 7A.2   Estimates of participation in further training in East Germany, 1989–93 (exponential model including episode splitting; standard error of β coefficient in brackets)

	Women	Women	Men	Men
Constant	−10.837*** (1.1784)	−8.183*** (0.8570)	−7.596*** (0.9512)	−7.020*** (0.8085)
Employment status and initial education+				
Discouraged unemployed worker	Reference category			
Full-time job	1.7775*** (0.3390)		0.3208 (0.4206)	
Part-time job	1.4815*** (0.3578)			
Short-time work	1.8709*** (0.3827)		0.1677 (0.4721)	
Unemployment	1.0834** (0.3706)		Reference category	
Education + training	0.2158*** (0.0169)	0.1513*** (0.0178)	0.2107*** (0.0158)	0.1482*** (0.0200)
Time effects				
Cohort 1930–34	Reference category		Reference category	
Cohort 1935–39	1.0889 (0.6004)		0.0887 (0.2614)	

Table 7A.2 (continued)

	Women	Women	Men	Men
Cohort 1940–44	1.2345*		0.2755	
	(0.5986)		(0.2460)	
Cohort 1945–49	1.2450*		0.1558	
	(0.6086)		(0.2568)	
Cohort 1950–54	0.9660		0.1792	
	(0.6165)		(0.2579)	
Cohort 1955–59	1.0445		0.0403	
	(0.6268)		(0.2654)	
Cohort 1960–64	1.0813		0.1257	
	(0.6421)		(0.2783)	
Cohort 1965–69	0.8612		0.3460	
	(0.6665)		(0.3006)	
Cohort 1970–74	0.9610		0.2588	
	(0.6939)		(0.3348)	
Cohort (linear)		−0.0131		0.0084
		(0.0092)		(0.0063)
Cohort^2 (linear)		−0.0009*		0.0001
		(0.0005)		(0.0004)
Trend + (months since	0.0409***	0.0410***	0.0380***	0.0369***
November 1989)	(0.0035)	(0.0034)	(0.0034)	(0.0034)
Life history in former GDR				
Duration of full-time	−0.0001	−0.0086	−0.0085	−0.0050
employment	(0.0092)	(0.0093)	(0.0050)	(0.0051)
Duration of part-time	−0.0073	−0.0084		
employment	(0.0060)	(0.0060)		
Duration out of labour	−0.0315	−0.0446		
force	(0.0250)	(0.0248)		
Job characteristics +				
Full matching of job		0.2195*		0.0046
skills and worker's skills		(0.0935)		(0.0846)
Weekly working time		0.0138***		0.0084***
		(0.0033)		(0.0024)
Social status +				
Discouraged		Reference		
unemployed worker		category		
Unemployed worker		0.3007		Reference
		(0.2169)		category
Professional		0.1916		0.4923
		(0.2878)		(0.2600)

Table 7A.2 (continued)

	Women	Women	Men	Men
Self-employed				−0.0498
				(0.1557)
White-collar worker in		0.3655*		0.1447
private sector		(0.1690)		(0.0964)
Blue-collar worker in		−0.6333**		−0.3523***
private sector		(0.2389)		(0.1020)
Civil servant				1.0090***
				(0.1837)
White-collar worker in		0.6350***		0.3064**
public sector		(0.1609)		(0.1053)
Blue-collar worker in		−1.1709***		−0.6829***
public sector		(0.1831)		(0.1771)
Sample selection bias+				
Probability of inclusion λ	−0.0133	−0.0399	0.0804	0.0382
	(0.1038)	(0.0994)	(0.0923)	(0.0910)
Number of episodes	51275	51275	50436	50436
Number of events	660	660	672	672
χ^2	510.05	587.54	353.79	423.85
Degree of freedom	18	16	14	15

Note: * $p \leq 0.05$; ** $p \leq 0.01$; *** $p \leq 0.001$; + time-dependent covariates.
Source: German Socio-Economic Panel (DIW, Berlin); own calculations.

8. Training transitions in the EU: different policies but similar effects?

Klaus Schömann[1]

1. INTRODUCTION

The strength, and the potential weakness, of policy making in the European Union lies in the fact that a policy agreed at European level can be implemented in very different ways in the various member states. As with European directives, policy guidelines issued by the Council of Ministers need to be 'translated' by each member state into its own specific institutional set-up. In the area of training there is a widespread consensus on the need for quality improvements and more precise matching of labour market policies to potential participants. The following quotation from a press release about the Eurobarometer (1997), a survey of individuals in all EU member states, reflects the beliefs and aspirations of European citizens: 'Response to the question as to whether continuing education and training can improve one's working life is a resounding yes, 76 per cent believe education and training will have a positive effect, only 19 per cent do not think so.' Such statements express the high expectations EU citizens have of the private and public organizations involved in formulating, financing and implementing education, training and lifelong learning policies in Europe.

The Commission of the European Union and the Organisation for Economic Cooperation and Development (OECD) continue to assess the causes of and possible solutions to the problem of high and persisting levels of unemployment in the advanced industrialized countries. Drawing on such earlier documents as the White Paper on 'Growth, competitiveness, employment' (European Commission, 1993) and *The OECD Jobs Study* (OECD, 1994), both organizations stress lifelong learning as an important component of a policy strategy aimed at overcoming structural barriers. In the White Paper, EU member states are encouraged to implement efforts 'to create the basis in each Member country for a genuine right to ongoing training' (European Commission, 1993, p. 17).

This is indeed a far-reaching policy target, particularly if this 'genuine right to ongoing training' is taken to apply to all groups of society irrespective of gender, ethnicity and employment status. Adopting a more restricted economic perspective on the labour market, *The OECD Jobs Study* (1994) states: 'Extending and upgrading workers' skills and competences must be a life-long process if OECD economies are to foster the creation of high-skill, high-wage jobs' (p. 47). The OECD is concerned more specifically with the effective implementation of strategies as part of a coherent approach to a range of policy areas that include labour market and social insurance policies.

The right to a basic general education serves only as the starting point or foundation for the right to some form of further training or retraining in the event of a person's labour market skills becoming obsolete. Women who have withdrawn from the labour market because of their domestic responsibilities are at particular risk of losing status and income on their return to paid work after a lengthy career break (Gustafsson, 1996). Labour market and education policies operating on various levels in the European Union are beginning to address this issue. Contractual and statutory rights to paid time off for training and education now exist in most EU member states (cf. Table 8.1). However, it is still important to evaluate whether the beneficiaries of these lifelong learning initiatives are drawn from a broad cross-section of the working population or whether participation is more restricted, particularly among groups at risk of social exclusion.

The spread of participation in training among various groups of the population can be interpreted as one indicator of social integration (cf. Chapter 2). Similarly, wider participation in training among individuals not currently in the labour force is one way of improving their chances of entering the labour force at some time in the future; in other words, it increases their chances of effecting a re-integrating transition in one of the transitional labour markets. Such indicators, as well as a more detailed analysis of who accomplishes integrative transitions, highlight the integration potential of training policies. Thus, throughout this book, the transition from unemployment to employment emerges from our comparisons of EU member states as one of the most important transitions, as does the prevention of transitions from employment to unemployment.

In this chapter, we first test whether training and skill formation is important for young people at labour market entry or whether training is generally important for persons wanting to make a transition into or within the labour market. Secondly, we see that transitional labour market theory (Schmid, 1995, ch. 2) indicates a need for a shift away from an education and training system centred upon the employed towards a training policy-based access, participation and completion irrespective of employment status. Thirdly, training aspirations and the acquisition of training certificates need to lead

Table 8.1   Contractual and statutory rights to paid time off for training in selected European countries

Austria	Denmark	Finland	France	Germany	Italy	Portugal	Sweden	UK
Employees (firms > 200 staff): after 3 years employment break for further training, unpaid study leave for 6–12 months. Payment from unemployment insurance: 5565 AS (approx. 400 ECU). Higher payments for special training possible. No compulsory replacement for job release for FT; otherwise (parental leave, sabbatical): replacement.	Employees, unemployed and self-employed have a right every 5 years to a year-long leave for further training, (in employment for a minimum of 3 yrs within the past 5 years, with the employer's consent). Further training during working time for low-skilled workers, additional collective agreements.	Leave of absence ('job alternation leave') with employer's consent after periods of continuous employment (as from first year). Condition: employment of unemployed substitute compulsory. Leave of absence may be used for any purpose. Additional collective agreements used.	Employees have a right to individual study leave. Low utilization, no state funding for the work release. Firms with more than 10 employees have to spend 1.5 per cent of the total wage bill on further training per year.	10 of the 16 *Länder* have educational leave regulations for employees (approximately 5 days annually). Federal laws for master and craftsman training. Additional collective agreements are widely used.	No general further training regulations. Educational leave possible. According to the 'Agreement on Employment', legal regulations are planned for work release, grants for further training and a levy for training.	Constitutional right to vocational training. Legal regulations exist for government funding for further training for employees. Regulations for unpaid further training leave are agreed upon with the unions.	Access to further training is guaranteed by the right of all employees to leave of absence. Since 1978 all employees can avail themselves of 25 working days for leave. No government funding for the work release.	No statutory rights or obligation to train, but incentives such as the 'Investors in People' standard. Access to training and paid education leave is negotiated between the employer and employee.

to the production of skills which are relevant for the labour market. Finally, we carry out an empirical assessment of the reach of training policies based on comparable individual-level data obtained from the European Labour Force Survey (hereinafter ELFS) and Eurobarometer, adding a comparative perspective to the three previous country-specific chapters on the Netherlands, Ireland and Germany with a comparative perspective.

The role of more broadly-based training policies and the design of public policies intended to advance social integration through such training policies, as well as institutions active in this field, are discussed only indirectly in this chapter. Policy making in the multi-level European Union governance structure will be dealt with in much more detail in the last two chapters of the book, as will the actors' perspectives on the issues at stake.

2. THE PROCESS OF SOCIAL EXCLUSION AND TRAINING SELECTIVITY

Drawing on previous reviews of the literature in the field of lifelong learning and training policies (Tuijnman and Schömann, 1996; OECD, 1999), we focus in this chapter on processes of social exclusion and integration in modern societies with specific reference to education and training policies. Both processes have a component of social selectivity which is not easy to pin down. Since we cannot observe the comprehensive nature of these processes directly, our research strategy is to indicate the presence of selective participation processes by identifying basic personal characteristics such as age, gender or level of qualifications. We believe that, despite the presence of unobserved heterogeneity, most of the factors contributing to social exclusion can be related to readily observable personal characteristics of individuals. Certain factors, including social background (cf. Chapter 3), 'soft' skills, such as communicational abilities, and motivation are known to be important determinants of successful transitions, but such information is not provided by most larger social science surveys and is unavailable to us for the purpose of this comparative analysis.

Participation in training and working life seems to be organized in such a way that particular groups in society are encouraged to be more involved in training than others. This means they have better chances of effecting transitions within the labour market, with only short spells of unemployment at worst. One of the indicators we have chosen to indicate fully as opposed to marginal social integration is the degree of selectivity of access to and participation in further training, since further training plays a key role in mastering technological progress in the workplace and in some spheres of private life.

A large part of the process of social exclusion can be attributed to social stratification in the early stages of the education system (cf. Chapters 3 and 4). Early experiences in the education system largely determine later access to further education and training. Many analyses of education and training systems are still based on the traditional, 'front-loaded' approach, which holds that learning is concentrated in the period before first entry into the labour market, despite the long-established notion that learning should be seen rather as a lifelong process of human development (Faure, 1972). The concept of lifelong learning implies that learning takes place over the life course and that it is confined neither to any specific age group nor to education administered by educational institutions. In practice, however, most if not all education systems produce a basic layer of social differentiation. Moreover, social differentiation at an early stage of the life course plays an influential role in labour market transitions over the entire life course and in processes of social exclusion or reintegration.

A broadly-based definition of lifelong learning might include, in addition to formal schooling, adult education, self-directed learning, continuing vocational training, on-the-job training and informal learning in the workplace or through the Internet. However, irrespective of the kind of learning process, participation in lifelong learning remains selective and dependent to a large extent on the educational experiences and qualification levels acquired during childhood or adolescence. A major hypothesis in the analysis of training as a means of furthering social integration is that the success of training strategies is still largely determined by social background and early experiences in the education and training system. If training is to work and to provide 'insurance' against the risk of social exclusion, training and learning processes need to be organized in such a way as to reach much broader segments of society irrespective of previous experiences of education, level of qualification, learning or work practices.

Lifelong learning or investment in training is expected to contribute to a high-skill, high-wage job strategy (OECD, 1994, 1999). If policy makers favour the investment-related over the integrative aspect of training, then the educational selectivity of further training is likely to be enhanced, since such a strategy is more likely to increase the returns to further training for individuals who already enjoy high returns to their investment. However, incorporating social rates of return to training into the analysis enlarges the scope for socially viable investment in training for those with low levels of qualifications, or none at all. But what is meant by social rates of return to training? We suggest a definition based on the notion of spill-over effects, for example the translation of training undergone by individuals into improvements in socially desirable fields of activity. One practical example would be the application of skills learned at work to voluntary work or to household activities such as the 'private production of goods and services' or care work.

The major thrust of a labour market policy designed to counter the social selectivity of further training is to work against the restriction of educational qualifications and further training opportunities for the few rather than the many. The social fabric of societies is at risk if the speed of knowledge and skill acquisition becomes even more selective and confined to certain social strata and age groups. Thus education selectivity is a major impediment to training policies intended to provide insurance against social exclusion both for individuals and for society at large. This issue will be addressed in the empirical sections of the chapter. Some recent examples of initiatives intended to counter this form of social selectivity in the European Union will also be presented.

The three previous chapters dealt with the impact of further training policies in the Netherlands, Ireland and Germany. All three chapters pointed out the selectivity processes at work, although it remains an open question whether this selectivity works in similar ways in each country. The institutions and policies relating to further training for young people in Ireland show the importance of market-oriented training programmes for participants' subsequent labour market success. Expressed in economic terms, it was found that marginal returns to investment in training are found to be higher for women than for men (Chapter 5). Increasing tertiarization seems to favour the return of women to the labour market and thus returns to training for women are currently higher for women than for men.

The Dutch studies show some slight positive effects for training in general and support the hypothesis that state-financed training should be aimed more towards reintegration programmes for the unemployed, since the returns to training for these persons are relatively high if they can be placed successfully. Labour market conditions during the late 1990s were quite favourable to such policies. Other labour market policies should directly address mismatch in the labour market. Such policies could build on the selectivity of measures and make positive use of participant 'creaming' in order to react quickly to skill shortages in some sectors of the economy (Chapter 6).

Drawing on the theory of transitional labour markets and life-course transitions, a set of hypotheses can be derived as starting points for the macro and micro levels of analysis, as already outlined in Chapter 2 of this volume. In this chapter we test hypothesis 3 from Chapter 2 at the macro level. This hypothesis states that the school-to-work nexus is susceptible to political influence. Thus each country in the European Union has a specific configuration of institutions and policies which may or may not favour labour market and further training transitions. Whereas Chapters 3 and 4 focused on first transitions into the labour market from a comparative perspective, this chapter emphasizes later labour market and training-related transitions (as do Chapters 5, 6 and 7). Taken together, initial and subsequent transitions constitute the transitional labour market of learning and working.

Apprenticeship-type links between initial education/training and the labour market were shown to have a smoothly functioning 'coefficient of coupling' that creates a sufficiently elastic bridge between learning and working that is not based solely on academic skills. Later training transitions certainly seem to be related to successful first entry, but the institutional features of the labour market, as a societal subsystem in its own right, make it necessary to determine a different 'coefficient of coupling' for further training transitions. It is reasonable to expect a high correlation between the two 'coefficients of coupling' (for first and subsequent transitions), but this is a hypothesis derived from a commonsense expectation about links between related institutions. So far there is no theory that would yield hypotheses about the links between educational institutions and their effects on the labour market. Transitional labour market theory has the potential to address this issue, but a more stringent deduction of hypotheses is beyond the scope of this chapter. Instead, we test the abovementioned hypotheses on the basis of comparable data sources for many European countries.

Hypothesis 4 from Chapter 2 can be tested by cross-country comparison. The 'coefficient of coupling' is more elastic in countries where transitions between education/training and the labour market occur more frequently and are combined with either more stable employment or higher wage profiles. A more elastic 'coefficient of coupling' in further training transitions is judged to favour the integration of wider sections of society into the labour market. Less selective participation in further training, which encourages larger numbers of women to participate, constitutes the first component of an elastic link between learning and the labour market. This characterizes the first transition into training. The second component consists of transitions back into the labour market after training participation. Both components are constituent parts of the transitional labour market and we shall proceed to empirical tests in a comparative analysis in this chapter.

At the micro level of analysis, we can evaluate hypotheses 10 and 11 as stated in Chapter 2. The first of these two hypotheses asserts the lasting effect of educational attainment prior to labour market entry on later transitions over the life course and the potential benefit of general and vocational education in mastering critical transitions. The presence of education selectivity in transitional labour markets as well, particularly in the further training and employment/unemployment transition, is viewed as evidence that employment systems are intrinsically linked to the dynamics of the education and training system in a country, and vice versa.

Evidence for education selectivity is interpreted, therefore, as a continuous form of coupling between societal spheres that perpetuates the social stratification arising out of pupils' social backgrounds and educational attainment. Hypothesis 11, a variant which could also be derived from labour market segmentation theory, calls for selective labour market policies and suggests that a 'coefficient of coupling' specific to each labour market segment should be established. Evidence on first labour market entry (Chapter 4) also indicates segmentation. Here we test for the persistence of such segmentation at later transitions. Besides education selectivity, selectivity in the labour market by age and gender is likely to lead to largely similar patterns of segmentation in the European Union, albeit of varying degrees of intensity.

In general, transitional labour market arrangements attempt to alleviate the persistent effects of labour market segmentation. The main thrust is to broaden the scope of social integration. The comparative analysis in this chapter is based on harmonized data sets from the ELFS; for most countries in the European Union, these data sets provide a sound basis for testing these hypotheses in the following sections.

3. COMPARING THE SELECTIVITY OF TRAINING

In order to compare how the selectivity processes function in the various EU member states, detailed longitudinal data for each country are required. The previous three chapters shed some light on selectivity processes in three countries. In this chapter, the selectivity issue is approached by comparing evidence from various EU data sources. The specific potential of each data source is exploited (the large sample size and the information on transitions provided by the labour force surveys, the expressed opinions in the Eurobarometer data), although the lack of detailed information on further training is a limitation that has to be taken into account.

Comparable estimates of participation in training or other formal learning activities in the European Union are hard to obtain. This is due in part to the difficulty of defining what constitutes learning. In a comparative analysis, differences in learning traditions give rise to differences in the indicators used to measure the extent and quality of learning. One example of the potential for bias in the indicators is the extent to which different countries report on more informal training and learning arrangements. However, despite such basic difficulties, the data collected by Eurostat in the course of the ELFS interviews now provide more than a decade's worth of comparable information derived from responses to the question on participation in education or training, including on-the-job training, in the four weeks prior to the reference date.

An initial comparative impression can be obtained from this general question on the various forms of training taking place during one month in each year (cf. Figure 8.1). During the four weeks prior to the interview in spring 1996, 3.6 per cent of people in the EU aged 30 years and older received some form of training (Eurostat, 1997). In the Scandinavian countries, Denmark, Finland and Sweden, the training participation rate for this age group was more than 10 per cent. The United Kingdom, the Netherlands and Austria are also countries with above-average participation rates in further education and training, whereas Germany, Spain, France and, to a lesser extent, Ireland show below-average participation. National averages derived from the Eurobarometer database show that France and Germany also reach the EU average of about 6 per cent for participation in further training in the 12 months prior to the reference date. In the case of France, this is due to the fact that the ELFS does not count in-company training, while for Germany we believe that a lot of training starts in the autumn and finishes before the spring, which is when the survey interviews take place. However, at 0.9, the correlation between the two measures of further training participation is very high. In other words, despite their different approaches, the two measures provide a fairly similar picture of the further training landscape in Europe.

Even simple descriptive analyses (Eurostat, 1997) show that those in employment in the EU are about ten times more likely than the unemployed to participate in some form of training, despite the fact that there are huge differences within the Union in the use of active labour market policies and, more specifically, of training measures aimed at the unemployed with a view to closing this gap (Schömann and Becker, 1995; OECD, 1999).

The gender distribution of training for adults in employment in 1996 (Figure 8.2) shows higher participation rates for women (6.5 per cent) among all people aged 30 and older in employment than for men (5.0 per cent). The Scandinavian countries, together with the United Kingdom, Ireland and the Netherlands, have substantially higher participation rates for women than for men when compared to all women or men in employment respectively. More than one in two women in employment receive further training in Scandinavian countries, with Denmark taking the lead with two out of three women. This raises interesting issues for policy making in the field of training and social integration. How can such a large-scale training effort be organized effectively? What are the effects of such efforts on the labour force? Do they truly benefit women, or is high training

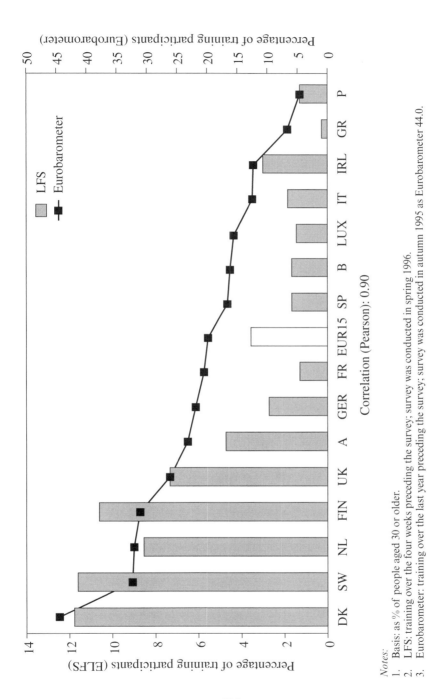

Notes:
1. Basis: as % of people aged 30 or older.
2. LFS: training over the four weeks preceding the survey; survey was conducted in spring 1996.
3. Eurobarometer: training over the last year preceding the survey; survey was conducted in autumn 1995 as Eurobarometer 44.0.

Figure 8.1 Adult participation in training, 1995–6

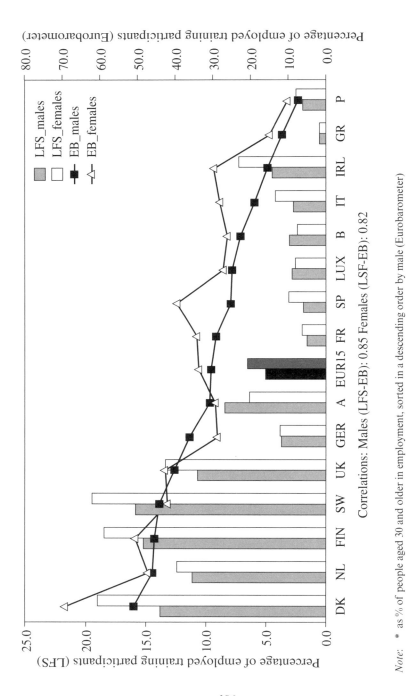

Note: * as % of people aged 30 and older in employment, sorted in a descending order by male (Eurobarometer)

Correlations: Males (LFS-EB): 0.85 Females (LSF-EB): 0.82

Figure 8.2 Training of adults in employment, by sex, 1995–6*

participation merely an indicator of a lack of suitable employment opportunities for them?

At first glance, this descriptive evidence is surprising, since the disadvantages women are known to suffer in the labour market do not seem to apply to access to further training. These descriptive statistics do not reveal any adverse selectivity effect to the disadvantage of women. More detailed analyses using multivariate techniques might yield a different picture if, for example, particular age groups or less well-qualified women experience disadvantages in access to training.

Age selectivity of training participation (Figure 8.3), on the other hand, is a common phenomenon in the European Union, except in Sweden. Even after excluding young people between 20 and 29 years of age from the comparison on the grounds that they return more frequently to full-time education, ELFS data show that the younger age groups between 30 and 39 have higher participation rates (7.3 per cent) than the 40 to 49 (5.6 per cent) and the 50 to 59 age groups (3.6 per cent). The Eurobarometer data are closely correlated to the ELFS results, although they show higher levels of participation in further training for the younger age groups.

Age is closely correlated to job tenure in Europe. Thus it would be reasonable to expect a tenure selectivity of training participation (Eurostat, 1997). The average training participation rate for employees with very short job durations of between one and six months is 7.5 per cent. This increases to 7.8 per cent for job durations between seven and 24 months, then drops to 6.9 per cent for durations of between two and five years and to only 5.2 per cent for job tenures above five years. These figures suggest that both increasing age and higher seniority in a firm reduce the probability of receiving training or of employees seeking training themselves.

Across the whole European Union, participation in training is highly selective by educational level (Table 8.2). With a participation rate of 11 per cent, university graduates receive the largest share of training opportunities. Only 5.5 per cent of employees who have completed the upper secondary cycle (A-levels, or a completed apprenticeship) participated in further training in spring 1996. Employees with only the compulsory minimum level of education are least likely to be offered further training: according to ELFS data, their participation rate was only 2.6 per cent (Eurostat, 1997).

The low correlation between the two data sources (cf. bottom of Table 8.2) shows how difficult it is to compare levels of education across Europe, particularly when the analysis is based on educational levels derived from information on 'age when a person left school' (as in the Eurobarometer data). What both sources show is that populations without any qualifications at all or with only the minimum compulsory level of education

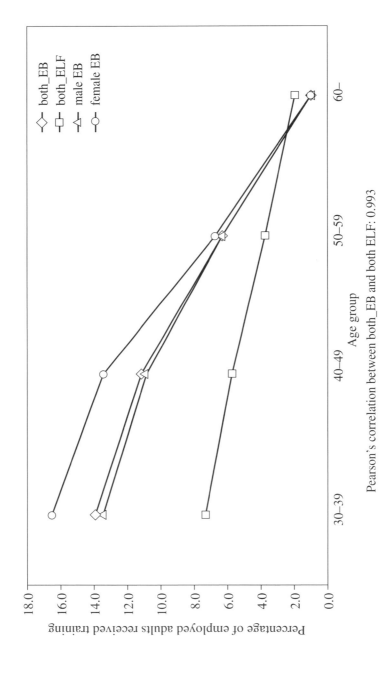

Pearson's correlation between both_EB and both ELF: 0.993

Figure 8.3   Training of adults in employment, by age, EU15, 1995–6

Table 8.2 *Training of adults by level of education*

ELF_Coun	ISCED_0	ISCED_3	ISCED_5	EB_Coun	G_15	G_16_19	G_20_	Corr.
EUR15_ELF	2.6	5.5	10.8	EUR15_EB	4.7	13.9	13.2	0.73
B_ELF	0.8	2.7	4.7	B_EB	0.8	8.0	15.2	1.00
DK_ELF	6.4	14.4	24.1	DK_EB	1.6	10.9	46.7	0.96
D_ELF	1.2	3.0	6.5	D_EB	5.8	14.7	12.5	0.59
EL_ELF		0.6	1.2	EL_EB	2.1	4.2	6.3	—
E_ELF	0.6	3.6	5.6	E_EB	9.2	8.3	12.9	0.68
F_ELF	0.7	1.5	3.6	F_EB	1.2	14.2	16.0	0.79
IRL_ELF	2.3	5.3	8.6	IRL_EB	2.3	9.4	7.0	0.63
I_ELF	1.0	4.9	7.5	I_EB	3.5	9.0	9.0	0.90
L_ELF	1.3	3.1	4.4	L_EB	3.5	10.5	11.8	0.96
NL_ELF	6.7	12.5	15.7	NL_EB	3.3	22.3	21.4	0.92
A_ELF	3.7	6.6	13.8	A_EB	5.1	15.9	9.3	0.15
P_ELF	0.7	6.6	6.9	P_EB	3.6	1.8	3.0	-0.73
FIN_ELF	8.1	14.0	31.7	FIN_EB	4.7	14.3	29.3	0.99
S_ELF	10.8	17.4	24.5	S_EB	5.8	16.6	21.0	0.97
UK_ELF	7.1	10.9	21.1	UK_EB	7.0	22.1	12.4	0.94
Correlation	0.196			0.523			0.69	

Note: ELF = European Labour Force Survey Data; EB = Eurobarometer Data; ISCED = International Standard Classification of Education.

(International Standard Classification of Education, level 0 and 1), together with those leaving school at age 15, have the lowest training participation rates. This indicates a higher risk of social exclusion, either at the time of leaving school or at later stages of the life course. The higher the level of educational attainment (as shown by the ISCED classification), the more likely it is that an individual will participate in training. The Eurobarometer data show that those who leave school between 16 and 19 years of age are most likely to return to further training in Germany, Ireland, the Netherlands and the United Kingdom when participation is measured over a one-year period.

In sum, the descriptive evidence from these two data sources, which applies a harmonized set of definitions across the European Union, reveals the education selectivity of further training participation as well as widespread and pronounced age selectivity. Contrary to our expectations, however, the empirical evidence does not uphold the gender selectivity hypothesis. The results so far suggest, in line with the conclusion to Chapter 4, that young employees and older employees face very different labour market conditions. For young employees, higher education levels and a high propensity to training participation, together with a track record in that respect, are highly valued in the labour market. For older employees, long labour market experience is a competitive advantage, irrespective of low participation in formal further training, although this applies mainly to stable or growing industries.

The multivariate evidence (cf. Table 8.3 for seven European countries and for the European Union as a whole) tests the selectivity hypothesis in more detail and with greater statistical rigour. In the year of the survey, employed persons in all the countries were – unsurprisingly – more likely to participate in further training during the course of a year (Eurobarometer data, description of data set and recoding scheme in the appendix) than the reference group, namely those not in the labour force. The unemployed are more likely to receive training than the inactive in Denmark, France and Germany and across the EU 15.

Education selectivity is confirmed, despite the crude measure available in the Eurobarometer data. Those who left full-time education after age 20 are most likely to resume further training, followed by those with intermediate-level education, while those who left school with only the compulsory minimum level of education are the least likely to participate in further training. Completion of a course of vocational training, whether one month or more than 24 months in duration, increases the probability of a return to further training, except in Germany. This indicates that vocational training has similar effects to general education in that it increases training probabilities for all persons, irrespective of gender or employment status, for example.

Table 8.3   Participation in training: results from the logistic regression*

Variable name and values	Param. estimate EU15	Param. estimate DK	Param. estimate ES	Param. estimate FR	Param. estimate IR	Param. estimate NL	Param. estimate UK	Param. estimate GER
INTERCEPT	−4.9795	−5.7980	−4.4861	−6.4011	−4.8734	−3.8554	−4.6303	−4.4477
OCCUP_6								
UNEMPLOYED	0.7601	1.1205	0.6489	1.5005	−0.2342	0.3601	0.5770	1.0336
EMPLOYED	1.2123	1.1788	1.3017	1.8305	0.4511	0.8417	1.5992	1.1525
SELF EMPLOYED	0.6829	0.9078	0.7282	1.1916	−0.2671	0.0383	0.6150	1.1285
EDUAGE								
16–19 YEARS	0.6850	1.1492	0.4425	1.2327	0.1031	0.2384	0.4024	0.5327
20+ YEARS	1.2409	1.2481	1.0204	1.7504	1.1945	0.4787	1.1800	1.1454
PROFEDU								
1–12 MONTHS	1.0523	0.6845	1.1768	1.9299	1.2455	0.6611	0.9395	0.1533
13–24 MONTHS	0.8882	1.0614	1.5566	1.8599	1.6651	0.6310	0.3385	0.0693
25 M AND MORE	0.9262	0.9364	1.6479	1.3486	1.0739	0.9948	0.4340	−0.0285
LLL_POS								
YES	0.9536	1.5742	0.7573	1.2690	1.5273	1.2913	0.5564	0.9567
NO	−0.1300	−0.3172	−0.0799	0.9711	0.6741	0.1297	−0.6764	−0.4658
GENEDU								
1–12 MONTHS	0.7056	0.5444	0.9866	1.5401	1.3104	0.5878	1.1685	0.4993
13–24 MONTHS	0.8242	0.1052	1.4984	0.8736	1.0695	0.3246	1.3139	0.8972
25 M AND MORE	1.0130	0.9008	1.0163	0.6375	0.9060	0.4332	0.9326	0.8327

Table 8.3 (*continued*)

Variable name and values	Param. estimate EU15	Param. estimate DK	Param. estimate ES	Param. estimate FR	Param. estimate IR	Param. estimate NL	Param. estimate UK	Param. estimate GER
AGE_6								
20–29	**0.9093**	**0.9857**	**1.0645**	0.2754	**1.3133**	**1.2231**	**1.2212**	**1.3269**
30–39	**0.9032**	**0.8004**	0.7543	0.6935	**1.3706**	**0.6907**	**1.2797**	**1.0963**
40–49	**0.8799**	**0.7412**	0.8773	0.4451	**1.1220**	0.4582	**1.2944**	**1.3018**
50–59	**0.5634**	**0.9399**	−0.0707	0.2407	0.3917	0.1841	**1.0999**	**0.7372**
INC_QART								
−	0.0114	0.4800	**−0.8150**	**−0.7276**	−0.6089	0.3136	−0.0434	−0.0533
+	0.1065	0.2037	0.2296	−0.4849	−0.3253	0.5233	0.1841	0.2091
++	**0.4146**	**0.9267**	−0.2557	0.2538	−0.1679	**0.9271**	0.5951	**0.4516**
DK/REFUSAL/NA	0.1409	0.4931	−0.0734	0.1153	−0.2297	**0.7541**	0.0310	**0.4558**
SEX								
FEMALE	**0.1807**	**0.5255**	0.2526	−0.0652	0.0453	0.0477	0.0645	0.0828

Note: *bold coefficients are significant at the 5% level; for further details, see appendix.

Source: Eurobarometer, own calculations.

To test the education selectivity or, to put it differently, the education accumulation hypothesis, we use the information provided by interviewees when asked whether they have resumed general education at all since leaving full-time education. For most countries, the results indicate that those persons who had resumed general education were also more likely to have participated in a training course in the previous 12 months (except in the Netherlands). This evidence confirms the education selectivity hypothesis stated in section 2 above. For a given 'coefficient of coupling' between the education system and the labour market, the stronger initial impetus given to an individual's human potential by the education system is transmitted to the labour market and is very likely to set in motion a mutual feedback structure allowing multiple transitions between the two societal subsystems, although such transitions may be restricted mainly to university graduates.

Those who believe that lifelong learning is an opportunity to be seized or an obligation to be fulfilled are also more likely to have participated in further training during the previous 12 months, although this result is statistically significant in Germany, Ireland and the EU as a whole. This reflects a kind of 'self-fulfilling prophecy'. For individuals whose experience of the education and training system has been positive, lifelong learning increases their potential for resuming training and the personal cost–benefit ratio of further training investments is likely to be positive. On the other hand, those who are reluctant to invest in lifelong learning are less likely to seek training themselves and are less likely to be chosen for training courses by their employers.

4. THE VICIOUS CIRCLE OF OPINIONS ON THE UTILITY OF TRAINING AND TRAINING PARTICIPATION

This section tackles the issue of training selectivity by age, gender and education level with a view to ascertaining whether those who believe training and lifelong learning is helpful also have higher further training participation rates. Some authors claim that many people are sceptical about the value of training and lifelong learning as a means of improving their employment prospects. Such expectations about training are likely to influence actual behaviour and thus the take-up of training measures.

The Eurobarometer is one of the few comparative data sources that regularly includes a set of questions concerning opinions on policies and satisfaction with general life conditions. This data source has rarely been used to date in socioeconomic assessments of the labour market. It contains a set of questions devoted to opinions on training, and particularly lifelong learning, in EU member states. Although a single snapshot of opinions is subject to spontaneous influences, a broad comparison of differences between countries can be assumed to be relatively stable.

A second advantage of this data set for our purpose is the more comprehensive question asked in the interviews about further training. Respondents are asked whether or not they have taken part in a training course in the past 12 months and whether they did so because their employer asked them to, because it was compulsory in order to get benefits (unemployment or other) or because they wanted to (see the appendix for more details). From this information we constructed a binary dependent variable on participation in training for the whole population which we consider to be a sufficiently well-defined indicator for assessing the probability of receiving training in any one year, despite the small sample size for each member state, as demonstrated in the previous section of this chapter.

Table 8.3 shows the estimation results of logistic regressions for training participation. The first three independent variables in the analysis indicate a person's employment status compared to the reference category of inactive people (see the appendix for definitions of variables). The employed are the most likely to participate in training in all countries shown in Table 8.3 with the exception of Ireland, where the coefficient does not pass the test for significance. Training as one form of social integration is much more prevalent among the employed. In Germany the self-employed have the second highest probability of training, although in France and Denmark the unemployed have a higher estimated probability of training participation. Thus employment status is an important predictor of training participation. The inactive, the unemployed and in some instances also the self-employed are at high risk of losing touch with new developments because of insufficient training activities.

The analyses based on the Eurobarometer confirm the social selectivity by age and education but not by gender. Those who leave education at the age of 20 or above are most likely to have taken up training during the previous 12 months. Similarly, selectivity by age is widespread, but specific national patterns and trends influenced by specific sets of active labour market policies do provide for some deviation from the overall trend. Positive and significant effects are found for people who have returned to either vocational or general education since they left full-time education.

In all European countries, those who responded affirmatively when asked whether they would like to be able to continue to learn or receive training throughout their lives were also more likely to have participated in training over the previous 12 months. The level of significance, however, is reached only in Ireland and Germany. This indicator sheds light on the integrative potential of training for people who are socially excluded, whether because of long-term unemployment, inactivity or poverty. Those who are sufficiently convinced that training might help them to escape social exclusion have a tendency actively to seek training. Conversely, it is difficult to persuade those with frustrating educational and training experiences, generally in school or the workplace, that training might be a way out of social exclusion for them as well.

Hypothesis 10 (cf. Chapter 2), which suggests that the effects of early experiences may be lasting, receives further support in this analysis, in conjunction with the still strong impact of social background on labour market entry, as indicated in Chapter 3. Hypothesis 11 holds that different labour market segments have their own specific links between learning and working (coefficient of coupling). Although this hypothesis is not pursued in detail for the various sectors of the economy, as in Chapter 4, the evidence in this chapter supports the view that people with only marginal attachment to the labour market, for example those in non-standard forms of employment, the unemployed and those engaged in unpaid household activities, have difficulty in gaining access to the same volume of training as those in standard employment.

Age selectivity is confirmed for all countries except France, which accounts for the explanation of training participation in terms of segmentation theory, and would also suggest there is need to derive age-specific 'coefficients of coupling' for younger and older employees. Gender selectivity is not confirmed, as the descriptive evidence already suggested. On average in the European Union, but particularly in Denmark, women's position in respect of access to training is a favourable one. In our view, this is evidence that the 'coefficient of coupling' is generally more elastic in Denmark than in the other countries. The Danish institutional arrangements generally favour multiple transitions and integrate broader segments of society into 'the training and employment nexus'.

Household income also has some influence on recent training participation. Low household income is still an impediment to participation. Most likely this reflects the immediate cost or opportunity costs of participation in training for those from low-income households. Forgone earnings seem to hinder individuals from low-income households. Even small payments for training or relatively low levels of forgone earnings are too high a price to pay, and restrictions on other expenditure are judged too costly to the household. The household income indicator supports the view that social exclusion due to lack of income is difficult to overcome, since even short training courses appear too costly for individuals from low-income households. This is likely to lead to exclusionary transition patterns at later stages or to an accumulation of social risks. The introduction of low-cost training measures for these individuals might be one way of breaking the vicious circle of low investment, low propensity to seek training and a lack of faith in lifelong learning as an insurance against the risk of unemployment or social exclusion.

5. EMPLOYMENT AND UNEMPLOYMENT TRANSITIONS AND THE ROLE OF TRAINING

The total sum of labour turnover in an economy can serve as a kind of baseline against which training investments can be evaluated. High job or employment mobility might not allow sufficient time for training investments to be viable for either employers or employees. High rates of job mobility, as found in the United Kingdom or the United States, allow less time for training costs to be recovered and increase the risk that trainees will be 'poached' by firms that do not train themselves. The second issue addressed in this section relates to transition probabilities and the social selectivity that occurs in labour market transitions. At the same time, our empirical analysis of transitional labour market theory is pursued.

Using calculations based on ELFS data, we find that labour turnover in 1995 was highest in Spain, Finland, Denmark, Italy, France and the United Kingdom, with more than 20 per cent of the dependent labour force changing jobs between spring 1994 and spring 1995 (Schömann, Kruppe and Oschmiansky, 1998). These figures on labour market transitions are calculated as a sum of all inflows into employment and outflows from employment between two points in time. The contrasting picture of generally low employment mobility, as observed in Belgium, Germany and Portugal, brings with it the risk of a stalemate in organizational dynamics, particularly when the inflow into employment is lower than the outflow. The three last-named countries are also the ones that show only average or below-average participation in further training, indicating a difficulty in accommodating rapid technological change in large sections of the labour force (cf. also Figure 8.1).

Estimating transition probabilities on the basis of the ELFS is a slightly risky exercise because of the cross-sectional design of the survey and its short-run retrospective content, such as the provision of information on employment status in the previous year only. Checks on the probability of effecting a transition within a 12-month period based on national panel data are still in progress, but preliminary results suggest that the transition probabilities are sufficiently well represented in the cross-sectional data, adjusted in some way for other seasonal job mobility effects not included in our analyses. In order to provide a sufficiently large number of cases for these transition probabilities to be calculated even for low-mobility countries, the ELFS for the years 1988 to 1996 was used for a pooled analysis of cross-sections for each country separately.

Our results from the logistic regressions of the probability of transition from employment to unemployment are based on a sample of persons aged between 15 and 65 living in private households who are neither in education nor inactive. A binary dependent variable is constructed in which the value one is assigned to cases where the employment status changes from one point in time to the other and the value zero to cases in which the employment status remained unchanged. This is a somewhat crude indicator, but the only feasible one available to us. Of course multiple changes between these two statuses cannot be dealt with in this analysis based on cross-sectional data. However, the data set does have the advantage of large sample size so that analyses with many covariates are still likely to yield sufficiently reliable estimates of coefficients.

Table 8.4 shows the estimated results for the probability of transition from employment to unemployment. In all countries the probability of losing a job and becoming unemployed is highest between 15 and 35 years of age (except in the Netherlands, where only up to age 30 is the probability greater than for the reference 36–40 age group). Older age groups, particularly in Spain, France, Germany and Ireland, have a significantly lower risk of becoming unemployed. In the Netherlands, transitions from employment into inactivity or retirement on grounds of disability seem to affect the estimations, at least indirectly. Age selectivity applied to employment transitions yields an age selectivity effect opposite to the one found for training participation in the previous section. Older employees are less likely to participate in training but are also less likely to become unemployed. Conversely, younger employees are the ones with the highest further training participation rates but are still the ones at highest risk of becoming unemployed. This calls for policy intervention if the labour market produces outcomes that are not consistent with the expected reward structure for training investments. This age selectivity paradox can be resolved by means of a more detailed investigation of employment protection systems and dismissal regulations which, in most European employment systems, have led to the establishment of a 'last in, first out' employment and dismissal structure (Schömann, Rogowski and Kruppe, 1998; OECD, 1999).

In Ireland and the UK, women have a higher chance of remaining in employment than men. In all other countries shown in Table 8.4, women move from employment to unemployment significantly more often. Compared with married people (the reference category), single and,

Table 8.4 Transitions from employment to unemployment

	Parameter estimate DE	Parameter estimate DK	Parameter estimate ES	Parameter estimate FR	Parameter estimate IR	Parameter estimate NL
INTERCEPT	**−3.6711**	**−3.201**	**−3.5542**	**−3.7801**	**−3.3657**	**−3.3099**
AGE1	**0.7087**	**0.2072**	**1.0353**	**1.8867**	**0.8311**	**0.3498**
AGE2	**0.2626**	**0.5965**	**0.8482**	**0.9925**	**0.5274**	**0.3888**
AGE3	**0.1164**	**0.2875**	**0.58**	**0.4688**	**0.251**	**0.2193**
AGE4	0.0929	0.1236	**0.2586**	**0.1719**	0.097	0.0793
AGE6	−0.0952	−0.1565	−0.0964	−0.1803	−0.1349	−0.1065
AGE7	−0.1251	−0.0171	−0.1679	−0.182	−0.3381	−0.1021
EDUC1	**0.4779**	**0.6156**	**0.7299**	**0.4522**	**1.3362**	**0.1759**
EDUC2	**0.0625**	**0.2813**	**0.3069**	−0.0519	**0.413**	−0.0932
FEDUC	**0.203**	**−0.7311**	**0.2392**	−0.0276	**−1.9371**	**−0.4921**
NATIOEC	−0.0388	0.2582	0.232	**0.2358**	**0.7632**	**0.5472**
NATIONEC	**0.4622**	**1.0365**	**0.406**	**0.7914**	**0.3251**	**1.1117**
FEMALE	**0.3427**	**0.2852**	**0.3378**	**0.2927**	−0.245	**0.4059**
AGRIC1Y	**1.0273**	**−0.5965**	**0.3628**	0.1146	−0.0446	−18.8966
ENEG1Y	**−0.6078**	**−1.5942**	**−0.6516**	**−1.0371**	**−0.8712**	−18.6239
MINC1Y	**0.1983**	**−0.8421**	**−0.3738**	**−0.7321**	**0.4058**	−18.5198
BUILD1Y	**0.2792**	−0.085	**0.8378**	**0.2872**	**0.8951**	−18.7199
TRADE1Y	−0.0698	**−0.7252**	−0.14	−0.0311	**−0.2273**	−18.9508
TRANS1Y	**−0.2979**	**−1.0318**	**−0.3279**	**−0.6258**	**−0.4493**	−18.7593
BANK1Y	**−1.4059**	**−1.2665**	**−1.0821**	**−0.8047**	**−0.9047**	−18.8379
PUBLIC1Y	**−0.7217**	**−0.9702**	**−0.6307**	**−0.8364**	**−1.5129**	−18.7157
OSERV1Y	**−0.4007**	**−0.4768**	**−0.3195**	−0.126	**−0.1461**	**−1.7548**

SINGLE	0.1762	0.5242	0.2874	0.4108	0.2295	0.4237
WIDISEP	0.5987	0.6795	0.4314	0.7014	0.4829	0.8367
YEAR88	−0.4635	−0.5052	−0.3207	−0.3343	−0.5249	−0.7092
YEAR89	−0.725	−0.3752	−0.4147	−0.3715	−0.6186	−0.5024
YEAR90	−0.7523	−0.4052	−0.3052	−0.0752	−0.8278	−0.6174
YEAR91	−0.2351	−0.2909	−0.1877	0.302	−0.4391	−0.6809
YEAR92	0.1052	0.1188	−0.0606	−0.1304	0.4412	−0.2196
YEAR93	0.0863	−2.1116	0.2883	0.0529	0.452	0.1066
YEAR94	0.1842	0.1867	0.1488	0.1207	0.1778	0.41
YEAR95	−0.1138	−0.1292	−0.0839	−0.105	−0.0428	0.1869
−2 LOG L	208559.68	30123.807	159493.63	147608.84	107315.81	55024.296
−2 LOG L(C)	201523.63	27892.256	148033.88	137345.18	100457.24	47041.138

Note: Results for the Netherlands without industry dummies yield similar results for all other coefficients; bold coefficients are significant at the 5% level; for further details, see appendix.

particularly, widowed and separated persons become unemployed more frequently in all countries under investigation. However, our analysis does not permit more precise conclusions as to whether it is family status alone or recent changes in family status that are associated with the risk of unemployment. One factor that might come into play here is the possible existence of flexible working-time arrangements, such as part-time work, that would provide alternatives to the employment/unemployment transition by facilitating moves from full-time to part-time employment, for example (O'Reilly *et al.*, 2000).

In addition to the substantial age selectivity in this transition we consistently find evidence throughout the European Union for education selectivity, which works against individuals without qualifications or with only the compulsory minimum level of educational attainment. In most countries, even those with the intermediate levels of educational attainment are at greater risk of unemployment than the reference group of persons with some form of higher education qualification. Education selectivity in flows into unemployment is likely to be reinforced by the education selectivity of participation in further training evidenced in the previous section.

Estimates of the probability of leaving unemployment to take up a new job between 1988 and 1996 suggest that the age profile of new entrants after unemployment is fairly similar in all EU member states (cf. Table 8.5). Younger employees have a higher probability of being recruited. After the age of 45 the probability of re-entering the labour market becomes negative compared to the reference 36–40 age group. There is also consistent education selectivity in the sense that lower levels of qualification make re-entry more difficult throughout the EU. New entrants seem to receive significantly more training than those who cannot achieve this transition. Only in the United Kingdom, the Netherlands and Ireland were women more likely than men to be among the re-entrants, probably on a part-time basis. Marriage also increases such transition probabilities. In order to control for temporal changes over the business cycle in each country, at least in a very crude way, we introduced year of survey dummy variables into the pooled data analysis (see also Schömann, Rogowski and Kruppe, 1998), with 1996 being the reference year. This procedure gives us some confidence that the micro-level estimation of transitions is purged of major differences in macroeconomic conditions and business cycle effects.

Labour turnover seems to work as a continuous employee sorting process. This process of social selection favours those best able to learn and to adapt quickly to new demands at the workplace. Whereas this process works to the advantage of young highly qualified persons and hastens their social integration, it works against older employees with lower levels of qualifications and puts them at risk of social exclusion through job loss.

Table 8.5   Transitions from unemployment to employment

	Parameter estimate DE	Parameter estimate DK	Parameter estimate ES	Parameter estimate FR	Parameter estimate IR	Parameter estimate NL
INTERCEPT	-0.2868	0.3779	-0.1623	0.0889	-1.2289	-0.2368
AGE1	0.353	0.9178	0.5619	0.4472	0.1311	1.1579
AGE2	0.4572	0.4336	0.5108	0.6009	0.2528	0.8457
AGE3	0.2879	0.21	0.2892	0.3011	0.2427	0.4427
AGE4	0.1462	0.1426	0.095	0.1103	0.1353	0.223
AGE6	-0.1495	-0.1249	-0.0476	-0.1427	-0.0212	-0.056
AGE7	-0.3707	-0.4553	-0.1555	-0.2468	-0.0161	-0.3085
EDUC1	-0.4962	-0.2035	-0.3409	-0.3291	-1.0119	-0.4877
EDUC2	-0.0327	0.0564	-0.2932	-0.0089	-0.2493	-0.1263
FEDUC	0.1241	-0.3423	0.912	0.3879	3.0423	0.4042
NATIOEC	0.1357	0.1857	0.4745	0.1337	-0.0125	0.0348
NATIONEC	-0.3005	-0.3589	0.0992	-0.4011	0.4556	-0.7494
FEMALE	-0.1251	-0.0988	-0.7935	-0.2539	0.4156	0.0918
SINGLE	-0.3605	-0.1716	-0.1999	-0.2872	-0.1297	-0.2831
WIDISEP	-0.395	-0.2518	-0.0364	-0.1867	-0.1742	-0.3081
YEAR88	-0.3701	0.0299	-0.062	0.0566	0.7458	-0.7846
YEAR89	-0.2701	-0.222	0.1379	0.1318	0.5974	-0.6684
YEAR90	-0.113	-0.3	0.2256	-0.2283	0.6905	-0.2033
YEAR91	0.0903	-0.3947	0.1887	-0.02	0.3879	-0.1696
YEAR92	0.4799	0.4149	0.1867	-0.0293	-0.2593	0.4396
YEAR93	-0.0247	-0.8959	-0.1511	0.0377	-0.1788	0.3375
YEAR94	0.0943	-0.3898	-0.2157	-0.0276	-0.017	0.1633

Table 8.5 (continued)

	Parameter estimate DE	Parameter estimate DK	Parameter estimate ES	Parameter estimate FR	Parameter estimate IR	Parameter estimate NL
YEAR95	**0.2917**	0.1198	−0.0315	0.0554	**0.2479**	**0.2151**
−2 LOG L	56312.355	9031.277	139257.90	66397.970	52905.847	20043.200
−2 LOG L(C)	54550.605	8623.162	134194.42	65116.058	49936.662	19162.463

Note: * bold coefficients are significant at the 5% level; for further details, see appendix.

Analysis of the labour market transitions of job losers and re-entrants shows that this tendency has been prevalent since the late 1980s and is quite evenly spread throughout the European Union.

The call for more equal participation in training as well as more equal entry opportunities for those previously unemployed still provides a major challenge to education and labour market policy making at the national and European level. New labour market arrangements in the form of transitional labour markets such as job rotation are indicated. And yet in large-scale quantitative analyses such tiny flowerings of the transitional labour market principle hardly show up because they are being piloted on a very small scale. Nevertheless, selectivity in labour markets by age and education can be identified as the two major challenges that will have to be addressed in any reforms or recommendations put forward in the field of education and labour market policy.

6.   CONCLUSION

The analyses in this chapter have added several new elements to the comparison of training and employment systems in the European Union. By way of conclusion, the evidence presented in the chapter will be summarized briefly in the light of the research hypotheses and some more general policy conclusions will then be drawn. The point of departure for the theoretical discussion was the basic hypothesis that the school-to-work nexus is subject to political design and that each country can, therefore, choose a set of institutions and policies that facilitate labour market and further training transitions. Although this might sound somewhat obvious, strong path dependencies in traditional education and labour market policies do seem to be the major impediment to the redesigning of these societal subsystems in such a way as to favour integrative transitions. Our results suggest that the Danish reforms have worked most favourably to enhance labour market transitions assisted by training policies. It can be concluded from the Danish example that social integration through training-related transitions is a viable policy target, despite the fact that the target is to some extent a moving one, since the target groups change quickly over the business cycle, for example, or in the course of the structural changes leading to the establishment of the service economy.

Although it appears reasonable, at first glance, to expect a high correlation between the two 'coefficients of coupling' (first and subsequent transitions between learning and working), our evidence in this chapter does not square well with this view. Countries in which the initial transition functions well, mostly those with apprenticeship-type education systems, are not necessarily equally successful in organizing later transitions. This applies to Germany, less strongly to the Netherlands, but no longer to Denmark. A more elastic 'coefficient of coupling' as observed in Denmark in first and subsequent training transitions makes it possible to integrate broader segments of society into the labour market and, more generally, into active participation in society. This works particularly to the advantage of women and improves their chances of achieving integration on a more equal footing.

The lasting effect of educational attainment prior to labour market entry is pervasive across the European Union (confirming hypothesis 10) and persists far beyond first entry into the labour market (cf. Chapters 3 and 4). Drawing on a comparable set of data for most European countries, this chapter confirms the education selectivity of labour market transitions. Apart from age, prior experiences with learning processes at school or in the workplace are the most serious impediment to the establishment of life-long learning policies and practices. Despite the considerable differences between the various national education and labour market systems across Europe, their effects are very similar, since there is pronounced education selectivity in all member states.

It is not an easy task to break the 'vicious circle' of disillusion with the employment effects of training among the less well-qualified segments of the population or to counter the adverse impact such disillusion has on the motivation to seek further training. Thus the indirect support for segmentation approaches to the labour market (hypothesis 11) no longer comes as a surprise after the evidence presented in this chapter. Particular policy efforts will be needed to motivate individuals in disadvantaged segments of the labour market in order to get them involved in the lifelong learning process and the transitional labour market of learning and working.

Additionally, we find some evidence of market failure in the area of training and general labour market performance. There is, therefore, a need to develop public policies in the area of lifelong learning that take account of both efficiency and equity. In the rapidly expanding field of training studies, analysis seems so far to have focused on the efficiency aspect. If the poaching of trained employees or restrictions on geographical or job mobility are problems in an economy, then the role of public policy must be to facilitate mobility and access to training. Since private-sector initiatives in the area of lifelong learning tend to operate in a very selective way, favouring those who already have higher-level qualifications or higher wages, public funds are needed to ensure more equal access to training opportunities. However, since growing budget deficits restrict the scope for spending increases, and since more spending does not necessarily mean better results, institutional and organizational reforms are needed to make policy design and the implementation of lifelong learning policies more efficient and, at the same time, accessible to a broader audience.

We started this chapter by asking whether different policies within the EU produce similar effects. The evidence can be summarized in the following statement. Even if education selectivity is hard to overcome, lifelong learning policies can make a difference. The integration of a higher share of the population into training and learning processes is a feasible objective, but if it is to be achieved the traditional European education and labour market institutions and policies will have to undergo a fundamental redesign in order to incorporate some of the major elements of transitional labour market theory.

NOTE

1. Excellent research assistance was provided by Thomas Kruppe, with his analysis of the European Labour Force Survey, and by Ralf Mytzek, with his analysis based on Eurobarometer data. Neither of them is responsible for any remaining errors in these analyses. Thanks are also due to the participants in the TRANSLAM network for comments on a previous version of the chapter.

BIBLIOGRAPHY

Becker, R. and Schömann, K. (1995), 'Berufliche Weiterbildung und Arbeitseinkommen – Eine Längsschnittstudie über der Einfluß beruflicher Weiterbildung auf Einkommensverläufe', mimeo Technical University of Dresden.

Bishop, J.H. (1990), 'Job performance, turnover and wage growth', *Journal of Labor Economics*, 8(3), 363–86.

Bishop, John H. (1991), 'On the job training of new hires', in David Stern and Jozef M.M. Ritzen (eds), *Market Failure in Training? New Economic Analyses and Evidence on the Training of Adult Employees*, Berlin: Springer-Verlag.

Blakemore, A. and Hoffman, D. (1989), 'Seniority rules and productivity: An empirical test', *Econometrica*, 56, 359–71.

Blaug, Mark (1976), *Introduction to the Economics of Education*, Harmondsworth: Penguin Books.

Blaug, M. and Mace, J. (1977), 'Recurrent education – The new Jerusalem?', *Higher Education*, 6, 277–300.

Breen, R. (1992), 'Job Changing and Job Loss in the Irish Youth Labour Market: A test of a general model', *European Sociological Review*, 8 (2), 113–25.

Brown, J. (1989), 'Why do wages increase with tenure? On the job training and life cycle wage growth observed within firms', *American Economic Review*, 79(4), 971–91.

Coleman, J.S. (1990), *Foundations of Social Theory*, Cambridge, Mass.: The Belknap Press of Harvard University Press.

Eurobarometer (1997), Press Release on Eurobarometer no. 47: November 1997 (*http://europa.eu.int/en/comm/dg10/infcom/epo/eb/eb47/eb47fr/alaune.html*).

European Commission (1993), 'Growth, competitiveness, employment: The challenges and ways forward into the 21st century', White Paper, *Bulletin of the European Communities*, Supplement 6/93.

Eurostat (1996), 'Continuing vocational training in enterprises – an essential part of life-long learning', *Statistics in Focus. Population and Social Conditions*, 1996 no. 7, Luxembourg.

Eurostat (1997), 'Training after 30 years of age', *Statistics in Focus. Population and Social Conditions*, 1997 no. 11, Luxembourg.

Faure, E. (1972), *Learning to Be. The world of Education Today and Tomorrow*, Paris: UNESCO.

Gehin, Jean-Paul and Méhaut, Philippe (1993), *Apprentissage ou Formation Continue? Stratégies Éducatives des Entreprises en Allemagne et en France*, Paris: l'Harmattan.

Gustafsson, S.S., Wetzels, C.M.M.P., Vlasblom, J.D. and Dex, S. (1996), 'Labour Force Transitions in Connection with Child Birth: A Panel Data Comparison between Germany, Great Britain and Sweden', *Journal of Population Economics*, 9, 223–46.

Knoke, D. and Kalleberg, A.L. (1994), 'Job training in US organizations', *American Sociological Review*, 59 (August), 537–46.

Korpi, T. (1994), 'Escaping Unemployment, Studies in the Individual Consequences of Unemployment and Labor Market Policy', *Swedish Institute for Social Research*, no. 24, Akademitryck AB, Edsbruk.

Mendes de Oliviera, M.E., Cohn, E. and Kiker, B. (1989), 'Tenure, earnings, and productivity', *Oxford Bulletin of Economics and Statistics* 51, 1–14.

Mincer, Jacob (1991), 'Job training: costs, returns, and wage profiles', in David Stern and Jozef M.M. Ritzen (eds), *Market Failure in Training? New Economic Analysis and Evidence on Training of Adult Employees*, Berlin: Springer-Verlag.

OECD (1994), *The OECD Jobs Study: Facts, Analysis, Strategies*, Paris: OECD.

OECD (1999), *Employment Outlook*, Paris: OECD.

Schmid, G. (1995), 'Is Full Employment Still Possible? Transitional Labour Markets as a New Strategy of Labour Market Policy', *Economic and Industrial Democracy*, 16(3), 429–56.

Schömann, K. and Becker, R. (1995), 'Participation in further education over the life-course: A longitudinal study of three birth cohorts in the Federal Republic of Germany', *European Sociological Review*, 11(2), 1–22.

Schömann, K., Kruppe, T. and Oschmiansky, H. (1998), 'Beschäftigungsdynamik und Arbeitslosigkeit in der Europäischen Union', *WZB Discussion Paper*, FS I 98-203.

Schömann, K., Rogowski, R. and Kruppe, T. (1998), *Labour Market Efficiency in the European Union, A Legal and Economic Evaluation of Employment Protection and Fixed-Term Contracts*, London: Routledge.

Tuijnman, A.C. and Schömann, K. (1996), 'Life-long learning and skill formation', in Günther Schmid, Jacqueline O'Reilly and Klaus Schömann (eds), *International Handbook of Labour Market Policy and Evaluation*, Cheltenham, UK and Brookfield, US: Edward Elgar, pp. 462–488.

Veum, J.R. (1993), 'Training among young adults: who, what kind, and for how long?', *Monthly Labor Review*, August, 27–32.

APPENDIX: DESCRIPTION OF THE EUROBAROMETER DATA SET

The Eurobarometer (Willem and Kaase, 1997) is a public opinion survey carried out on behalf of the DG X, 'Public Opinion Surveys and Research' Unit, of the European Commission. It was established in 1974 and is usually carried out twice a year (spring and autumn). The cross-country, cross-sectional survey covers all the member states of the European Union in the respective year. The size of the representative national samples usually approximates 1000 interviews which are conducted as face-to-face interviews in the respondent's home. The Eurobarometer 44.0 served as data source for our analysis. These data were collected from October to November 1995. Its total sample size is 16 641 cases. The distribution of the cases among the participating countries is as follows:

France	1 007
Belgium	1 016
Netherlands	1 018
Germany	2 208
Italy	1 024
Luxembourg	957
Denmark	1 000
Ireland	1 005
United Kingdom	1 358
Greece	1 006
Spain	1 000
Portugal	995
Finland	1 032
Sweden	1 010
Austria	1 005

In connection with the European Year of Lifelong Learning, 1996, a thematic focus in this survey is questions concerning the respondents' experiences with and attitudes towards lifelong learning and further education. Table 8A.1 describes the variables and the recalculation of variables we used in our analysis.

Table 8A.1   Eurobarometer data set analysis

Variable name	Description	Question in the original questionnaire
TRAIN	Training participation during the last 12 month preceding the survey. Coding: 0 = no, 1 = yes, 9 = not available	Q60: 'Have you done a training course in the past 12 months, or not?' (If YES) 'Did you do the course because your employer asked you to, because it was compulsory in order to get benefits (unemployment or other), or because you wanted to?'
OCCUP_6	Occupation, recalculation into 6 groups. Coding: 0 = inactive, 1 = unemployed, 2 = employed, 3 = self-employed, 4 = student, 5 = not available, fisherman, farmer	D15: 'What is your current occupation?'
EDUAGE	Age R finished education, recalculated into 4 groups. Coding: 1 = up to 15 years, 2 = 16–19 years, 3 = more than 20 years, 4 = still studying	D8: 'How old were you when you stopped full-time education?'
PROFEDU	Time R resumed professional education. Coding: 1 = 1–12 months, 2 = 13–14 months, 3 = 25 months and more, 4 = never taken any	D9a: 'Since stopping full-time education, have you taken apprenticeship or professional training for your job?'
LLL_POS	Positive attitude towards lifelong learning. Coding: 0 = not available, 1 = yes, 2 = no, 3 = don't know	Q56: 'Some people say that "learning stops when you leave school and start work". On the other hand, others think that "you have to make the effort to learn throughout your life". Would you personally like to be able to continue to learn or be trained throughout your life, or not?'

Table 8A.1 (continued)

Variable name	Description	Question in the original questionnaire
GENEDU	Time R resumed general education. Coding: 1 = 1–12 months, 2 = 13–14 months, 3 = 25 months and more, 4 = never taken any	D9b: 'Since stopping full-time education, have you resumed general education at all?'
AGE_6	R age, recalculated into 6 groups. Coding: 0 = 20–29, 1 = 30–39, 2 = 40–49, 3 = 50–59, 4 = 60 and over, 5 = under 20	D11
INC_QART	Income quartile of the household the respondents are living in. Coding: 1 = low, 2 = low–medium, 3 = high–medium, 4 = high, 5 = don't know, refusal, not available	D29
SEX	R gender Coding: 1 = male, 2 = female	D10

Bibliography

EUKom DG X http://europa.eu.intlenlcommldg10linfcomlepoleb.html

PART III

The Firm's Rationale for Training

9. Training practices and management of older workers: a typology from the French case

Annie Jolivet

Studies of company training practices in France have clearly shown inequality of access with age. This result is consistent with the conclusions drawn from human capital theory: for a given initial endowment, a firm is less interested in financing training as a worker's age increases. If these inequalities can be explained by the necessity of training new employees first, they can also lead to a weakening of the position, or even to the exclusion, of workers not in receipt of training, whose skills would be less frequently updated.

Thus training practices are connected to recruitment and lay-off practices, in particular as regards older workers. According to the internal market approach, firms can select one of two opposing strategies. They can either stabilize and train their workforce, or make it flexible and not provide any training. A wide range of hybrid strategies exists between these two poles. What are these mixed behaviours, and how do they affect ageing workers?

Our aim here is to analyse, by means of a typology, the differences in firms' training practices, in particular access to training for older workers, and to connect them to recruitment and lay-off behaviours towards the same group. This will allow us to understand to what extent access to training for older workers contributes to the prevention of their exclusion and to their re-employment. The data for this study come from a survey carried out in 1992 by the French Ministry of Labour. This survey is actually the most recent one linking data on workforce movements to data on workforce structure, and in particular age structure.

We begin by summarizing the existing conclusions about older workers' access to training in French firms, and we specify our data and method (section 1). The six clusters derived from an upward classification are then analysed (section 2). Finally, in section 3, we outline some of the findings of our study and discuss how they affect not only the exclusion of older workers but also the potential for developing training and transitions for this group.

1.   ACCESS TO TRAINING FOR AGEING WORKERS

Two types of data relating to training provide an insight into age-related access to training financed by firms: the vocational training and skills surveys (*Enquêtes Formation Qualification Professionnelle*) carried out in 1977, 1985 and 1993 and the annual statements of training expenditures (*Déclarations 2483*) submitted by firms under a legal obligation to provide training.[1]

According to the 1985 vocational training and skills survey,[2] a worker aged between 25 and 35 has the highest chance of having received training during the five years preceding the survey. Training opportunities then decline with age, with the reduction becoming really noticeable from age 45. This threshold seems to have risen, since it was age 40 or thereabouts in 1977.

Examination of the annual statements of training expenditures submitted by firms in the early 1990s (the so-called *Déclarations 2483*) confirms this threshold.[3] The training actions financed by firms are aimed mainly at workers under 45 years of age. In 1991, this group accounted for 80 per cent of all trained workers.[4] Moreover, the access rate to training[5] decreases very little for the 35 to 44 age group, whereas it decreases by almost one-third for workers aged 45 and over (see Table 9.1). However, we cannot be sure that training efforts really do decrease from age 45

Table 9.1   Access rate (per cent) to training in 1991, by age group and firm size*

Number of employees	−25	25 to 34	35 to 44	45+	All
10 to 19	3.7	4.2	4.0	2.6	3.7
20 to 49	12.5	14.1	12.3	7.8	11.9
50 to 499	28.9	32.4	28.5	17.5	27.0
500 and over	96.1	75.6	65.6	47.3	65.1
All	36.3	40.6	38.6	27.2	36.3

Note: * Access rates are underestimated by 50 per cent for firms of 10 to 19 employees, and overestimated in the order of 15 per cent for firms of 500 employees and over.

Source: Déclarations fiscales 24.83 and Enquête Emploi 1991 (exploitation CEREQ – Centre d'Etudes et de Recherches sur les Qualifications); Aventur 1994.

onwards, because no detailed information is available for the older age groups. The 1993 vocational training and skills survey[6] also shows that access to training falls with age. Here, however, the decline does not set in until 50 years of age: between January 1992 and May 1993, in fact, workers aged between 40 and 49 had the greatest access to training. Because the age clusters used are wide (nine years), it is difficult to draw any real conclusions from this study as to the point at which access to training opportunities begins to decline.

On the basis of these data, the threshold is around 45 or 50 years. Whatever the underlying reasons for it are, older workers' reduced access to training is compounded by other age-related differences. According to the 1993 vocational training and skills survey,[7] training seems to reinforce the links between employer and employee: the proportion of trained workers leaving firms is six times smaller. Thus reduced access to training weakens the position of older workers, making then increasingly vulnerable to exclusion. It can also reduce promotion opportunities when training constitutes preparation for a potential promotion. However, the relationship between training and promotion weakened during the 1990s, so the primary function of training is to adapt workers to jobs. Moreover, the reduced access to training may be the consequence of reduced access to promotion, since training may be needed for a promotion. Lastly, it may be due to a lower average level of educational attainment among older employees, a sort of 'vintage' effect, as the most qualified workers in each occupational group enjoys greater training opportunities.

Both sources of data on training reveal the determining impact of firms' characteristics on older workers' access rate to training. The gap between older workers and their younger colleagues in this respect is particularly wide in small firms, while access inequality is reduced in large firms. Firms in industries that have the highest levels of training offer older workers virtually the same training opportunities as younger workers. Finally, the access rate to training is higher among older workers when there is not a high concentration of workers aged 45 and over in the workforce. Thus access to training opportunities depends not only on age but also on certain characteristics of firms and on their organizational structures.

Our purpose here is to examine differences in training practices, but this time using establishment data rather than focusing solely on the sector of economic activity. To this end, we used the survey on 'Management of an ageing workforce' which was carried out in 1992 by the French Ministry of Labour[8] and provides data on some 1069 establishments with ten or more employees.

Among the available data, few give information on firms' training effort.

Training refers here to a range of different actions, all financed by firms, but excludes on-the-job training, which is not easily measured. The survey provides data on training expenditures as a proportion of the total wage bill, that is the financial contribution rate as defined by CEREQ,[9] on the number of workers trained and on the number of workers aged 45 and over given training. Older workers' access to training is analysed by calculating the ratio of the number of workers aged 45 given training to the total number of workers trained. It is not possible here to define an access rate to training for older workers. The distribution of workers by age includes permanent workers only, whereas some of the workers in receipt of training may be temporary. Moreover, most establishments did not provide information about their temporary workers. Overall access to training is measured here by dividing the total number of trained workers by the number of workers employed in 1991, that is both those already present at the beginning of the year and those recruited during 1991, whatever their employment duration.

It is thus possible to see, at the establishment level, how access to training for older workers is connected to the intensity of the training effort and to recruitment and departure behaviour.

An earlier analysis of the three variables relative to training was carried out by means of a principal component analysis. It revealed a disjunction between the overall training effort and the specific training effort directed towards older workers. The first axis (explaining 49.7 per cent of the variance) is determined only and strongly by the proportion of trained workers and by the rate of training expenditures, whereas the second axis (33.3 per cent of the variance), at right angles to the first, depends exclusively on the proportion of workers aged 45 and over given training. Behaviour at establishment level could not be analysed from just one of these variables, and for that reason a classification method was chosen.

A typology of training practices was built from the three training variables using an upward classification.[10] The level of aggregation chosen had to limit the number of clusters analysed while maximizing inter-cluster variance. Finally, six clusters were chosen, explaining 65.2 per cent of the total dispersion between establishments. The way the six clusters group together reveals, firstly, an opposition between the establishments training a lot (cluster 6) and the others. This opposition explains 28.9 per cent of the inter-establishment dispersion. Only subsequently does a differentiation appear between establishments with a moderate or weak training effort (clusters 4 and 2), establishments with a fairly strong effort but one that does little to benefit older workers (clusters 1 and 5) and establishments whose training effort is strongly aimed towards older workers (cluster 3).

2. SIX TRAINING PRACTICES DIRECTED TOWARDS OLDER WORKERS

In 1991, establishments trained on average 29.7 per cent of their workers, and 20.2 per cent of these were aged 45 or over. They devoted 2.8 per cent of their wage bill to continuing vocational training. The six clusters to be analysed here diverge from this average behaviour in three respects: the scale of the training effort, the share of the over-45s among those trained and the targets of training. Each cluster is described and analysed in great detail below.

Cluster 6: a Very Intensive Training Effort of Benefit to Older Workers

This category contains 257 establishments, representing 24 per cent of the sample. It is characterized by a very intensive training effort, in terms of both the share of workers trained and the level of training expenditure. On average, 59.2 per cent of the workers were trained, twice as many as the sample average. Training expenditures accounted for 4.7 per cent of the wage bill, compared with 2.8 per cent for the establishments as a whole. This training effort benefited older workers, as 26.3 per cent of the trainees were aged 45 and over, but they are not the main target group. Indeed, this figure is only six percentage points above the sample average.

This analysis is confirmed by the study of average hiring and departure rates for older workers. The share of the 45 and over age group in the in-flows is 1.8 times smaller than for the establishments as a whole (15.8 per cent, compared with 28.4 per cent in the sample). Moreover, in-flows in the form of transfers are more frequent (14.5 per cent of recruitment compared with 6.4 per cent in the sample as a whole) and involve a higher share of older workers (12.5 per cent of the workers hired this way, compared to 7.3 per cent). Older workers account for a slightly lower share of outflows (33.8 per cent of departures in 1991, compared with 39 per cent). While the overall shares of redundancies, retirements and early retirements are quite similar to those for the sample as a whole, a slightly greater share of older workers are made redundant, retire at age 60 and over or take early retire-ment between ages 55 and 59. Overall, older workers in this sample account for 22.6 per cent of all collective dismissals and early retirements between ages 55 and 59 (compared to 13.4 per cent in the sample). The share of transfers in total outflows is greater than average (one departure out of ten compared with one out of 20 in the sample as a whole), and a slightly greater share of those aged 45 and over is affected by such transfers (14.9 per cent compared to 10.8 per cent).

The behaviour of these firms is linked to the structure of their workforce.

Firstly, seniority is much higher than it is in the sample as a whole: on average, 62.1 per cent of permanent workers had at least ten years' seniority (compared to 51 per cent). Secondly, there is a higher concentration on the intermediate age groups (25 to 44 years) and, above all, on the 45 to 54 age group. Thus, despite the underrepresentation of workers aged 55 and over, the average share of older workers is rather more than the average for the sample (33 per cent, compared to 31.2 per cent). Finally, the skill structure shows a clear underrepresentation of skilled and unskilled workers (23.8 per cent and 5.6 per cent of permanent workers, respectively, compared to 29.7 per cent and 10.2 per cent on average in the sample).

Almost 80 per cent of the establishments are concentrated in four sectors: intermediate goods industries (23.7 per cent, compared to 16.7 per cent in the sample), capital goods industries (20.6 per cent, compared to 15.6 per cent), finance, insurance, real estate and leasing (11.7 per cent, compared to 4.5 per cent) and not-for-profit services (24.1 per cent, compared to 16.5 per cent). This cluster includes the only insurance establishment.

Three-quarters of the establishments have at least 200 employees, and 45.1 per cent have at least 500 (compared to 24.2 per cent of the sample as a whole). They are also more likely to be part of a group (71.2 per cent, compared to 54.7 per cent) and make greater use of manpower planning (39.3 per cent, compared to 22.3 per cent).

For the firms in this cluster, the intensive training effort seems to be part of a workforce adaptation policy, in both quantitative and qualitative terms. Having previously been stabilized, older workers are either trained or redeployed to other establishments within the firm, with exclusion being used as a strategy of last resort.

Cluster 3: a Weak Training Effort, Devoted Mainly to Older Workers

This cluster includes 98 establishments, representing 9.2 per cent of the sample. On average, these establishments are characterized by a weak training effort, in terms of both numbers trained and expenditure. Only 11.9 per cent of workers receive training, 2.5 times less than the sample average. Training expenditures represent on average only 1.2 per cent of the wage bill, compared to 2.8 per cent for the sample as a whole. In spite of its weakness, however, this training effort is devoted largely to older workers: on average 58.9 per cent of those receiving training are aged 45 and over, three times more than the sample average.

The high level of training directed at older workers is explained in part by recruitment behaviour. Workers aged 45 and over account on average for 44 per cent of all new hires in establishments in this cluster, 1.6 times higher than in the sample as a whole. Yet older workers are also more affected by terminations of employment: they accounted for 49 per cent of departures in 1991. 'Other departures' (ending of temporary contracts, individual dismissals, resignations and so on) do not account for a higher share of total departures but are more likely to involve older workers: 46.1 per cent of such departures affected workers aged 45 or over, as against 32.8 per cent in the sample as a whole. Retirement and early retirement are more frequent, accounting for 13.1 per cent of total departures, compared to a sample average of 8.6 per cent. In contrast, collective dismissals are a little less frequently used, and older workers are far less affected (4.8 per cent of the workers laid off are aged 45 and over, as against 13.5 per cent in the sample as a whole). Moreover, early retirements between ages 45 and 59 are very rare. Thus the older workforce seems to be both flexible in terms of individual turnover and stable in terms of total share of employees.

The scale of the training effort devoted to older workers is due at least in part to the characteristics of the permanent workforce. The age structure has a much greater than average share of older workers. The intermediate age groups are strongly underrepresented (53.1 per cent, as against a sample average of 62.1 per cent). On the other hand, the 45 to 54 age group and those aged 55 and over are very strongly represented: 28.4 per cent of permanent workers are aged between 45 and 54, compared to an average of 23.1 per cent in the sample, and 12.7 per cent are 55 and over, as against 8.1 per cent. Thus the average share of older workers is 41.1 per cent (compared to 31.2 per cent). Yet average seniority is slightly lower than the sample average. Finally, the share of skilled workers is higher than the sample average (34.6 per cent, as against 29.7 per cent).

Six economic activities are particularly well represented: not-for-profit and for-profit services (respectively 23.5 per cent and 17.3 per cent of the establishments, compared to 16.5 per cent and 16.8 per cent in the sample as a whole) and above all distribution (12.2 per cent, as against 8 per cent), consumer goods industries (11.2 per cent, compared to 7.9 per cent), construction (9.2 per cent, as against 6.7 per cent) and transport and telecommunications (6.1 per cent, compared to 3.3 per cent). These sectors account for almost eight out of ten establishments.

The low level of training expenditure is consistent with the establishments' size: 83.4 per cent have fewer than 200 employees and 49 per cent fewer than 50 (as against 53.3 and 25.8 per cent, respectively, in the sample as a whole). Firms in this cluster are more likely to be operated by firms that are not part of a group (59.2 per cent, as against 43.3 per cent) and use very little manpower planning (11.2 per cent of establishments, compared to 22.3 per cent). The weak training effort is strongly aimed at older workers, who represent a large share of the workforce. This behaviour is coupled with both a flexibilization and a stabilization of their workforce.

Cluster 4: a Moderate Training Effort of Benefit to Older Workers

This category is the largest one, since it contains 279 establishments, representing 26.1 per cent of the sample. The training effort is weaker than in the sample as a whole: on average, only 21.3 per cent of the workers already in post or hired in 1991 benefited from training (compared with an average of 29.7 per cent) while expenditures represent only 1.7 per cent of the wage bill (as against 2.8 per cent). On the other hand, the average share of workers aged 45 and over among those receiving training is slightly greater: 24.4 per cent, compared to 20.2 per cent. The moderate training effort thus benefits older workers quite well.

On average, the establishments in this cluster recruit a smaller share of older workers: 23 per cent of the persons hired in 1991 were aged 45 and over, compared with 28.4 per cent for the sample as a whole. Less use is also made of transfers from other establishments as a form of recruitment. Older workers are also less affected by terminations of employment: they account for 34.5 per cent of out-flows (compared with 39 per cent). 'Other departures' involve a lower share of older workers (27 per cent as against 32.8 per cent). Moreover, the share of retirements in the total retirements and early retirements is more important (45.2 per cent versus 39 per cent), whereas those types of out-flows are not more frequent than in the sample. The incidence of other forms of departure is similar to that in the sample as a whole. Thus older workers account for a lower share of hires but are more stabilized than in the previous cluster.

The age structure of the permanent workforce shows a slight bias towards older workers, but to a much smaller extent than in cluster 3. Workers aged between 25 and 44 are slightly underrepresented, whereas workers aged 45 and over are slightly overrepresented. Thus the average share of older workers is 32.9 per cent, compared to 31.2 per cent for the sample as a whole. Seniority is very similar to the sample average: 52.4 per cent of permanent workers have been employed in the establishment for at least ten years (as against 51 per cent). Finally, the skill structure differs little from the sample as a whole, with the exception of the technician category, which is slightly underrepresented (9.3 per cent of permanent workers, compared to 11 per cent). On the other hand, the proportion of women is higher: 42.2 per cent, as against 39.1 per cent.

The distribution by economic activity is also quite similar to the sample as a whole. Agriculture and food processing, consumer goods industries, transport and telecommunications and services in general are slightly overrepresented. The relative weakness of training cannot be explained by the size of establishments. Although very large establishments are under-represented, this is also the case for small ones. The share of establishments that are part of a group is similar to that in the sample as a whole (52 per cent, as against 54.7 per cent). However, they make less frequent use of manpower planning (17.9 per cent, compared to 22.3 per cent). Moreover, they have to deal with 'difficulties' more frequently (40.5 per cent, as against 36.5 per cent). In these establishments, the moderate training effort seems to be aimed at a fairly well-stabilized workforce.

Cluster 2: a Weak Training Effort Almost Excluding Ageing Workers

This category includes 175 establishments, representing 16.4 per cent of the sample. The training effort is weak, in terms both of the share of employees receiving training and of expenditure levels. On average, only 10.6 per cent of the employees receive training, 2.8 times fewer than in the sample as a whole. The average training expenditures amount to 0.9 per cent of the wage bill, compared to 2.8 per cent for the sample as a whole. Thus establishments in this cluster have an even lower propensity to train than those in cluster 3. Older workers are seriously affected by the weakness of the training effort: on average only 1.3 per cent of the trainees are aged 45 and over.

Like cluster 3, cluster 2 is characterized by a high proportion of older workers in both inflows and outflows. On average, 47.1 per cent of the persons hired are aged 45 and over, 1.7 times more than in the sample as a whole. Recruitment is mainly for temporary jobs, to a greater extent than in the sample as a whole or in cluster 3. Older workers are also particularly affected by terminations of employment: on average 48.6 per cent of the workers who left in 1991 were aged 45 and over. The share of outflows in the 'other departures' category is higher than the sample average (88.2 per cent, as against 78.9 per cent), and 47.6 per cent of the workers involved are aged 45 and over (compared to 32.8 per cent). Thus flexibility in the older age groups seems to be very high, which partly explains the weakness of the training effort.

The virtual absence of training for older workers is due in part to the characteristics of the workforce. The age structure is in fact younger than the sample as a whole, contrary to cluster 3. Workers under 25 account for 10.7 per cent of the permanent workforce, the highest proportion among the six clusters (compared with a sample average of 6.7 per cent). Moreover, there are far fewer older workers, especially those aged 45 to 54 (18.8 per cent, as against 23.1 per cent). Thus the overall share of older workers is particularly low: 26.4 per cent, as against 31.3 per cent for the sample as a whole. Average seniority is much lower than in the sample as a whole and the average for cluster 3: 36.8 per cent of permanent workers have been in post for at least ten years, compared with 51 per cent in the sample as a whole, and 47.2 per cent in cluster 3. The managerial, supervisory and technician categories are underrepresented in the skill structure, to the benefit of clerical and, in particular, unskilled workers (14.4 per cent of permanent workers, as against 10.2 per cent). Women are also slightly underrepresented (37.7 per cent, as against 39.1 per cent).

It is hardly surprising, therefore, that the establishments in this cluster are strongly concentrated in areas of economic activity that typically have a very flexible workforce. Four sectors account for 61.7 per cent of the establishments (compared to 39.4 per cent for the sample as a whole): consumer goods industries (12 per cent of the establishments, as against 7.9 per cent), construction (11.4 per cent, as against 6.7 per cent), distribution (16.6 per cent, compared to 8 per cent) and for-profit services (21.7 per cent, compared to 16.8 per cent).

The weakness of the training effort is consistent with the size of the establishments: 86.8 per cent have fewer than 200 employees and 51.4 per cent have from ten to 49 employees (25.8 per cent in the sample). They are less likely to be part of a group (40 per cent, as against 54.7 per cent), more likely to be sole establishments (63.4 per cent, compared to 48.6 per cent) and less likely to use manpower planning (8 per cent, as against 22.3 per cent). A greater than average share declares itself 'to be in fairly good health' (57.7 per cent, compared to 51.6 per cent). The very weak training effort is consistent with a flexible workforce.

Cluster 1: a Fairly Strong Training Effort of Little Benefit to Older Workers

This category includes 240 establishments, some 22.5 per cent of the sample. These establishments provide much more training than those in the three previous clusters, in terms of both the share of workers trained and the level of expenditures. The average proportion of employees receiving training is 30.4 per cent. As for the average training expenditures, they account for 3.4 per cent of the total wage bill, far higher than the 2.8 per cent sample average. However, older workers benefit very little from this fairly intensive training effort: on average, only 7.6 per cent of the workers receiving training are aged 45 and over, that is to say 2.7 times less than in the sample as a whole.

The recruitment and departure behaviour hardly explains this lack of training provision for older workers. The average share of workers aged 45 and over in total hires is very similar to the sample average (26.4 per cent, as against 28.4 per cent). The same applies to departures: the 45 and over age group accounted for 36.6 per cent of the workers leaving an establishment in 1991, as against 39 per cent for all establishments. The shares of the various types of departures are similar to what they are for the sample as a whole. Only a slightly higher share of older workers is affected by redundancies, early retirements and transfers. Thus 16.9 per cent of all redundancies and early retirements affect the 45 and over age group (compared to 13.4 per cent for all establishments).

The age structure of the permanent workforce provides a better explanation of the training behaviour of these establishments, which appears to diverge markedly from that of the sample as a whole. Workers under 25 and those aged between 25 and 44 are slightly overrepresented, while the 45 and over group is underrepresented, particularly the 45 to 54 category (19.8 per cent of the permanent workforce, as against 23.1 per cent). Thus the share of older workers is only 26.9 per cent (31.2 per cent in the sample as a whole). However, workers have only slightly less seniority than the sample average: 49.3 per cent of the permanent workforce have been in post for at least ten years, as against 51 per cent. Finally, skilled manual and, especially, unskilled manual workers are overrepresented (31.2 per cent and 14 per cent of the permanent workforce, respectively, as against 29.7 per cent and 10.2 per cent).

Unlike the picture in the other clusters, establishments are not strongly concentrated in a small number of sectors. Nevertheless, two sectors are overrepresented relative to the sample as a whole, namely the capital goods industries (22.9 per cent of establishments, as against 15.6 per cent) and construction (9.6 per cent, as against 6.7 per cent). On the other hand, for-profit services and finance, insurance, real estate and leasing are significantly underrepresented. Likewise, this cluster includes establishments of all sizes, although establishments with over 200 employees are more frequent (57.5 per cent of the establishments, as against 46.7 per cent in the sample). They are more likely to be part of a group (60 per cent, as against 54.7 per cent) but use manpower planning only slightly more than the sample average (25 per cent, as against 22.3 per cent). The significant volume of training provided is of little benefit to older workers, but there seems to be no particular link with workforce flexibilization or destabilization.

Cluster 5: an Intensive but Selective Training Effort of Some Benefit to Older Workers

This category includes 20 establishments, 1.9 per cent of the sample. Compared to the other clusters, the training effort here appears quite distinctive. While training expenditures are very high (9 per cent on average of the total wage bill, that is to say 3.2 times the average proportion in the sample), the share of employees receiving training is low (only 11.3 per cent of people employed during 1991 received training, 2.6 times less than the sample average). Older workers tend to fare quite well: 11.3 per cent of workers receiving training are aged 45 and over, only 1.8 times less than the sample average. Thus the high level of expenditure on training can be explained as a limited attempt to adapt the skills of one part of the workforce.

The establishments in this cluster have the greatest proportion of older workers in both hires and departures. On average, 51.9 per cent of recruitment involves the over-45s. Fixed-term contracts predominate. As for departures, 62 per cent involve older workers. As in cluster 2, 'other departures' are much more frequently used than in the sample as a whole: they account for 88.6 per cent of total departures, compared to an average of 78.9 per cent for the sample as a whole. Given the share of fixed-term hirings, this is readily explained by the ending of fixed-term contracts. This kind of departure affects a far greater share of older workers: 58.1 per cent of all those leaving the establishments are aged 45 and over, as against 32.8 per cent. Moreover, there were no redundancies in 1991.

The weakness of the training effort directed towards older workers may be partly due to the characteristics of the permanent workforce. The age structure of the workforce is quite young in this cluster, with workers under 25 being particularly overrepresented (11.9 per cent, compared to 6.7 per cent in the sample as a whole), while workers aged between 45 and 54 are underrepresented (18.8 per cent, as against 23.1 per cent). Overall, 27 per cent of the workers are aged 45 and over (as against 31.2 per cent). Seniority is also lower than average for the sample: only 38 per cent of the workers have been in post for at least ten years (compared to a sample average of 51 per cent). The skill structure is also specific, since skilled workers are considerably overrepresented relative to the sample average (49.2 per cent, compared to 29.7 per cent). This is consistent with the lower than average share of women, who account for only 33.1 per cent of the permanent workforce (as against 39.1 per cent).

Three sectors are overrepresented, accounting for 65 per cent of the establishments in the cluster: consumer goods industries (10 per cent of establishments, compared to 7.9 per cent in the sample), for-profit services (30 per cent, as against 16.8 per cent) and, above all, construction (25 per cent, compared to 6.7 per cent). The establishments are mainly small and medium-sized: three-quarters have fewer than 200 employees, and half have from ten to 49 employees. They are also mainly single establishment firms (70 per cent, compared to 48.6 per cent) and tend to be independent rather than part of a group (70 per cent, as against 43.3 per cent). Few of them use manpower planning (10 per cent, as against 22.3 per cent). Finally, a greater than average share is either 'in fairly good health' (55 per cent, as against 51.6 per cent for the sample as a whole) or 'in a somewhat difficult position' (10 per cent, as against 3.7 per cent). The intensive but selective training effort is intended to adapt the skills of a small section of employees. Access to training is also reduced for older workers. This training practice is consistent with workforce flexibilization.

3. RESULTS AND IMPLICATIONS FOR TRANSITIONS AND IMPROVEMENTS IN TRAINING PRACTICES

On the basis of the six clusters discussed in the previous section, we first analyse some determinants of training practices towards older workers. Establishments data point out some differences with the results obtained with firms data (see Section 1). Then we consider the implications of the observed behaviours on transitions and training access for older workers.

Determinants of Training Access for Older Workers

The six clusters presented in the previous section reflect a broad range of training practices within firms. Firstly, they indicate a relative disjunction between intensity of the training effort and access for older workers. While an intensive training effort benefits older workers quite significantly (cluster 6), a weak training effort can be related either to good training opportunities (cluster 3) or to very poor access to training (cluster 2) for the 45 and over age group. This is consistent with the result of a principal component analysis carried out using the three training indicators as active variables: the first axis, corresponding to the training effort, is at right angles to the second, corresponding to the rate of access to training among older workers.

Secondly, the empirically derived clusters modify the conclusions relating to the establishment features that determine access. Contrary to CEREQ's findings, our classification reveals a positive relationship between training opportunities for older workers and their share in the permanent workforce: establishments providing the greatest training opportunities for older workers have the oldest age structures (see cluster 6 and, to a lesser extent, clusters 3 and 4), whereas a younger age structure tends to be associated with reduced opportunities for ageing workers (see clusters 2 and 5). An unbalanced age structure can reduce natural movements and limit the use of involuntary departures. Thus, when firms cannot renew skills by recruiting young workers, they have to find ways of adapting the skills of the current workforce. Moreover, seniority reflects a stable workforce, which is consistent with the notion of internal labour markets. Training is thus provided inside the firm rather than outside.

Our analysis based on establishments also reveals strongly heterogeneous practices within sectors. This heterogeneity may partly explain the differences between our classification results and those provided by sectoral studies. As shown in Table 9.2, two types of training practices are needed to account for at least half of the establishments in a given sector, with the exception of finance, insurance, leasing and real estate.

Table 9.2   Percentage distribution of all establishments in a given sector, by cluster

	Clusters						
Sector	6	3	4	2	1	5	All
Agriculture and food processing	14.3	9.5	**33.3**	19.1	**23.8**	0	100
Intermediate goods	**34.1**	3.3	**23.5**	14.5	22.9	1.7	100
Capital goods	**31.7**	4.2	25.2	6.0	**32.9**	0	100
Consumer goods	11.9	13.1	**27.4**	**25.0**	20.2	2.4	100
Construction	4.2	12.5	16.7	**27.8**	**31.9**	6.9	100
Trade	8.1	14.0	**24.4**	**33.7**	18.6	1.2	100
Transport, telecommunications	11.4	17.1	**34.3**	14.3	**22.9**	0	100
For-profit services	11.7	9.4	**30.6**	21.1	**23.9**	3.3	100
Finance, insurance, leasing and real estate	**62.5**	6.2	14.6	2.1	14.6	0	100
Not-for-profit services	**35.2**	13.1	**29.0**	9.6	11.4	1.7	100

Likewise, while small establishments largely exclude older workers from training, Table 9.3 shows that this is also the case in quite a high proportion of large and very large establishments. The relationship between size of establishment and training effort aimed at older workers has thus to be smoothed.

Thirdly, the link between training practices, on the one hand, and recruitment and departure practices, on the other, seems to be weak. The clusters are not markedly different with regard to the hiring and departure of older

Table 9.3   Percentage distribution of establishments, by size and cluster

Number of employees	Clusters						
	6	3	4	2	1	5	All
10 to 49	9.0	17.4	16.7	32.6	20.7	3.6	100
50 to 199	13.9	11.6	36.4	21.1	15.3	1.7	100
200 to 499	31.2	4.2	29.2	6.7	27.5	1.2	100
500 and over	44.8	2.3	21.6	2.7	27.8	0.8	100

workers. A comparison between clusters derived from training practices alone and clusters based on the three types of practices, that is recruitment, departures and training,[11] makes it clear why this is the case. Highlighting the differences in training practices leads to the near disappearance of the observed differences in recruitment and departure practices. Training practices can thus be considered to be partially independent of recruitment and lay-off practices. In particular, this means that the use of early retirement schemes or large-scale redundancies, which mainly affect older workers, cannot be related to a specific training practice. An apparent paradox remains, however: greater training opportunities are offered to older workers by those establishments that exclude them the most (see cluster 6). This can be explained by the practice of using training courses to screen employees or by a selection of workers before training (for example, excluding employees who approach the retirement or pre-retirement age).

Transitions and the Improvement of Training Practices Aimed at Older Workers

The results presented above raise two main questions. Firstly, do reduced training opportunities lead to the exclusion of older workers? Secondly, how can these opportunities be increased?

Access to training for older workers represents a challenge for firms. Besides contributing to the efficiency of these workers, it improves the opportunities for older workers to move into other jobs both inside the firm (tutorial, redeployment) and outside it (outplacement). Of course this does not mean that each establishment has an equal interest in training its workforce. The perceived need for training depends on certain environmental variables, and in particular the influence of technological developments on job content and work organization. Thus a weak or selective training effort does not necessarily result in a skills shortage if the pace of technological change is slow. Moreover, on-the-job training is generally excluded from training statistics, although it makes a very significant contribution to the maintenance of skills, particularly for senior workers.

Training is not the only way of adapting the workforce. Another strategy is to recruit workers with the required skills on the external labour market. Against a general background of 'downsizing', the scope for hiring is closely linked to departures. Training and labour flows are thus connected, but not necessarily in the expected way. A firm may have to maintain the skills of its remaining older workers because recruitment is weak and/or large-scale lay-offs are not possible. Cluster 6 illustrates this logic: a strong training effort appears to go hand in hand with the exclusion of a segment of the older workforce. On the other hand, a firm that makes its workforce flexible may not train them only because the tasks they have to perform are not really evolving (see cluster 2). Thus the relationship between reduced training opportunities and the exclusion of older workers is not evident.

With regard to the improvement of access opportunities and transitional labour markets, the diversity of practices in establishments with weak or moderate training provision makes it virtually impossible to propose a simple general solution. Firms with low training intensity are frequently small or medium-sized, with between 50 and 200 workers. Any attempt to improve training opportunities might require the removal of the obstacles to training for these firms. For instance, the introduction of arrangements for providing a temporary workforce to replace employees on training leave could encourage more widespread training. This replacement workforce could be made up of unemployed or semi-retired individuals, and could contribute to the reintegration of other workers. Another limit to the training effort may be the difficulty for some firms, especially the small ones, to finance a certain level of training expenditures. Creating funds to which firms contribute could help to raise the training effort of the less active firms. This 'mutualization' already exists in France, but it is compulsory only for firms with more than ten employees.

Developing schemes whereby workers could share the cost of training with their employer could also encourage greater training efforts and increase access opportunities for ageing workers. A lack of training opportunities could also be countered by training schemes allowing workers to decide on their training. Two schemes already existing in France, the 'individual training contract' (*contrat individuel de formation*, or *CIF*) and the 'training time reserve' (*capital de temps formation, compte épargne formation*), are examples of such an approach. In particular, the training time reserve gives a worker the right to a number of hours' training within the framework of a company's training plan, allocated on the basis of his/her seniority. The recent working time reduction favours this 'coinvestment': to avoid a raise in training costs, some company-wide agreements allow training to be partly done during free time.[12] However, the effectiveness of such schemes depends on whether or not they are taken up by those who have less access to training. An evaluation of the CIF beneficiaries reveals for example quite the same inequality of access with age than the continuing vocational training.[13]

Besides increasing firms training effort and access opportunities for ageing workers, a more qualitative aspect has to be considered: the validation of training, the validation of skills in general. Ageing workers are quite distinctive compared to other workers because they have experience, mainly through on-the-job training. However, they are often not credited for these skills, the result being a problem of transferability and transition is more difficult if they are laid-off. Creating a validation system for vocational skills is thus a crucial mean of improving labour market transitions for ageing workers.

4. CONCLUSION

The training practices observed in 1991 show a diversity of attitudes towards ageing workers. Firstly, there is no close relationship between training effort and training access for ageing workers. While an intensive effort benefits ageing workers, a weak or moderate effort can lead to either good, or to very few, opportunities for ageing workers.

Secondly, there is a relative independence of training practices from recruitment and departure practices. Training of ageing workers helps them to preserve and update their skills but they are not necessarily excluded when this effort is poor. Good access to training can also go hand in hand with the exclusion of some older workers, particularly when it becomes necessary to adapt skills and/or rejuvenate the age structure.

Opposing situations can be derived from the analysed behaviours. A large majority of ageing workers are stabilized within firms, either staying in the same firm, or being transferred to related firms. For these workers, training access seems to be quite good. In contrast, some ageing workers are forced to become adaptable and experience recurrent unemployment. They also benefit from fewer training opportunities. This unequal access to training has then two implications: on one hand less training can lead to less transferable skills, on the other hand skills adaptation can be limited.

Finally, improving training access for ageing workers highlights the challenge of continuous vocational training: confronted with greater precariousness and skill mobility, training has to ensure both adaptability and employability of ageing workers.

NOTES

1. The Act of 16 July 1971 imposed an obligation on the firms with ten or more employees to devote a minimum proportion of their annual wage bill to continuing vocational training. The Act of 31 December 1991 extended this obligation to firms with fewer than ten employees. The minimum contribution was initially set at 0.8 per cent of the total wage bill, and has been gradually raised to the current 1.5 per cent.
2. See Laulhé (1990).
3. See Aventur (1994).
4. See Bentabet and Santoni (1994).
5. The access rate to training is calculated by CEREQ; the number of trainees in each age group is divided by the number of employees in the same age group.
6. See Goux (1994).
7. See Goux and Maurin (1997).
8. For more details on this survey, see the appendix and Le'Minez and Baktavatsalou (1994).
9. See Bentabet and Santoni (1994).
10. The aggregation criterion used here is the usual Ward criterion (minimization of intra-cluster variance and maximization of inter-cluster variance).
11. A principal components analysis on the whole recruitment, departure and training indicators of older workers' access to training reveals the predominance of indicators related to in- and out-flows. Training ranks only fifth (see Jolivet, 1999).
12. See Liaisons sociales (1999).
13. See Lerenard (1998).

BIBLIOGRAPHY

Aventur, François (1994), 'La formation continue des salariés à partir de 45 ans', in Liliane Salzberg and Anne-Marie Guillemard (eds), *Emploi et vieillissement*, Collection Cahier Travail et Emploi, DARES-Ministère du travail, La Documentation Française, pp. 89–95.

Bentabet, Elyes and Santoni, Françoise (1994), *La formation professionnelle continue financée par les entreprises. Exploitation des déclarations fiscales des employeurs n°2483. Année 1991*, Série Observatoire, Document no. 92, CEREQ, janvier, 179 pp.

Crocquey, Edwige (1995), 'Les capacités de formation dans les établissements de plus de 10 salariés: de l'alternance à la formation en situation de travail', *Premières Synthèses*, no. 79, 16 January, 6 pp.

Crocquey, Edwige (1995), 'La formation professionnelle continue: des inégalités d'accès et des effets sur la carrière peu importants à court terme', *Premières Synthèses*, no. 107, 8 August, 8 pp.

Gauron, André (2000), 'Formation tout au long de la vie', *Les Rapports du Conseil d'Analyse Economique*, no. 22, La Documentation française, 163 pp.

Goux, Dominique (1994), 'La formation professionnelle continue', *INSEE Première*, no. 314, May, 4 pp.

Goux, Dominique and Maurin, Eric (1997), 'Les entreprises, les salariés et la formation continue', *Economie et Statistique*, no. 306, pp. 41–55.

Guillemard, Anne-Marie (1996), '*La gestion des âges dans l'entreprise en France. Combattre les barrières d'âge au recrutement et à la formation*', en collaboration avec Annie Jolivet, Sandrine Melan, Julien Faure, Alexandre Iellatchitch,

Rapport pour la Fondation Européenne pour l'Amélioration des Conditions de Vie et de Travail, Dublin, 97 pp.

Jolivet, Annie (1999), 'Entreprise et gestion de la main-d'œuvre vieillissante: organisation, discrimination', doctoral thesis in economics, supervised by Bernard Gazier, Université Paris I, 408 pp.

Laulhé, Pierre (1990), 'La formation continue: un avantage pour les promotions et un accès privilégié pour les jeunes et les techniciens', *Economie et Statistique*, no. 228, January, pp. 3–8.

Lerenard, Agnes (1998), 'L'effet du congé individuel de formation sur les carrières individuelles', *Premières synthèses*, no. 04.1, 8 pp.

Le Minez, Sylvie and Baktavatsalou, Ravi (1994), 'Les modalités de sortie de la vie active et le vieillissement au travail', *Dossiers statistiques*, no. 4–5, December, Ministère du travail.

Liaisons sociales (1999), '35 heures: temps de travail et formation', *Conventions collectives et accords*, no. 64, C3, 21 June, 10 pp.

APPENDIX: EXPLOITATION OF THE SURVEY

The data analysed come from the pairing of two sources: on the one hand, a postal survey carried out in 1992 with an adequate sample of establishments and, on the other, monthly surveys on labour flows (*Enquête sur les Mouvements de Main-d'Œuvre, Déclarations des Mouvements de Main-d'Œuvre*).

The final sample of this survey on the 'Management of an ageing workforce' comprises 2100 establishments, a quarter of the 8533 establishments that were contacted. This gap is due, on the one hand, to the incoherent or inadequate responses given to some questionnaires and, on the other, to pairing difficulties.

A new selection of establishments was made in order to analyse data relating to training. Because of the indicators chosen, some checks were necessary in order to exclude those establishments which did not supply the responses to be analysed or whose responses were incoherent. Of the 2100 establishments in the final sample, 911 did not provide all the data relating to training and were therefore excluded. The reduction in the size of the analysed sample is due mainly to the impossibility of calculating the rate of access to training for older workers. Finally, only 1069 establishments satisfied the various checks, that is to say 51 per cent of the final survey sample and only 12.5 per cent of the establishments contacted. However, the excluded establishments show hiring and departure behaviours similar to those of the selected establishments.

Nevertheless, this selection deeply modifies the analysed sample structure by size and by sector of economic activity (see Tables 9A.1 and 9A.2). As far as size is concerned, the sample structure is reversed: establishments with under 200 employees are underrepresented, especially small establishments, while large establishments are overrepresented, especially very large ones (500 employees and over). As for sector, establishments in the intermediate goods, capital goods and not-for-profit service sectors are overrepresented, whereas establishments from the construction, distribution and for-profit services sectors are underrepresented.

Table 9A.1   Distribution of establishments, by size

	10 to 49 employees	50 to 199 employees	200 to 499 employees	500 employees and over	All
Adequate sample* (%)	38	30	15	16	100
Survey sample	42.3%	25.8%	14.9%	17.0%	100
	888	*541*	*313*	*358*	*2100*
Analysed sample	25.8%	27.5%	22.5%	24.2%	100
	276	*294*	*240*	*259*	*1069*

Note: *The adequate sample was defined according to the UNEDIC data at the end of 1990.

Table 9A.2   Distribution of establishments, by sector of economic activity

	Adequate sample (%)	Analysed sample (%)	Analysed sample (No.)
Agricultural and food processing	3.1	3.9	*42*
Intermediate goods	6.3	16.7	*179*
Capital goods	6.6	15.6	*167*
Consumer goods	8.2	7.9	*84*
Construction	11.7	6.7	*72*
Distribution	19.4	8.0	*86*
Transport, telecommunications	5.3	3.3	*35*
For-profit services	29.2	16.8	*180*
Finance, insurance, leasing and real estate	3.4	4.5	*48*
Not-for-profit services	7.0	16.5	*176*
All	100	100	*1069*

10. Exclusion of older workers, productivity and training

Arie Gelderblom and Jaap de Koning

1. INTRODUCTION

This chapter uses individual company data to investigate the relation between labour productivity and wages, on the one hand, and the age composition and training intensity of workers, on the other. It is based on a study conducted for the Dutch Institute for Labour Studies, OSA (Gelderblom and de Koning, 1992a).[1] The main purpose of the chapter is to investigate the extent to which training can help to lower the wage–productivity ratio of older workers. If training had a significant effect in this respect, it could enhance activity rates among the over-55s, thereby helping to prevent their being excluded from the labour market.

Table 10.1 clearly illustrates the low activity rate among older people in the Netherlands. In the potential labour force as a whole, the activity rate is almost 60 per cent. Among those aged between 55 and 64, however, the rate falls dramatically to about 25 per cent. Moreover, this rate has remained stable in recent years, bucking the overall trend of increasing participation.

Table 10.1   Activity rates, by age group, in the Netherlands (per cent)

	1988	1992	1996
15–24	42	42	39
25–34	67	73	76
35–44	64	69	71
45–54	56	61	64
>55–64	26	25	26
Total	53	57	59

Source: Labour Force Survey, Central Bureau of Statistics, The Netherlands.

Relatively low employment–population ratios for older age groups can be found all over Europe. However, the Netherlands is among the countries with the lowest ratios (see Table 10.2).

If labour market participation decreases with age, what kind of transitions take place out of the labour market? In the Netherlands, the following transitions out of the labour market are particularly widespread.

1. Some people, especially women, withdraw from the labour market to concentrate on domestic responsibilities. However, this does not explain the decrease in labour market participation in the older age groups, because most of these withdrawals take place between ages 25 and 40, that is during the main child-raising phase of the life cycle. Quite a lot of the women who leave the labour market for this reason return when their children have grown up.
2. People become unemployed. However, the unemployment rate in the 55–64 age group is only 4 per cent, compared with 7 per cent for the total labour force (1996). If older people do become unemployed, they tend to remain unemployed for a long time. However, the incidence of unemployment is so low that this cannot explain the low participation rates among older workers.

Table 10.2   Employment–population ratios in older age groups in a number of EU member states (per cent), 1995

	50–54	55–59	60–64
Belgium	58	35	12
Denmark	76	64	33
Germany	73	52	18
Greece	60	49	32
Spain	52	40	24
France	72	49	11
Ireland	54	45	34
Italy	55	36	17
Luxembourg	60	36	11
Netherlands	64	43	14
Austria	69	43	14
Portugal	69	53	38
Finland	75	48	19
Sweden	87	77	48
United Kingdom	74	60	35

Source: Labour Force Survey, Eurostat, Results 1995.

3. People take early retirement. Early retirement schemes expanded in the 1970s and 1980s and sometimes helped to prevent dismissals in companies that were restructuring. A lot of schemes still offer retirement at age 61 or 62, although there is some pressure from employers' organizations and government to put an end to them on grounds of cost, particularly since the population is continuing to age.

4. Workers flow into disability schemes. In the mid 1990s the number of registered workers in disability schemes totals some 900 000, nearly one-sixth of the labour force. About 40 per cent of the disabled are aged between 55 and 65 and more than 30 per cent between 45 and 55. This means that a significant share of the non-participating older population is to be found in the disability schemes.

Why has the use of early retirement and disability schemes become so 'popular' among individual employees and employers? One hypothesis put forward is that labour productivity has been increased too much, and that workers are, in consequence, 'worn out' long before retirement age. This hypothesis seems to be supported by the fact that average labour productivity in the Netherlands is higher than in some other industrialized countries. However, it should be borne in mind that capital-intensive activities have a large share in the Dutch economy and that the disability rate in these industries is no higher than in other industries. Moreover, average productivity growth has not exceeded that of other countries since the 1960s (van Paridon, 1991). Thus we tend to conclude that this explanation is not very plausible.

An alternative explanation is that most 'disabled' persons are not in ill-health at all, but have been pushed out of the labour market for economic reasons (see also Aarts and de Jong, 1990). It is well known that companies have used the Disability Act and early retirement schemes during periods of recession as means of reducing their internal labour reserves. Gelderblom and de Koning (1992a) show that employment growth in a company has a strong negative influence on the disability rate, confirming that this rate depends on the economic situation. The fact that the disability rate is higher the more export-oriented a company is also points to the role of economic factors. Workers and trade unions tended to go along with these practices because disability benefits and early retirement benefits were more generous than unemployment benefits. Older workers are more likely to become 'disabled' than younger workers because inactivity is more or less acceptable for them.

However, this is not the whole story. Even during the recovery phase of the economy at the end of the 1980s, the number of workers on disability benefit was still rising. Our hypothesis is that older workers are less attractive to employers because their productivity tends to be low compared to their wages. Age–income profiles show that older workers' wages tend to be rather stable. If productivity declines with age – which remains to be proved – this could imply that older workers become economically obsolete.

The low participation rate among older people (from age 45 to 50 onwards) is a threat to the economy. Demographic trends suggest that the share of young people in the population will decline, while that of older people will rise. If participation rates among older people continue to be low, the overall participation rate will decline, leading to higher social security premiums and higher wage costs, which would in turn reinforce the mechanism responsible for the expulsion of older workers.

How can this vicious circle be broken? There are at least two possible options. First, the attractiveness of early retirement and disability schemes for individual employers and employees could be broken. This is the route taken by the Dutch government. Benefit payments under the disability schemes have dropped to a minimum level after a certain time. Moreover, employers have to pay a certain penalty when employees join the disability scheme.

Second, older employees could be encouraged to participate in training. This would be one way of improving older workers' productivity and postponing their obsolescence. It is also important for the following reason. As the number of school leavers declines, companies will no longer benefit from the latest knowledge and skills in the way they used to. This fact, combined with the ever-faster pace of technological development, makes post-initial education and training increasingly important.

This chapter is concerned with two main issues. The first is the relationship between age, productivity and wages. The analysis shows that productivity does indeed decline with age, making the productivity–wage ratio unfavourable for older workers. The second is the influence of training on productivity. Training has much more effect on productivity than it has on wages, thus improving the productivity–wage ratio and postponing expulsion from employment.

The chapter is structured as follows. Section 2 gives a short overview of theories behind age-productivity and age-wage curves. This is followed, in section 3, by the empirical analyses. Finally, section 4 gives a summary of the results and relates them to social exclusion issues.

2. THEORIES OF AGE-PRODUCTIVITY AND AGE-WAGE CURVES[2]

Neoclassical theory tells us that wages reflect marginal productivity. However, modern theories of the labour market have tended to move away from positing such a close connection between productivity and wages. Thus, according to human capital theory, investment in training by individuals and firms is concentrated in the younger age groups because training is most profitable at a young age. In Becker's original model (1964), companies pay for firm-specific training, on the assumption that wages will exceed productivity in the younger age groups and that the reverse is true in the older age groups. Wages and marginal productivity will not be equal at a given point in time, but will be equal on average over the working period. According to this theory, the employment of older workers is not a particular problem, because their productivity exceeds wages. This theory is not confirmed by the facts, however.

Later contributions made some adjustments. First, it was shown that, in the case of firm-specific training, companies and workers would share both the costs and revenues of training (Ritzen, 1989). Second, there is ample empirical evidence that companies also pay for a considerable share of their workers' general training (de Koning, 1991). However, this does not alter the basic predictions of the theory concerning the form of the age–productivity and age–wage curves. These curves are shown in Figure 10.1.

Human capital theory seems to be of little assistance in explaining the expulsion of older workers. In human capital theory, productivity is the result of two factors, ability and investment in training.

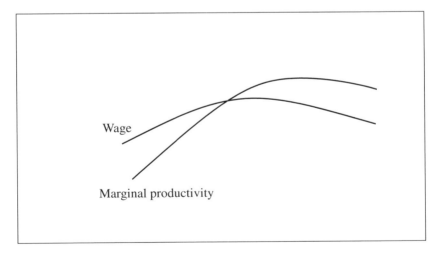

Age

Figure 10.1   Age–productivity and age–wage curve according to human capital theory

Table 10.3   Proportion of civil servants by age group who perceive difficulties in several aspects of their work (answers on each aspect only from those for whom the aspect is relevant to their jobs)

Work aspect	Proportion of age group with perceived difficulties (%)				
	<35	35–44	45–54	>54	Total
Heavy physical work	7	21	35	49	19
Social abilities	10	14	18	15	13
Working under time constraints	28	33	40	52	33
Great responsibility	16	16	9	22	15
Routine work	31	26	15	18	26
Many contacts outside civil service	7	6	3	11	7
Creativity	10	13	13	22	12
Irregular working hours	27	24	27	27	26
Working on several tasks simultaneously	24	27	29	47	28
Negotiating	24	22	15	26	23
Managing others	30	27	11	15	23

Source: Gelderblom and de Koning (1992c).

From the ergonomic literature, we know that physical and mental ability remains fairly constant until relatively old age (see, for example, Sweetland, 1978; Meier and Kerr, 1976; Winnubst *et al.*, 1995). There are indications, however, that around the age of 45–50 workers tend to experience more problems in their work. This is illustrated for civil servants in Table 10.3. In particular, they experience difficulties in dealing with high work pressure.

Since training will be concentrated in the early years of the working life,[3] this would imply that productivity increases quickly among younger workers, stabilizes at middle age and declines in old age.

Human capital theory does not distinguish between potential and actual productivity, but simply assumes that workers perform to their maximum potential. Recent economic theories of the labour market stress the behavioural aspect of productivity and no longer assume that actual productivity automatically equals potential productivity. There is a wide variety of these so-called 'efficiency-wage models' (see Akerlof and Yellen, 1986). They cover various aspects of the problem. One is the uncertainty about the productivity of newly recruited workers. Firms have to incur costs in order to acquire information about this productivity, which is why they will offer relatively low pay to young workers. Secondly, because turnover is costly and workers are risk-averse, contract theory[4] predicts that employment relationships will tend to be long-lasting. However, this makes it necessary to keep workers motivated. One possible strategy is to hold out the prospect of wage increases.

So contract theory and efficiency-wage models predict that wages will be below productivity in the early stages of a career and will exceed productivity at the end of it (see Figure 10.2 for a graphic representation). This is precisely the reverse of the pattern predicted by human capital theory.

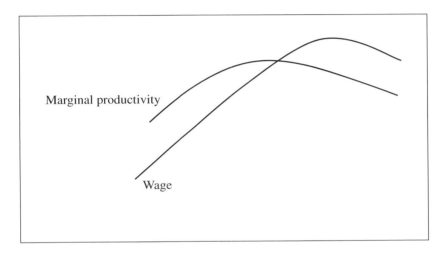

Age

*Figure 10.2   Age–productivity and age–wage curve according to the
            efficiency-wage theory and contract theory*

It should be noted, however, that contract theory deals with implicit contracts. In practice, companies employing older workers with a relatively low productivity–wage ratio may be inclined to find ways of circumventing the implicit arrangements in order to get rid of them. Thus contract theory can explain the expulsion of older workers from the labour process.

We have concentrated thus far on economic theories. However, psychological and sociological factors are also likely to influence productivity. For instance, older people may have a different attitude to work from younger people. There is also evidence of prejudice against older workers, which can turn out to be a self-fulfilling prophecy. Thus, while potential productivity may still be high among older workers, actual productivity may decline.

In sum, we can say that (actual) productivity will probably increase in the early stages of a career but will gradually stabilize and finally decline. Theory is not so clear about the age–wage curve. Human capital theory predicts that older workers will have a favourable productivity–wage ratio, whereas contract theory suggests that older workers have relatively high salaries compared to their productivity. Psychological and sociological factors seem to point in the same direction as the latter theory.

3. EMPIRICAL RESULTS

Measurement of Productivity

The relationship between age and wages is measurable because wages can be determined at the individual level. But what about productivity? In only a limited number of jobs, mainly those in which an individual physical output is produced, productivity can be measured 'objectively'. Jablonsky *et al.* (1988) provide an overview of productivity research in the few jobs that fall into this category.

For most jobs, however, such objective measurement is not possible. In these cases, judgments by management could be a way out. One study using these judgments is that by Medoff and Abraham (1980). Another possibility is to ask employees how they perceive the (change in) performance over a certain period. This is the method adopted by Gelderblom and De Koning (1992c).

All these types of measurement have a subjective basis. The type of measurement used in this chapter has a more objective character, since it makes use of aggregate productivity data at company level and relates these to the age composition of the workforce, using several other control variables, such as production technology, capital stock and characteristics of the workforce other than age.

The Data

The data are taken from the 1989 wave of the Institute for Labour Studies (OSA) company survey.[5] This survey includes about 2000 private companies and non-profit-making organizations. However, our analysis will be based exclusively on the private sector, because the data do not contain a usable production indicator for non-profit-making organizations.[6] Furthermore, not all the companies provided all the necessary data required for our analysis. As a result, the number of companies on which our analysis is based is far fewer than 2000; it varies between 431 and 651, depending on the equation. The questionnaire used in the survey covers a wide range of topics, including the following:

- employment broken down by gender, age, education, type of contract and so on,
- company training,
- labour turnover, recruitment and outflow,
- wages,
- working conditions,
- internal organization,
- production technology,
- value added (with the exception of a number of non-profit-making organizations,
- an indicator of physical production,
- capital stock, investment and depreciation rate,
- utilization rates for capital and labour,
- characteristics of output markets.

Even this list omits aspects that are important to our analysis. For instance, we have no information on the distribution by age and educational level of the workers participating in company training and those leaving their company for various reasons. This, of course, will make it more difficult to interpret the results.

The empirical analysis deals with two equations explaining productivity and wages on the company level. Is the age composition of a company's workforce a determining factor of productivity and wages? Does company training have an influence on the latter variables? On the basis of the productivity and wage equations, conclusions will be drawn about the productivity–age and the wage–age curves and the effect of training on both of them.

The Productivity and Wage Equations

How is the productivity–wage ratio affected by age? Is it really true that this ratio is unfavourable for older workers and, if so, can company training improve it, postponing the economic obsolescence of older workers? To answer these questions, both productivity and wages were related to the age composition of the workforce and participation in company training. Table 10.4 shows the results of the partial relation between productivity and age composition. From the figure we conclude that companies with a relatively young labour force and those with a relatively old labour force have low productivity, which would point to a quadratic relation between productivity and age.

Is it possible to draw conclusions about the productivity–age curve from an aggregate analysis relating company productivity to age composition?

Table 10.4   Productivity and age

Shares	Mean productivity per FTE (full-time equivalent of workers) in the companies concerned (thousands of guilders per FTE per annum)
Share of under-20s	
Less than 3%	175
3–6%	163
6–9%	123
More than 9%	107
Share of 20–29-year-olds	
Less than 15%	161
15–25%	154
25–40%	169
More than 40%	127
Share of 30–39-year-olds	
Less than 15%	96
15–25%	150
25–40%	154
More than 40%	170
Share of 40–49-year-olds	
Less than 10%	128
10–20%	142
20–30%	157
More than 30%	177
Share of over-50s	
Less than 5%	144
5–10%	156
10–20%	154
More than 20%	163

This can be argued as follows. Suppose that productivity p_i of worker i depends on age (l_i) in the following way:

$$\log(p_i) = \alpha + \beta l_i + \gamma l_i^2.$$

Company productivity could be conceived as the expected value of individual productivity:

$$\log(\bar{p}) = E(\log(p)) = E(\alpha + \beta l + \gamma l^2) = \alpha + \beta\, E(l) + \gamma E(l^2).$$

This equation can be rewritten as follows:

$$\log(\bar{p}) = \alpha + \beta\, E(l) + \gamma\, E(l^2) \approx \alpha + \beta\, u + \gamma(\sigma^2 + u^2),$$

where u and σ denote mean and standard deviation of the age distribution in the workforce, which can be computed using data on age composition available from the survey. Parameter α will depend on other variables such as training, education and capital intensity. These variables were added to the equation and OLS was applied. The results are shown in Table 10.5. They show that the productivity–age curve has a quadratic form, with middle-aged workers being most productive. External company training has a positive effect on productivity, as does internal training, but not significantly.

Table 10.5 A selection of explanatory variables in the productivity and equation

Variable	Coefficient (t-value)
Average age	0.160 (2.1)
Quadratic age term	−0.002 (−1.9)
Share of external training	0.612 (2.6)
Share of internal training	0.299 (1.5)

What about the wage–age curve? Table 10.6 shows a similar pattern to that in Table 10.4. Companies with a young labour force and those with an older labour force have a relatively low average wage level, pointing to a quadratic form of the wage–age curve. The same kind of equation used for productivity was estimated for the wage level. Age was included in the same way and again variables such as education, labour conditions, training and so on were added.

The results shown in Table 10.7 indicate that the wage–age curve has a quadratic form too. However, this curve is much 'flatter' than the productivity–age curve, suggesting that the productivity–wage ratio is relatively low for both young and old workers. Comparing this result with the theories treated before, we find that it combines elements of the predictions of human capital theory (a low ratio for young workers) with elements of the wage-efficiency theory (a low ratio for old workers). Both curves are shown in Figure 10.3 (variant training 0). In the case of the wage equation, too,

Table 10.6   Wages and age

Shares	Average wage level[a]
Share of workforce under 20 years	
Less than 3%	48
3–6%	43
6–9%	43
More than 9%	41
Share of workforce 20–29 years	
Less than 15%	50
15–25%	47
25–40%	45
More than 40%	41
Share of workforce 30–39 years	
Less than 15%	41
15–25%	43
25–40%	46
More than 40%	49
Share of workforce 40–49 years	
Less than 10%	40
10–20%	43
20–30%	47
More than 30%	48
Share of workforce over 50 years	
Less than 5%	44
5–10%	45
10–20%	47
More than 20%	45

Note: [a] Thousands of Dutch guilders per annum per FTE.

Table 10.7   A selection of explanatory variables in the wage equation

Variable	Coefficient (t-value)
Average age	0.053 (3.0)
Quadratic age term	−0.001 (−2.7)
Share of external training	0.124 (2.4)
Share of internal training	0.083 (1.7)

company training has a positive effect. Again the effect of external training dominates that of internal training, although the difference is less than in the case of productivity.

Effects of Training

We have seen that the productivity–wage ratio is unfavourable for older workers. Now we will concentrate on the question of how useful training is in improving this ratio for older workers.[7] Can training improve productivity, while at the same time leaving wages relatively stable? To answer this question we use the results from the analysis of productivity and wages already presented, in which training is one of the explanatory variables.

From Tables 10.5 and 10.7, we conclude that the effects of training on productivity exceed the effects on wages. The corresponding coefficients are higher in the equation for productivity. The elasticity of productivity with respect to training lies around 0.1. So a doubling of training participation leads to a 10 per cent increase in productivity. The elasticity of wages with respect to training is much lower, namely around 0.025.

This last conclusion can be illustrated in a graph. What happens if participation in internal training and external training both increase by 10 percentage points, while the remaining explanatory variables remain fixed on their sample mean? The effects of this increase are illustrated in Figure 10.3.

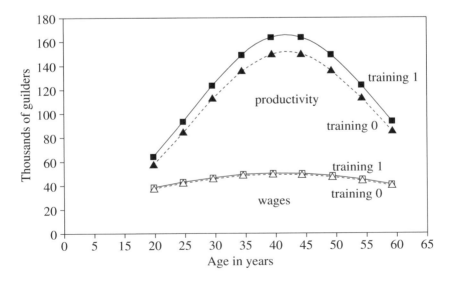

Figure 10.3   The effect of an increase in training

The original situation equates to variant training 0. The situation with increased training corresponds to variant training 1. The graph shows that the productivity curve moves up much further than the wage curve. This would imply that training improves the productivity–wage ratio for older workers.

One implicit assumption made is that the increase in training is spread out evenly over all age groups. Because of the nature of the data (no information on training participation per age group), it is not possible directly to test the separate effect of increasing training for older workers. A more indirect test using training participation by the share of older workers in the regression for productivity does not indicate that the effect of training older workers is less than the effect of training younger groups. Thus increasing the participation of older workers in training would play an important role in keeping them employed, particularly since older workers are underrepresented in training and training improves their (unfavourable) productivity–wage ratio.

Finally, it is important to make a few further remarks on some of the assumptions made in the analysis used above.

1. We have not taken into account the costs of training.
2. The relation between training participation and productivity and wages is measured in one period. For a complete picture, it is necessary to measure the effects in several periods. For example, it is possible that the effects on productivity disappear quickly, while the effects on wages remain.
3. We have assumed that training has an influence on productivity, but it is possible that productivity also influences the training effort. For an example of an analysis which takes into account this interdependency, we refer to De Koning and Gelderblom (1992b). This analysis leads to a similar coefficient for the effect of training on productivity, however.

4.   CONCLUSIONS

In recent years, labour market research has shown an increasing interest in older workers, partly because of the strong growth of early retirement and disability schemes releases. In this chapter we have concentrated on the following questions: Are older workers overrepresented among those receiving disability benefits? Is the productivity–wage ratio unfavourable for older workers? Can training reduce discrepancies between productivity and wages?

Our investigation made use of a large-scale survey of companies. The average wage and productivity level are both separately explained by a number of factors, including the age structure of the workers. The analyses provide positive answers to all the above questions. For example, wages tend to develop along a far flatter curve than productivity. The latter initially rises fast with the years, but beyond a certain age also declines rapidly. Wages also decline beyond a certain age, but less fast. Training is a means of improving the productivity–wage ratio, and in this way training could be effective in reducing the expulsion of older workers from the labour market.

What is the relevance of these findings? Because of the changing age structure of the population, the share of people aged between 55 and 65 years in the potential labour force will increase dramatically in the coming decades. Continuation of the current low participation and activity rates in this age group would have a considerable negative impact on the size of the total labour force. In the Dutch situation, this could lead to structural labour shortages.

Can economic inactivity among people aged between 55 and 65 really be seen as social exclusion? To some extent it can. At least some of the people concerned would have strongly preferred to continue working. In their view, society no longer considers their contribution to be of value. Furthermore, benefit regimes become increasingly unattractive. Many of those in disability schemes end up with low incomes and have virtually no chance of returning to the labour market. Thus preventing inactivity among older workers is extremely important, from both an economic and a social point of view.

NOTES

1. An earlier version of this chapter was presented at the 1992 EALE conference.
2. This section relies on, among others, Oliviera *et al.* (1989).
3. There are two reasons for this. First, learning on the job will automatically take place for the most part at a younger age. Second, the pay-off period is the longer the earlier the investment in training is made.
4. In this text we speak of 'the' contract theory. However, this is a broad category referring to theories dealing with the consequences of (implicit) contracts between employers and employees for the labour market. Only a part of these types of studies dealt with the relationship between age and wages. For examples see Lazear (1984), Oliviera *et al.* (1989) and Parsons (1986).
5. A sort of repeat measurement took place for the 1991 wave. However, the questions asked were less suitable for determining overall productivity per company. Only a very limited number of companies could be included in the analysis, which made the analysis of productivity less interesting.
6. Non-profit-making institutions were asked to give a physical indicator of production, such as the number of patients and the number of clients. Because the survey is repeated among the same companies and institutions it will be possible to calculate a measure for the change in production volume that could be used for analysis. This is a subject for future research.

7. From analyses using the survey of civil servants mentioned before (Gelderblom and De Koning, 1992c), it appears that there are more instruments for improving the performance of older workers, such as increasing mobility and improving management involvement.

BIBLIOGRAPHY

Aarts, L.J.M. and de Jong, P.R. (1990), *Economic aspects of disability behaviour*, Rotterdam.

Akerlof, G. and Yellen, J. (1986), *Efficiency Wage Models of the Labour Market*, Cambridge: Cambridge University Press.

Becker, G.S. (1964), *Human Capital*, Princeton: Princeton University Press.

Bishop, J. (1987), 'The recognition and reward of employee performance', *The Journal of Labor Economics*, 5, 36–56.

Brown, W. and Nolan, P. (1988), 'Wages and labour productivity: the contribution of industrial relations research to the understanding of pay determination', *British Journal of Industrial Relations*, 26, 339–61.

Clark, R.L. and Spengler, J.J. (1980), *The Economics of Individual and Population Ageing*, Cambridge: Cambridge University Press.

Gelderblom, A. and de Koning, J. (1992a), 'Meer-jarig, minder-waardig? Een onderzoek naar de invloed van leeftijd op produktiviteit en beloning' ('More aged, less valued? An inquiry into the influence of age on productivity and wages'), OSA voorstudie V 39, Netherlands Economic Institute, The Hague.

Gelderblom, A. and de Koning, J. (1992b), 'Company training: volume, underinvestment and return', paper for the fourth EALE conference, Warwick, 3–6 September.

Gelderblom, A. and de Koning, J. (1992c), 'Leeftijd en functioneren. Een aanzet voor een beleid bij de rijksoverheid' ('Age and individual performance. A start for a policy in the civil service'), published by the Ministry of Internal Affairs, The Hague.

Jablonsky, M., Rosenblum, L. and Kunze, K. (1988), 'Productivity, age, and labour composition changes in the U.S.', *Monthly Labour Review*, 111(9), 34–8.

Koning, J. de (1991), 'Evaluating Training at the Company Level', paper for the International Conference on the Economics of Training, Cardiff, 23–4 September.

Lazear, E. (1976), 'Age, experience and wage growth', *American Economic Review*, 66(4), 548–58.

Lazear, E.P. (1981), 'Agency, earnings profiles, productivity, and hours restrictions', *American Economic Review*, 71(4), 606–20.

Lazear, E.P. (1984), 'Incentives, productivity and labour contracts', *Quarterly Journal of Economics*, 99(2), 275–96.

Medoff, J.L. and Abraham, K.G. (1980), 'Experience, performance, and earnings', *Quarterly Journal of Economics*, 95(3), 703–36.

Medoff, J.L. and Abraham, K.G. (1981), 'Are those paid more really more productive? The case of experience', *The Journal of Human Resources*, 16(2), 186–216.

Meier, E.L. and Kerr, E.A. (1976), 'Capabilities of middle-aged and older workers: a survey of the literature', *Industrial Gerontology*, 3, 147–56.

Oliviera M.M. de, Cohn, E. and Kiker, B.F. (1989), 'Tenure, earnings and productivity', *Oxford Bulletin of Economics and Statistics*, 51(1), 1–14.

Paridon, C.W.A.M. van (1991), 'Hoe produktief is Nederland?' ('How productive is the Netherlands?'), *Economisch Statistische Berichten*, 3821, 830–1.

Parsons, D.O. (1986), 'The Employment Relationship: Job attachment, Work effort and the nature of contracts', in O. Ashenfelher and R. Layard (eds), *Handbook of Labour Economics, Volume 2*, Amsterdam: North Holland.

Ritzen, J.M.M. (1989), 'Market Failure for General Training and Remedies', paper presented at the symposium on Market Failure in Training, Madison, May 11–12.

Rosen, B. and Jerdee, T.H. (1985), *Older Employees, New Roles for Valued Resources*, Homewood, Illinois: Dow Jones-Irwin.

Schwab, D.P. and Heneman, H.G. (1977), 'Effects of age and experience on productivity', *Industrial Gerontology*, 4, 113–17.

Sweetland, J. (1978), *Mid Career Perspectives: The Middle Aged and Older Population*, New York: Work in America Institute.

Winnubst, J.A.W., Schabracq, M.J., Gerrichauzen, J. and Kampermann, A. (eds), (1995), *Arbeid, levensloop en gezondheid* ('Labour, course of life and health'), Utrecht: LEMMA.

11. Training and the transition from work into unemployment

Arie Gelderblom, Pieter van Winden, Ruurd Kunnen, William Praat and Marian de Voogd-Hamelink[1]

1. INTRODUCTION

Education and training are widely regarded as effective weapons in the fight against unemployment, one of the principal social evils facing Europe in the late twentieth century (EU, 1998; OECD, 1997). However, they are only two of a multitude of factors affecting employment, unemployment and the transitions between them. Careful research is therefore needed to determine the net effects of education and training on unemployment and to identify the conditions under which these effects are most favourable.

In terms of labour-market transitions, education and training can contribute to the reduction of unemployment in two ways. They may play a *curative* role by improving the chances of the unemployed finding a job and they may play a *preventive* role by improving the position of those still in work but who are threatened by job loss in the (near) future.

The Netherlands Economic Institute (NEI) has surveyed existing data and studies on the curative role of training in the Netherlands.[2] The available evaluations of training measures for the unemployed run by the Public Employment Service suggest these may have positive, albeit relatively small, effects. In recent years, however, hardly any studies have been carried out in this field and there is a particular lack of studies into the effects of the training of employed workers as a means of preventing unemployment in the later stages of their careers. Some studies relating to other countries show that these types of effects do exist (see, for example, Schömann et al., 1996).

Preventive training deserves the full attention of policy makers and researchers in the field of social and labour market policy. Previous research has demonstrated that unemployment itself, particularly long-term unemployment, becomes an impediment to a return to work (Graafland, 1990; Blanchard and Summers, 1986). Adaptation to changing working conditions and job requirements may be easier for employees than for those not in work. Moreover, unemployment among skilled workers leads to waste of human capital and the costs of reactivating this capital may be relatively high.

The main objective of this chapter is to ascertain whether training measures might reduce the likelihood of workers becoming unemployed. Longitudinal data sets on the Dutch labour market, collected by the Institute for Labour Studies (OSA), provide a launching pad for our investigations.

The OSA–Labour Supply Panel started in April 1985 and was repeated in the autumn of 1986. Since then, between 4000 and 4500 people in about 2000 households have been questioned every two years. One limitation of the data is that members of the sample must be at least 16 years old and not attending formal education or in military service. Non-responding persons or households are replaced in such a way that each *wave* is also a representative cross-sectional sample of the potential labour force in the Netherlands in each year of data collection. About one thousand respondents in the data set were included in the original panel started in 1985. We have used the panel data of the waves of 1994 and 1996.

The OSA–Labour Demand Panel is a database consisting of about 2000 firms and organizations in both the market and public sectors. It started in 1989 and has been repeated every two years. At first only organizations with ten employees or more were included, but in 1995 the minimum size was reduced to five employees. If possible, the same organizations are surveyed in each wave. Non-responding organizations are replaced. Information is collected at individual establishment level. In the case of small firms, the establishment generally coincides with the firm or organization as a whole. This is not usually the case with large firms. For such firms, only the main establishment is included in the survey. This is because it would be too complicated to complete the questionnaire properly for all establishments. Information is provided by the company director or, in the case of larger organizations, by the personnel manager. Our analysis uses data from 1994.

We expect to find a negative relationship between participation in training and the likelihood of a transition from employment to unemployment. Although there are many factors that may affect the chance of becoming unemployed, obsolescence of occupational skills is an important one. This is true for the short term, as shortages of skills may cause decreasing productivity, but also for the long run, as firms' adaptability to changes in the economy may diminish. If a worker's occupational skills are up-to-date, his or her labour market position will be fairly strong, other things being equal.

On the other hand, firms will tend to retain highly trained workers, since they represent valuable human capital.

Our analysis is conducted in two stages. In the first, the background to workers' participation in job-related training and the relation between such participation and the transition from employment to unemployment are examined, using longitudinal data from the OSA–Labour Supply Panel. In the second, the background to firms' training policy and the relation between that policy and the number of dismissals as a proportion of the total workforce of individual firms (forced outflow) are investigated, using the 1995 wave of the Labour Demand Panel.

These two parts of the analysis are intended to be complementary. Analysis of the longitudinal data of the Labour Supply Panel allows us to take into account the employment histories of individuals and to measure precisely the effects of their personal characteristics. The analysis of the training policy of firms, using data from the Labour Demand Panel, seems to be a logical addition to the analysis of workers' training behaviour, as previous research has demonstrated that it may be the organization they are working in that provides strong encouragement to workers to participate in job-related training. Moreover, a number of company characteristics can play a role in the forced outflow of employees.

It must be recognized, however, that these two phases differ in some respects. The first stage involved modelling the behaviour of the various agents, that is individual workers and firms. However, since the behaviour of firms and that of individual workers are obviously connected, workers' personal characteristics are used not only in the analysis of training participation but also in the analysis of firms' training policy, and vice versa, despite the fact that, in the Labour Demand Panel, workers' personal characteristics are measured on an aggregate level, that is at the level of the workforce in each firm. Characteristics of firms as measured in the Labour Supply Panel are treated in the analysis as if they were characteristics of workers.

Finally, it is important to stress again that the analyses at both individual and company level also pay attention to the determinants of training participation. This is also relevant information for the investigation of 'social exclusion'. As will be discussed further below, some types of individuals and some types of firms seem to have easier access to training than others. In other words, there seem to be inequalities in training opportunities between working people. These inequalities may affect the employment opportunities of those who have restricted access to training. In the long run, they may even affect the employment structure of the economy. A clear view on the determinants of training participation can help policy makers in developing measures to spread training effects more evenly.

The analyses of worker participation in training and the effects of training on the transition from employment to unemployment are presented in section 2. The results of firms' training policy and the forced outflow of workers are presented in section 3. Section 4 presents some of the conclusions that might be drawn from the analysis.

2. TRAINING AND THE TRANSITION FROM EMPLOYMENT INTO UNEMPLOYMENT: AN ANALYSIS AT THE INDIVIDUAL LEVEL

Methodology

The aim of section 2 is to examine to what extent training reduces the risk of becoming unemployed through an analysis at the individual level. To this end, we selected a particular group of people who at a certain point in time (in the present research, the survey date of the OSA–Labour Supply Panel 1994) were employed. Next, we examined the risk of a person from this group becoming unemployed within a certain time after the survey date (by 1996, the date of the next OSA labour supply survey). This risk is explained by taking into account the following factors:

- whether or not the person received any training in the period under examination (from 1994 to 1996),
- what training the person received prior to this period,
- initial education and work experience,
- personal characteristics,
- job and company-specific characteristics.

Our hypothesis is that the risk of becoming unemployed declines as more human capital is invested in a person. Human capital is determined by education, training and work experience. In addition, personal characteristics may also play a role. For example, young people are often still looking for a suitable job and are consequently relatively mobile, which may increase their risk of becoming unemployed. The risk may also be higher for older people who, generally speaking, are likely to be perceived by employers as having an unattractive wage–productivity ratio.[3] One characteristic that may be of relevance here is the type of employment contract: people on a temporary contract will probably be at greater risk of becoming unemployed.

In this research report, training is defined as the number of courses taken (c) in the period between the two survey dates. By definition, this number is greater than or equal to 0, and is therefore a *censored* variable. Unemployment (u) is defined as a *dichotomous* variable, which equals 1 if a person has been unemployed for some time in the period in question and 0 if there is no question of unemployment.

In setting up our analyses, training (c) and unemployment (u) are assumed to affect each other. It is further assumed that job-related training has a negative influence on the risk of becoming unemployed and, conversely, that unemployment also influences the number of job-related courses attended: the longer a person is unemployed during a certain period of time, the less the likelihood of his receiving job-related training. Thus the question of whether courses actually do influence the risk of becoming unemployed needs to be determined by means of a simultaneous model:

$$u = \gamma_1 c + \beta_1 x_1 + \varepsilon_1$$

$$c = \gamma_2 u + \beta_2 x_2 + \varepsilon_2,$$

where:

u = unemployed (or not) at any point in the period 1994–6;
c = the number of job-related courses attended in the period 1994–6;
x_1 = other explanatory factors for becoming unemployed;
x_2 = other explanatory factors for the number of courses.

This simultaneous model cannot be estimated with a standard method, as unemployment is a dichotomous variable and course participation a censored variable. However, the model can also be reformulated as follows:

$$u^* = \gamma_1 c^* + \beta_1 x_1 + \varepsilon_1$$
$$u = 1 \text{ if } u^* > 0$$
$$u = 0 \text{ if } u^* < 0$$

$$c^* = \gamma_2 u^* + \beta_2 x_2 + \varepsilon_2$$
$$c = c^* \text{ if } c^* > 0$$
$$c = 0 \text{ if } c^* < 0$$

This model includes latent and continuous variables for course participation and unemployment. It can be estimated by means of a two-stage method as described by Maddala (1983). In the first stage, a PROBIT analysis is performed on the unemployment variable and a TOBIT analysis on the course variable. In both equations all explanatory variables are taken into account (both x_1 and x_2). On the basis of these analyses, forecasts for the latent variables u^* and c^* are calculated. In the second stage, these forecasts are used as explanatory variables in the original equations. One precondition for effective application of this method, however, is that the number of courses can be predicted with some accuracy. Our research will include an examination of whether this condition has been met.

One problem in conducting these analyses is the relatively low number of respondents that became unemployed in the period 1994 to 1996. For this reason, the number of explanatory elements in the equation for unemployment has to be limited. In the following, the equations for the risk of becoming unemployed and for course participation will be estimated separately. Training course participation and unemployment are explained by means of a multivariate analysis. First, course participation between the two survey dates is modelled by means of a TOBIT model. The risk of becoming unemployed during the same period is then estimated by means of a PROBIT analysis. Given the low number of transitions, the number of explanatory variables in the unemployment analysis is kept at a low level. In the first instance, the interdependence of unemployment and training is not explicitly accounted for. Finally, the simultaneous model will be estimated.

Analysis of course participation

Table 11.1 lists the results of a TOBIT analysis of course participation. The variable to be explained, training course participation, is the number of courses followed while being employed in the period 1994–6. About a third of those working in 1994 attended at least one course in the following period. Course participation is explained by taking into account a number of characteristics. Apart from gender, age and highest completed level of initial education, other variables, such as courses attended in the past, type of company and employment contract, home situation and individual unemployment history were included in the analysis.

The results show that gender does not have any influence on course participation. Working women and men seem to have equal opportunities for increasing their level of knowledge by attending courses. A relatively greater number of young people appear to attend courses. The initial education received does not always provide the level of knowledge that is needed for a particular job. Moreover, human capital theory states that the expected pay-off period is long for this group. The level of initial education also influences course participation. It appears that a relatively low number

Table 11.1   Results of TOBIT analysis of the number of job-related courses between 1994 and 1996

Variable	TOBIT	
	Coefficient	t-value
Constant	−1.6228	−5.5
Female	0.1829	1.1
Age under 25	0.1450	0.6
Age between 25 and 34	0.4093	2.5
Age between 35 and 54	ref.	ref.
Age 55+	−1.0754	−3.2
Primary education	−0.4739	−1.8
Lower vocational education	0.0569	0.3
Lower general secondary education	0.1556	0.7
Secondary vocational education	ref.	ref.
Upper general secondary education/pre-university education	0.1532	0.6
Higher professional education/university education	−0.0179	−0.1
Modern apprenticeship	0.2626	1.0
Number of courses attended before 1994	0.1723	6.8
Number of job-related courses attended in period between 1992 and 1994	0.1221	1.4
Organization encourages job-related training	0.5908	3.8
Civil servant	0.2667	1.5
Self-employed	−0.8646	−2.6
Company with fewer than 10 employees	−0.4768	−2.1
Elementary and lower professions	−0.6547	−4.1
Temporary contract	0.4744	1.1
Second job	−0.6883	−2.5
Working more than 35 hours per week	0.5535	3.2
Number of months worked with the same employer in 1994	−0.0019	−2.5
Unemployed at some point in period between 1992 and 1994	0.1676	0.2
Unemployed at some point in period between 1994 and 1996	−0.7341	−2.0
Variance	5.0747	16.4
Number of observations	2001	

of people with primary education attend courses. Differences between the other types of initial education seem to have little effect on course participation.

The more courses workers have attended in the past, the more they are likely to attend in the future. Our results show that the number of courses attended in the period before 1994 had a major effect on course participation between 1994 and 1996. Apparently course participation has a self-reinforcing effect. This is in line with the so-called 'accumulation hypothesis', which states that continuing training is concentrated on a specific group who gradually build up more human capital. An overview of studies confirming this hypothesis can be found in Tuijnman and Schömann (1996). It is also possible, however, that a person's training history is an indicator of unobserved factors which continue to influence course participation. Encouragement by the employer also leads to higher course participation.

Being a civil servant has a positive effect on course attendance, while self-employment has a negative effect. Relatively few people working in lower positions and people doing additional subsidized work[4] participate in courses. Participation by part-timers is also lower. Employees who had been working in a company in 1994 also attended courses less often. The age factor might again play a role here.

In other variants of the equation, company training policy was included as an explanatory factor. However, this variable did not have a significant effect on course participation. Further research showed that the partial connection between company policy and course participation is also weak.

The analysis shows that workers who were unemployed at some time during the period under investigation took fewer training courses than those who were in unemployment throughout the period. This suggests that unemployment spells reduce the likelihood of attending courses. However, there may also be a technical explanation for this result. By definition, a person cannot take a job-related course during a period of unemployment. This partially explains the negative effect of the unemployment variable on the course variable. In the next section, in which a simultaneous model is estimated, the interdependence of unemployment and course participation is taken into account.

Despite the significance of many of the explanatory factors, the overall explanatory force of the equation is relatively small. About 650 of the respondents in the random test had attended a course at some point between 1994 and 1996. However, the forecast of training participation is positive for only 177 individuals in this group.[5] In a later stage, the relatively low predictive power of the model will be discussed in more detail.

From work to unemployment
The risk of becoming unemployed has been analysed by means of a PROBIT model (see Table 11.1). Apart from data relating to gender, age and the highest completed level of initial education, variables relating to course participation, employing organization, type of contract, home situation and individual unemployment histories were included.

Table 11.2   The risk of becoming unemployed between 1994 and 1996

Variable	Coefficient	t-value
Constant	−1.7026	−7.9
Female	0.2147	1.8
Age under 25	−0.3636	−1.7
Age between 25 and 34	0.0278	0.2
Age between 35 and 54	ref.	ref.
Age 55+	−0.4141	−1.1
Primary education	−0.0264	−0.1
Employed in a private company	0.4422	2.6
Company with fewer than 10 employees	0.1834	1.3
Permanent contract	−0.5258	−3.5
Number of months worked with same employer in 1994	−0.0015	−2.0
Single	0.2192	1.5
Unemployed at some time in period between 1992 and 1994	0.4759	2.3
Number of job-related courses attended in period between 1992 and 1994	−0.0599	−0.7
Number of courses attended in period between 1994 and 1996	−0.1274	−1.7
Number of observations	1972	

Table 11.2 shows that female employees are more likely to become unemployed than male employees. Young workers below age 25 have a relatively small risk of becoming unemployed, although the difference between this group and the over-55s is not significant. Education does not seem to have much influence on the risk of becoming unemployed. Owing to the limited number of transitions and the insignificance of the education variables, these variables have not been included in the final analysis.

Course participation reduces the risk of becoming unemployed. For courses taken before 1994, however, the negative sign is not statistically significant. The result for courses taken between 1994 and 1996 is stronger. This result seems to confirm the research hypothesis: course participation reduces the risk of becoming unemployed. A simultaneous analysis, in which course participation in 1994 and 1996 is partially explained by the unemployment rate in this period, would be necessary to confirm this hypothesis.

Those working in private companies have less job security than civil servants and the self-employed. The risk for single people is also relatively high. As might be expected, individuals on permanent contracts run less risk of becoming unemployed. The same is true for people who have been working for the same employer for a long time. Moreover, the risk of becoming unemployed is partly determined by a person's unemployment history over the previous two years.[6]

Towards a Simultaneous Model

The analysis presented above shows that job-related training reduces the risk of becoming unemployed. A problem with this analysis, however, is that the causal connection might also be reversed. In this section, a model is estimated in which account is taken of the mutual influence of unemployment and course participation. To this end, training course participation was remodelled and the forecasts of the number of courses incorporated into the unemployment model. Table 11.3 presents the results of the simultaneous analysis. The analysis indicates that course participation does not have a significant influence on the risk of becoming unemployed.

Statistical arguments probably play an important role here. Earlier analyses showed that course participation can be only partially explained. The forecasts of the number of courses included in the equation are

Table 11.3   Influence of job-related courses on the risk of becoming unemployed between 1994 and 1996, in a simultaneous model

Variable	Coefficient	t-value
Constant	−1.6680	−7.4
Female	0.2418	2.0
Age under 25	−0.3600	−1.7
Age between 25 and 34	−0.0124	−0.1
Age between 35 and 54	ref.	ref.
Age 55+	−0.2676	−0.7
Primary education	0.0612	0.3
Employed at a private company	0.4839	2.9
Company with fewer than 10 employees	0.2999	1.8
Permanent contract	−0.6064	−3.8
Number of months worked with same employer in 1994	−0.0014	−1.8
Single	0.1924	1.3
Unemployed at some time in period between 1992 and 1994	0.4365	2.1
Number of job-related courses attended in period between 1992 and 1994	−0.1304	−1.4
Forecast of number of job-related courses attended in period between 1994 and 1996	0.0828	0.9
Number of observations	1972	

consequently inaccurate. Furthermore, a partial analysis shows that the forecasted number of courses bears little relation to the risk of becoming unemployed. There is a significant relation, however, between the forecasts and the other explanatory factors in Table 11.3. The small number of transitions from work to unemployment may also influence the results. Thus, on the basis of the available data, it is not really possible to draw up a simultaneous model that takes account of the interdependence of training and unemployment.

This conclusion does not change if the job-related courses are further differentiated. We have carried out some analyses in which employer-subsidized courses were distinguished from other courses. Opportunities for making distinctions according to the length or significance of training are limited.

The problem of mutual causality does not play a role if we examine the effect of courses taken in the two years prior to 1994 on the risk of unemployment between 1994 and 1996. Table 11.4 presents the results of such an analysis. These show that previous job-related training also fails to have a significant influence on the risk of becoming unemployed. The minus sign of the coefficient of this variable, however, is as we expected.

Table 11.4   Influence of job-related courses in the past on the risk of becoming unemployed between 1994 and 1996

Variable	Coefficient	t-value
Constant	-1.7562	-8.3
Female	0.2233	1.9
Age under 25	-0.3714	-1.7
Age between 25 and 34	0.0177	0.1
Age between 35 and 54	ref.	ref.
Age 55+	-0.3776	-1.0
Primary education	-0.0125	-0.1
Employed in a private company	0.4547	2.7
Company with fewer than 10 employees	0.2118	1.5
Permanent contract	-0.5439	-3.7
Number of months worked with same employer in 1994	-0.0015	-2.0
Single	0.2025	1.4
Unemployed at some time in period between 1992 and 1994	0.4549	2.2
Number of job-related courses attended in period between 1992 and 1994	-0.0871	-1.0
Number of observations	1972	

3. COMPANY TRAINING POLICY AND THE FORCED OUTFLOW OF WORKERS

This chapter focuses on the relationship between training and unemployment. In section 2, this relationship was examined at individual worker level; here it is the behaviour of firms that is investigated. Two aspects of that behaviour are examined.

1. Earlier research indicates that an active employer training policy has a strong stimulating effect on employee participation in training (Kunnen and de Voogd-Hamelink, 1997). This was confirmed in section 2. In this respect, training policy is more important than the characteristics of the workers themselves and of their jobs. However, the motives of firms in pursuing a training policy are supposed to be different from those of the employees who participate. Training policy and the intensity of companies' training effort are analysed below.
2. Dismissal is one cause of unemployment. The number of dismissals as a proportion of a firm's total workforce is called the *forced outflow*. The forced outflow is distinguished from the involuntary outflow, because the former does not include the outflow of ill or disabled workers. We are interested in ascertaining whether the forced outflow is smaller in training-intensive firms than in less training-intensive firms. This is investigated later.

Company Training Policy and Training Intensity

Hypotheses
We hypothesize that firms' training policies are intended to enhance the occupational skill of the workforce and the ability of workers to adapt to technological and organizational change. For firms, training can be considered as an investment in human capital intended to increase productivity and improve quality (Mincer, 1958; Becker, 1964).

In human capital theory, an important distinction is made between general and firm-specific training. General training is supposed to be profitable for individual workers, because it strengthens their position in the external labour market. Firm-specific training, on the other hand, does not improve workers' position in the external market. For these reasons the worker pays the costs of the general training and the firm pays for specific training. However, our data set does not contain any direct information on whether the training was general or specific, so in our analyses we will not make this distinction. There is also a theoretical reason for not doing so, however. In our opinion, the distinction between general and firm-specific training is not so clear. In fact, firm-specific training often contains elements that are broadly applicable outside the firm (Hövels and Van den Berg, 1992). On the other hand, general skills always have to be made specific before they can be used in the context of an actual firm (Moerkamp, 1991, 1996).

It is assumed that companies providing training expect positive rates of return. Thus a firm's training policy will be related to the characteristics of its workforce: if the personnel is relatively young, if there are more men than women and relatively few temporary and part-time workers, firms will tend to expect relatively high rates of return from training and their investment in training will therefore tend to be greater. In these cases the expected pay-off period of the investment is expected to be longer.[7] Training policy can be further encouraged by external constraints, such as an insufficient supply of skilled employees in the labour market.

However, the attitude of many companies towards training is ambivalent. On the one hand, they realize that training is a useful and profitable investment in human capital; on the other, they fear that trained workers may use their enhanced labour market position to seek more highly paid jobs in other companies. This leads us to the central research questions of this section.

The first hypothesis is that *company training policy will be less active the greater the voluntary outflow of workers* (H_1). This hypothesis will be rejected if our analysis does not reveal a significant and negative relation between the training effort and the voluntary outflow. If a significant and positive relation is found, the hypothesis that *voluntary outflow increases with company training effort* (H_0) will be confirmed. With this hypothesis, it is explicitly assumed, for theoretical reasons, that voluntary outflow depends on the training effort, in contravention of the model analysed.[8] If this H_0 hypothesis is confirmed, there are probably companies recruiting employees trained by other firms that are not doing much training of their own. Thus we expect to find *a negative relation between the inflow of newly hired workers and company training effort* (H_2) if H_0 is true ('train or buy').

It might be expected that a lot of firms would take countermeasures to prevent the outflow of recently trained workers. Examples of such measures are an obligation on workers to pay back the training costs to the employer if they leave the company after a short time and the linking of training to career development within the firm. In fact, the existence of training opportunities may attract workers in the first place. Linking training to career development may make it attractive for workers to stay with the firm. The third hypothesis is that *internal labour markets and firm-based training are often related to each other* (H_3).

Model

In most research on training by firms, the number of employees taking training courses is used as a measure of training policy. This measure is somewhat superficial, as it says nothing about the training courses themselves. What is needed is information on the amount of money spent on training, but the Labour Demand Panel does not provide reliable data on expenditure. However, the data set does contain other relevant information, which we will use to construct a dependent variable that is somewhat more sophisticated than simply the number of participants.

Firstly, a distinction can be made between training courses taken on the initiative of the employer/firm and those taken at the employee's initiative. Research on labour market problems in Dutch municipalities (Taes *et al.*, 1992) has demonstrated that management and workforce sometimes differ in their perception of the quality of the link between workers' competencies and those required by the organization, that is, the link between education/training and work. This may be because management evaluates this link with an eye to future developments, while workers are concerned mainly with the status quo. However, it is not known how each kind of initiative should be weighted. Indeed, the weighting may differ by type of firm. In traditionally organized firms, the employer's initiative is the more important indicator of training policy; in so-called *learning organizations*, on the other hand, employer's and employee's initiative may be equally relevant.

We have analysed several models. In the first one, a weighting of 3 is attached to courses taken on the employer's initiative, a weighting of 1 to courses taken on the employee's initiative and a weighting of 2 if the initiative was a joint one. In the second model, these weightings are $2\frac{1}{2}$, $1\frac{1}{2}$ and 2, respectively, while in the third they are all the same (1). The models with the same weightings were found to have the highest rate of explained variance and the best fit. The structure of the explanatory variables was very similar in the different models. For these reasons, we decided to attach equal weight to employee's and employer's initiative, so this variable was not used in our analyses.

Secondly, the data set contains information on the number of working hours spent on training. This information will be used in the following analyses, because it seems to be an additional indicator of company training effort. Although the number of cases on this item decreased somewhat because of non-responses, the rate of explained variance and the goodness of fit increased.

No distinction is made in our analyses between internal and external training courses. The reason is that we do not know whether these types of courses represent different training policy measures and, if so, how big these differences are. The greater the supply of firm-specific courses from professional training providers is, the more efficient it may be for companies to externalize their training policy. This does not necessarily mean that training policy becomes less active.

In the following analyses we make use of the indicator of company training intensity S_i:

$S_i = (Dic_i + Dec_i - Deic_i) * 1/L_i * Wd_i/Dc_i = Wd_i/L_i$, where
Dec = number of employees taking external training courses in 1994,
Dic = number of employees taking internal training courses in 1994,
$Deic$ = number of employees taking internal and external training courses in 1994,
Dc = $Dec + Dic - Deic$ = number of employees taking courses in 1994,
Wd = number of working days spent on taking training courses in 1994,
L = number of employees in 1994.

Actually S_i is a conditional variable, because firms first need to develop a training policy before they can make more or less intensive use of it. It is assumed that the considerations underlying the decision to develop a training policy are different from those influencing the decision to make use of the policy. The latter decision is probably linked to short-term economic fluctuations, while the former may be related to structural factors.

The data set provides no direct information on the existence of a training policy. For about 10 per cent of the organizations in the analysis the value of S_i is zero. These organizations (firms) may include those that do not have a training policy, as well as those that may not have made use of the training facilities in the period examined (1994). To test our supposition that two separate decisions are involved, two analyses were conducted: (a) an estimation of the probability that a training policy exists in all firms ($S_i = 1$ or 0); (b) an explanation of training intensity in firms that have a training policy ($S_i > 0$).

Results
The results of the analysis (Table 11.5) show that the explanatory structures of the models are not identical. Existence of training policy and intensity of training have significant relations with different variables. Sometimes they relate significantly to the same variables, but with opposite signs. These results support our hypothesis that the decision to develop a training policy is taken, in part, for reasons other than those underlying the decision to make use of it. The use of two separate models is thereby legitimated.

This section focuses on the relationship between training policy and training intensity, on the one hand, and flows of workers, on the other.

Table 11.5   *Presence of training policy and intensity of training in firms*

	Model (a) training policy (probit)	Model (b) training intensity (tobit)
1. Flows of workers		
% voluntary outflow	−0.11	1.24*z*
% internal mobility	5.15*s*	0.45
% inflow	0.31	−0.90*z*
2. Characteristics of the workforce		
% under 30 years of age	0.31	0.07
% between 30 and 39 years of age	ref.	ref.
% over 40 years of age	−0.11	−0.20
Level of education		
academic or higher vocational	0.36	−0.74*
upper secondary or secondary vocational	ref.	ref.
basic, lower vocational or lower secondary	−0.84*s*	−0.45*
Part-time factor	−0.47	1.11*
% temporary workers	−0.77	0.39
% female workers	−0.46*	−0.07
3. Technology		
New technology introduced in 1994	−0.05	0.42*s*
Rate of innovation (newest →totally obsolete)	−0.09*z*	−0.15*
Indicator R&D products and services	0.50*	−0.07
Indicator R&D production process	−0.50*m*	0.35
4. Organization		
Outsourcing of activities during the last 2 years	−0.08	−0.01
Average settling in time for new employees	0.10*z*	0.29*s*
Number of executives	0.02	1.61*
Number of hierarchical levels	0.25*s*	0.08
HRM department or HRM functionary present	−0.04	−0.02
Log(size) (number of employees)	0.39	0.09
Squared log(size)	−0.02	−0.02
Sensitivity to market fluctuations	−1.08*	0.58*z*
Sensitivity to market*log(size)	0.41*s*	−0.09
Sector		
manufacturing	ref.	ref.
commercial services	0.24*	0.15
non-commercial services	0.73*s*	0.91*s*
5. Labour market		
Undermanning as a consequence of labour-market		
shortages	0.03	0.42*z*
% hard-to-fill vacancies	−0.88	−5.41*

Table 11.5 (continued)

	Model (a) training policy (probit)	Model (b) training intensity (tobit)
6. Reorganization of firms		
Change of position in larger organization coupled with:		
expansion of the labour force	0.50	0.29
reduction and dismissal	0.18	1.89s
reallocation of employees within the firm	−0.28	−0.55z
training of workers	−0.12	0.16
Internal reorganization coupled with:		
expansion of the labour force	0.54*	0.32*
reduction and dismissal	−0.07	−0.48*
reallocation of employees within the firm	−0.50*	0.41*
training of workers	0.67*	−0.05
Constant	−0.05	−0.52

Notes: s = very significant ($p < 0.01$); * = significant ($0.01 < p < 0.05$); m = moderately significant ($0.05 < p < 0.10$); z = weakly significant ($0.10 < p < 0.20$).

Many other variables, such as workforce characteristics, the jobs and the environment of the firm, are of relevance in explaining training, however, and they have been included in both models.

Our main interest is the relationship between worker flows and training. The other variables have been included primarily to make a multivariate analysis possible, that is in order to make a reliable estimate of the probability that a training policy will occur and of the intensity of that policy, if present. The results are discussed first with regard to the hypotheses formulated in the preceding section and then some other interesting outcomes are reviewed.

Presence of training policy is strongly related to the percentage of workers changing jobs within the firm (internal mobility). This indicates that internal labour markets and company-based training policy often go together. Hypothesis H_3 is confirmed.

The analyses do not show a clear relationship between the presence of a training policy and the inflow and voluntary outflow of workers. These variables are probably less structural than the internal labour market.

A large voluntary outflow is associated with high intensity of training, although the relationship is hardly significant. Since we do not find a significant and negative relationship, hypothesis H_1, that firms will be discouraged from training their workforce when the voluntary outflow is high, has to be rejected.

However, there are reasons to confirm the hypothesis that a high training intensity encourages workers to quit for a better paid job elsewhere (H_0). Firstly, the relation between training intensity and voluntary outflow is positive and (weakly) significant. Secondly, the larger the inflow of newly hired workers is, the less intensive the training in the firm becomes. The latter can be seen as an indication that companies that do not train their own employees recruit trained employees from other firms.

It seems that employers who are ambivalent towards training because they fear that the trained workers will quit are, to some extent, justified in their views. However, this is more a matter of attitude than of behaviour, because a high voluntary outflow does not in practice prevent firms from training. Moreover, those employers who rely on the internal labour market to retain trained employees also seem to be justified.

Some remarks on the question of causality are apposite here. Firstly, the question of causality may not be considered to have been answered satisfactorily because no information on the sequence of events has been used. What we do have information on is training intensity and the outflow of workers in the year 1994. A solution to this problem might be found by analysing panel data from different years, so that the outflow in year x can be explained by the training in year $x - 1$. This may be a topic for further research.

Secondly, there may be a relationship between training intensity and voluntary outflow, but that does not necessarily mean that voluntary outflow is high because the workers who quit have just enhanced their occupational competencies by training. Why would employers continue training if that were the case? Another explanation may be that, where training intensity is relatively high, it is the workers who have not taken training courses who have to quit. Some selection mechanism may have been operating, ensuring that workers who do not fit well into the organizational structure seek and find a better job elsewhere.

The age composition of the workforce does not seem to have much influence on training policy and training intensity. Although the coefficients have the expected signs, the relations lack statistical significance. The much-touted theory that it is not profitable for firms to train older workers is not supported by the data. The theory cannot be rejected either, however, because it is possible that the training in firms with a relatively old workforce may benefit the younger employees most.

As far as educational attainment is concerned, it appears that firms with a large share of workers with low educational attainment are more likely not to have a training policy. In those firms that do have a training policy, training intensity is lower when the workforce is relatively ill-educated and, conversely, when it is more highly-educated than in firms where a majority of the workforce has completed secondary education (craft training). Firms with a highly feminized workforce often do not have a training policy, but, in those that do, training is no less intensive than in firms with a more male-dominated workforce. The results of the analyses on the influence of age and gender confirm the results found by Kunnen and De Voogd-Hamelink (1997).

We expected to find that a high proportion of part-time workers would have an adverse impact on training intensity. A part-time factor is included in the analyses. This factor indicates the number of part-time workers in the total number of full-time equivalents. The larger the part-time factor (maximum 1), the smaller the proportion of part-time workers. There is no significant relation to the presence of a training policy. The part-time factor relates positively to training intensity; that is, the lower the number of part-time workers, the more intensive the training, which is in accordance with our expectations.

We expected technologically innovative firms to pursue an intensive training policy. To test this hypothesis, four variables were included: the introduction of a technological innovation in 1994, the rate of innovation (evaluation of the present production techniques on a five-point scale from newest to totally obsolete), the proportion of R&D related to product innovation and the proportion of R&D related to process innovation. The analyses show that firms with more modern equipment at their disposal than other firms in the same industry are more likely both to have developed a training policy and to have a more intensive training policy. There is no link between the mere existence of a training policy and the recent introduction of a new technology. However, if a training policy is in place, a new technology has an intensifying effect.

Organizations that devote a relatively high share of their R&D budget to the development of new products are fairly likely to have a training policy. R&D expenditure on the production process has a negative effect, however. This may be connected to the employment effects of R&D. While most R&D expenditure related to process innovations has labour-saving effects, R&D expenditure on new product development leads more often to the creation of new jobs (Reijnen and Kleinknecht, 1992; Brouwer and Kleinknecht, 1994).

We also expect to find that organizations introducing organizational innovations into the production process pursue an intensive training policy. Thus several indicators have been included in the models. Neither 'outsourcing', a characteristic of *lean production*, nor flat organizational structures appear to encourage the development of a training policy. The probability of developing a training policy would even seem to increase with the number of hierarchical levels: the more managerial staff there are, the more intensive the training. This may be explained by the fact that executives are generally overrepresentated in training courses (Gelderblom and De Koning, 1992).

Every newcomer in a company needs time to adjust. The more complex the organization, the longer this so-called 'settling-in period' usually is. The length of the settling-in period is also often considered as an indication of additional human capital built up within the firm. The average length of the settling-in period seems to have a weak effect on the presence of training policy, but relates clearly to intensity. This seems to confirm that training can play a role in building up human capital during the settling-in period.

The probability that a firm has a training policy depends on the number of employees. Table 11.5 shows a parabolic relationship to training intensity which reaches a maximum at about ten employees. It seems that firms with more than ten employees profit from economies of scale: as a result of efficiency gains, a less intensive training policy has the same effects.

The fifth group of variables in Table 11.5 relates to the effects of the labour market on training policy. These effects appear to be moderate. Small companies that are sensitive to market fluctuations are less likely to abandon their training policy than larger firms.

Finally, a couple of variables related to reorganizations have been included for analytical reasons. It turns out that internal reorganizations have a stronger impact on training and training policy than a change of position within the larger organization to which the firm belongs.

Training and Forced Outflow of Workers

The main question to be addressed here is whether job-related training can prevent employees becoming unemployed. We focus on the relationship between company training policy and dismissals, that is the forced outflow. We will test the hypothesis that *the forced outflow of workers is smaller the more intensive company training is*. The theoretical basis for this hypothesis is that an employer who has made an investment in training will seek to maximize the return on that training and will therefore try to retain the employees who have taken training courses. Moreover, as training should have reduced mismatches between workers' occupational competencies and the qualifications and competencies required in jobs, dismissals for reasons of skill gaps should no longer be necessary. However, there may be other reasons that make dismissals unavoidable. In the following multivariate analysis reorganizations will be taken into account. Workforce characteristics,

*Table 11.6   Explanation of the forced outflow of workers
            (tobit-regression)*

1. Flows of workers	
% voluntary outflow	0.04
% internal mobility	0.17*s*
2. Characteristics of the workforce	
% under 30 years of age	−0.03
% 40+ years of age	−0.08*
Level of education	
academic or higher vocational	0.00
upper secondary or secondary vocational	ref.
basic, lower vocational or lower secondary	0.01
Part-time factor	0.07*z*
% temporary workers	0.06
% female workers	0.03
3. Organization	
Outsourcing of activities during the last 2 years	0.01
Average settling-in time	0.02*
Number of executives	0.00
Number of hierarchical levels	0.00
HRM department or HRM functionary present	0.01
Log(size) (number of employees)	0.09*s*
Squared log(size)	−0.01*s*
Sensitivity to market fluctuations	0.09*
Sensitivity to market*log(size)	−0.01*
Sector	
manufacturing	ref.
commercial services	0.00
non-commercial services	−0.00
4. Labour market	
Undermanning as a consequence of labour-market shortages	0.04*m*
% hard-to-fill vacancies	−0.47*m*
5. Reorganization of firms	
Change of position in larger organization coupled with:	
expansion of the labour force	0.03
reduction and dismissal	0.19*s*
reallocation of employees within the firm	−0.01
training of workers	−0.01

Table 11.6 (continued)

Internal reorganization coupled with:	
expansion of the labour force	0.02m
reduction and dismissal	0.07s
reallocation of employees within the firm	0.03*
training of workers	−0.04
6. Intensity of training (S_i)	−0.05s
Constant	−0.38s

Note: s = very significant ($p<0.01$); * = significant ($0.01<p<0.05$); m = moderately significant ($0.05<p<0.10$); z = weakly significant ($0.10<p<0.20$).

technological and organizational innovations (which may be labour-saving) and the labour market will also be included.

In contrast to the analyses in the preceding section, no distinction is made between the presence of a training policy and training intensity. In other words: $S_i \geq 0$. The results are shown in Table 11.6.

Two models were tested. In the first, the firms' profits in 1994 are taken into account; in the other, profits are excluded. Inclusion of the profits variable led to a decrease in the number of cases as a consequence of non-response to this part of the questionnaire. The goodness of fit also deteriorated. Unexpectedly, the effect of profit per head on forced outflow appeared to be very weak. For that reason, only the model excluding profits is presented.[9]

The most important finding is that training intensity is significantly and negatively related to the forced outflow: the more intensive the training policy, the lower the number of dismissals. Thus the main question addressed in this section can be answered affirmatively.

The analysis produced other results worth mentioning. It is noticeable that in firms with a relatively old workforce the forced outflow is relatively small, even though older and, possibly, less productive workers might be expected to be at greater risk of becoming unemployed than younger ones. Maybe the relationship between age and productivity is less self-evident than is often thought. However, it could be that the less productive older workers have departed, not via dismissals, but through other channels, for instance the social security system. Another explanation may be that forced outflow among younger workers is also high, as a consequence of the adaptation process school leavers usually go through.

Another noteworthy result is the positive relation between the number of in-firm job changers and the forced outflow (dismissals). At first glance, it seems contradictory that, the more workers change jobs within the firm, the larger the number of dismissals. Probably, the workers who change job are not those who are fired. A possible explanation may be workforce segmentation. Some workers form part of the core workforce, enjoying well-paid, secure jobs with good career prospects, while others have a more precarious or, from the firm's perspective, more flexible employment relationship.

The average settling-in time is a customary indicator of the human capital of the firm. The longer the average settling-in time, the larger the forced outflow. This is a striking result for which there is no obvious explanation. Further research is required. The relation between organizational size and forced outflow is parabolic, with a maximum at 90 employees. In large firms that are sensitive to market fluctuations, forced outflow is relatively small, while in small firms sensitivity to market fluctuations seems to stimulate forced outflow. Finally, in-firm reorganizations coupled with an expansion of the workforce seem to lead to a larger forced outflow. It is likely that many reorganizations require an adjustment of the total composition of the workforce that cannot be achieved solely through in-firm reallocations and training measures and makes forced outflows inevitable.

4. CONCLUSION AND COMMENT

Expectations of the role of company training are often high. There are good reasons why this should be so. Chapter 10 in the present volume shows, for example, that it increases productivity. It is also a largely self-regulating labour market instrument, with only limited state intervention, which increases its attractiveness. However, less is known about its role in tackling problems of social exclusion and individual transitions in the labour market. The central question this chapter has sought to address is whether training can reduce the risk of unemployment.

Our analyses do not provide a definite answer. On the one hand, our analyses of individual behaviour do not, ultimately, show any significant relation between the number of job-related courses taken in 1994–6 or in 1992–4 and the probability of workers becoming unemployed in 1994–6. The coefficients have the expected signs in most cases, but are not statistically significant. This result may be due in part to the small number of transitions in the database.

The analysis of the effects of company training policy, on the other hand, clearly shows that the more intensive the training policy is, the smaller the number of dismissals becomes.

For the moment, there do not seem to be sufficient grounds for answering our research question in the negative. The role of company training in preventing unemployment is, therefore, still open to further research. However, another of our findings is relevant to the issue of social exclusion. Some categories of workers were found to have more access to training than others. Thus older workers, those with low educational attainment and those in second jobs participate less than others. Moreover, those who have participated in the past are more likely to attend training courses in the future. Thus some workers seem to embark on a process of lifelong learning, while others are excluded from training opportunities that might improve their labour market position. Policies designed to encourage company training should pay special attention to these groups.

NOTES

1. Thanks are due to Dr J. de Koning and Dr M.A. van der Ende who contributed to the methodology and data-processing, respectively.
2. See Chapter 6 of this volume. An extended version of this chapter can be found in De Koning (1998).
3. This issue of the position of older workers is examined in greater detail in Chapter 10 of this book.
4. Additional subsidized work means that they work in a job which is created in order to give the unemployed work experience. 'Additional' refers to the fact that the subsidized job should not substitute or displace allready existing jobs. These jobs are subsidized in the framework of labour market policy schemes.
5. The TOBIT analysis is used here. We assert that the model forecasts course participation if, according to the model, the chance of participation is higher than 0.5.
6. This is sometimes referred to as hysteresis. A detailed discussion of hysteresis can be found in Graafland (1990).
7. To what extent this really is the case for the groups mentioned remains to be seen. For example, young people have indeed many working years ahead of them, but also a higher tendency than older workers to leave to work for another employer.
8. One method of testing hypotheses H_0 and H_1 might be to use a model in which voluntary outflow and training policy are each separately explained. In that case, hypotheses H_0 and H_1 do not have to be mutually exclusive. Another option would be to analyse more carefully the time sequence of voluntary outflow and training by using panel data, thereby gaining some insight into causality. However, we will not go so far in this section.
9. These types of relations could be tested in greater detail in a longitudinal framework, because there can be time lags in the effects of profits.

BIBLIOGRAPHY

Barrett, Alan and O'Connell, Philip J. (1998), 'Does training generally work? The returns on in-company-training', Discussion Paper No. 1879, Centre for Economic Policy Research, London.
Becker, Gary S. (1964), *Human Capital. A Theoretical and Empirical Analysis, with Special Reference to Education*, Princeton: Princeton University Press.

Bernasco, W., de Voogd-Hamelink, A.M., Vosse, J.P.M. and Wetzels, C.M.M.P. (1998), *Trendrapport Vraag naar arbeid 1998 (Trendreport Labour Demand 1998)*, Tilburg: Institute for Labour Studies (OSA).

Blanchard, O.J. and Summers, L.H. (1986), 'Hysteresis and the European unemployment problem', in Stanley Fischer (ed.), *NBER Macroeconomic Annual*, vol. 1, Cambridge, Mass.: MIT Press, pp. 15–18.

Brouwer, N.M. and Kleinknecht, A.H. (1994), 'Technologie, werkgelegenheid, winsten en lonen in Nederlandse bedrijven (Technology, employment, profits and wages in Dutch companies)', OSA, W114, The Hague

EU (1998), 'The 1998 Employment Guidelines', Council Resolution of 15 December 1997.

Gelderblom, A. and de Koning, J. (1992), 'Meer-jarig, minder-waardig? (More aged, less valued? An inquiry into the influence of age on wages and productivity)', voorstudie V 39, OSA: The Hague.

Graafland, J.J. (1990), 'Persistent Unemployment, Wages and Hysteresis', VU dissertation, Amsterdam.

Hövels, B. and van den Berg, J. (1992), *Beroepsonderwijs in de grafische industrie (Vocational education in the printing trade)*, Nijmegen: ITS.

Koning, J. de (1998), 'Training for the unemployed in the Netherlands: what do we know after more than 50 evaluation studies?', NEI working paper 1998/2.

Kunnen, R. and de Voogd-Hamelink, M. (1997), 'Scholingsgedrag in Nederland 1986–1992 (Training behaviour in the Netherlands 1986–1992)', OSA-W153, The Hague.

Kunnen, R., Praat, W.C.M., de Voogd-Hamelink, A.M. and Wetzels, C.M.M.P. (1997), 'Trendrapport Aanbod van arbeid 1997 (Trend Report Labour Supply 1997)', OSA-rapport nr. 25, The Hague.

Maddala, G.S. (1983), *Limited Dependent and Qualitative Variables in Econometrics*, Cambridge: Cambridge University Press.

Mincer, Jacob (1958), 'Investment in Human Capital and Personal Income Distribution', *Journal of Political Economy*, 66, 281–303.

Moerkamp, T. (1991), 'Leren voor een loopbaan (Education for a career)', OSA-W92, The Hague.

Moerkamp, T. (1996), 'Transitievaardigheden en transfer in de beroepsloopbaan (Transitional skills and transfer during the professional career)', OSA-W140, The Hague.

OECD (1997), 'Meeting of the employment, labour and social affairs committee at ministerial level', Paris.

Reijnen, M. and Kleinknecht A.H. (1992), 'Technologie en de vraag naar arbeid (Technology and the demand for labour)', OSA, W107, The Hague.

Schömann, K., Becker, R. and Zühlke, S. (1996), 'Further education and occupational careers in East Germany', paper, July.

Taes, C.G.J., Allaart, P.A. and Kunnen, R. (1992), 'De gemeentelijke arbeidsmarkt (The labour market of municipalities)', A&O-fonds, sectie gemeenten, The Hague.

Tuijnman, A.C. and Schömann, K. (1996), 'Life-long Learning and Skill Formation', in G. Schmid, J. O'Reilly and K. Schömann (eds), *International Handbook for Labour Market Policy and Evaluation*, Cheltenham, UK and Brookfield, US: Edward Elgar, pp. 462–88.

12. Does enterprise-sponsored training aggravate or alleviate existing inequalities? Evidence from Ireland

Philip J. O'Connell

1. INTRODUCTION

In recent years there has been a resurgence of interest in the importance of investment in skills and competencies in furthering the goals of economic progress, fuller employment and social integration. The importance of such investment in human capital is emphasized both by the OECD (1994, 1998, 1999) and by the European Commission (1994). This resurgence of interest in human capital coincides with a new emphasis on the need for 'lifelong learning', both to respond to current rapid changes in the organization and technology of production and service delivery and to counter the socially disruptive effects of increased labour market flexibility.

Investments by firms play an important part in overall investments in human capital, and enterprise-sponsored training of employees plays a particularly large part in lifelong learning. The principal rationale driving training investments by enterprises is the belief that such investments will enhance company performance. While it is believed that investment in training also has the potential to reduce inequality and prevent unemployment, much less is known about the contribution of enterprise-sponsored training to these social goals.

Most of the research on training and education focuses on the individual as the unit of analysis, with the result that the labour market effects of education and training are well understood. Far less attention has been paid in the empirical literature to the enterprise as the unit of analysis, despite the obvious importance of enterprise-related training to human capital formation. This chapter seeks to fill some of the gaps in our knowledge of training by studying the determinants and effects of job-related training at firm level.

Increased international interest in education and training is driven partly by a belief that training can be a means of reducing social exclusion (OECD, 1998). There is now a very substantial body of work showing that the labour market prospects of individuals, including both employment prospects and earnings, are closely related to the skills and competencies accumulated through participation in initial education and in continuing vocational education (OCED, 1994, 1998). Moreover, the greater importance now accorded to continuing training, or lifelong learning, is a reflection of both the pace of change in the technology and organization of production and of increased flexibility in labour markets. Increased training over the life cycle, can, it is argued, equip individuals to adapt to changes in production and render them more employable in flexible labour markets, and by so doing, help to reduce social exclusion.

For continuing training to play such a role in countering social exclusion, it is of course necessary that access to training be distributed widely across society, and in particular that training opportunities be available to those disadvantaged in the labour market. In most societies, however, participation in continuing training is highest among those relatively advantaged in the labour market. Internationally comparative data published by the OECD (1998) show that individuals in employment have substantially higher average rates of participation in vocational training than the unemployed, who in turn have higher participation rates than those outside the labour market. Moreover, among those employed, most studies find that employers tend to provide more training for their better educated workers (Lynch, 1994; Schömann, 1998).

Table 12.1 shows participation by employed adults in job-related training in ten countries for 1994–5, derived from the *International Adult Literacy Survey* (IALS). These individual-level data show substantial variation between countries in the incidence of training, with over half of all employed adults in the United Kingdom participating in some form of training in the previous 12 months, compared to 16 per cent in Poland. The data also show, however, a universal pattern in which participation in continuing training is related to initial educational qualifications. Across all countries, those with higher levels of education receive more training than those with lower qualifications. O'Connell (1999) shows that both the incidence and duration of continuing training are strongly related to initial education, suggesting that current patterns of continuing training are likely to exacerbate rather than mitigate labour market inequalities and processes of social exclusion.

Comparative data on training also show that there are important differences at enterprise level in the incidence of training. Most commentators on job-related training argue that small firms are less likely to provide training for their workers, mainly because of diseconomies of scale.

Table 12.1   Participation by employed adults aged 25–64 in continuing education and training, by educational attainment, 1994–5

	Below upper secondary (%)	Upper secondary (%)	Tertiary (%)	All (%)
Australia	26.2	36.4	53.4	38.1
Belgium (Flanders)	7.4*	20.2	32.7	20.0
Canada	20.8	28.9	52.7	37.5
Ireland	14.8	24.1	37.8	23.4
Netherlands	20.9	34.5	45.5	32.5
New Zealand	37.0	46.7	62.3	46.9
Poland	8.0	25.0	29.1	16.5
Switzerland	9.0	34.4	43.8	31.7
United Kingdom	40.8	55.4	73.2	51.9
United States	17.4	34.4	63.1	45.6
Unweighted mean	20.2	34.0	49.4	34.4

Note: * indicates fewer than 30 cases in the sample cell.

Source: O'Connell (1999).

Firstly, smaller firms may have higher training costs *per employee* than larger firms because of difficulties in spreading fixed training costs over a small group of employees. Secondly, the loss of production incurred by having even one employee in training may be higher for smaller than for larger firms. Table 12.2, which presents data on the incidence of education and training of individuals by the size of the firm in which they work, confirms that expectation. In general, those working in larger firms are more likely to participate in training than those in smaller firms. Thus averaging across the IALS countries, 23 per cent of those working in firms with fewer than 20 employees received some form of education or training, compared with 46 per cent of those working in firms with 500 or more employees.

Most of the advances in our knowledge of the impact of education and training on labour market outcomes are derived from analyses of individual-level data. Empirical evidence of the impact of training at enterprise level is much less developed than that relating to individuals, although there is a growing literature which suggests that training increases the productivity of firms and leads to higher earnings for trained personnel. Quantitative analysis of enterprise-level data has tended to focus more on the effects of

Table 12.2   Participation by employed adults aged 25–64 in continuing education and training, by firm size, 1994–5

	Fewer than 20 employees (%)	20–99 employees (%)	100–499 employees (%)	500 or more employees (%)
Australia	23.3	36.3	45.5	54.7
Belgium (Flanders)	15.2	15.9	25.4	25.0
Canada	30.8	40.8	24.5	46.7
Ireland	10.8*	17.4*	29.6	34.8
New Zealand	29.6	56.0	56.6	63.7
Poland	9.0	21.9	17.6	24.3
Switzerland	26.9	25.0	32.0	41.8
United Kingdom	27.7	46.4	52.0	63.8
United States	30.9	36.3	42.0	59.3
Unweighted mean	22.7	32.9	36.1	46.0

Note: * indicates fewer than 30 cases in the sample cell.

Source: O'Connell (1999).

training on company performance (for example, Barrett and O'Connell, 2001; Bartel, 1989; Holzer *et al.*, 1993), although several studies have found evidence of positive effects of training on wages (Bartel, 1995; Booth, 1991, Loewenstein and Spletzer, 1997). Moreover, a number of studies have found that training enhances both company performance and workers' wages (Bishop, 1994; Groot and Osterbeek, 1994).

This chapter draws on a survey of companies' training activities in Ireland in 1993, and on a follow-up survey designed to measure the impact of training in 1995, in order to investigate the extent to which enterprise-sponsored training contributes to social goals. It looks first at the determinants of company-sponsored training to assess the extent to which the incidence and volume of training undertaken by firms is related to the quality and structure of employment in the firm. It then investigates the impact of training on two outcomes which affect workers' well-being. It looks first at the extent to which training is related to changes in employment levels within firms: does training prevent 'downsizing'? Second, it analyses the impact of training on changes in average workers' compensation: what benefits do workers derive from engaging in training sponsored by their employers?

2. THE DATA

The starting point for this research is a survey undertaken in 1993 and reported in Fox (1995). The survey was designed to collect detailed information on the training practices of a nationally representative sample of 1000 enterprises operating in Ireland. The survey covered companies employing more than ten people in manufacturing industry, construction and private services. Its focus was on continuing vocational training, rather than initial training, and so apprentices and trainees are excluded.

A total of 650 useable returns was obtained from this survey. The data obtained provide information on the economic activity of each company, whether or not different types of training were undertaken, the number of days employees spent in training and company expenditure on training courses, including the labour costs incurred for employees participating in courses. The data from this survey are used below to investigate firm-level determinants of the level of training activity. Descriptive statistics on the principal variables used in that analysis are reported in Table 12.3.

In order to measure the effects of training on changes in employment and labour costs, I draw on a follow-up survey of the 650 companies in April

Table 12.3 Descriptive statistics on main variables used in the analysis of the determinants of training

Variable	Mean	Std dev.	Minimum	Maximum
Trainees/employees	33.26	34.48	0.00	100.00
Training days/employees	1.45	2.20	0.00	15.18
Training expenditure/payroll	1.34	1.95	0.00	14.50
Employment, 1993	180.91	538.59	8.00	7094.00
Labour costs/employment	13.37	6.47	1.71	38.80
Percentage managers	15.08	11.90	0.00	93.75
Percentage technical workers	6.36	11.33	0.00	80.00
Percentage clerical	31.74	28.36	0.00	100.00
Percentage craft	10.13	19.31	0.00	100.00
Percentage operatives	36.69	30.73	0.00	97.64
Percentage women	37.77	26.80	0.00	100.00
Percentage temporary or seasonal	7.24	26.57	0.00	357.14
Recruits/employment	9.84	15.49	0.00	110.00
Foreign-owned	0.21	0.41	0.00	1.00
Finance sector	0.04	0.20	0.00	1.00
Trade sector	0.35	0.48	0.00	1.00
Industry sector	0.50	0.50	0.00	1.00
Other sector	0.10	0.30	0.00	1.00

and May of 1997 undertaken to study the effects of training and company performance (Barrett and O'Connell, 2001). Given that the sample which we resurveyed was quite small, we sought to maximize the response rate by minimizing the amount of information sought. The main pieces of information sought were as follows: output in 1993 and 1995 and the value of fixed assets, the size of the workforce and labour costs at the two points in time. Eliminating responses with incomplete or poor-quality data reduced the number of useful cases from the follow-up survey to 203.

Descriptive statistics on the main variables used from the follow-up survey to analyse the effects of training on changes in employment and wages are reported in Table 12.6 below. Comparison of the descriptive statistics for the two surveys shows that the mean value of company size and training measures are very similar in the two surveys, although the follow-up survey contained a higher proportion of companies in the industry sector.

3.   THE DETERMINANTS OF FIRM-LEVEL TRAINING

On average, the firms in our sample provided training for about one-third of their employees, although there was considerable variation around the mean. Measuring the incidence of training represents one dimension of training effort, but it does not capture the intensity of that effort. We use two indicators to measure training intensity: (a) the total number of training days received as a ratio of total employment in the company, and (b) total expenditure on training as a percentage of total payroll. The training expenditure measure includes both the wage costs of personnel undergoing training and direct training costs, mainly the cost of providing training or of purchasing training from external providers.

Our principal interest in estimating models of the determinants of training is to investigate the relationship between training and the proportion of relatively advantaged workers in firms. Table 12.1 above showed a near universal pattern at the individual level, with participation in continuing education and training increasing with the level of initial education and those with the lowest educational qualifications being least likely to receive further training. Unfortunately, our company-level data set collected no direct measures of the educational qualifications of company personnel. We do, however, have two measures which can be used to capture company differences in the average market capacities of their workforces. First, we use the ratio of total labour costs to total employment. Labour costs represent all expenditures borne by employers to employ workers and consist of wages and salaries, bonuses and other incentive payments and social security and pension contributions. The survey also included companies' vocational training costs, but we exclude these from our measure of labour costs since we are interested in explaining differences in company training. The measure of labour costs per employee thus represents a comprehensive measure of average employee compensation, including direct wages as well as other elements of the total compensation package. My hypothesis is that, in firms with higher labour costs per employee, the incidence and intensity of training is higher than in firms with lower labour costs.

A second measure of firm-level variation in workers' market capacity is occupational structure. Here the expectation is that firms characterized by greater proportions of workers in higher occupational grades, particularly managerial and technical occupations, show greater levels of training activity than those with high proportions of workers in lower occupational grades.

As already noted, most commentators on job-related training argue that small firms are less likely to provide training than large firms, mainly because diseconomies of scale raise the unit costs of training for workers in small companies and because the loss of production incurred by training workers may be greater for larger than for smaller firms. Table 12.2 above confirms that this is true across a number of industrial countries at the individual level. In attempting to model the company-level determinants of training, two size variables are specified: total employment in 1993, and total employment squared. The squared term is included in order to capture non-linearities in the size–training relationship.

The equations also include a number of control variables, believed to influence the training activity of firms. The percentage of women in each company is included to control for possible gender differences in the allocation of training. Employers are likely to provide less training of temporary workers because of the difficulty in capturing the return on the training investment in workers on fixed-term contracts, so the percentage of temporary workers in a company should have a negative influence on training. Recruitment, on the other hand, should necessitate training, so the percentage of recent recruits in total employment should increase training activity.

The Irish economy is characterized by a dualism, which can be roughly characterized as a division between a dynamic, modern, high value-added, high-technology, foreign-owned sector oriented towards international markets and an indigenously owned sector characterized by lower productivity and oriented more to the domestic market. This crude dichotomy does not accurately reflect the diversity within the indigenous sector, which is becoming increasingly export-oriented and more productive, but it is likely nonetheless, that firms in the foreign-owned sector remain, on average, more likely than those in the indigenous sector to face continuing

Table 12.4 Establishment-level determinants of training

Variable	Trainees as % of employment		Training days per employee		Training expenditure as % of payroll	
	Coefficient	t-value	Coefficient	t-value	Coefficient	t-value
Employment	0.037***	6.621	0.002***	4.277	0.002***	4.071
Employment^2	0.000***	−5.456	0.000***	−3.253	0.000**	−3.030
Labour costs/employment	1.020***	4.391	0.056***	3.569	0.031*	1.997
% managers	0.318**	2.728	0.016*	1.987	0.019**	2.422
% technical	0.350**	3.039	0.022**	2.804	0.025***	3.235
% craft	−0.070	−0.953	0.004	0.784	0.001	0.204
% clerical	0.071	1.137	−0.004	−0.892	−0.003	−0.674
% women	−0.010	−0.174	−0.001	−0.151	0.001	0.204
% temporary	−0.002	−0.033	−0.005	−1.733	−0.004	−1.413
% recruits	0.083	1.046	0.001	0.152	−0.003	−0.582
Foreign ownership	14.323***	4.293	0.640**	2.830	0.592**	2.645
Finance sector	0.046	0.007	−0.100	−0.214	0.015	0.032
Trade sector	−8.686*	−2.266	−0.710**	−2.733	−1.009***	−3.919
Other sector	−6.275	−1.313	0.196	0.606	0.146	0.456
(Constant)	6.396	1.249	−2.277	−6.561	−1.931	−5.618
Adjusted R^2	0.239		0.209		0.206	

Note: *** P<0.001, ** P<0.01, * P<0.05.

competitive pressures to maximize company performance. To the extent that this is the case, we would expect foreign-owned companies to exhibit greater commitment to training their workers.

Table 12.4 reports the results of three simple OLS equations for the three measures of training. Labour costs per employee have a positive and highly significant effect on the incidence of training (equation 1, trainees as a percentage of employment), its intensity (equation 2, the ratio of total training days to total employment) and its cost (equation 3, training expenditure as a percentage of payroll). Companies with higher proportions of employees in managerial and technical occupations train more of their employees and engage in more training activity compared to the reference category, operatives. Larger firms engage in more training, and the positive coefficient in respect of total employment combined with the small negative coefficient for the squared employment term indicates that training increases with firm size, but the rate of increase tapers off at the higher end of the size distribution.

Foreign ownership stimulates training, in line with expectations. The effects of the percentages of women, of recruits and of temporary workers are as anticipated, although they fail to reach statistical significance. The coefficients in respect of the dichotomous sectoral variables indicate that companies engaged in retail and wholesale trade provide less training than those in the manufacturing sector, the reference category, but that the other sectors controlled for, namely finance and 'other', do not differ significantly from manufacturing.

The results of these models provide clear support for the general hypothesis that both the incidence and the intensity of training are greater in firms characterized by relatively advantaged workforces – that is, in companies where average compensation packages are more valuable and in those characterized by greater proportions of workers at the higher end of the occupational hierarchy. This suggests that, at the level of the company, training allocation tends to be distributed in proportion to the distribution of labour market advantage. To the extent that this is the case, the current allocation of training is likely to maintain, if not reinforce, existing inequalities between workers, rather than mitigating them.

4. DO WORKERS BENEFIT FROM TRAINING?

Who benefits from enterprise-sponsored training? The empirical literature suggests that such training can lead to productivity gains for those enterprises that train and to increased wages for trained workers (OECD, 1994). Barrett and O'Connell (2001), using the follow-up survey of in-company training described above, show that training measured in 1993 had a

Table 12.5   Descriptive statistics on main variables used in the analysis of the effects of training

	Mean	Std. dev.	Minimum	Maximum
% change in employment, 1993–5	10.83	28.72	−70.00	154.54
% change in labour costs, 1993–5	15.32	31.80	−48.03	136.78
% change in assets, 1993–5	10.79	28.83	−78.96	146.32
Total workforce, end 1993	178.52	463.78	10.00	5269.00
Trainees as % of employees, 1993	38.98	34.78	0.00	100.00
Training days per employee, 1993	1.80	2.95	0.00	30.87
Training expenditure/payroll, 1993	1.51	1.89	0.00	10.64
Labour costs per employee, 1993	14.53	6.42	4.37	38.88
Proportion managers	0.15	0.11	0.01	0.82
Proportion technical	0.06	0.09	0.00	0.50
Proportion clerical	0.25	0.25	0.00	0.95
Proportion craft	0.12	0.20	0.00	0.89
Finance sector	0.03	0.18	0.00	1.00
Trade sector	0.26	0.44	0.00	1.00
Industry sector	0.66	0.48	0.00	1.00
Other sector	0.04	0.21	0.00	1.00

positive effect on productivity over the 1993–5 period. Here we are concerned to ascertain whether the positive effects of training also extend to workers in those companies. We look at two potential effects of training that affect workers' welfare. First, we investigate the relationship between training and changes in employment. There has been little attention in the empirical literature to the employment effects of training, although Ottersten Kazamaki *et al.* (1996) did find that training yielded long-run increases in labour demand in their panel survey of small firms in Sweden. If training is successful in generating increased productivity or enhanced corporate performance, this should lead to competitive gains for companies. But the effects of increased productivity on employment are unclear. Increased productivity could have the effect of reducing employment if market share remains constant, and is only likely to increase employment if productivity gains are translated into increased market share.

Second, we look at the effects of training on changes in labour costs. This relationship has received some attention in the empirical literature and the weight of the evidence suggests that the productivity gains realized from enterprise-sponsored training are shared between firms, on the one hand, in the form of increased profits or performance, and workers, on the other, in the form of increased wages (OECD, 1994).

Table 12.5 shows descriptive statistics for the main variables in the analysis of the impact of training. Average employment in 1993 was 178, and employment increased by an average of 11 per cent over the next two years; labour costs per employee increased by 15 per cent and investment, measured by the change in corporate assets over the 1993–5 period, rose by 11 per cent. There was considerable variation around these means.

Table 12.6 shows the results of the OLS models of change in employment between 1993 and 1995. Three equations are estimated, one for each of the measures of training. While the effects of training are positive, they are non-significant in each equation. Moreover, none of the equations explains much of the variation in employment. These results suggest that training has little discernible influence on subsequent employment in companies. If this is the case, training does little to protect total employment at the level of the firm. It is important to acknowledge here that these findings relate to companies; they suggest that training may do little to protect employment levels within firms, since firms engaging in a great deal of training seem no more likely to increase employment than those with less training. It remains entirely possible, however, that training may increase individual workers' job security, by increasing their probability of being kept on in a firm, or individuals' employment security, by enhancing their employability and hence the probability that they will quickly find another job if they lose their jobs with the current employer.

Table 12.7 shows the results of the OLS models of changes in labour costs per employee, which measure the total average compensation package in each company. Again, three equations are estimated relating to the three training measures. The effects of the ratio of trainees to total employment and of training days per employee are both positive and significant, indicating that both the incidence and the intensity of training lead to increases in employees' total compensation packages. This positive effect of training on workers' compensation is consistent with empirical findings derived from enterprise-level data in other countries (for example, Groot and Osterbeek, 1994). The effect of the training expenditure variable, while positive, is not significant. The effects of the initial level of labour costs per employee are negative but significant only in the equation analysing the effects of training incidence. These negative coefficients of initial levels of labour compensation suggest some tendency for labour costs to increase more slowly in companies with higher average labour costs. This finding is consistent with other recent studies that have found that earnings gains from training are larger for workers lower down the occupation, skill or earnings distribution: among less skilled workers in the United States (Bartel, 1995), among workers with intermediate educational qualifications in the United Kingdom (Blundell *et al.*, 1996) and among women in the United Kingdom (Booth, 1991) and in Germany (Pischke, 1996).

Table 12.6   OLS models of employment change, 1993–5

| | Training variable: | | | | | |
| | Trainees as % of employment | | Training days per employee | | Training expenditure as % of payroll | |
	Coefficient	t-value	Coefficient	t-value	Coefficient	t-value
Training	3.035	0.531	0.984	1.106	1.085	1.035
Investment 1993–5	6.300	0.981	5.979	0.937	6.002	0.940
Total workforce, end 1993	−0.003	−0.338	−0.003	−0.352	−0.003	−0.323
Workforce^2	0.000	0.061	0.000	0.074	0.000	0.078
Trade sector	7.644	1.769	8.083	1.867	8.034	1.855
Finance sector	−11.020	−1.075	−9.586	−0.943	−10.346	−1.020
Constant	7.619	2.278	7.045	2.291	7.052	2.259
Adjusted R^2	0.002		0.006		0.006	

Table 12.7   OLS models of change in labour costs per employee, 1993–5

| | Training variable: | | | | | |
| | Trainees as % of employment | | Training days per employee | | Training expenditure as % of payroll | |
	Coefficient	t-value	Coefficient	t-value	Coefficient	t-value
Training	14.289*	1.967	2.217**	2.945	1.683	1.356
Investment	−1.542	−0.199	−3.352	−0.438	−2.707	−0.348
Total workforce, 1993	0.017	1.423	0.020	1.720	0.021	1.696
Workforce²	0.000	−1.461	0.000	−1.663	0.000	−1.607
Labour costs per employee, 1993	−0.839*	−2.162	−0.719	−1.935	−0.660	−1.750
% managers	28.230	1.241	21.329	0.953	19.190	0.835
% technical	6.329	0.227	17.162	0.646	13.044	0.471
% clerical	6.731	0.534	9.409	0.753	7.296	0.575
% craft workers	−0.221	−0.019	−4.277	−0.378	−1.576	−0.138
Trade sector	−11.436	−1.625	−10.770	−1.550	−10.767	−1.522
Finance sector	25.553	1.833	29.511*	2.160	29.094*	2.093
Constant	15.833*	2.185	15.290*	2.141	16.566*	2.279
Adjusted R^2	0.057		0.080		0.047	

Note: *** $P<0.001$, ** $P<0.01$, * $P<0.05$.

These are very simple models, largely because of the restricted number of variables collected in the follow-up survey and the relatively small number of cases – just over 200 – available for the analysis. Nevertheless, the models do indicate that training does yield positive material gains for workers in firms which undertake training. The findings also suggest that, while training does generate increased earnings, broadly conceived, it has little discernible impact on enterprise-level employment.

5.   CONCLUSIONS

This chapter has focused principally on the distribution and effects of job-related training sponsored by enterprises. A great deal of attention has been paid in recent years to the importance of lifelong learning as a strategy to increase social integration, reduce inequalities and enhance individuals' employability. However, the evidence from individual-level data gives cause for concern. In most countries the distribution of training is closely related to initial education, with the result that those most in need of continuing training are less likely to receive it than those who are already relatively well equipped to compete in modern labour markets.

Given the important role played by enterprise-sponsored training in continuing education and training, it is essential to increase our understanding of individual-level variation in training participation in order more clearly to apprehend the processes that cause differences between firms in their training activity. We also need to understand the effects of enterprise-sponsored training: does it promote such social goals as employment and increased material well-being for workers?

This chapter has examined both the determinants and the effects of enterprise-sponsored training in a nationally representative panel survey of firms in Ireland. The results show, first, that both the incidence and the intensity of job-related training are greater in companies characterized by relatively advantaged workforces; that is, in companies where average worker compensation packages are more valuable and in companies with greater proportions of workers at the higher end of the occupational hierarchy. This suggests that, at the level of the firm, training is distributed in proportion to labour market advantage. The models also confirm that the volume of training is greater in larger firms.

With respect to the effects of training, the analysis suggests that, in companies where there is a high incidence of training, or a large amount of training is undertaken, the growth in worker compensation is higher than in companies which engage in less training. The findings also indicate that these 'wage returns' to training are inversely related to average labour costs per employee in companies, suggesting that the earnings gains from training may be higher among less advantaged workers, and among groups of workers less likely to receive training. Training does not, however, appear to have any discernible impact on changes over time in employment.

These findings from the enterprise-level analysis are consistent with training patterns and outcomes that are already well established at the individual level. In general, those who are relatively advantaged in the labour market tend to receive more training than the less advantaged, and training confers material benefits on those who participate in training. This suggests that current patterns of access to continuing training are more likely to reinforce than to reduce existing inequalities in the labour market. If it is true that knowledge, skills and competencies constitute a vital asset, not only in supporting economic growth but also in reducing social inequality and combating unemployment, low pay and poverty, then current training patterns within enterprises represent a perverse allocation principle, with participation in continuing training being distributed in inverse proportion to need. From a broader social perspective, the goal of greater social integration is likely to be advanced only if access to continuing training is widely extended to encompass the developmental needs of all workers. Given the importance of the enterprise as a site of continuing training, this suggests a need for intervention in order to alter the incentive structures facing firms in such a way as to promote greater access to training across the entire skill and occupational structure, but particularly among those in less skilled occupations.

BIBLIOGRAPHY

Arulampalam, W. and Booth, A.L. (1998), 'Training and Labour Market Flexibility: Is There a Trade-off?', *British Journal of Industrial Relations*, 36(4), 521–36.

Barrett, A. and O'Connell, P.J. (2001), 'Does Training Generally Work? The Returns to In-Company Training', *Industrial and Labour Relations Review*, 54(3), 647–67.

Bartel, A. (1989), 'Formal employee training programmes and their impact on labour productivity: Evidence from a human resources survey', *Working Paper*, No. 3026, National Bureau of Economic Research, Cambridge, Mass.

Bartel, A. (1995), 'Training, Wage Growth, and Job Performance: Evidence from a Company Database', *Journal of Labor Economics*, 3, 401–25.

Bishop, J. (1994), 'The impact of previous training on productivity and wages', in L. Lynch (ed.), *Training and the Private Sector*, Chicago: University of Chicago Press.

Black, S. and Lynch, L. (1996), 'Human-Capital Investments and Productivity', *AEA Papers and Proceedings*, 263–7.

Blundell, R., Dearden, L. and Meghir, C. (1996), *The Determinants and Effects of Work-Related Training in Britain*, London: Institute for Fiscal Studies.

Booth, A. (1991), 'Job-Related Formal Training: Who Receives it and What is it Worth?', *Oxford Bulletin of Economics and Statistics*, August, 281–94.

European Commission (1994) *Growth, Competitiveness, Employment: The Challenges and Ways Forward into the 21st Century*, White Paper, Luxembourg: European Commission.

Fox, R. (1995), *Company Training in Ireland*, Dublin: FAS.

Groot, W. and Osterbeek, H. (1994), 'Bedrijsopleidingen: goed voor produktivviteit in loon', *Economisch Statische Berichten*, 3988, 1108–11.

Holzer, H., Block, R., Cheathem, M. and Knott, J. (1993), 'Are Training Subsidies for Firms Effective? The Michigan Experience', *Industrial and Labour Relations Review*, 46, 625–36.

Loewenstein, M.A. and Spletzer, J. (1997), 'Belted Training: The Relationship Between Training, Tenure and Wages', US Bureau of Labour Statistics, mimeo.

Lynch, L. (ed.) (1994), *Training and the Private Sector: International Comparisons*, Chicago: University of Chicago Press.

O'Connell, P.J. (1999) 'Adults in Training: An International Comparison of Continuing Education and Training', OECD Center for Educational Research and Innovation, WD(99)1, Paris.

OECD (1994), *The OECD Jobs Study, Evidence and Explanations, Part II*, Paris: OECD.

OECD (1998), *Human Capital Investment: An International Comparison*, Paris: OECD.

OECD (1999), 'Training of Adult Workers in OECD Countries: Measurement and Analysis', *Employment Outlook*, Paris: OECD, pp. 137–75.

Ottersten Kazamaki, E., Lindh, T. and Mellander, E. (1996), 'Cost and Productivity Effects of Firm-Financed Training', Industrial Institute for Economic and Social Research, *Working Paper*, no. 455, Uppsala, Sweden.

Pischke, J.S. (1996), 'Continuous Training in Germany', National Bureau of Economic Research, *Working Paper*, no. 5829.

Schömann, K. (1998), 'Access to Life-Long Learning and Implications for Strategies of Organizational Learning in the European Union', in Horst Albach, Meinolf Dierkes, Ariane Berthoin Antal and Kristina Vaillant (eds), *Organisationslernen – institutionelle und kulturelle Dimensionen*, WZB Jahrbuch 1998, Berlin: edition sigma, pp. 433–46.

PART IV

Actors in the Field of Training

13. Firms' further training practices and social exclusion: can industrial relations systems provide greater equality? Theoretical and empirical evidence from Germany and France

Olivier Giraud[1]

The academic and public debates in Western Europe on further training (FT) in firms both revolve around two different issues: the fight against inequalities among individuals (Croquey, 1996; Schömann *et al.*, 1996) and the improvement of firms' economic performance (Streeck, 1991; Mason *et al.*, 1996; Carriou and Jeger, 1997). The institutional arrangements for FT in most European countries reflect this tension and usually combine public with private financing and public with market regulation of firms' FT provision (Auer, 1994). The positive and mutually reinforcing social and economic effects it is said to produce have even made FT one element in the consensual strategies on lifelong learning that have been advocated by the labour ministers of OECD countries as part of the fight against social exclusion (OECD, 1997).

In spite of these voluntarist claims, the results of most qualitative or quantitative studies of the effects of FT on labour force segmentation are pessimistic. Firstly, companies seem to select employees for FT courses in a way that tends to reinforce segmentation in internal labour markets and to exclude women, the less skilled and the new recruits. Secondly, the returns on further education in terms of remuneration or upward mobility are becoming more and more unclear. The improvement of firms' economic performance through FT could also have positive side-effects on the integration of those groups in the economically active population most exposed to precarious conditions. However, these effects on productivity and quality are equivocal (Auer, 1994) and are still being hotly debated in the economic literature (OECD, 1997).

In addition to public actors seeking to mitigate both the financial and political costs of social exclusion, trade unions and, more generally, industrial relations systems as a whole are institutions and collective actors within or close to companies that would seem to have an interest in defending a solidaristic conception of FT.[2] In some cases, the unions are consulted on every decision relating to FT within the firm. In other cases, the unions negotiate on all matters linking FT to opportunities for closer integration into the internal labour market; that is, upward mobility rules, wage levels, job classification systems and so on.

This chapter adopts an institutionalist perspective in order to examine the possible interactions between industrial relations systems and the effects of firms' FT practices on the prevention of social exclusion. Taking case studies of firms as a starting point, as many determinants as possible of firms' FT investment decisions are considered. A distinction is made between those factors linked to market pressures, such as technical change or changes in company ownership, and institutional factors, such as the structure of industrial relations systems, national incentive systems for FT and labour market structure. Two countries are compared, each one exemplifying a particular model. Germany is taken as the archetype of the occupational labour market model, while France represents the internal labour market model (Marsden, 1990).

The first section of this chapter briefly outlines the comparative approach adopted in the research and presents the case studies. The second section examines the internal coherence hypothesis (*effet sociétal*) in terms of the industrial relations systems, labour market structures and training systems in both countries. The third section presents both institutional FT systems and analyses the available comparable data on firms' FT practices, their effects on labour market segmentation and the industrial relations strategy toward firms' FT practices. The fourth section outlines the conclusions drawn from the case studies and analyses different modes of interaction between industrial relations systems and firms' training practices.

1.   THE COMPARATIVE APPROACH AND THE CASE STUDIES

In order to investigate the influence of industrial relations systems on the effects of FT practices, a comparative approach based on company case studies was adopted. Interviews with FT specialists from both unions and employers' associations were also conducted in both countries. It was assumed that French and German firms of comparable size, operating in the same industry and competing in the same product market, would be exposed to quite similar market pressures. In contrast with other comparative research, it was decided not to explain each country's 'product strategy' in terms of 'differences in skill levels' or 'process skills' (Mason *et al.*, 1996, p. 186). However, even though narrow product markets are the focus of attention, it seems very likely that similar market pressures might make themselves felt in different ways in different national and corporate contexts. Depending on national social, institutional or economic conditions and the specific circumstances of individual companies, the same market pressures might be countered through investment in technology, reorganization of the work process, changes in the workforce, adaptation of skill profiles and so on.

Among the numerous, complex and interlinked determinants of firms' FT practices, we focus only on the most important elements of the labour market structure in both countries (section 2) and on the institutional variables shaping the national FT systems (section 3). These two sets of variables will be used as a means of analysing firms' FT policies. The only company-specific factors taken into account are industry, size of firm, product market position, workshop-specific production and ownership structure.[3]

Since sectoral governance regimes are as important as national ones (Hollingsworth *et al.*, 1994), our research was conducted in a number of different but highly internationalized industries, namely laboratory chemicals, telecommunications and the railway rolling stock industry. Two out of the three chosen industries, telecommunications and laboratory chemicals, are currently undergoing important technological changes. The telecommunications industry is also experiencing a radical change in its market configuration, but is used to dealing with constant technological change. All three industries are affected by the general trend towards the decentralization of production brought about by long-term market pressures (Piore and Sabel, 1984).

These industries were chosen because of their specific industrial relations configurations. In Germany, the homogeneity of the industrial relations system is based in part on the unions' ability to cooperate (Katzenstein, 1987). This general inclination towards cooperation is restricted by the split between the relatively militant engineering and metal workers' union IG-Metall and the more moderate positions adopted by the unions in the chemical industry (IG-Bergbau, Chemie Energie). The railway rolling stock and laboratory chemicals industries exemplify these two industry configurations. In France, the most important dividing line within the industrial relations systems coincides more and more clearly with the public/private split. Strikes and other trade unions are concentrated in the protected public sector. The telecommunications carriers in both countries still have most of the characteristics of typical public-sector organizations.

All the case studies in both countries were conducted in large companies, because the influence of industrial relations institutions is supposed to be greater, and therefore more easily assessed, in larger firms.

2. LABOUR MARKET STRUCTURES, INDUSTRIAL RELATIONS AND FURTHER TRAINING: TWO COHERENT MODELS?

Researchers involved in comparative studies of labour markets and industrial relations systems in France and Germany can now look back on almost two decades of research that has produced a rich body of work. The tradition was established in the early 1980s by economists and sociologists at LEST (Laboratoire d'Economie et de Sociologie du Travail), whose research brought to light two internally coherent national models. In both models, firms' productive systems (work organization, hierarchy, cooperation/competition and so on), pay, promotion and job classification rules are linked in a specific way to the entire training and education system inside and outside the firm. What the LEST researchers uncovered, in other words, was a strong connection between dominant models of work organization, industrial relations systems and national educational systems (Maurice *et al.*, 1986).

According to their conclusions, the German model rests on a company hierarchy and promotion system based on training, certification and competence and a wage system linked to productivity. The corresponding system of work organization is characterized by a fairly low supervisor-to-worker ratio and a fairly high degree of autonomy for production workers. The model is said to be underpinned by the structure of the German education and training system, which is characterized by a largely positive attitude towards basic vocational training in firms. In contrast to the German model, the management hierarchy, promotion and wage rules in the French system revolve largely around seniority. Wages and promotion are also influenced by on-the-job training. The system of work organization is characterized by a higher proportion of foremen and managers and less autonomy for production workers. The structure of the French education system, which makes the school-based vocational training system a refuge for dropouts, is one of the factors that explain the low status of vocational qualifications in France.

A similar divide separates the two industrial relations systems. The dualistic structure of the German system produces a clear division of labour between, on the one hand, a more consensual mode of bargaining at company level, the scope of which is restricted by law to topics such as work organization and regulation of the internal labour market and, on the other hand, a more conflictual mode of negotiation at industry level dealing with issues such as wages and working time (Schmidt and Trinczek, 1991). The structure of the French industrial relations system does not permit a similar distribution of consensual and conflictual issues. Furthermore, employers' associations and unions are weak and divided along political and industrial lines. The capacity for reaching consensus has recently deteriorated still further. Strong internal divisions have emerged in most employers' associations and unions, making it even more difficult for the organizations themselves to unite around common positions and interests.

Other scholars pursued this comparative analysis of the two models, showing that the German system was more likely to lead to the development of occupational labour market structures and the French one to internal labour markets (Marsden, 1990). This latter dichotomy is especially relevant to our main concern in this chapter, namely the integration of the less skilled elements of the workforce. On the face of it, the French system should provide better opportunities for the integration of unskilled workers. Indeed, since the French job classification, wages and promotion rules rest on seniority and on-the-job training, the failure to acquire an initial vocational qualification should not be an impediment to upward mobility. In Germany, promotion is based on certification. Even after the certificate of qualification as a skilled worker (*Facharbeiterbrief*) has been awarded on completion of training, each step up the promotion ladder requires successful completion of an FT course (usually individually financed) and acquisition of the corresponding certificate. Upward mobility in Germany seems to be attainable only in a way that tends to exclude the less skilled elements of the workforce.

However, it should also be borne in mind that the general trend towards the decentralization of production is tending to homogenize production systems. Furthermore, the consequent 'flattening' of hierarchies to the lowest possible level reduces the space available for blue-collar workers to move upwards. Géhin and Méhaut, and Drexel have shown in their comprehensive comparative studies of the German and French FT systems that these internally coherent models are being affected by the changes currently taking place in industrial production systems and have stressed the key role played by FT in those changes (Géhin and Méhaut, 1993; Drexel, 1996).

3.   FURTHER TRAINING SYSTEMS, ASSESSABLE EFFECTS AND INDUSTRIAL RELATIONS STRATEGIES

The basic institutional arrangements for FT in Germany and France are often said to be very different (Dubar, 2000; Drexel, 1996). However, a description of the two systems and analysis of their effects in terms of labour market segmentation will show that the differences are not as great as is often suggested. The linkages between industrial relations systems and FT will also be examined in detail.

The National FT Systems

In France, the Further Training Act of 1971 (frequently updated since) placed certain legal constraints on firms' FT practices. The Act has three main provisions. Firstly, companies with more than ten employees[4] are obliged to spend at least 1.5 per cent of their wage bill on FT or to pay an equivalent amount into a fund. Secondly, it establishes an individual right to FT, financed out of a fund set up for the purpose. Thirdly, it seeks to clarify the roles of state, firms and social partners at industry and firm level. According to the provisions of the Act, the state's sphere of competence is confined to general FT provision and regional regeneration and retraining schemes (so-called 'reconversion' programmes). Firms are responsible for training needs arising out of adjustment and technical change. For their part, the social partners are responsible for regulating FT at both industry and company level (Dubar, 2000).

The FT levy on firms has been raised and differentiated many times. Since the last reform introduced in 1994, companies have to dedicate 0.1 per cent of their wage bill to the financing of the individual right to FT (individual training leave), 0.1 per cent to a new scheme which tries to balance individual training needs with the interests of firms (*Capital Temps Formation*), 0.4 per cent to sandwich courses for young people and the remaining 0.9 per cent to training for the existing workforce. The various industries, regions, sizes of company, business associations and types of training activity have their separate FT funds, a total of about 100 in all (Brochier and Mériaux, 1997). These funds are supposed to be managed by joint union/employer bodies. However, this turns out to be the case only at national or regional level: all the local bodies charged with implementing FT are jealously controlled by employers' associations alone.

In comparison with this seemingly comprehensive and frequently altered legal framework, the German system appears to be quite sophisticated. There are four federal laws dealing with FT, and in theory they form the basis for an all-encompassing system for the promotion of FT. The Employment Promotion Act (*Arbeitsförderungsgesetz*) lays down the framework for FT schemes for the unemployed and also makes provision for financial support for employed individuals seeking to upgrade their qualifications. Resources for this area of training, which is publicly funded, have been much reduced over the last few years. The Vocational Training Promotion Act

(*Berufsbildungsförderungsgesetz*) makes much of the need for training to be planned, but its actual impact has been minimal. The Vocational Training Act (*Berufsbildungsgesetz*) lays down the framework for the German vocational training system, from initial to further and continuing training. This (partially) unified structure enables individuals to avail themselves of training opportunities throughout their working lives. Finally, the Workplace Labour Relations Act (*Betriebsverfassungsgesetz*) stipulates training rights and regulates the joint management of FT at company level. Despite this extensive legal framework, there is no general individual right to FT in Germany, and the legal incentives to invest in FT are aimed at individuals rather than companies. Since the early 1980s, almost all the *Länder* have made provision for individual training leave, generally for one week per year. This leave is usually a 'right' which has to be agreed to by the employer. The basic ambiguity of this measure is a major impediment to uptake, and the brevity of the leave allowed prevents individuals from embarking on training courses leading to a recognized qualification.

From the societal effect perspective, therefore, both national FT systems would appear to be consistent with the model of which they are a part. The German system is based on a coherent set of training paths rooted in the solid base provided by the dual system of vocational training. The French system, on the other hand, was designed to supplement the national model. In this system, FT is intended to compensate for the weakness and overly academic nature of initial vocational training in France, and represents an attempt to develop an area of activity based on joint management and consensus within a largely conflictual industrial relations system.

Despite the considerable differences between the two FT systems, it will be argued in the next section that their assessable effects in terms of labour market segmentation are not dramatically different.

Further training practices and labour market segmentation

Before trying to assess the effect of FT in terms of labour market segmentation, it is necessary to ascertain the overall level of firms' investment in FT. The available data (see Table 13.1) indicate that French firms invest more in FT than their German counterparts.

Both the access rate to FT courses and the training costs per employed person are consistent with the hypothesis that French firms invest much more in FT than their German counterparts in order to compensate for the lack of firm-specific initial training (Géhin and Méhaut, 1993). However, it should be noted that individual investment in vocational FT is more widespread in Germany than in France. Total expenditure on vocational FT, including individually financed measures, is higher in Germany than in France (BMBF, 1996, p. 354).

Table 13.1   Firms' investment in FT, 1993

	Access rate to firms' further training courses (in %)	Average duration of training courses	Training costs as a percentage of overall labour costs	Training costs per employed person (PPS[a])	Hourly training costs
France	36	52	2.2	564	29.7
Germany	24	34	1.2	292	35.6
EU average	28	43[b]	1.6	431	35.0

Notes:
[a]   Purchasing Power Standard.
[b]   Excluding Portugal, Greece and Ireland.

Source: Céreq/Eurostat data, results from the Continuing Vocational Training Survey 1994 (CVTS), panel data comparing further training practices in the 12 European Union member states in 1990, quoted in Céreq (1998, p. 11).

Table 13.2   Diversity of firms' further training practices

	Formalized training courses	Training on the job	Conferences, workshops, seminars	Job rotation	Self-training	% of companies using at least one training procedure
France	48	36	24	20	11	62
Germany	60	57	72	18	21	85
EU average	43	38	34	14	13	57

Source: Céreq/Eurostat data, results from the Continuing Vocational Training Survey 1994 (CVTS), quoted in Céreq (1998, p. 14).

The results presented in Table 13.2 introduce the question of inequality of access to FT within firms. The proportion of firms that use continuing training is higher in Germany than in France. Furthermore, even if the training practices of German firms are more diversified and tend to rely more often on on-the-job training, they also use formalized training courses more often than French firms. These figures suggest that the use of FT is more generally prevalent among German firms, but that a small group of French firms makes intensive use of FT. In terms of equality of access, these data imply that a large group of French employees working in firms that do not utilize FT are virtually excluded from this activity. These assumptions are congruent with a recent French analysis based on a house-hold panel (INSEE, 1994; Croquey, 1996).[5] According to this survey, 8.5 per cent of employees in small firms (those with between three and nine employees) benefited from FT during the relevant period; the figures for companies with between 100 and 499 employees and with more than 500 were 22 per cent and 31.1 per cent, respectively. CVTS data[6] indicate that the proportion of employees working in companies offering FT is 84.1 per cent in Germany and only 57.6 per cent in France (Eurostat, 1994, p. 56). All the CVTS results indicate that company size is a much stronger factor

Table 13.3   Participation in courses per 100 employees of all enterprises

Industry (selection)	Germany	France
Mining and quarrying	31	39
Food, beverages, tobacco	14	32
Non-metallic products	34	47
Transport equipment	21	49
Electricity, gas, water	48	56
Construction	13	17
Retail, trade, repair	32	28
Hotels and restaurants	9	30
Post and telecommunications	—	70
Banking and Insurance	55	68

Source: Eurostat, CVTS (1994, p. 72).

in determining inequality in France than in Germany (Table 13.3).[7]

On the other hand, industry affects access to FT in both countries in a similar way. White-collar industries provide the best opportunities for FT and the situations in manufacturing industries are disparate, while con-struction and personal services offer the lowest level of access to FT. In Germany at least, this sectoral distribution of firms' FT involvement is con-sistent with the distribution of firms' involvement in youth vocational training (Lutz, 1992). If this assumption held true at company level and in both countries, it would provide evidence that the most important determi-nants of firm's investment in training are sector-specific. The distribution of training investment between initial training and FT could then be explained largely by institutional factors (Table 13.4).

Among the individual factors determining access to FT, gender appears to

Table 13.4   Most relevant inequalities in access to firm-level further training[a]

	French data: access rate to firm-level further training between January 92 and May 93	German data: access rate to firm-level further training in the last 12 months (October 91/92 to January 91/92)
Gender		
Male	21.6	30
Female	19.5	23
Initial education		
Tertiary education	30.4	45
Upper secondary leaving certificate or technician's certificate	30.2	31
Vocational training certificate	19.4	22
No certificate	7.4	12
Occupational status		
Managerial	31.8	35[b]
White-collar	18.4	31
Manual worker	9.2	16

Notes:

[a]   The data presented here are taken from studies based on different methods and are not to be used for term-by-term comparison. The French FQP panel data are based on a sample of 18,300 people of working age. Of this sample, 10,117 were employed and constitute the sample for the present study. The German data presented here (Kuwan and Waschbüsch, 1994) is based on the German version of the 92/93 Labour Force Survey which comprises 2,095 people. German data from the BIBB/IAB panel (Jansen and Stooß, 1993) or from the BSW panel (BMBF, 1996), which are based on samples and methods comparable with the French FQP, combines firm-level further training with all other kinds of further training, so that it is almost impossible to isolate and analyse firms' activity in this area.

[b]   The German questionnaire asks whether the employee is in a managerial position.

Sources: French data: Enquête FQP INSEE 1993, quoted by Croquey (1996, p. 65). German data: Labour Force Survey 1992/93, quoted by Kuwan and Waschbüsch (1994).

be a much more significant cause of inequality in Germany than in France. Until the late 1980s, women's participation in FT was much lower than that of men in France as well. Dubar argues that the 1984 reform of the Further Training Act, which compels companies and works councils to negotiate on the gender dimension of company training plans, is one of the reasons for the rapid bridging of the gender gap in this area (Dubar, 2000, p. 70).

The other sources of inequality in access to FT seem to be more analogous in Germany and France (Table 13.4). In both countries, initial education levels and classifications are the most discriminating personal characteristics. Indeed, employees occupying the highest positions in firms and those with the highest level of education tend to absorb a very large share of firms' FT budgets. In that respect, and contrary to expectations, the French and the German situations are comparably poor as far as social exclusion is concerned. The FT access rate among the less skilled segments of the labour force is even worse in France than in Germany. Other factors such as employment contract duration or company seniority clearly reinforce the assumption that access to firms' FT provision is highly dependent on the extent to which individuals are integrated into the internal labour market.[8]

Despite certain differences, the provision of FT in Germany and France is marked by strong inequalities in access to courses. This finding could be interpreted as evidence that very different institutional systems actually produce similar effects (Regini, 1997). This assumption needs to be examined in greater detail.

Further training and industrial relations systems
In spite of the extensive legislative framework surrounding FT, the German system is much less institutionalized than the French one. Apart from detailed rules on joint decision making at company level, there is almost no legal constraint on employers in the area of continuing training in Germany. The social partners do not really play a decisive role in this area either, in contrast to the situation with initial vocational training (Giraud and Lallement, 1998). Géhin and Méhaut list a few regional industry-level agreements that aim to improve the returns on FT for the employed or seek to link working time reduction and the encouragement of individual FT (Géhin and Méhaut, 1993, pp. 123–4). Such agreements are still rather few in number, however, and the worsening of the general economic situation after German unification has not encouraged unions to go on the offensive in this field. From January 1996 to September 1998, only four out of 83 national or regional industry-level agreements laid down new rules for FT (WSI, *Tarivarchiv*, September 1998). Two of them, concluded in 1996 and 1997 in the textile and clothing industry, introduced a levy intended to finance a system of initial and continuing training within the industry. The others were concluded within Deutsche Telekom, the publicly owned telecommunications carrier. The company agreement[9] of July 1996 lays down collectively negotiated quality norms for FT, while the agreement of May 1998 established decentralized joint committees on FT, the main function of which is to make available grants for individually initiated training

schemes, most of which lead to a recognized qualification. In the same agreement, the company agreed to dedicate 10 per cent of all continuing training expenses to this particular programme.

Apart from these few examples, the overall influence of unions at industry level is weak. The unions are trying to strengthen their bargaining position on this issue by demanding more state regulation and public funding (DGB, 1998). In the German context, a mixed system of public and private regulation for FT would afford the unions greater room of manoeuvre, since the regulation of market policies such as those relating to the labour market is usually based on the strong involvement of the social partners. In the general field of training, moreover, the situation in the initial vocational market has become so difficult in recent years that the unions have concentrated their bargaining power on the preservation of apprenticeships. Between January 1996 and September 1998, 15 of the 83 industry agreements concluded seek to promote initial vocational training and youth employment by laying down tough training rates for companies[10] or guaranteeing employment for six or 12 months for those trainees who pass their final examinations (WSI, *Tarifarchiv*, September 1998).

The position of employers' associations is more ambiguous. Firstly, they claim there is no need for any kind of regulation of FT practices.[11] On the other hand, however, they are heavily involved in the FT market and regard the provision of FT as one of the services with which they provide their clients in order to help them manage the considerable constraints imposed on them by the agreements they negotiate with the unions at industry level (Soskice and Hancké, 1997, pp. 255–6). In particular, by trying to help small and medium-sized firms develop their FT activities, the employers' associations intend to make any other kind of regulation superfluous.

At company level, FT is one of the areas covered by the legislation on codetermination. According to the Workplace Labour Relations Act, in cases where firms fund FT for their employees, the works council can suggest or indeed require that individual employees or groups of employees be included in the scheme (section 98, *Betriebsverfassungsgesetz*). However, at this level too, unions and works council members tend to focus their bargaining power on the issues of particular concern to the unions.

This apparent lack of investment in FT by all actors in the German industrial relations system can be explained by at least three factors. Firstly, the FT system itself does not place them in a very strong position on the issue. Secondly, the unions have in recent years developed a strategy aimed at safeguarding employment. Thirdly, interventions in the area of training are already focused on the worsening problems faced by the initial vocational training system.

Given the level of public regulation in the French FT system, the situation in our second country should be different. The Further Training Act of 1971 introduced consultation and bargaining procedures on firms' provision of FT at both industry and company level. As a result, the regulatory framework governing the provision of FT took on many of the characteristics of the corporatist model (Mériaux, 1998, p. 112). These procedures have been modified and extended several times since 1971. The current regulations stipulate that management at company level has to 'consult' the works council on the company's annual FT plan. This 'consultation' is close to the spirit of the 1982 Auroux Acts and maintains the 'company director's responsibility for training' (quoted by Dubar, 2000, p. 33). In other words, the company must disclose and discuss the content of its FT programme for the next year but does not have to take the views of the works council into account. In spite of the reluctance of the French unions to cooperate with management, this annual obligation to negotiate might, in the medium or long term, lead to the joint management of company FT policy.

Up to the early 1990s, several waves of negotiation at industry level led to a series of reforms of the FT system.[12] Between the 1970s and 1990s, continuing training was one of the few objects of consensual bargaining between management and labour at industry and even inter-industry level. The various actors now seem to be increasingly dissatisfied with the outcomes of this bargaining, as well as with their further effects.

The first reason for this discontent is that very little use has been made to date of the right of individual workers to initiate FT. In 1996, less than 1 per cent of all employees participated in an FT course financed by their employer.[13] In an attempt to balance company FT policy and the interests of individual workers, the 1993 Labour Act drawn up by the conservative government introduced an individually initiated training scheme known as *Capital Temps Formation* (CTF). Companies pay a levy of 0.1 per cent of their total wage bill into a training fund and the costs of all training courses they allow their employees to attend are then refunded, provided that the courses satisfy the conditions laid down at industry level. This scheme is aimed primarily at employees wishing to prepare for training leading to a recognized qualification, with priority being given to the lower-skilled elements of the workforce (Centre INFFO, 1997). In spite of vehement opposition from the radical CGT trade union confederation (Joubier, 1998, p. 45) and the deep divisions within the moderate CFDT on the matter (Guilloux, 1997, p. 30), 32 industry-level agreements were concluded between 1994 and 1995 (Centre INFFO, 1997, p. v) and 16 in 1997 (Ministère de l'emploi et de la solidarité, 1998, pp. 108–9). The explanation for the dynamism of industry-level regulation in this area is that the moderate unions hoped initially that they would be able to enlist the support of the state in linking continuing training and working-time reduction (Besson, 1997).

Preliminary data from some industries would suggest that, once again, it is more highly-qualified employees seeking to improve or diversify their skills who are making most use of CTF.[14] It would also seem that, in most industries, a considerable share of the levies paid into the fund ends up in the state's pocket, since far too few employees avail themselves of the opportunities open to them under the scheme. More generally, the increasing inability of the actors in the French industrial relations system to reach any kind of consensus would seem considerably to reduce the efficiency of FT regulation (Mériaux, 1998, pp. 121–2).

French firms spend considerable sums of money on FT. Most larger companies spend well in excess of the minimum laid down and the average expenditure rate reached 3.31 per cent of the total wage bill in 1993 (Céreq, 1995).[15] Nevertheless, companies concentrate their expenditure on training courses closely related to their production or human resources management (HRM) needs. The objectives of the industry-level negotiations, which seek to establish different forms of individual rights to FT and to put in place training programmes offering recognized qualifications to those with the lowest skills, are not reflected in the reality of company FT. The joint regulation of FT practices at company level, reinforced by the legislation of the 1980s, has turned out to be the key locus of attempts by the social partners to influence the actual outcomes of continuing training. However, the question of cooperative governance at company level is a problematic issue in France, not only for management and unions but also for employee representatives at company level.

4.   CASE STUDIES

The case studies undertaken in three manufacturing industries in Germany and in France reveal the considerable influence exerted by the industry-specific determinants of company FT policy. French and German firms competing in the same product markets not only share certain technological and organizational characteristics: decision-making structures and procedures also seem to be converging. However, the differences between the national industrial relations systems also play an important role in shaping companies' training policies.

In this section, the findings of the case studies are outlined and company FT practices are categorized in accordance with the motivations driving firms' investment in training. For each category of training identified, the decision-making process leading to the design and funding of the training programme is analysed. In each case, an attempt is made to identify the actors responsible for deciding to implement a training programme, the decision-making procedure involved, the level of employee selectivity and the extent to which joint decision-making bodies are involved. The term 'selectivity' is used to denote the propensity of firms to exclude from training provision those employees for whom the returns on training are reckoned to be low. In theory, lower returns to FT might be expected for unskilled workers, part-timers and those on limited contracts. The focus here is on the larger training schemes implemented in each company. The various programmes are differentiated from each other according to the extent to which the decision-making procedures are centralized. In this way, the degree of customization can be assessed and the possible access and bargaining level for employees or employee representatives identified.

For instance, centralized decision making involving the human resources (HR) department might open up opportunities for negotiation on FT issues that could be linked with other issues such as pay (bonuses), working time or working conditions. In a decentralized production unit, training decisions are more likely to be shaped either by the actual needs identified by middle management or by the personal relationships between middle managers and the various members of the unit. Unless a democratic form of management has been established, a highly decentralized form of decision making might reduce the space available for collective action, representation and any kind of organized bargaining.

Laboratory Chemicals

Company-initiated FT in this industry is subject to many constraints. All workers handling chemical and biochemical products must attend regular health and safety and quality-assurance training courses and acquire the corresponding certificates. In recent years, the production processes in the industry have undergone drastic changes and have rapidly become industrialized and automated. These changes have led to a sudden increase in companies' skill requirements. The lower average level of skills among production workers in the French firm investigated has made it necessary for the company to increase its investment in training. Both of the firms studied have decentralized their system of work organization and removed at least two levels of the management hierarchy. They have also both applied for ISO accreditation.

1.　The health and safety and quality certificates are acquired through training that is largely internal and involves the whole of the workforce.

In both companies, management of this kind of production-related FT is decentralized. In the German company, team leaders inform production managers of the likely training needs in their groups. Managers check the training budget and establish priorities for the various FT applications. In the French company, the decision-making process is equally decentralized but the organization and budget check is handled by specialists in the HR department and not by the head of the production department. In neither case is there any selectivity for this kind of health and safety training.

2. Other production-related training programmes linked to technical change or to new products are reserved in the first instance for the core labour force. The selection process is decentralized, but in both the German and French companies the courses are developed in cooperation with the head of the production department or the relevant engineers. In the French company, the HR department is involved in the budgeting of the training.

3. Both companies supplement their core workforce with younger, more flexible, workers employed on short-term contracts. The German company uses this flexible, peripheral workforce to cover for the *Gastarbeiter* among its permanent employees, who tend to take their holidays at the same time, and to cope with seasonal variations in demand. In the French firm, the use of flexible contracts has become an established practice involving some 20 per cent of all production workers. The HR department of the French company maintains a continuous training programme aimed at all employees on short-term contracts. The firm is located in a rural area and uses a local non-mobile pool of low-skill young people as a flexible source of labour. The company's FT department keeps records on the gradual training of these regular/occasional workers. Team leaders can consult files on individual skill profiles and adapt their flexible hiring practices to this long-term strategy.

4. All new permanent recruits in the French company have passed the *baccalauréat* and completed two years of specialist training in higher education. The German company used to recruit skilled bakers or plumbers but now hires only young people trained by the company in one of the recognized trades or occupations related to laboratory chemicals or people from a higher educational level. In both firms, these young, skilled people are useful in implementing the strategy of production decentralization, since they are both mobile and keen to obtain rapid promotion. Both firms have developed FT programmes leading to recognized qualifications for their unskilled labour force. In both cases there is little demand from the target group. Both compa-

nies in fact concentrate their expenditure on skill enhancement training on the newly recruited and already highly skilled sections of the workforce (Table 13.5).

Table 13.5 Further training practices in laboratory chemicals firms

Goal of further training	German firm		French firm	
	Selectivity	Joint decision making	Selectivity	Joint decision making
1. Health and safety and quality certification	− − D	− −	− − D	− −
2. Other production-related training	+ D/C	− −	+ D/C	− −
3. Labour force flexibility	− − D	− −	− − D	− −
4. Skill enhancement	+ + D/C	+/− D/C	+ + D/C	− −

Note: Each row relates to a specific type of training and to the numbered sections in the text; D = decentralized decision making, C = centralized decision making.

In the French company, the level of involvement of employee representatives in both the development and implementation of the four different kinds of FT is low. Management is obliged by law to disclose the main objectives of the annual company training plan to the works council, but consensus on the matter is seldom reached. Union representatives have requested more FT courses leading to recognized qualifications and more joint decision making in the day-to-day running of the various courses. Management doubts that employee representatives have sufficient expertise to make a useful contribution in that respect.

The works council in the German firm also makes little contribution to decisions on FT. However, the good relationship between labour and management means the works council is in a position to support applications from individual workers seeking company funding in order to attend training courses leading to recognized qualifications. The works council's activities in this respect do not give it any influence over the general development or implementation of company FT policy and smacks more of clientism than joint decision making.

Telecommunications Carriers

In both countries, the ending of the public monopoly in the telecommunications market has been reflected in changes to many aspects of company management. Partial privatization and the emergence of new telecommunications companies have forced both public carriers to face competition for the first time. As a result, they have had to deal with new kinds of price and quality pressures. In both companies, the workforce has maintained its civil service status but management is trying to develop new types of company-wide and local agreements in order to increase employee mobility. In both Germany and France, the dominant telecommunications carriers use FT as one of the main channels for negotiation with the workforce and as an instrument of internal change and adjustment at local level. In this particular sector, the public-sector organizational structures are still affecting the institutional environment.

The German carrier is used to negotiating company agreements at central level, but the management of the French company has only recently discovered the advantages of company-level bargaining. In the past, the French government was the negotiating party for all matters relating to the labour/management relationship, with the result that any linkage between company policies and human resources management was constrained by political considerations. The radical change in the French government's attitude to its public telecommunications carrier has enabled the company to negotiate new types of company agreements similar to those already long established in the German company.

Disparate types of FT coexist in both companies.[16] An attempt has been made, therefore, to organize this wide range of practices into categories based on the level of appropriateness of each kind of training to the companies' requirements.

1. The telecommunications sector is subject to constant technical change. For decades now, both the French and German carriers have been developing a company culture of continuing training that reflects the centrality to both companies of technical performance. They both maintain their own training centres that provide a wide range of mostly technical training. These training centres periodically publish catalogues of available courses, which all company employees are invited to consult. This type of technical FT seems to be clearly related to the need to adapt to technical change. In fact, depending on the various hierarchical relationships pertaining locally, this type of FT is implemented at a very decentralized level and is the subject of negotiations between individual employees and their immediate superior. In the French and German public-sector environment, in which priority is given to FT, ordinary employees actually enjoy greater autonomy than in private firms even in the matter of FT implementation. Under these conditions, FT can quite easily be used as a reward or other kind of

compensation. However, the new downward pressure on costs is forcing both public carriers to increase the effectiveness of their FT expenditure, and both companies are trying to develop new procedures for managing that expenditure.

2. The ending of the telecommunications monopoly has forced the public carriers drastically to reduce and reallocate both general and labour costs. The German carrier plans to shed thousands of jobs over a fairly short time span. This redundancy programme is going to give rise to an enormous amount of job rotation, and a corresponding share of FT will be dedicated to internal retraining. A centrally negotiated company agreement lays down highly detailed rules for selecting employees to be retrained and allocated to new jobs. At local and regional level, joint committees made up of representatives of works councils and management are responsible for deciding on disputed cases, of which there are many.

   The French company has followed a different path in its drive to combine cost reduction and workforce reallocation. It seems to have adopted a less aggressive approach to the overmanning problem than its German counterpart, at least for the time being. Important reforms in industrial relations have to be tested and implemented with great caution in the French public sector because of the unpredictability of workforce–management relations. The company is slowly shedding jobs and offering career opportunities in occupations and divisions where there are manpower shortages. The company pays any retraining costs that might be incurred.

3. In recent months, the French telecommunications carrier has been testing a new use of FT as both an instrument for workforce redeployment and a source of new HRM rules. In one division of the company, whose vertical structuring has been reinforced, management has cut jobs, redeployed some of the workforce and changed the rules governing promotion and job classification. All these processes have been linked to FT courses. After lengthy and complex negotiations conducted at central level, the moderate unions signed an agreement whereby the traditional promotion rules of the French public service, based on competitive examinations in general subjects, will be replaced in one division by a varied process of job-related and skill-based self-evaluation, initial selection and guidance, training, fair examination and, finally, job reclassification. This centrally negotiated but locally implemented reform of company HRM strategy should not be linked to codetermination. French unions generally refuse to be associated with any kind of screening or selection process in the company. The unions apparently accepted this reform of the promotion rules because

it replaces general with technical, job-related knowledge in the selection process.

Unlike the German public carrier, The French company still cannot rely on unions being willing to accept the social costs of jobs reduction and labour force reallocation in exchange for power sharing in both the development and the implementation of the measures[17].

4. Finally, mention should be made of the company agreement concluded in the spring of 1998 between management and unions in the German public carrier. In partial compensation for the large-scale redundancy programme, the union was able to negotiate a substantial contribution by the company to individually initiated FT leading to recognized qualifications. Ten per cent of all company expenditure on continuing training now has to be dedicated to individually initiated FT, most of it leading to the award of recognized qualifications. These special budgets are to be managed at a decentralized level by joint works council/management committees. The unions were able to negotiate joint management rights over an important source of funding for training and may turn it into an effective tool of workforce solidarity. However, it should be noted that such codetermination practices may also lead the union to concentrate its bargaining power on its core clientele, which is for the most part the skilled elements within the workforce (Table 13.6).

Table 13.6   Further training practices in telecommunications carriers

	German firm		French firm	
Telecommunications carriers	Selectivity	Joint decision making	Selectivity	Joint decision making
1. Technical change	− D	+/− D	− D	+/− D
2. Internal mobility and labour force adjustment	+ + D/C	+ D/C	+ D	+/− C
3. Change in HR management rules			+ + D/C	+/− C
4. Individually initiated further training	+/− D/C	+ + D/C		

Note: As for Table 13.5.

Railway Rolling Stock Industry

The general economic situation in this sector is more serious than in the other two. The position of the companies investigated as appointed suppliers to their national public railway companies and to many local transport companies is becoming less and less comfortable: the public transport sector is also facing renewed cost competition. At the same time, new products and technologies, such as high-speed train systems, developed by these market competitors have achieved worldwide success. Their positive effects on international markets have until recently guaranteed a stable workforce but increased the pressures on both companies to keep on performing well. Increased productivity has become the primary objective in an industry that has recently been affected by drastic cost reduction plans and lay-offs.

Thanks to its stable market position, the French company has been able to avoid redundancies or even job losses in the plant we investigated. Nevertheless, in 1995, the company introduced an ambitious programme of productivity increase. The plan involved reorganization of the production process, simplification of the management structure, a general improvement in quality management and, lastly, the introduction of project-based organization. FT packages specifically designed to facilitate work or process reorganization and quality improvement have been bought in from specialist firms and used to train all employees (2). More generally, the company's satisfactory market position provides sufficient resources for investment in FT for adaptation to technical change (1). The management of this kind of FT is still fairly centralized and the training courses are monopolized by managerial staff; in this sense, it is still characteristic of top-down management practices. The decentralization of the production hierarchy has not been accompanied by a corresponding decentralization of HRM. Neither type of FT leads to recognized qualification, but both are closely matched to company requirements. There is virtually no individually initiated FT in this company, nor any other types of FT linked to promotion.

The German company tried to implement similar quality and productivity improvement measures in a less certain and stable market situation. The plant is unprofitable, and the FT budget is consequently small and selectivity for all kinds of FT high (1, 2). Continuing training is organized by the firms' engineers and is only made available if absolutely necessary. Moreover, instability of employment in this plant generates considerable labour turnover, which in turn increases the need for training. There is no joint management of FT expenditure. However, employees of all levels and positions are theoretically able to apply for any kind of FT and a considerable amount of training is provided by the corporation. Applicants are selected at central level by the head of the production department in collaboration with the human resources department. Considerable disparities between blue- and white-collar working in the allocation of FT opportunities have been reported. Virtually all applications for FT from production workers have been rejected in recent years. Even the new work group leaders, who have been allocated many new tasks as a result of the decentralization of work organization, have been unable to obtain basic training in organization or HR management. The only FT courses offered to production workers as a whole are those linked to safety certification and specific technical changes (1). The German firm has made only very limited use of FT as a means of mobilizing the workforce during periods of organizational change, unlike its French counterpart, which has made extensive use of FT for precisely that purpose (Table 13.7).

Table 13.7   Further training practices in the railway rolling stock industry

Rail transport manufacturing	German firm		French firm	
	Selectivity	Joint decision making	Selectivity	Joint decision making
1. Technical change	+/− C	− −	+/− C	− −
2. Work reorganization and quality management improvement	+ + C	− −	− − C	− −

Note: The numbers relate to specific references within the preceding text.

5.   CONCLUDING REMARKS

Our comparative approach, based on pairs of companies supplying very similar products or services, has not confirmed the coherent national systems hypothesis. On the contrary, similar trends in the evolution of work organization and of firms' FT policies were observed, not only across countries but also within sectors. Significant long-term disparities, such as those in skills structures, do of course persist. However, contrary to the argument advanced by Mason, van Ark and Wagner, the disparities observed in the case of laboratory chemicals, for instance, are not an impediment to the successful development of both firms in the same product market (Mason *et al.*, 1996, p.191). In that case, the skill supply cannot explain the firms' product strategies. In the other two cases, the skills structures are quite similar to each other, which would suggest that, in the telecommunications and railway rolling stock industries at least, the recruiting strategies of German and French companies, and maybe both educational systems as well, have been following converging paths over the past few years, which does not accord with the explanations offered by the 'societal effect' approach.

The second conclusion that can be drawn concerns the substitution hypothesis advanced by Géhin and Méhaut (1993), who suggest that French firms might use FT to compensate for the failure of the overly academic vocational training system to equip workers with specific skills. The rather constraining French system of incentives to invest in FT could thus be regarded as an institutional opportunity for firms to develop their FT practices. However, this argument, which is a further development of the societal effect approach and is confirmed in the case of laboratory chemicals, has to be qualified in certain respects. Firstly, it was observed that the effects of the legal incentive system in France vary considerably according to industry and size of firm. The pattern of variation is quite similar in Germany. This strongly suggests that there are other, industry-specific factors shaping FT in firms. In Germany, moreover, industries such as banking and insurance and energy combine considerable investment in initial training with investment in FT, which indicates that the substitution phenomenon is not supported by our evidence, at least in these industries.

The third set of conclusions that can be drawn here relates more directly to the initial question we addressed in our comparison of both FT systems: how successful are the two systems in fighting social exclusion?

In statistical terms, it was noted that, apart from those related to gender, the inequalities in the allocation of FT in companies are comparable in both countries. In both cases, training is a strongly cumulative process, and in both systems the lack of an initial qualification is the most discriminating factor in determining access to company-financed training opportunities. This first observation indicates that the effects of the two sophisticated but very different FT regulatory frameworks are rather weak.

In France, the unusual corporatist nature of the regulatory framework was nourished by dynamic bargaining over two decades. In the 1990s, it seems to have been affected by the increasing inability of employers' associations and labour organizations to act effectively. Even though an effective regulatory framework has been maintained in some industries, there is little evidence that companies make use of the most advanced types of FT. The rudimentary joint management procedures introduced at company level in the 1980s have had little effect on firms' day-to-day FT practices. Continuing training, which has often been presented as the one consensual element in the conflictual French industrial relations environment, has not been sufficient to initiate a 'velvet revolution' leading to the development of joint management practices at firm level. One possible reason for this failure in the French case might be the adverse combination of the late recognition of unions as bargaining partners in French companies and the dispersion of bargaining power and responsibility on the management or government side (Lallement, 1997, p. 308).

In Germany, the legal incentive system for FT is generally weaker than in France. The most effective resource available to actors in the industrial relations system seeking to turn company FT practices into a weapon against social exclusion is the Workplace Labour Relations Act, which provides the work council with extensive rights of codetermination in respect of the implementation of company-financed FT. However, these company-level workforce representative bodies are highly dependent on the general strategies adopted by the unions, and in recent years there has been a failure to provide adequate opportunities for extending the strategic role of FT.

In both Germany and France, there has been a reduction in the linkage between FT and firms' promotion strategies. In both countries, companies are tending to recruit new employees with skills specific to each vacancy. The decentralization of production has eliminated a high proportion of intermediate positions in firms, thereby doing away with the most accessible internal promotion opportunities for production workers. Support for the traditional upgrading paths in German firms is becoming increasingly eroded, and the French FT system has been unable to contribute to the development of upgrading in French companies. It was evident from all the case studies that firms' use of FT is related to their needs in terms of technical change, work or process reorganization and human resources management or mobilization. In two out of three sectors, the general trend towards production decentralization has led to a similar trend in FT development and implementation.

However, joint management practices are still weak in both countries. This is hardly surprising in the case of France, but a more detailed explanation is required in the German case. Decades of codetermination in Germany have led to the incorporation of a number of economically significant outcomes, such as quality or productivity management, into plant-level collective bargaining. However, work councils have been unable to make the regulation of FT a subject for plant-level bargaining, in spite of the provisions of the Workplace Labour Relations Act. This again raises the question of the fairness of such microcorporatist arrangements.

The transitional labour markets approach demonstrates that the transitions that are most risky for individuals and most expensive for society at large are those that take place without preparation or support. FT is a transitional market to which both industrial relations systems are closely and continuously related. From the centre of the industrial relations system to company level, unions have been able to implement a long-term and coordinated strategy aimed at putting FT expenditure to use for more solidaristic purposes. The breakdown of production accounting into cost centres is threatening firms' most vulnerable employees (Gazier, 1998, pp. 344–5). The current rapid expansion in companies' use of flexible employment forms is further evidence of the gaps now opening up between the various segments of the labour market. Industrial relations systems have to find new solutions to a problem that is no longer new but is threatening further to exacerbate social exclusion within European societies. Models of working-time redistribution could be adapted to be applied in the field of training, mobility, promotion and careers. If employment can be considered as a collective good that can be shared, then, other determinants of social integration such as skills could be regarded as possible objects of innovative forms of redistribution. The current trend towards the decentralization of industrial relations tends to make the company a resilient locus for bargaining and the development of new types of solidarity. The state could provide incentives, in terms of certification procedures or rights to company-level bargaining on FT, which might help firms become more effective instruments of labour market integration, thereby providing some form of quid-pro-quo arrangement for the many flexibilization measures they have benefited from in all Western countries in recent years.

NOTES

1. I would like to acknowledge the helpful comments and suggestions received from the following in response to an earlier draft of this chapter: Florence Audier, Michel Lallement, Gilbert Lefèvre, Olivier Mériaux, and the editors of this book. For his help at a preliminary stage of the work, I thank Dick Moraal.
2. This assertion needs some qualification. Many scholars have shown that unions can be tempted to set clear priorities in their interest representation strategies and might well favour a stable, core labour force over outsiders or newcomers. This classic debate on collective action should not be forgotten here (Olson, 1982; Offe and Wiesenthal, 1980).
3. Other relevant criteria such as location (rural or urban), finance, workforce skill structure and so on will be considered only in the analysis of the case studies.
4. Smaller companies are required to spend only 0.15 per cent of their wage bill on further training.
5. A sample of 18 300 individuals were asked in 1993 about further training participation in the previous 17 months.
6. Continuing Vocational Training Survey in Enterprises, based on a survey of 50 000 enterprises in 12 member states (Eurostat, 1994).
7. A study by the Institut der Deutschen Wirtschaft corroborates this point (Weiss, 1994, p. 51).
8. Data for these two situations are available only for France. The access rate to further training for employees with more than five years' tenure is 1.5 times higher than that for those with less than one year's tenure. The access rate for employees on permanent contracts is 2.7 times higher than that for those on fixed-term contracts (Data FQP, quoted by Croquey, 1996, p. 65).
9. Company agreements within huge companies such as Deutsche Telekom, which has almost 200 000 employees, are regarded by the social partners as industry agreements.

10. The training rate is the ratio of trainees/employees. Unions and work councils keep a vigilant eye on this ratio, particularly in periods of tension in the apprenticeship market.
11. Interview with employers' association, Berlin, September 1998.
12. The national inter-industry agreements of 1982 and 1991, for example, have been incorporated into more comprehensive legislation.
13. This assessment of the take-up of the individual right to further training is modified by more detailed examination. Eighty-one per cent of the periods of training granted under the terms of the scheme led to the award of a recognised qualification. More than 17 per cent of these periods were granted to employees on short-term contracts and 59 per cent to people aged between 25 and 34. Only 8 per cent of the people taking part in courses were unskilled workers; 40 per cent were white-collar workers, 17 per cent foremen or technicians and more than 11 per cent engineers and managers (cadres) (COPACIF, 1996).
14. Interview with Fédération Chimie Energie CFDT, Paris, July 1998.
15. Expenditure by smaller firms (those with between 10 and 19 employees) is 1.6 per cent, very close to the compulsory minimum.
16. It is likely that companies employing more than 150 000 people in the French case and almost 200 000 people in the German case actually make use of many more types of continuing training than the categories used here. Nevertheless, these categories do correspond to the main further training activities that can be compared within equivalent divisions of these big companies.
17. The risks linked to this kind of union strategy in the German context have already been pointed out (Mahnkopf, 1989).

BIBLIOGRAPHY

Auer, Peter (1994), 'Further Education and Training for the Employed: Systems and Outcomes', in Günther Schmid (ed.), *Labor Market Institutions in Europe: A Socioeconomic Evaluation of Performance*, New York: M.E. Sharpe, pp. 121–50.

Becker, Rolf and Schömann, Klaus (1996), 'Berufliche Bildung und Einkommensdynamik – Eine Längsschnittstudie mit besonderer Berücksichtigung von Selektionsprozessen', *Kölner Zeitschrift für Soziologie und Sozialpsychologie*, 3, 426–61.

Besson, Virginie (1997), 'Capital de temps de formation – Critiques et louanges d'un nouveau dispositif', *Entreprises-Formation*, 104, December, 26–8.

BMBF – Bundesministerium für Bildung, Wissenschaft, Forschung und Technologie (1996), *Berichtssystem Weiterbildung VI – Integrierter Gesamtbericht zur Weiterbildungssituation in Deutschland*, Bonn: BMBF.

Brochier, Damien and Mériaux, Olivier (1997), 'La gestion paritaire des fonds de la formation – Genèse et enjeux d'un nouveau système', *Céreq-Bref*, 131, May, 1–4.

Carriou, Yannick and Jeger, François (1997), 'La formation continue dans les entreprises et son retour sur investissement', *Economie et Statistique*, 303, 45–57.

Centre INFFO (1997), 'Capital de temps formation: le démarrage', *Inffo Flash*, 469, 1 February.

Céreq (1995), *La Formation continue en France*, 113, Marseilles: Céreq.

Céreq (1998), *La formation professionnelle continue dans les entreprises françaises en 1993 – Résultats d'une enquête européenne*, Documents série observatoire 133, February, Marseilles: Céreq.

COPACIF (1996), 'Le congé individuel de formation – Repères et tendances 1987–1994', journées techniques du 28 mars 1996 (working document).

Croquey, Edwige (1996), 'La formation professionnelle continue: des inégalités d'accès et des effets sur la carrière peu importants à court terme', *Travail et Emploi*, 65, 61–8.

DGB (1998), 'Allianz der Aufbruchs – Plattform Weiterbildung', *Einblick*, 13–14.

Drexel, Ingrid (1996), 'Kosten und Nutzen unterschiedlicher Weiterbildungs-systeme – Schlagartiger und offene Fragen aus international vergleichender Perspektive', in Richard von Barbeleben, Axel Bolder and Helmut Heid (eds), *Kosten und Nutzen beruflicher Bildung*, Stuttgart: Franz Steiner Verlag, pp. 42–54.

Dubar, Claude (2000), *La formation professionnelle continue*, Paris: La Découverte.

Eurostat (1994), Continuing Vocational Training Survey, Luxembourg: Eurostat.

Gazier, Bernard (1998), 'Ce que sont les marchés transitionnels', in Jean-Claude Barbier and Jérôme Gautié (eds), *Les politiques de l'emploi en Europe et aux Etats-Unis*, Paris: Presses Universitaires de France, pp. 339–55.

Géhin, Jean-Paul and Méhaut, Philippe (1993), *Apprentissage ou formation continue? Stratégies éducatives des entreprises en Allemagne et en France*, Paris: L'Harmattan.

Giraud, Olivier and Lallement, Michel (1998), 'Construction et épuisement du modèle néo-corporatiste allemand – La Réunification comme consécration d'un processus de fragmentation sociale', *Revue française de sociologie*, XXXIX(1), 36–69.

Guilloux, Patrick (1997), 'Le CTF n'est pas un droit!' (interview by Virginie Besson), *Entreprises-Formation*, 104, December, 30.

Hollingsworth, J. Rogers and Boyer, Robert (1997), 'From National Embeddedness to Spatial and Institutional Nestedness', in J. Rogers Hollingsworth and Robert Boyer (eds), *Contemporary Capitalism – The Embeddedness of Institutions*, Cambridge: Cambridge University Press, pp. 433–84.

Hollingsworth, J. Rogers, Schmitter, Phillipe C. and Streeck, Wolfgang (eds) (1994), *Governing Capitalist Economies. Performance and Control of Economic Sectors*, New York: Oxford University Press.

INSEE (1994), 'La formation professionnelle continue', *INSEE-Première*, 314, May.

Jansen, Rolf and Stooß, Friedemann (1993), 'Qualifikation und Erwerbssituation im geeinten Deutschland', *BIBB/IAB Erhebung 1991/92*, Berlin/Bonn: Bundes-institut für Berufsbildung, Institut für Arbeitsmarktforschung.

Joubier, Jean-Michel (1998), 'Une réforme de la formation professionnelle continue', *Le Peuple*, 1482/1483, July, 45–7.

Katzenstein, Peter J. (1987), *Politics and Policy in West-Germany – the Growth of a Semi-Sovereign State*, Philadelphia: Temple University Press.

Kuwan, Helmut and Waschbüsch, Eva (1994), *Betriebliche Weiterbildung – Ergebnisse einer Befragung von Erwerbstätigen und betrieblichen Experten in Deutschland*, Bonn: Bundesministerium für Bildung und Wissenschaft.

Lallement, Michel (1997), 'Du gouvernement à la gouvernance de l'emploi', *Cahiers Internationaux de Sociologie*, CIII, 295–311.

Lutz, Burkart (1992), 'La hiérarchie interne du système dual', in Martine Möbus and Eric Verdier (eds), *Le système de formation professionnelle en République Fédérale d'Allemagne – Résultats de recherche françaises et allemandes*, Collection des Etudes, *CEREQ*, 61, February, 143–5.

Mahnkopf, Birgit (1989), 'Gewerkschaftspolitik und Weiterbildung – Chancen und Risiken einer qualifikationsorientierten Modernisierung gewerkschaftlicher Tarif-Politik', *WZB Discussion paper*, FS-I, 89–11, Wissenschaftszentrum Berlin.

Marsden, David (1990), 'Institutions and Labour Mobility: Occupational and Internal Labour Markets in Britain, France and West Germany', in Renato Brunetta and Carlo Dell'Aringa (eds), *Labour Relations and Economic Performance*, Basingstoke: Macmillan.

Mason, Geoff, van Ark, Bart and Wagner, Karin (1996), 'Workforce Skills, Product Quality and Economic Performance', in Alison L. Booth and Dennis J. Snower (eds), *Acquiring Skills: Market Failures, their Symptoms and Policy Responses*, Cambridge: Cambridge University Press, pp. 177–97.

Maurice, Marc, Sellier, François and Silvestre, Jean-Jacques (1986), *The Social Foundations of Industrial Power – A Comparison of France and Germany*, Cambridge, Mass.: MIT Press.

Mériaux, Olivier (1998), 'Logiques d'échange politique et régulation du système français de formation professionnelle continue', in Bruno Lamotte (ed.), *Les régulations de l'emploi – Les stratégies des acteurs*, Paris: L'Harmattan, pp. 111–22.

Ministère de l'emploi et de la solidarité (1998), *La Négociation collective en 1997 – Tome I, Tendance et dossiers*, Paris: La Documentation Française.

OECD (1997), 'Labour Market Policy: New Challenges – Life Long Learning to stay employable all life long, Meeting of Ministers for Employment', *Labour and Social Affairs*, Paris, 14–15 October.

Offe, Claus and Wiesenthal, Helmut (1980), 'Two Logics of Collective Action: theoretical notes on social class and organizational form', *Political Power and Social Theory*, 1, 67–115.

Olson, Mancur (1982), *The Rise and Decline of Nations – Economic Growth, Stagflation and Social Rigidities*, New Haven, Conn.: Yale University Press.

Piore, Michael and Sabel, Charles (1984), *The Second Industrial Divide*, New York: Basic Books.

Regini, Marino (1997), 'Different Responses to Common Demands: Firms, Institutions, and Training in Europe', *European Sociological Review*, 13(3), 267–82.

Schmidt, Rudi and Trinczek, Rainer (1991), 'Duales System: Tarifliche und betriebliche Interessenvertretung', in Walther Müller-Jentsch (ed.), *Konflikt-partnerschaft – Akteure und Institutionen der industriellen Beziehungen*, Munich: Rainer Hampp Verlag, pp. 167–99.

Schömann, Klaus, Becker, Rolf and Zühlke, S. (1996), 'Further Education and Occupational Careers: A Longitudinal Study on Participation in Further Training and its Impact on Employment Prospects', paper presented at the GSOEP Conference held in Potsdam 10–12 July 1996.

Soskice, David and Hancké, Bob (1997), 'De la construction des normes industrielles à l'organisation de la formation professionnelle – Une approche comparative', in Martine Möbus and Eric Verdier (eds), *Les diplômes professionnels en Allemagne et en France: Conception et jeux d'acteurs*, Paris: L'Harmattan, pp. 245–62.

Streeck, Wolfgang (1991), 'On the Institutional Conditions of Diversified Quality Production', in Egon Matzner and Wolfgang Streeck (eds), *Beyond Keynesianism: the Socio-Economics of Production and Employment*, Aldershot, UK and Brookfield, US: Edward Elgar.

Weiss, Reinhold (1994), *Betriebliche Weiterbilung – Ergebnisse der Weiter-bildungserhebung der Wirtschaft*, Cologne: Deutscher Instituts-Verlag.

WSI (1998), *Tarifarchiv*, on-line information service, September.

14. Assessing the impact of experimental EU training policies in France, Germany and Ireland

Sophie Rouault

If 'the essence of federalism is not to be found in a particular set of institutions but in the institutionalization of particular relationships among the participants in political life' (Sbragia, 1993), then European integration can be understood as a long-standing 'process of institutional creativity' (Hooghe, 1996). Within this theoretical framework, this chapter seeks to scrutinize policy change through empirical investigation of some experimental training programmes financed by the European Social Funds (ESF) and monitored by DG V of the European Commission (Directorate General for Employment, Industrial Relations and Social Affairs).

The regulatory and redistributive policies that make up the social dimension of the EU are indeed the outcomes of long-standing processes of consultation, conciliation and bargaining that constitute both a quest for information, expertise and legitimacy and the essence of a 'European policy style' (Mazey and Richardson, 1998). The formulation of European policies could thus be characterized as a specific form of negotiated and coordinated collective action, relying not only on hierarchical but also on more informal and societal forms of interaction, involving forms of mutual learning and leading to more or less institutionalized policy arrangements.

In the first section of this chapter, the policies in question are located within the broader context of the reforms of EC structural funds and of their links with mainstream labour policies in member states. These experimental policies are the result of a historical process of institutional creativity and are underpinned by a legitimizing rhetoric that attributes a specific role to the Union in the field of active employment policies.

In the second section, the implementation of these policies in France (an historically centralized state now partially decentralized), in Ireland (a relatively small and virtually non-decentralized state) and in Germany (a federal state) is compared. The focus of attention here is on the ways in which supranational policy input disrupts firmly embedded administrative structures and sets of political relationships at the national and subnational levels and gives rise to particular forms of learning from which local forms of 'transitional labour markets' (Schmid, 1995) might emerge.

The third section is an attempt to use 'multi-level governance' theory in order to specify the forms of policy change observed. It is argued that European policies are elements of a wider process of competitive policy building.

1. COMMUNITY INITIATIVES AS A 'LABORATORY FOR SOCIAL INNOVATION'

The ground-breaking 1988 reform of EC structural funds was the result of the Commission's long-standing tradition of 'entrepreneurial' activity in the sphere of policy formulation. Very gradually, the Commission succeeded in replacing a system of inter-state compensatory payments with what appears to be a European grammar of economic and social development and experimentation. The development of the Community initiatives took place just as the 'fight against social exclusion' was being incorporated into both national and European policy agendas; in policy instrument terms, these EC programmes reflect the Commission's desire to move away from national income support policies and to bolster training programmes that would later come to be known as 'active employment policies'. In other words, the European Commission, while presenting itself as an enabler of experimentation in the field of employment policies, was at the same time subsidizing training transitions orientated towards local forms of labour market regulation.

The European Commission as Policy Entrepreneur

A 'window of opportunity' (Kingdon, 1984) for major reform of the structural funds in 1988 was opened up by the conjoining of two streams of initiatives, one political, the other policy-oriented. The process of European integration had been relaunched by the Single European Act of 1987, which laid the foundations for the '1992' single market project. In the wake of the SEA, the Commission, led by Jacques Delors, managed to forge a strategic link between market integration and social issues. The removal of all barriers to the free movement of goods, services and workers gave rise in turn to a discourse on social and economic solidarity and cohesion, based on the argument that market making produced negative externalities and inequalities requiring market-correcting mechanisms. Social initiatives and reforms, therefore, stemmed from market integration, in keeping with a long judicial tradition of policy making in the EC (Leibfried and Pierson, 1995). This political activism on the part of the Commission was backed up by a series of policy initiatives, projects and ideas.

It began by establishing a system of quotas and margins designed to constrain the room for manoeuvre enjoyed by member states in the allocation of structural funds (ESF and ERDF, European Regional Development Funds). A non-quota section, accounting for some 10 per cent of the total volume of funds, was then established in order to finance programmes not intended, unlike those receiving mainstream funding, to supplement national social and regional policies.

A European Grammar for the Fight against Social Exclusion

The 1988 reform of the structural funds laid down certain principles governing the formulation and implementation of EC regional programmes by member states. Sometimes perceived as a new set of regulations (Smyrl, 1995), these principles could equally well be said to provide the framework for a 'constitutive policy' (Lowi, 1964; Duran and Thoenig, 1996) or incentive policy (Quermonne, 1994) intended to prompt the development of new policy practices among public actors and between public and private actors.

Some of those principles concerned more particularly the relationships between national executives and the European Commission. Structural policies now had to complement and not replace national regional policies; funding was to be concentrated in the neediest areas in order to improve the regional impact of those policies. They were formulated on the basis of programmes lasting several years and in accordance with negotiated guidelines in order to stop them being a mere collection of unrelated projects. A system of continuous (that is, ex ante, running and ex post) evaluation was established in order to help legitimate this multiannual commitment. Finally, national programmes were to be formulated and implemented through partnerships involving not only national and regional executives and the relevant departments of the Commission but also 'all parties concerned' (the social partners, local associations and so on).

This apparently forbidding list of principles does shed some light on the Commission's standpoint, which is not entirely devoid of ideology. It lay down organizational rules and procedures constituting a framework for collective action without defining too precisely the problems to be tackled, policy content or the degree of formality in the interaction between the actors involved. Rather, it created 'spaces' for political exchange and expert debates, in short for experience in the processes of collective policy making aimed at providing both the participants and the initiator of such exchanges with values and legitimacy. In the light of these characteristics, the policy-making framework established in 1988 and modified in 1993 can be described as a constitutive as well as an incentive policy reform that formalized the growing power of the Commission in this policy field. However, it was also intended to give the European Community, and more precisely the Commission, a specific role in the field of employment policies; this role is particularly visible in the case of the Community human resources initiatives (consisting, from 1994 onwards, of the Employment and Adapt programmes), which were the heirs of the 'non-quota section' (monies spent in accordance with 'European' rather than national priorities) and intended to encourage experimentation with new policy approaches based on negotiation and collective regulation in the field of training policies and social exclusion.

The Employment Initiatives as a Laboratory for Policy Experimentation

Tracing the conceptual genesis of the Employment and Adapt initiatives through several interorganizational or informal networks of specialists and experts inside and outside the Commission illustrates the policy activism of an institution able to capitalize on expert knowledge in order to push through its policy initiatives.

One of the conceptual sources of the Commission's activism in this area is to be found in its participation in certain OECD initiatives. At the beginning of the 1990s, the OECD set up a network of specialists on local development (ILE, or local job creation initiatives). At the same time, DG V launched a programme of action research dealing with similar issues and named LEDA (Local Employment Development Action). The aim was to collect examples of 'successful local experiments' that were used to construct an argument in suport of the Commission's intervention in promoting local experiments.

Implementation of the Community HR (Human Resources) initiatives (1990–94) coincided with a debate conducted inside the OECD and the Commission (DG V) on the need for more active employment policies to promote more efficient interaction between the supply and demand for labour, to encourage the mobilization of the labour supply (job search training, work experience schemes), to develop employment-related skills (on-the-job training) and to stimulate the demand for labour through public subsidies (Schömann, 1995). The Commmunity HR initiatives are, in fact, perfectly consistent with the definitions of 'active labour market policies' formulated by both institutions (as demonstrated below), and member states continue to use this policy framework to experiment with active labour market policies. This approach was enshrined in Delors'

White Paper on Growth and Competitiveness (Commission Européenne, 1993).

The Commission's search for policy concepts and expert knowledge is characteristic of its search for a 'space' in which it could engage in policy formulation in a way that would complement existing national policies and therefore be politically acceptable while gaining legitimacy through the contacts with national and international officials, researchers and voluntary organizations fostered by the networks it initiates and cultivates. These networks are also typical of one style of EU policy making. They perfectly illustrate the strategy of 'soft dominance' (Tömmel, 1994), whereby informal relationships are built into EU policy-making rules, becoming vehicles for the production of norms (beneficial mutual learning) and altering the usual relationships between the actors involved (with exchanges taking place in a 'neutral' space, beyond bureaucratic routines and constraints and sectoral boundaries). At the same time, these networks provide the Commission with technical information and functional legitimacy by means of an exchange mechanism that both epitomizes and compensates for the EU's notorious 'democratic deficit'.

As the Commission put in place its HR initiatives in the wake of the 1988 reform, it presented them as spaces for experimenting with new policy approaches in transnational forums, where political and societal actors could exchange views on national and local experiences in the field of economic and social development. In addition to the general principles for implementing EU structural policy laid down in the 1988 reform, the Commission made eligibility for funding under the initiatives dependent on the development of 'transnational partnerships' and the exploration of 'innovative approaches' to vocational training and the reintegration of certain target groups into the labour market. In other words, it established basic rules for taking part in the game of experimentation without providing too much in the way of policy content for public bodies or project teams charged with implementation of those programmes. This was consistent with the principle of constitutive policy making: the Employment Initiative was akin to an 'incomplete contract' (Majone, 1993) offered by the Commission to a multiplicity of national and subnational actors. The Commission limited itself to providing a very broad definition of the problem, namely the exclusion from labour markets of certain underprivileged target groups, including women, young people, the long-term unemployed and handicapped people, and saw itself as restoring to national and regional policy makers some scope for conceptual manoeuvre at the margins of firmly embedded national policies and national systems suffering from the inevitable structural inertia. It offered national and local actors an opportunity to develop new practices and new partnerships through collective action. In so doing, it strongly underscored the complementary nature of its action. In fact, the Commission is condemned by EU treaties to define such action as vaguely as possible: in the field of social and labour market policies, the policy 'space' is almost wholly filled by firmly embedded national arrangements within which the Commission had to carve out its own 'niche'.

As noted above, the HR initiatives were intended to provide incentives for experimentation with new training methods. In both phases (1990–94 and 1994–9), the aim has been to meet economic and social needs at both national and local level, notably by improving existing systems of vocational guidance and training and renewing the content and the objectives of training policies (with an emphasis on adaptation to technological change). It differentiates between several target groups: women in NOW (New Opportunities for Women), disabled people in Horizon, young people and the long-term unemployed in late-Euroform, young unemployed people in Youthstart, the long-term unemployed in Integra and employed people threatened by technological change in Adapt.

The genesis of the Employment and Adapt initiatives illustrates perfectly some of the structural characteristics of EU policy making. The underlying concepts were developed over a long period through informal networks of experts and political and societal actors in order to give the policy a certain functional legitimacy. Further, its constitutive and incentivizing nature (in the field of structural and redistributive policies at least) means that it remains consistent with the EU's treaty base. This form of incomplete contract for experimentation burdens the actors responsible for implementation with the task of reintepreting this vague European grammar of social integration in order to make it literally 'viable' but also to leave scope for the reappropriation and reinterpretation by regional and local actors of the policy problems associated with social exclusion.

2.   ASSESSING THE ORGANIZATIONAL AND COGNITIVE IMPACT OF THE EMPLOYMENT AND ADAPT INITIATIVES

It is to the completion of this constitutive policy contract, by nature incomplete, that we now turn. Who are the actors and organizations willing and/or able to 'translate' (Callon, 1986) and 'transfer' (Dolowitz, 1996) these general principles into action and, above all, to give meaning to this policy (Muller, 1996)? We will begin by analysing why an institutionalist approach (in its historical version) can be used to investigate both the organizational and cognitive impacts of EU policy. Both these aspects of policy implementation in the three countries chosen (France, Ireland and Germany) will then be investigated, before some guidelines for assessing the common impact of EU experimental policies on three national 'policy communities' are proposed.

Defining Institutions as Brokers and Educators

In contrast to pluralist and (neo-)corporatist approaches, which consider institutions as politically neutral elements in an organizational landscape, whose function it is to facilitate societal and political exchange (see Moravcsik, 1993, for an application of pluralist theories to the EC), the institutionalist approach, as revived by March and Olsen (1984), emphasizes that institutions can, under certain conditions, be treated as political actors. To do so, it has to be proved that they enjoy relative autonomy, that is they are able to choose some of the rules and means by which they act, and to determine their own preferences. Even on the basis of this 'first-stage' definition, it is clear – if such acknowledgment were still necessary – that the European Commission has, over the years, used subtle interpretation of the treaty base and the functional legitimacy acquired through development of its expertise to turn itself into a genuine political actor.

Historical institutionalism can provide a highly developed definition of institutions that can be used as a basis for specifying the functions that an institution must develop in order to assert its relative autonomy. The same definition can also be used to construct a guideline for assessing the role of the Commission and the other institutions involved in the implementation of the HR initiatives. To this end, March and Olsen used a double metaphor: a relatively autonomous institution is, at one and the same time, 'a broker, providing information, identifying possible coalitions, and facilitating side-payments and logrolls' and 'an educator, stimulating and accepting changing worldviews, redefining meanings, stimulating commitments'. This analytical framework, which encompasses the organizational and cognitive input of institutional political actors in policy making, helps to underline the European Commission's capacity to act as a broker of political and functional interests. The neoinstitutionalist argument that 'the processes of politics may be more central than their outcomes', which reduces the overwhelming importance normally attributed to formal decisions, underlines the importance of policy-making processes as social or even socialization rituals. Through processes of exchange, the actors involved discover, express and jointly construct the significance of their action and imbue it with values and history.

The challenge here was to determine who were the actors able to complete the contract proposed by the Commission and to initiate these socialization processes. This function is indeed especially difficult to perform in a policy context involving several levels of governance and a multiplicity of public and private actors. The concept of institution is, therefore, a tool for observing how the Commission's guidelines were adapted and reinterpreted within three national contexts, in accordance with a comparative approach in which EU policy is seen as disrupting nationally (or regionally) established sets of political and functional relationships in the field of training and social policies.

Dealing with the Organizational Constraints of EU Training Policies

This section focuses more particularly on the implementation at national level of this experimental policy, that is on the solutions adopted by national executives seeking to implement the contract proposed by the European Commission. Given the constraints inherent in the policymaking 'grammar' set out in the 1988 reform, the aim of which was to promote cooperation in policy planning and implementation between national and subnational levels of governance and representative societal actors, the question was: who was allowed to participate and did the set of participants evolve over time (between the 1990–94 and 1994–9 funding waves)? As implementation equates in structural terms to the reappropriation and reinterpretation of the 'letter' of the law (that is, the 1988 reform and the experimental rules of the Community initiatives), the purpose of this section is to ascertain the extent to which a relatively autonomous space for discretionary action by public and quasi-public actors was created.

During the first wave of the Employment Initiative (1990–94), the three countries studied (France, Ireland and Germany) put in place fairly centralized frameworks for the implementation of Commission policy, although in all cases there was considerable reliance on external (that is, non-governmental) organizations, which were thought to be more flexible than traditional public-sector bodies. In all three cases, the principles laid down by the Commission implied adaptation at the margin (through the creation of new administrative structures, for instance) rather than integration into existing policies in the area. This state of affairs was slightly modified in the second wave of funding (1994–9), notably under pressure from the Commission, which advocated genuine decentralization of funding and greater involvement by subnational political actors in order to devolve regulation of the public employment service to a more local level, thereby improving efficiency. Responses differed in accordance with the historical patterns of existing political exchange (Parri, 1989).

Delegation and subcontracting as first choices

In France, the Ministry of Labour and Social Affairs set up a special ESF office in 1990. Somewhat isolated from other departments, it was given responsibility for the Employment Initiative but delegated almost all the operational tasks associated with it to external bodies. One of these external organizations was Racine, which was put in charge of Euroform and Horizon and, from 1994 onwards, of all sub-initiatives. At first, it did not have any formal status but later it became a non-profit association. Its de facto area of specialization was the monitoring of European training programmes (Force, Petra, Eurotecnet) and it was staffed initially by civil servants on secondment, most of whom were positively committed to the European project.

The operational programme (OP) of the Employment Initiative, which consists of the negotiation of national priorities for action with the Commission as well as the public tendering and project selection processes, has been the subject of close collaboration between the ESF office and Racine. More precisely, it would seem that Racine was given the task of building, from scratch, all the frameworks required for completing the national part of the experimentation contract and compiling the information for the Ministry to take the final decisions (that is, designing the application forms, informing civil servants in contact with likely project leaders, setting deadlines and putting in place financial management mechanisms).

This delegation of virtually all operational tasks quickly led to Racine becoming the sole source of expertise in the area. It was not long before this quasi-governmental body (a private organization with a 'public service' mission) acquired a solid base of European know-how. This created an imbalance of information and expertise between the hybrid organization and its creator. In 1994, this dependence on external expertise, which was synonymous with a certain degree of isolation, prompted the Ministry to formalize Racine's subordinate position. From that point on, Racine was to be defined as a provider of technical assistance to the Ministry and not just to the project leaders as before.

The delegation of tasks took a different form in Ireland. Here, the Department of Labour (nowadays the Department of Enterprise and Employment) also established an ESF office to which Employment Initiative officials were deployed. It also chose to delegate responsibility for the operational aspects of the Employment Initiative, but to existing representative organizations (National Women Council of Ireland for NOW, for instance) and quasi-public bodies (Leargas for Euroform) rather than to newly established entities. The decision was taken, therefore, to share responsibilities and expertise, giving each subcontractor political or functional recognition and a de facto right of participation (and even decision-making powers) in European policy matters. A consensus soon developed around this division of tasks, due in no small measure to the informal nature of the hierarchical relationships involved, which was itself characterized by fairly short lines of communication (most contact with the Department takes place through telephone calls). This enabled officials to retain a degree of expertise and to 'keep in touch' with projects on the ground. In this case, there seems to be no real imbalance of information between the managing partners, each of them having a fairly comprehensive overview of the implementation of the programme and of the network of relationships linking all the actors involved.

In Germany as well, implementation of this European training programme ended up by being largely privatized. In 1991, only one sub-initiative (Horizon) was monitored by a private company (EFP, or *Europa Büro für Projektbegleitung*), the others being delegated to a public institution (BiBB, or the *Bundesinstitut für Berufsbildung*, the Federal Institute for Vocational Training Affairs) as a result of pressure exerted by the federal Department of Vocational Training on the Ministry of Labour in a dispute over their respective spheres of competence. This dispute led eventually to further privatization of the management of the Employment Initiative, with EFP became the provider of technical assistance to the Department in 1994. The federal Ministry of Labour seems to try to compensate for this high level of delegation by taking responsibility for the continuing evaluation of all the organizations involved, over and above the formal requirements laid down by the European Commission.

After reunification (in 1994 in fact), the *Länder*, including the new ones in the former East Germany, chose their own technical assistance providers. Most of the new *Länder* delegated responsibility for implementation to the private companies (with BBJ Servis GmbH acquiring a virtual monopoly before the work began to be shared systematically with a partner company) in charge of implementing the main instruments of labour market policy. These companies, modelled on the so-called *Gesellschaften zur Arbeitsförderung, Beschäftigung und Strukturentwicklung* or ABS (Hild, 1995), had moved eastwards after reunification to put in place the infrastructure for implementing 'internally imported' labour policies and had acquired experience in the restructuring of declining industries. Their advantage over public-sector bodies was reckoned to lie in their flexibility and speed. The implementation of European training policies followed this trend and was incorporated into this 'mixed economy' of labour policies as part of a large-scale experiment in labour policy.

This privatization of the implementation of the Employment and Adapt initiatives took place for different reasons in the three countries. In France and Germany, it met a need for greater flexibility, a fact acknowledged by officials in interviews. In Ireland, it was seen as a means of including new social partners in the policy-making process. It should also be stressed that the constraints exerted by the European Commission have contributed to the privatization of the provision of social services by the state, in a general move towards a 'mixed economy' in social policy making (Lewis, 1995). In consequence, both the state and the original initiator of the policy (the Commission) may well be deprived of the ability to 'make sense' of these experimental programmes by integrating them into existing training and labour market policies. This lack of visibility (and discourse) at the national level is raising doubts about the political will to transfer the results of these training experiments into mainstream policies. This in turn raises questions about the legitimacy of both European and national levels of governance in this area of training policy.

Having assessed the extent to which implementation of the Employment and Adapt initiatives was privatized, we now turn to the question of the sharing of political authority between levels of government, that is to the impact of European policy making on the power relations and political exchanges taking place between central government and regional and local authorities.

Decentralization under supranational pressure?

The 1988 reform of the structural funds was intended to establish a set of principles promoting partnership between the different levels of government (national, regional, local) as a core public philosophy. This intrusion into national politics is often seen as a result of the Commission's desire to improve the access of the regions to the European polity and policy making. The European Commission at least intended to enlarge the circle of participants in European policy making, although national governments had already demanded and acquired the right to decide who would participate (Marks, 1992; Hooghe and Keating, 1993). This also applies to the Community initiatives, although in the case of the Employment and Adapt Initiative, the picture varies over time and from country to country. Cross-country comparison provides some clues as to the role of the Commission in the establishment of polycentric political exchanges, and in particular provides evidence of its disruptive effect. Thus what is of interest here is the vertical dimension of power sharing. The horizontal dimension, that is the local commitment of regional executives to individual training projects, is analysed in the third section. The strategies adopted by national authorities in order to retain the power and expertise threatened by the Commission's promotion of cooperative policy making provide, in turn, a basis for assessing the degree of disruption caused by European policy.

The French government opted first to centralize implementation of the Employment Initiative, albeit with a strong element of delegation. However, in the light of the co-funding principle, regional authorities were often asked to provide funds but were reluctant to co-fund projects and programmes in which they had no voice and about which they had, initially, very little information. Eventually, under the influence of the mechanism adopted for mainstreaming funding (Community Support Framework by objectives) and the hostile reaction of some regions to a Green Paper on the Community Initiatives (1992), the Commission succeeded in getting 80 per cent of the funds allocated at regional level. The French government chose to 'deconcentrate' rather than decentralize funding by transferring competences to state authorities in the regions and not to regional authorities. Thus the Regional Departments of Vocational and Further Training were given responsibility for managing 80 per cent of ESF funding in 1994. Central government's desire to retain control of this (relatively small) amount of money (see Table 14.1 below), albeit at regional level, may well reflect a shift, at a broader level, towards more constitutive policies and the retention of most experimental policies at the national level (urban policy is characteristic in this respect; Donzelot and Estèbe, 1994). As observed in the next subsection, however, the implementation of such policies is de facto decentralized at the local or project level, given the need to build strong political support at local level for individual projects.

Table 14.1   *ESF (and ERDF) funding under the Human Resources Community Initiatives, 1989–99 (ECU millions)*

	Employment initiative	Sub-programmes		France	Ireland	Germany
1989–93	Approx. 600	Euroform NOW Horizon	262.2 104.2 158.2	 61.5	 24.1	 48.3
1994–99	Approx. 1400	NOW Horizon Integra Youthstart	496 513 385 441	 146.5	 45.1	 197.4
1994–99 Employment +Adapt	Approx. 3470			473.5	616.9	454.6

Source: OPOCE (Office de publications officelles des Communautés Européennes/Office for official publications of the European Communities).

The Irish case provides a strongly contrasting picture, since it represents an attempt to engage in regional policy without a genuine tier of regional government. A regional tier of government was set up around 1987 in order to satisfy Brussels' demands, but it consisted mostly of functional management bodies established to monitor the implementation of programmes funded by the European structural funds. This strategic move, designed to bring Ireland into line with the Commission's grammar of regional development, did not prevent Commissioner Bruce Millan (DG XVI, regional policies) from denouncing the 'cosmetic nature of regional involvement' in Ireland (Laffan, 1996). This regional tier does indeed seem to have very little input into the policy-making process, that is into the definition of problems, the devising of solutions or the sharing of policy roles: expertise and political power remain concentrated in the hands of central government. Nevertheless, the grammar of intergovernmental partnership devised by the Commission might have indirectly led local officials, entrepreneurs and societal groups to mobilize around the theme of local economic development (concern in this area being particularly acute around the issues of training and the fostering of new economic activities).

The picture in Germany is rather blurred. As in France, the federal government has retained some competence in experimental training and labour market policies. However, it has completely decentralized 80 per cent of the Employment Initiative funding to the *Länder*, while remaining solely responsible for negotiating the operational programme (OP) with the Commission and supervising the comparative evaluation of implementation frameworks and the performance of the *Länder*. It retained 20 per cent of the funding in order to subsidize projects with a national dimension. EFP, the national provider of technical assistance responsible for the development of transnational partnerships between local projects, supervises relations with other national implementation infrastructures from Bonn. In the light of EFP's recognized transnational expertise, this division of labour is a consensual one. It would appear that these choices were made in the wake of the 'turf war' with the Department of Vocational Training simply in order to avoid such political/administrative complications in future. In this case, therefore, the balance of gains and constraints created by the Employment Initiative led to a functional form of decentralization, with the federal government retaining control over the political negotiations with the Commission, as well as over evaluation procedures.

This brief survey of the vertical dimension of power sharing in the implementation of the Employment and Adapt initiatives confirms that national governments continue to act as gatekeepers in the field of EU redistributive policies. Direct links between subnational tiers of government and the

Brussels bureaucracy are always encouraged (or tolerated) by central governments when they remain on an informal or technical level. However, pressure from Brussels is likely to disrupt the status quo in countries where subnational executives are already constituted as political actors with strong territorial interests and experience of multi-level governance (in a federal system, for instance). This suggests that, in its desire collectively to define policy and devise solutions in the fight against social exclusion, the intervention of the European Commission is not so welcome. Solutions to problems are still not being devised collectively by a plurality of political authorities; rather, they are the object of tough negotiations held behind closed doors between governments and the Commission.

These observations should not be allowed to overshadow the vital role played by regional and local representatives at the level of project implementation, where they often participate in monitoring committees which enable local projects to acquire their social and policy meaning. Indeed, it is mainly at the subnational level that this experimental policy 'makes sense', is perceived by the actors involved (mainly project teams and training organizations, but also local officials working in related fields) to have explanatory and/or symbolic power over and above the norms and obligations laid down by the Commission and member states.

Beyond State Regulation: Giving Effect and Meaning to EU Policies

As we have seen, implementation of the Employment and Adapt initiatives has been delegated to a greater or lesser extent to private-sector organizations. This means not only that the operational aspects of the initiatives have been taken out of the ambit of government but also that the actors in a position to regulate the policy, to make it work and make sense in terms of providing solutions to problems (local unemployment, social deprivation and so on) are not state actors but quasi-public or private actors. As a result, the state is being partially deprived of one of its traditional functions, namely articulating the social utility of public policies in order to justify them.

Shifting constraints: the many forms of substitution effect

There would seem to be a substitution effect between national and supranational funding for experimental training programmes, with national authorities shifting part of the financial burden onto the European level in order to mitigate the effects of budget cuts. Some non-profit organizations in France, for example, have been pointed in the direction of European funding by the Ministry of Agriculture: 'There is not much money left for this kind of project, but there is a European tender out on a related topic which might suit you. . . .'. Conversely, organizations that have received subsidies from Community HR initiatives have acknowledged that some projects could not have been financed within a purely national framework because of excessive structural and regulatory rigidities. Thus Teagasc, the quasi-public national organization in charge of training in the farming sector in Ireland, was able to change its highly formalized curricula into a modular form of training thanks to Community funding. Even more strikingly, the Irish police launched a project under the Employment Initiative to develop training in equal opportunities within the force.

In some ways, the Adapt and Employment initiatives were also seen by national governments as an opportunity to experiment with policy initiatives that were considered too innovative to be integrated into mainstream policies but were legitimized to some extent by their supranational funding. In France, the Adapt initiative was used to subsidize the development of training modules aimed at seasonal workers. Giving seasonal workers training in harvesting techniques and ergonomics and providing them with a certificate on successful completion of the course is thought to facilitate their hiring by other farmers throughout the year. Funding has also been used to conduct studies of multiple job holding, with this kind of training being used as an example of how to facilitate transitions between several part-time jobs and to develop, on the basis of concrete and feasible local experiments, new 'activity contracts' to replace the 'outdated' employment contract providing full-time employment for life with a single employer. Similarly, EU funding (under the Adapt Initiative) was used to import the 'job rotation' concept from Denmark to Germany (see below) in order gradually to familiarize the *Länder*, small and medium-sized firms and corporate organizations with this new instrument of labour market policy.

In both cases, EU funding gave these initiatives higher visibility and provided sufficient finance to cover the costs of dissemination and promotion. Participation in these EU training programmes enabled project promoters to gain greater acceptance among politicians and policy makers for the methods and arrangements tested. This in turn imposed an exogenous constraint on policy makers, who are all the more open to new ideas if a positive-sum game of this kind, in which all players are winners, offers some degree of respite for their hard-pressed budgets.

Experimenting with transitional labour market policies at a local level

'Policy innovation' was established by the European Commission as an essential precondition for eligibility for funding under the Employment and Adapt initiatives. Given its limited scope for the exercise of judicial power, the Commission had to remain vague in its demands, the aim of these initiatives being to 'develop new policy practices' and to 'initiate new partnerships'. The criteria for defining and selecting innovative projects were initially only loosely formalized at the national level. Indeed, it would seem that the degree of innovation was defined territorially, with policies implemented for the first time in a given geographical area being considered innovative. National governments limited themselves to establishing a few national priorities for action which were enshrined in an operational programme (OP) negotiated with the Commission. In all three cases analysed here, priority was given to the activation of labour market policies through employment-oriented training, employment counselling and career guidance, upgrading of skills, sandwich courses, assistance with business start-ups, and so on. Two main policy-making innovations were common to all three countries studied and were recognized as such by the actors involved.

Firstly, the HR initiatives opened up opportunities to initiate new political and professional dialogues in a local context. The establishment of local committees to monitor individual projects (which happened more or less automatically in France and Ireland) was intended to garner political and expert support and advice for project promoters by bringing together on a regular basis local and regional officials, civil servants, entrepreneurs and, in some cases, researchers. Not infrequently, there appeared round the table people who previously had either refused to enter into dialogue because they were in conflict or in competition with each other (particularly on a political level) or had simply never had the occasion to engage in dialogue because they were operating in different spheres. Since they were 'experimental', and 'European' into the bargain, local projects of this kind provided a relatively neutral and prestigious forum for dialogue, with discussion focused on the technical or professional aspects of a specific project. As a result, local antagonisms could be unblocked, enabling new sources of funding to be tapped and information on administrative or banking regulations to be made available, thereby facilitating the completion of projects.

These rather informal forums seem to have an important educating role for participants: government departments acquire information on each other's activities, local politicians become familiar with the training methods and day-to-day problems of non-profit organizations, and so on. Local project promoters are de facto entrusted with the task of 'territorial mediation', and their 'marginal' position enables them to question local political and policy practices and representations. As Andy Smith puts it, 'structural funds strengthen the recomposition not of a territorial tier (the region here) but rather of local territories' (Smith, 1995). In this case, the same can be said of local labour market mechanisms.

Secondly, the HR initiatives have provided local labour market policies with additional tools and flexibility. European funding has made it possible to complement local training policies, for example by financing pre- and post-training phases intended to facilitate transitions between family life (in the NOW programmes, for instance) or between long-term unemployment and training (in Integra) and then between training and employment.

In France, EU monies are used, for instance, to finance so-called 'territorial analyses' which have the dual function of mobilizing future trainees as both individuals and groups while at the same time helping them to conduct an inquiry into local employment needs through documentary research (employment statistics) and interviews with local entrepreneurs and politicians. This preparatory inquiry is intended to give trainees ideas about possible job opportunities by assessing local employment needs and to help them to evaluate the feasibility of any ideas they may come up with. This is especially valuable when the ultimate goal of the training is a business start-up. EU funding is also used to finance a post-training phase, for example to provide medium-term support for those starting up their own businesses. These complementary services are often made available through providers of technical support and consultancy services, whose ability to speak the appropriate administrative 'language' provides a mechanism of adjustment between the formal and often rigid criteria for funding (whether national or European, they must always be measured in hours of training provided) and the real policy aims of training organizations. Thus quasi-public intermediate bodies often act as facilitators or 'brokers' between a plurality of conflicting policy norms and interests, allowing them to sit more easily alongside each other and creating the conditions under which individual processes of trial and error and maturation can unfold (particularly crucial in business start-ups).

Germany provides another example of an experiment aimed at implementing local forms of transitional labour markets. At the invitation of the Commission, a consultancy organization was commissioned to import a new labour policy instrument based on the Danish 'job rotation' scheme. The core principle of this experiment is that it combines continuing training for employed people on training leave and work experience for unemployed people temporarily filling the posts vacated by those taking leave. The consultancy organization acts as an intermediary between employers and a pool of unemployed people. This combination of two different forms of training provision (advanced further training and retraining) gives rise to a complex configuration of actors, institutions and funding structures that has already been investigated above. The 'import' of this instrument, which involves a sort of two-way transition, introduces an exogenous concept that challenges the regional training system and, ultimately, the national regulatory framework by reorganizing and regulating on a local and informal basis individual transitions into and out of the labour market, in a positive-sum game for all participants (firms, public authorities, training organizations, employee and substitute worker). Here too, a societal body acts as an educator and broker for all the parties involved in the project, managing steering committees and information sessions and garnering enough political acceptance and legitimacy for the project to turn it into an instrument of regional labour market policy.

In Ireland, Community HR initiatives provided funding for a local project in the suburbs of Dublin set up by a charity with the aim of facilitating multiple transitions into and out of the labour market. EU monies were used to build a three-storey building housing a kindergarten for mothers returning to training or work and help for teenagers with their schoolwork provided by pensioners living in the building. By virtue of its European dimension and the persuasive powers of the women in charge of the project, in which multiple transitions and forms of integration into the community and the labour market were gathered together under one roof, a whole bundle of administrative and judicial intricacies was unpicked and resolved.

Experiments in multi-level governance: policy mediation beyond the State
Meso-level analysis would suggest that the institutions acting as 'brokers' and 'educators' in the implementation of the Human Resources initiatives are mainly societal rather than state actors. This calls into question the role of political authorities as creators of public spaces or forums for the expression of societal interests (Rouault and Muller, 1997). In the case analysed here, the regulation of societal and professional interests takes place through intermediary and quasi-public bodies; their role as experts and subcontractors to public institutions gives them legitimacy, while their position on the margins of the state apparatus offers them a certain degree of political and policy-making autonomy. This form of 'sub-state' policy regulation can be illustrated by the quasi-public networks that have developed in France and Ireland around the organizations providing technical assistance for local projects. Our hypothesis here is that these partly public, partly private organizations epitomize a new kind of relationship between state and civil society in the policy-making sphere, and more especially in the field of social policies, which needs to be more precisely defined. European policies provide an opportunity to do so, since they highlight this shift in the traditional functions of the state. By providing a forum for the expression of a plurality of societal and professional interests, these quasi-public organizations act as institutional brokers.

Some technical assistance providers organize 'seminars' or 'workshops' for project leaders in order to familiarize them with the intricacies of European programmes and funding and to translate for them the rules of this complex grammar of experimentation. In the Irish and French cases, the basic principle of these meetings is the cost-free exchange of information and technical competences in a mutually profitable positive-sum game (all the partici-pants having already been funded). Once again, this philosophy of mutual-ity, together with the relative neutrality of the exchanges, facilitates dialogue between parties not normally involved in such exercises. These working groups indeed bring together a diversity of project organizers: non-profit associations, public training providers, organizations representing the social partners and even government departments (the Police and Post Office in Ireland, national and regional government officials in France).

These relatively loosely organized forums set up by the intermediary bodies provide a locus for the representation of societal interests and, on occasions, of conflicting public and private interests. All participants can choose between the 'voice' and 'exit' options; most of the time, they choose the first option. In France, for instance, more and more large and public-sector organizations are being funded under HR initiatives, since small associations do not have the resources to handle European projects (that is, to wait one or two years for the money to arrive). Quasi-public organizations are sometime able to mediate between them by underlining their common problem (dealing with local unemployment), by offering a forum for the exchange of views on possible solutions and by proposing mutually beneficial collaborative projects (development of new training curricula). By pooling information and expertise, these intermediary organizations act as educators, questioning and changing attitudes and policy practices.

Over and above the challenge to organizational habits and prejudices, these meetings are also a locus for confrontation between conflicting pro-fessional cultures and working methods. Over time, this leads to change in the organizations involved. This is especially true of management methods. The constraints of European experimentation, including the obligation to provide interim reports, has forced all the organizations involved to strengthen their competence in forward-looking management (funding being spread over several years). Moreover, delays in receiving funds have given rise, over time, to a need to select projects in accordance with well-established management criteria. This in turn has forced train-ing organizations to hire new personnel or to train existing personnel to deal with this 'management burden'. This is particularly true of public training providers in France, long used to relying on state funding and investing mainly in their educational and training competences. Participation in those collective learning processes can also lead to gradual changes in participants' professional practices. For example, proponents of social integration and proponents of economic integration – two dis-tinct schools of thought in France – have been made aware of the possible complementarity of their approaches, while male trainers in France have become acquainted with the application of the gender approach to training courses aimed at women starting their own businesses.

At a deeper level, however, this new process of professional socialization heralds the entry of these organizations into the 'multi-level governance game' (Scharpf, 1994). Against a background of financial constraint, they have to ensure their survival (a totally new concept for some of them) by diversifying their sources of funding (European/national/regional/local). The cofinancing principle underlying the Employment and Adapt initiatives formalized a recently established practice, whereby the obtaining of a grant increases the probability of being awarded additional funding by another institution or government department. The pooling of information and competences, therefore, enables project organizers and other participants collectively to map the sphere of multi-level policy making, in which a plurality of authorities and funders are competing for control over policy and the definition of problems (if not of solutions). In this way, project organizers gradually become more familiar with the informal and opaque policy style of the European Commission and get used to cultivating direct contacts in the search for further funding. This collective learning process can even lead to the constitution of professional lobbies able to construct a policy argument and to defend it at the various levels of governance. This practice was formalized during the Irish Youthstart projects by the organization charged with providing technical assistance. Playing a politically rather ambiguous role, it developed the notion of 'clustering': project organizers were invited to meet in topic-based clusters in order to accumulate written material, develop conceptual arguments and initiate the collective lobbying of officials and other training providers.

This collective initiation into the workings of multi-level governance has led to changes in the policy theory and practice and to the emergence of a hybrid regulatory mode in the sphere of social and employment policies. In this hybrid mode, public policies are regulated by a combination of public, quasi-public and private actors and organizations. The latter are better suited to a multi-level policy-making context, since they operate at the margins of historically embedded systems and gain their legitimacy through their functional expertise. The striking element is here that state authorities have delegated not only the operational aspects of policy but also most of the symbolic and rhetorical activities that give meaning to public policies and political legitimacy to the institutions engaged in such activities. This 'sub-state' mode of policy regulation, which is also advocated in transitional labour market theory, challenges standard theories of state building. In this sense, the disruptive effect of experimental social policies designed by a supranational authority sheds light on this acutely problematic phenomenon.

3. THE ROLE OF SUPRANATIONAL POLICIES IN BRINGING ABOUT POLICY CHANGE

The definition of the European Union as a political entity producing legitimate public policies underlines its 'state-like' character. This unorthodox comparative strategy helps to focus attention on the way in which the European Commission has managed, through a long-term process of institutional creativity, to carve out for itself a role as political actor or policy regulator at the margins of deeply rooted national policies on training and other social issues. Examination of the implementation of an experimental employment policy in three member states, thereby adding a second comparative dimension to the analysis, makes it clear that this inescapably constitutive or incentive policy framework requires a sub-state or quasi-public mode of regulation if the incomplete contract concluded with the Commission is not completed. This hybrid mode of regulation and policy mediation, operating in a context of multi-level governance, uncovers possible mechanisms for policy change and labour market transitions that are not entirely monitored by political authorities.

Policy Changes above and beyond State Regulation

The implementation of the Community HR initiatives offers an example of 'competitive policy building' (cf. the concept of 'competitive state building' outlined in Leibfried and Pierson, 1995), where policy change occurs at the interface between political systems. A plurality of public authorities (supranational/national/regional) compete to define a problem ('unemployment and social exclusion') through a strategy of differentiation (from established national policies), offering policy actors a plurality of programme models and sources of funding. If 'policy makers are inheritors before they are choosers' (Rose, 1993), the European Commission is reintroducing the notion of choice for policy implementers, albeit within certain constraints. By virtue of its position as a young and developing institution, it can act as a source of ideas and a producer of policy concepts, but within the structural constraints laid down by member states.

The elaboration and operationalization of solutions to social exclusion are delegated to quasi-public organizations, in accordance with a general trend towards the privatization of social policy provision, especially in the field of labour market policies (Schmid, 1994). The result of this privatization of policy implementation is the constitution of a pool of labour policy expertise at the margins of the state apparatus, with public authorities losing to some extent their ability to construct a legitimate political discourse on the regulation of regional or local labour markets. However, if the private or semi-public bodies in possession of the policy-making expertise have the task of making policies work, it would seem that they are also, de facto, vested with the political function of 'making sense' of them. They do so by offering societal actors as well as government officials a forum in which to forge links with each other and to express their professional interests. Within these forums, the role of these semi-public bodies is to act as mediators, helping the other professionals to breathe new life into a particular policy sphere. It is through such informal contacts that changes in policy practices can occur, mostly within a regional or local context.

In other words, a supranational policy input in the form of an incentive training policy has the effect of fostering the development of a sub-state and partly public, partly societal mode of regulating policy making in the employment sphere. This in turn calls into question the policy role of both European and national authorities and the political legitimacy and accountability of these more traditional institutional mediators.

Transitional Labour Markets and Social Exclusion: a European Effect?

European funding seems to assist experimentation with transitional labour markets at a local level by encouraging the development of new forms of social and political regulation mediated mainly by private or societal actors. Local networks based on an unusual combination of non-profit organizations, training providers, government officials, local authorities and firms are being developed on a temporary basis around a single training course cofinanced by the EU. These networks are acting as facilitators of individual transitions (between family work and economic activity, between unemployment and work, between single and multiple job holding, between seasonal and permanent work, and so on) and are therefore alleviating social exclusion. At a national level, networks are bringing together professionals, many of whom are not used to pooling their technical knowledge and competences, officials and researchers. Their experience in the networks is prompting them to construct methodologies and arguments they can use to diffuse within their region, ministry or administration the training experiments they have analysed collectively. One quantitative evaluation (they are, regrettably, in short supply) shows that the 'return to work' rate (or rate of successful transition) of these experimental training policies is notably higher than those of 'traditional' national policies (about 35.6 per cent of trainees on the Horizon-Germany programme returned to work or undertook further training between 1991 and 1995; Seyfried *et al.*, 1995). However, the main achievement of those European programmes – which is underlined in qualitative evaluations based on interviews with local project organizers –

seems to be the local 'partnerships' and 'networks' that develop between mutually complementary organizations; that is, between vocational coun-selling organizations, training organizations, local policy makers and firms. Such partnerships and networks ensure better coordination of supply and demand in the local labour market, thereby facilitating transi-tions and social 'inclusion' – but only for some 'privileged' trainees.

Can Policy Legitimacy Stem from Policy Expertise?

In state-building theories, nation states have constituted and legitimized themselves through policy making and a public discourse of justification for their actions and by creating an identity for a mythological (national) community (Obradovic, 1996). This clearly does not apply to policy making at the European level: among the populations of the member states, there is very little sense of belonging to a supranational community. So what kind of legitimization processes are at work?

'State actors' (including here the European Commission) are legitimized in their actions in so far as they formulated the principles that guide the implementation of policies and make experimentation 'possible'. However, they are unable to 'build on' this initial legitimacy by producing, for instance, a symbolic discourse on those policies. Because of the constraints contained in the EU's treaty base, the Commission has to proceed with great caution in seeking to expand the scope of its policy making (Scharpf, 1994). Furthermore, in the absence of a true European community of citi-zens able to listen to its discourse of political justification, it is able to exert very little influence on the implementation of policies it has launched. Nevertheless, it would be untrue to say that no political discourse on the Community HR initiatives has been produced. However, those discourses that have been produced are largely technical in nature and aimed at a very limited number of professionals in the sector concerned rather than at the average citizen. National states are also unable to build on these constitu-tive policies, since they delegate most aspects of policy implementation and regulation and are therefore unable to incorporate the experimental tools into mainstream national policies.

However, while the 'traditional' political actors are not producing any discourse on these policies and their effects, such discourses are being pro-duced by professionals and 'experts' in forums such as seminars and con-ferences that could be described as local and professional public spaces. While some authors proposed the concept of 'administrative democracy' (Duran and Thoenig, 1996) to describe this trend in policy making, this shift away from purely representative mechanisms of legitimization seems to indicate that we are dealing here rather with a 'para-administrative democracy', in which a discourse of policy justification is developed collectively in forums bringing together private and public actors and organizations. However, this European process of socialization and the collective production of policy expertise and political discourse, far from creating a transnational space for public policy debate (Muller, 1996), tends rather to produce here a plurality of unintegrated local professional forums open to expert debate.

The kind of citizenship being exercised in these public debates might well be described as 'a performance-based citizenship'. The citizens able to express themselves in the new forums are those capable of grasping the complex game of multi-level governance. Is this not, in fact, a foretaste of the new forms of citizenship likely to emerge in complex societies?

BIBLIOGRAPHY

Callon, M. (1986), 'Eléments d'une sociologie de la traduction', *L'Année sociologique*, 36, 169–209.

Commission Européenne (1993), *Croissance, Compétitivité, Emploi: Livre Blanc*, Luxembourg: OPOCE.

Dolowitz, D.P. (1996), 'The British welfare-to-work system: a reinterpretation through the eyes of policy transfer', *Contemporary Political Studies*, 3, 1784–94.

Donzelot, J. and Estèbe, P. (1994), *L'Etat animateur: Essai sur la politique de la ville*, Paris: Edition Esprit.

Duran, Patrice and Thoenig, Jean-Claude (1996), 'L'Etat et la gestion publique territoriale', *Revue Française de Science Politique*, 46(4), 580–624.

Hild, P. (1995), 'ABS-Gesellschaften – eine problemorientierte Analyse bisheriger Befunde', *Mitteilungen aus der Arbeitsmarkt- und Berufsforschung*, 4, 503–15.

Hooghe, L. (ed.) (1996), *Cohesion Policy and European Integration: Building Multi-Level Governance*, Oxford: Oxford University Press.

Hooghe, L. and Keating, M. (1993), 'The Politics of European Union Regional Policy', *Journal of European Public Policy*, 1(3), 367–93.

Kingdon, J.W. (1984), *Agendas, Alternatives and Public Policies*, Boston: Little, Brown.

Laffan, B. (1996), 'Ireland: A Region Without Regions – The Odd Man Out?', in L. Hooghe (ed.), *Cohesion Policy and European Integration: Building Multi-Level Governance*, Oxford: Oxford University Press.

Leibfried, St. and Pierson, P. (eds) (1995), *European Social Policy: Between Fragmentation and Integration*, Washington, DC: Brookings.

Lewis, J. (1995), *The Voluntary Sector, the State and Social Work in Britain*, London: Macmillan.

Lowi, Th. (1964), 'American Business, Public Policy, Case Studies, and Political Theory', *World Politics*, 16(4), 677–715.

Majone, G. (1993), 'The European Community between Social Policy and Social Regulation', *Journal of Common Market Studies*, 31(2), 153–70.

March, J.G. and Olsen, J.P. (1984), 'The New Institutionalism: Organizational Factors in Political Life', *American Political Science Review*, September, 734–79.

Marks, G. (1992), 'Structural Policy in the European Community', in A. Sbragia (ed.), *Euro-Politics: Institutions and Policymaking in the 'new' European Community*, Washington, DC: Brookings.

Mazey, S. and Richardson, J (1998), *Lobbying in the EU*, Oxford: Oxford University Press.

Moravcsik, A. (1993), 'Preferences and Power in the European Community: A Liberal Intergovernmental Approach', *Journal of Common Market Studies*, December, 473–524.

Muller, P. (1996), 'La mise en œuvre des politiques de l'Union européenne', in F. Arcy and L. Rouban (eds), *De la Ve République à l'Europe*, Paris: Presses de la FNSP.

Obradovic, D. (1996), 'Policy legitimacy and the EU', *Journal of Common Market Studies*, 34(2).

Parri, L. (1989), 'Territorial Political Exchange in Federal and Unitary Countries', *West European Politics*, 196–217.

Quermonne, J.-L. (1994), *Le système politique de l'Union européenne*, Paris: Montchrestien.

Rose, R. (1993), *Lesson-Drawing in Public Policy*, New York: Chatham.

Rouault, S. and Muller, P. (1997), 'Une grammaire européenne de l'expérimentation sociale: la mise en œuvre de l'Initiative Emploi', *Cultures et Conflits*, 28, 60–75.

Sbragia, A. (ed.) (1992), *Euro-Politics: Institutions and Policymaking in the 'new' European Community*, Washington, DC: Brookings.

Sbragia, A. (1993), 'The European Community: A Balancing Act', *Publius*, 23, 23–39.

Scharpf, F.W. (1994), 'Community and Autonomy: Multi-Level Policy-making in the European Union', *Journal of European Public Policy*, 1(2), 219–42.

Schmid, G. (1994), 'Reorganisation der Arbeitsmarktpolitik: Märkte, Politische Steuerung und Netzwerke der Weiterbildung für Arbeitslose in der Europäischen Union', WZB Discussion Paper FS I 94-213, WZB, Berlin.

Schmid, G. (1995), 'Is Full Employment Still Possible? Transitional Labour Markets as a New Strategy of Labour Market Policy', *Economic and Industrial Policy*, 16, 429–56.

Schömann, K. (1995), 'Active Labour Market Policy in the European Union', WZB Discussion Paper FS I 95-201, WZB, Berlin.

Seyfried E., Gmelin, A., Bühler, A. and Schütte, E. (1995), *Abschlussbericht. Evaluation der Gemeinschaftsinitiative Horizon in der BRD*, Berlin: Forschungsstelle für Berufsbildung, Arbeitsmarkt und Evaluation.

Smith, A. (1995), *L'Europe au miroir du local: les fonds structurels et les zones rurales en France, en Espagne et au Royaume-Uni*, Paris: L'Harmattan.

Smyrl, M.E. (1995), 'From Regional Policy Communities to European Networks: Inter-Regional Divergence in the Implementation of EC Regional Policy in France', *EUI Working Paper RSC*, No. 95/20, Florence.

Tömmel, I. (1994), *Staatliche Regulierung und europäische Integration: Die Regionalpolitik der EG und ihre Implementation in Italien*, Baden-Baden: Nomos.

15. From the market for qualifications to the transitional labour market of learning and working: summary and conclusion

Klaus Schömann and Philip J. O'Connell

The volume, focusing on training-related transitions, represents a core component of the ambitious research programme on social integration through transitional labour markets. Training-related transitions constitute the transitional labour market of learning and working which goes beyond the study of the first school-to-work transition. Further training and related labour market transitions have a direct link to previous experiences in the education system and, therefore, we treat the two spheres of initial learning and work-related continuing training as one market for qualifications, which we name the transitional labour market of learning and working. Institutional structures of education systems and employment systems are known to vary widely from one country to another. The comparative nature of the studies collected in this volume allows us to take this claim seriously and test the implications of different institutional arrangements on learning and working processes.

In this final chapter of the book we give a brief overview of the topics dealt with in the book and a short summary of the major substantive findings of individual contributions. The second part of this chapter discusses the evidence relating to the hypotheses derived from the theoretical treatment of transitional labour markets developed in Chapter 2. This critical assessment of the contribution of a more formalized model of transitional labour markets is followed by a 'mise en perspective' by the editors of the individual contributions to develop an overview of the findings reported in each chapter. Our guiding perspective contrasts social integration versus social exclusion, market orientation versus market failure and policy intervention versus policy failure in the organization and outcomes of learning and working processes.

This volume started with a chapter of basic definitions of what is meant by terms like 'social integration' and 'social exclusion' and the presentation of a new approach to the development of hypotheses based on the institutional theory of transitional labour markets. The empirical work is organized in four major parts of the book. The first part focuses on the first transition from education to the labour market. Initial education is still an important predictor of subsequent labour market prospects and potential. The first transition is also a particularly troublesome transition featuring high rates of youth unemployment throughout Europe, despite considerable political efforts devoted to this target group of labour market policies. Chapters 3 and 4 deal with two aspects of first entry: demand for more education and segmentation at entry into the labour market.

In the second part of the empirical results, Chapters 5 to 8 address the role of training in the fight against unemployment. Cross-section evidence across a range of European Union countries on transitions between unemployment and employment is complemented by in depth-longitudinal evidence and cost–benefit assessments of public policies concentrated on this transition. These chapters focus on the extent to which training policies promote social integration in both access to and outcomes of programmes. While the findings in this part identify inefficiencies in past and current approaches to active labour market policies, they also suggest several ways in which public policies can be improved.

Social integration, nowadays, operates to a large extent through integration into stable and well-paid employment. Therefore, in Part III of the volume, Chapters 9 to 12, we present analyses of training provided by firms to their employees. Firms are an important place of continuing training and lifelong learning processes in the broadest sense possible. Learning in organizations is increasingly important to organizational performance, and learning does not only take place in structured forms of training courses but may often become embedded in the standard operating procedures of high-performance work organizations (Ichniowski *et al.*, 1995). One of the larger concerns at issue here is the apparent trade-off between the firm's economic performance and the societal goal of broad social integration in the working life of individual employees.

Besides the efforts of individuals and firms there are a number of collective actors involved in influencing both the nature and scale of training activities, and the extent to which such training facilitates socially integrative labour market outcomes or training transitions. Negotiations of social partners largely determine within firm training efforts, but they are also powerful players in the game of institution building and institutional change. In Part IV of this volume, Chapters 13 and 14 address the issue of 'change management' of institutional arrangements through social actors. One important aspect is the distinction of bipartite versus tripartite negotiations within a single country. Another aspect of increasing importance is the multi-level issue involved in policy making in the field of training and labour market policies through a complex setting of cofinancing of public policies from the local, national and European level. From this broad overview of the content of the whole volume we move to the more detailed discussion of results from each of the empirical parts.

1. SUMMARY OF MAJOR RESULTS ON TRAINING TRANSITIONS

The major data sources for the study of these processes is the European Community Household Panel (ECHP), the European Labour Force Survey (ELFS), the Eurobarometer, specific country longitudinal surveys and recently available firm-level data in three countries. The role of actors in the field of training is approached by in-depth case studies to grasp the multidimensional and multi-level aspect of the rationale for training activities by social actors. The studies mainly present analyses for five countries: France, Germany, Ireland, the Netherlands and Spain. Larger comparisons of outcomes of training transitions across the European Union based on harmonized data sets and methodological approaches are presented at the end of Part II in Chapter 8 of this volume.

Empirical Results on Demand for Education and First Entry into the Labour Market

Estimates of education demand models for Spain, Ireland and Germany on the basis of the ECHP highlight that labour market and income expectations are less important incentives in influencing the demand for higher education than factors related to parental social background and the current institutional framework of the education system and the labour market. The observed patterns of access to higher education were strongly driven by the supply of higher education and professional training. At the individual level a higher level of parents' educational attainment and a higher socioeconomic status are likely to increase the demand for education among their children (see Chapter 3 of this volume; Becker, 2000; Bonmati, 2000). Institutional change such as the widening of access to university-level education with the intention of increasing the opportunity for social integration of larger groups through higher education has led to the paradoxical effect that it also increased the negative signalling effect for dropouts and labour market difficulties for the least qualified.

These signals, or 'group-level influences' according to Parkin (1974), are embedded in educational credentials originating in the full-time education system. They are largely responsible for the sorting of individuals at labour market entry to specific industrial segments in France, Germany, Ireland, the Netherlands, Spain and the United Kingdom (Audier, in this volume; Gangl, 2000a). The analysis shows that young labour market entrants are not in competition with older employees in firms' recruitment processes. Moroever, educational sorting leads to labour market segmentation according to skill levels among the young. This finding indicates that second-chance education needs to be reformed to include more elements of transitional labour markets, such as improved opportunities and incentives for such education, career breaks for further education and training, as well as combining part-time work and education, in order to avoid stigmatization and negative signalling effects. Gender-specific recruitment practices at ports of entry are still prevalent across the European Union (Audier, in this volume; Gangl, 2000b; Müller and Shavit, 1998) and recruitment patterns in both advantaged and disadvantaged labour market segments still fail to offer sufficient equality of access for women. This suggests that the transitional labour market reforms outlined above should also incorporate interventions designed to promote equality of opportunity.

Evaluation of Further Training Policies in the European Union

The second part of this volume deals with further training transitions, with in-depth studies of Ireland, the Netherlands and Germany. A comparative chapter with a wider spread of European countries but less detailed data completes this part. The Irish study (Chapter 5 in this volume) demonstrates that training programmes characterized by strong labour market linkages are more likely to enhance the subsequent employment prospects of both women and men. A similar pattern can be seen in the studies on the Netherlands and Germany. A closer linking of publicly supported training activities to the labour market and firms' skill needs is an important element to improve the integration chances of participants in labour market measures (O'Connell and McGinnity, in this volume). Public training policies too far removed from the functioning of labour markets do not achieve the intended effects of social integration, although they may, at least temporarily, alleviate the risk of social exclusion. For young persons a closer institutional link between general education policies and labour market concerns advances their post-programme earnings and employment chances. Education for its own sake as well as temporary employment programmes in activities that are only loosely related to the labour market are less likely to promote long-term social integration in Ireland.

The cost–benefit reanalysis of evaluations of training measures has shown that while training may improve the chances of transitions from unemployment to employment, the net effects are relatively small. Improved selectivity of training policies for unemployed persons who would be unlikely to achieve integration on their own initiative and/or resources increases the cost-effectiveness of these programmes. For those from ethnic minorities or women with long career interruptions, programmes aimed at their specific needs work best. The Dutch findings suggest that relatively high net rates of return to such specific training investments can be achieved for these target groups where courses are completed. Even if gross placement rates in employment are relatively low for 'hard-to-place' target groups, these programmes may nevertheless yield positive social returns, since economic inactivity is frequently the costly alternative (de Koning, in this volume; Gelderbloom and de Koning, in this volume). The analysis shows the value of training measures designed specifically for target groups who are, in the absence of public programmes, at risk of social exclusion. Linking the design of training programmes more closely to qualification needs in the labour market represents a promising and cost-effective policy development.

The long-term evaluation of further training in West Germany revealed low levels of investment in further training of less well-educated employees (Schömann and Becker, in this volume). The reluctance to seek training of these employees indicates either low payback to initial investments in education or negative experiences during earlier participation in schooling. Lifetime earnings are, therefore, likely to fall further behind the earnings of the well educated. For most women in West Germany, institutional impediments, such as caring responsibilities largely left to private households, have made training participation difficult to organize. Capitalizing on training investments was only achieved through long-term employment relationships.

Additionally, for the transformation of the economy of East Germany in the early 1990s, it can be shown that employment prospects of job-related training are highest while pursued on-the-job even if this job is scheduled to be terminated in the near future. This highlights the superior cost-effectiveness of preventive measures, since no unemployment benefit payments are necessary, despite the difficulty of early identification of future marketable skill needs. In both East and West Germany important social selectivity effects were found, which leads us to the conclusion that 'adverse selection' in training participation may well be an early sign of higher risks of exclusionary transitions at later stages of the life course. Social selection for training participation can be interpreted as an early warning indicator for 'at risk' groups of society.

Comparative results across most European Union countries show that social selectivity according to age and level of initial education is a major predictor of participation in further training. Evidence based on European

Union-wide surveys like the small sample Eurobarometer and the large size European Labour Force Survey suggests that this selectivity is difficult to overcome. It appears that the logic of human capital investment results in higher risks of unemployment and long-term unemployment for those with low skills and little marketable work experience. The social selection operating in labour markets is in some instances complemented rather than mediated by selective training policies, which can lead to a twofold selection process operating as first step social exclusion. Hence market failure combined with government or policy failure can generate increased risks of social exclusion (see Chapter 8 in this volume). At the institutional level there is no necessary link between a well functioning system of initial education and an equally well performing system of further training. The prevention of unemployment through on-the-job training appears to be a more promising policy strategy than counting solely on curative measures aimed at the already unemployed.

Assessing the Firm's Rationale for Training

Theoretical approaches to the firm's rationale for training postulate a close link between firm productivity and wages. In practice, however, seniority-based wage structures frequently dominate the link between age of an employee and individual productivity. Since individual productivity is difficult to observe and to measure, particularly in sectors where productivity is largely dependent on teamwork and production in networks, we do not expect to find clear-cut trends across industrial sectors. The rationale of the firm is driven by the imperative to enhance organizational performance and profitability and this differs from a social rationality driven by concerns with social integration.

The first chapter in Part III, Chapter 9 by Jolivet, analyses the training practices of French firms with the specific focus on the relationship between employee wage structures and firms' training efforts. The French levy on the wage bill to finance further training operates to some extent in favour of older workers. If a firm's training expenses are high, usually older employees can also benefit from this. An important caveat remains. In some instances more training is offered to older employees, but at the same time these firms dismiss large numbers of older employees. Training, in these cases, can work as a screening device during episodes of 'downsizing' of the firm's workforce. Older employees who show less potential for future productivity increases in screening courses are more likely to be laid off. This usage of training as a screening device to weed out weaker workers may represent an unwelcome potential of lifelong learning strategies from societal and individual perspectives.

Gelderblom and de Koning (Chapter 10, in this volume) present evidence that productivity and wages do not evolve in proportion to each other. Productivity rises rapidly among younger employees, but declines rapidly in later working life. In contrast, wages follow a more moderate growth and decline before retirement. Training of older employees is found to yield an improved productivity wage ratio for older employees, and could thus promote a less exclusionary tendency in the labour market for older workers. Prevention of economic inactivity for persons beyond the age of 55 appears to be feasible with training which takes account of specific learning approaches of older employees. In the Dutch case a substantial proportion of those who withdraw from the labour market because of disability would have preferred to remain economically active in the labour market. Lifelong learning as a means to narrow the productivity–wage ratio in middle and older age may facilitate the economic sustainability of more generous social security systems, delaying retirement transitions, and broaden the scope for social integration of older employees, and can thus contribute to transitional labour markets between employment and retirement.

Chapter 11 examines whether lifelong learning reduces the risk of individual unemployment or collective dismissal. The first part of the question, relating to individual risk, is investigated using longitudinal individual data, similar to the approaches in Part II of this volume. Despite the usual findings of selection effects, there is no statistically significant evidence that lifelong learning can prevent risks of unemployment. However, the Dutch firm level data confirm the hypothesis that firms with a higher level of training effort show lower rates of subsequent dismissals (individual or collective). Gelderblom and others have undertaken several attempts to reject the unemployment-prevention hypothesis, but it appears quite resistant to falsification in statistical modelling and effects are rather small. Their conclusion reiterates the segmentation approach: some employees have 'internalised' lifelong learning on an individual basis, whilst the majority of employees appear to be excluded from company training. The latter group of persons is also less likely to find a way back to learning outside the labour market.

O'Connell reports a similar pattern of results for Ireland (see Chapter 12). Companies which offer more valuable compensation packages to their employees show both a higher incidence and a greater intensity of training. Industrial sectors with higher productivity, or firms in the primary segments, offer better current terms of employment, in the form of higher wages, as well as better future prospects by investing in continuing training to enhance enterprise competitiveness and sustainability. However, training does not appear to influence enterprise-level changes in aggregate employment, a finding which casts doubt on the validity of the prevention hypothesis for Ireland. The Dutch finding that the returns to training of a less qualified workforce are higher than training of already well-equipped employees is supported by O'Connell (this volume).

Throughout the European Union labour market segmentation is related to productivity patterns of industrial sectors. Labour market segmentation at entry into the labour market is perpetuated and reinforced by company training policies. In order to prevent market failure, leading to underprovision of training, as well as career paths leading to labour market exclusion, it is necessary to increase participation in publicly financed but, at the same time, market-oriented and firm-based training to encompass the developmental needs of all employees, irrespective of age, levels of qualifications and current earnings.

We can observe very low rates of participation in continuing vocational training among ageing workers in most member states of the European Union (France, Ireland and the Netherlands are analysed in some detail: see Chapters 9 to 12, in this volume; see also O'Connell, 1999). This situation is combined with a seniority-based wage structure reflecting the greater employment insecurity of older employees in most firms. The greater the discrepancy between worker productivity and wages, the more likely the risk of job loss and transitions into unemployment, early retirement or other forms of withdrawal from the labour market (for example, disability benefits or pension dependency). The chapters reported in the present volume suggest that there are important differences in the extent to which continuing training by enterprises can serve to prevent social exclusion. In the Netherlands, firms engaging in greater training efforts show lower rates of dismissals in subsequent years, but this is less true in France and least in Ireland. On the basis of firm-level and individual-level data it seems to be possible to identify persons on positive career tracks with greater levels of participation in training and those with high risks of exclusion from the labour market owing to failure to participate in or be selected for training by the firm or public policy initiatives. Creaming practices by both firms and public agencies, in selecting those who are already well-equipped in the labour market for further training, tend to exacerbate existing skills gaps between employees and can increase the exposure of those who lack skills to even greater risks of social exclusion.

The Impact of Political Actors in the Field of Training

Part IV of this volume adds a new dimension to the predominantly economic and sociological analyses presented in the previous parts. This consists of a political science approach to the analysis of actors in the field of lifelong learning, national education, training and labour market systems in the multi-layered political system of the European Union. The first contribution, by Giraud, examines the role of industrial relations in firms' further training practices and the extent to which such practices promote social integration as opposed to social exclusion. Matched plant comparisons of France and Germany lead to the conclusion that joint trade union–management practices in the realm of further training are still weak in both countries. Moreover, neither of the very different regulatory frameworks of both initial and further training appear to overcome the limited participation in company-sponsored training among less well-equipped workers and others facing high risks of social exclusion.

The development of a common market within the European Union may be expected to lead to a convergence of education and training systems across the Union within sectors. Giraud argues that in France and Germany this convergence process has resulted in the evolution of greater similarity in training systems between companies in similar product or service markets across countries. So the training system of a company in Germany could have more in common with a French company in the same product or service market than with other German companies in different sectors. This means that traditional comparison between national systems – mainly initial education in Germany, further training in France – has become less applicable. Rather than substitutes, the two forms of training have become indispensable complements, thereby reinforcing the trend to set up positive career paths with upward mobility and frequent training rather than static career tracks which are likely to lead to exclusion from the labour market (see Part III of this volume). Improved comanagement and cofinancing of further training, combined with changes in working-time arrangements, could contribute to the further development of transitional labour markets that would facilitate continuous upgrading and updating of skills in a manner that would promote enhanced performance and competitiveness for enterprises and increased employment security for workers.

The disengagement of the link between further training and internal promotion ladders has largely reduced internal promotion opportunities for employees. Despite extensive codetermination arrangements in the realm of further training in France this practice has not really reached the collective bargaining at plant-level. However, company-level bargaining on further training is the most effective strategy either to prevent exclusionary trajectories or to increase plant level acceptance of integrating strategies.

The second contribution in this part, by Rouault, deals with the impact of experimental European Union initiatives in the field of employment and training. Governance in the European Union is presented as a complex multi-level governance and in the field of training it is dominated by the selection and financing of pilot projects and experimental policy designs, and subsequent evaluations and 'benchmarking' to reveal best practice. This undoubtedly contributes to the development of an improved policy expertise across the Union, but in order to spread legitimacy of this policy beyond expert groups a larger public discourse is needed. So far this discourse is restricted to discussions among representatives of governments, social partners, pressure groups and appointed experts. Since the organization of such policy forums is left to administrators, this procedure has been dubbed 'administrative democracy'.

Sponsorship of experimental interventions, particularly by the European Social Fund, means that European integration brings with it a process of institutional creativity (Rouault, in this volume). The European Union initiatives function as laboratories for social innovation. In order to find and define a role for the European Commission in the fight against social exclusion, implementation of policies is largely delegated to semi-public, expert or non-governmental organizations (NGOs). Decentralization and privatization of social policy provision has, therefore, gained a stronger impetus through European level policy making than had previously been the case in most member states of the Union. It remains to be seen whether such institutional creativity can generate adequate strategies to increase social integration while not simultaneously increasing the risk of social exclusion for other groups less well represented in the policy formation process.

Overall, the evidence reveals that social exclusion is a result not only of market failure but also of a combination of market failure with policy failure. Since the number of policy approaches and the differing social protection arrangements vary widely within the European Union, more rigorous evaluations of the kind presented in this volume are needed to build solid and multiple bridges between the worlds of learning and working. The next section will review the theory of transitional labour markets in the light of the above evidence.

2. THE THEORY OF TRANSITIONAL LABOUR MARKETS REVISITED

The theory of labour market transitions allows us to identify the multi-dimensional and multi-level issues affecting the goal of social integration. In addition to human capital theory, segmentation approaches and insider–outsider theory, our theory of transitional labour markets points to several changes in the way education and training transitions can be linked to the labour market in order to further the objective of social integration. Institutional arrangements are especially useful to complement the role of the market if there is need to correct market failure. Market failure in training arises for example in the form of underinvestment in continuing training by specific social groups who could have high returns. The opposite process of overinvestment in training is similarly wasteful from the perspective of human capital investment (Büchel, 1998), although it is not easy to identify and measure overeducation precisely (Borghans and de Grip, 2000).

The analyses presented throughout this volume provide ample evidence in favour of hypothesis 1 of the institutional theory of transitions and transitional labour markets (see Chapter 2, section 4): *Stronger demand for skills and competences in the initial education system leads to greater labour market success.* This basic hypothesis is close to the rationale of the human capital theory, albeit the emphasis is put on skills and competence as well as the motivational aspect of schooling – to learn how to learn – rather than simple number of years of schooling or achievement of a school leaving certificate. It needs to be acknowledged that the correlation of educational certification with possession of marketable skills and competence is, in most cases, fairly high, but a one-to-one translation is misleading and hides important parts of the process of skill acquisition, market values and implicit signalling values. The empirical tests of this hypothesis have made use of individual-level data on initial educational attainment and subsequent earnings and are thus similar to empirical approaches to test human capital models (compare OECD, 1999). The additional efforts to model social selectivity in initial education and further training and to estimate employment and unemployment probabilities for different education levels and labour market segments reveals the limited extent to which the theory of human capital can be applied in its 'pure' form (see Chapters 3 to 8 of this volume and OECD, 1999, pp. 135–8).

Well-known institutional and societal factors have proved persistent over time, for example: (a) the continuing relevance of parental and social background for educational trajectories (Chapter 2); (b) segmentation of the labour market from the very beginning of employment trajectories at the point of labour market entry (Chapter 3); (c) differential access to further training and marketable use of further training (Chapters 4 to 8); (d) continued high investments in training of those with higher levels of education and skill versus the exclusion of older workers or those groups with low achievements in initial education; (e) persistent wage differentials between women and men in the returns to education and training (Chapters 5 and 7). The 'ensemble' of the evidence presented suggests that the basic human capital theory applies mainly to prime-age male dependent employees in high profit-generating industries, who come from favoured social and parental backgrounds. For most other groups of society the human capital approach seems to have limited application and little explanatory power. Moreover, that approach is unlikely to yield practical escape routes from social exclusion since the explanatory power of the theory is confined to situations in which no other 'institutional and societal effects' need be taken into account (see also Lynch, 1994; Acemoglou and Pischke, 1999; OECD, 1999).

The second hypothesis is of a more general nature and should be tested at the aggregate level: *a higher level of educational investment in a society, either in the form of wider access to higher education or improved quality of education, will lead to higher average labour productivity and earnings.* The transition theory states that, under the assumption of an appropriately defined link between the education system and the labour market, a larger share of participants in higher education or further training will subsequently translate into higher productivity and earnings. The evidence across the chapters in this volume supports the general hypothesis but suggests an additional generalization: that training provided to the least qualified is likely to achieve the highest returns, despite the widespread reluctance of firms to invest in the less qualified or older employees (see Chapters 9 to 12).

The findings for Ireland show that participation in training and employment programmes with strong market linkages improves subsequent employment prospects and earnings (Chapter 5), and thus provide support for the need of market orientation as a second element of the second hypothesis. The term 'market orientation' is less clearly defined in relation to general education, but at tertiary level, market orientation can simply relate to the extent to which courses respond to skill needs in the labour market. This could include organizational reforms, such as the flexible provision of modular courses, or the ability to shift the allocation of training slots in accordance with feedback from the labour market. Such a strategy may appear to work in the short to medium run, although the longer-term sustainability of orienting general education to current market needs is a subject that requires further research. 'Herd behaviour' of education and training providers and labour market agents might introduce sizeable cycles of enrolments and could distort post-participation reward structures (Neugart, 2000).

Hypothesis 3 states that *countries can influence not only the duration and quality of their education systems and their likely consequences for the labour market, but also the school-to-work transition in its own right.* This addresses the role of institutions in both education systems and the labour market and thus calls attention to the transitional labour market at entry into the labour market. Chapters 3 and 4 deal with the first entry into the labour market from a comparative perspective. The evidence shows that public policies can address education and the labour market separately without taking into account the link between the two spheres of action. Better results in terms of social integration are obtained if transitions from school to work are influenced by the nature of the linkage between the two spheres, which we termed the 'coefficient of coupling' in Chapter 2. Specific public policy efforts and coordination mechanisms, such as an apprenticeship system, make it possible to establish a transitional labour market with the aim of easing transitions between institutions.

European employment guidelines have focused attention on youth unemployment and therefore indirectly on the school-to-work transition (Serrano, 2000; Fondeur and Lefresne, 1999). Specific policy interventions, either as part of a reform of the education system – for example greater market orientation, or combining general education with on-the-job training in apprenticeships – or as part of active labour market policy (for example subsidizing wages of young entrants) are applied throughout the European Union. The evidence suggests that the functioning of the youth labour market in particular is quite different from the neoclassical model of the labour market and that institutions are an important determinant of how well markets operate: for example, apprenticeship-based integration patterns appear to perform better than transition processes in which pure market forces dominate.

Hypothesis 4 postulates that *the more frequently transitions between education/training and the labour market occur, the higher will be the level of social integration of participating groups.* This takes up the long-running debate regarding economic flexibility, but defines flexibility more narrowly than usual, as frequent transitions between education/training and the labour market. From the wider debate on economic flexibility, understood as mobility in the labour market, we know that it is crucial to differentiate between forced and voluntary job mobility, particularly concerning changes between standard and non-standard work arrangements (Schömann *et al.*, 1998). Similar information on voluntary/involuntary changes are not available for moves between education and the labour market. However, information for Ireland, Denmark and the Netherlands suggests that in countries with higher rates of transitions between training and working we tend to find higher levels of integration of women into the labour market. Reintegration of women through training appears to be working in these societies, although this is still only available to a few women (see Chapters 5–8 of this volume). Theories of labour market segmentation probably focus too narrowly on overall job mobility and neglect the evidence on multiple training transitions. Only evaluations over the long term will allow us to differentiate between the short-term training transitions which allow short term integration and longer-lasting, more durable integration into the labour market and society as a whole.

The fifth hypothesis deals with the role of social partners in the design of the link between education and the labour market: *in countries where the social partners play a prominent role in the institutional arrangements governing the link between education/training and the labour market, a more dynamic and mutually enhancing exchange between the two spheres is likely to arise*. Chapter 13, by Giraud, takes up this issue in a French–German comparison of industrial relations in the field of training and further training. Frequent bargaining at firm, regional or industry level, as well as at the national and increasingly European level, has created a complex interplay of levels and issues of bargaining. It appears that in both countries bargaining on wages, working time and conditions are complemented by bargaining on 'presumably' soft issues like initial training, vocational training and further training. Stalemate in one field of bargaining is likely to be counteracted by progress of negotiations in another field. In France and Germany, this interdependence of bargaining fields can lead to situations where deadlock in wage negotiations occurs in parallel with progress on 'soft' issues such as the reform of curricula in vocational education. Countries with a well established and historical tradition of bargaining at various levels seem to be better equipped to address also the link between training and integration into the firm or the labour market in general. In Germany there are numerous examples of collective agreements which specify the duration and a number of apprentices who are guaranteed employment after completion of the apprenticeship in the firm. In France the link between participation in further training and career prospects, including wages and occupational grades, seems to be strong. In both countries, however, there is a negotiated link. In Germany the principal linkage is related to *initial* training, while in France the linkage is predominantly related to *further* training. The Scandinavian countries apparently have integrated systems of negotiating in terms of both initial and further training-related transitions which favour multiple and integrative transitions (Schömann, 2001).

Hypothesis 6 states: *small-step experimental policy making is the preferred way of policy making in the multi-level governance structure of the European Union*. This is mainly addressed by Rouault in Chapter 14 of this volume. Labour market policy reform and first steps towards a more harmonized set of labour market policies have been rather careful throughout the European Union. This is principally due to the absence of a legal basis for such a harmonized European policy, with the result that policy must be guided by annual agreements on policy priorities in the fields of employment and social affairs. The Employment Guidelines and the so-called 'Luxembourg process' have become a standard 'modus operandi' of consultation. The major policy initiatives work through the social funds and the employment initiatives, but experimental policy innovations usually start at the margins of the existing legal context and administrative routines in the countries under study (France, Ireland and Germany). Several years of experimenting with new policies – for example, job rotation – may eventually lead the national authority to incorporate elements of, or lessons learned from, the experimental policy into the mainstream national or regional policy framework. The example of the employment initiative studied in Chapter 14 shows that this is a rather slow process of adaptation and, so far, more the exception than the rule. On the level of the theory of coupled oscillators this seems plausible since rapid changes of the coefficient of coupling of two subsystems may give rise to dynamics which will be difficult to control afterwards.

Whereas the six hypotheses above mainly deal with the macro and institutional level of analysis related to education, training and the labour market, the second set of hypotheses alters the focus of attention to the micro level of analysis and the impact of institutional links and influences on micro-level processes. Hypothesis 7 holds that *achieving higher education levels, usually combined with longer durations in education or better quality of education in terms of relevance for the labour market, will lead to higher labour productivity and subsequently higher labour earnings under the premise of a well established link between the two subsystems.* This can be understood as a more general hypothesis than the basic human capital investment model (Becker, 1964). Since the human capital theory builds on a well established link between the general education system and the labour market, relaxing this assumption and making it the basic element of another theory, the theory of transitions as formulated in Chapter 2, allows us to define the transitions theory as the more general case. Owing to the importance of the institutional link between education and the labour market and to important national variation in institutional structures and relevant actors (Shavit and Müller, 1998), we argue that it is essential to give more importance to the institutional context for this transition, rather than considering it just as an assumption falling under the usual clause of 'ceteris paribus'. Therefore hypothesis 7 restates to some extent hypothesis 1 as a micro-level process. In this respect human capital theory could be regarded as a special case of the transitions theory that is applicable where a well established link between the two subsystems exists. This would presuppose the presence of fully informed agents, a transparent certification practice, wide access to recruitment routines of firms and intermittent agents, and the absence of internal labour markets, insider–outsider processes or generational crowding or specific cohort effects. Whenever such ideal conditions do not prevail, and this appears to be the case in many instances (OECD, 1999), a more detailed modelling and empirical tests of the type of link between institutions becomes necessary. We would submit that the transitional labour market approach is better equipped to deal with departures from the basic assumptions of the human capital approach.

Estimates of returns to human capital investment, as presented in Chapter 5 by O'Connell and McGinnity for Ireland and in Chapter 7 by Schömann and Becker for East Germany, suggest that returns to human capital investment are higher for women than for men. This should not lead to the conclusion that for women there exists a better link between their educational attainment and subsequent labour earnings. In the case of Ireland and Germany, both countries with below-average rates of female labour force participation in the European Union (Eurostat, 2000), a selection process is at work which reduces the number of women who continue to stay in the labour market. The selective group of women who accumulate longer work experience may enjoy higher returns than men with the same level of qualifications. The same rationale can be applied to explain longer spells of unemployment and higher levels of unemployment for women than for men. Institutional features of the labour market, perceptions about women's participation patterns and recruitment practices of employers form part of the link between the two subsystems and seem to have a negative impact on the institutional link between the two societal subsystems.

Hypothesis 8 postulates that *higher levels of education will increase the duration of labour force participation and of employment over the lifetime*. The micro-level analyses of individual data from Chapters 4 to 8, as well as the micro-level analyses using employers' information in Chapters 9 to 12, provide substantial support for this contention. Chapter 4 shows that those with higher qualifications are more likely to enter more favourable segments of the labour market than the less educated. Similarly, the better educated are more likely to be selected for further training programmes and tend to be more successful in finding jobs after completion of training (Chapters 5 to 8).

The analysis of firms' training practices in France reveals that employees not selected for training are subsequently at greater risk of dismissal. On the other hand, selection of an employee for company-sponsored training tends to prolong the duration of an employment contract. This is especially the case for older employees, but in some cases poor performance in training may also increase the probability of leaving the firm. Gelderbloom and de Koning, in the analysis for the Netherlands of firms' training effort and job mobility (Chapter 10), argue that the narrowing of the productivity to wage gap through further training of older employees is likely to extend labour force participation of ageing workers. However, the results of Chapter 11, also for the Netherlands, indicate that it is not easy specifically to identify older employees who need training to prevent an early departure from the labour market. The results from Ireland (Chapter 12) which suggest that more highly educated or skilled employees receive higher shares of firms' training efforts and are, therefore, more likely to stay longer with the same firm, or if not in the same firm to remain economically active longer, reinforce the findings from the other two countries.

We now turn to hypothesis 9: *students' successful performance and completion of full-time initial schooling is largely dependent on their parental and wider social background.* Higher educational attainment of parents has a positive impact on children's educational attainment and subsequently on the first transition into the labour market (Chapter 3). In addition to parental background, the wider social background, including the presence of high-quality schooling in the local neighbourhood, is also influential. Economically depressed regions frequently lack resources to provide sufficient support to the schooling system and this may reinforce unequal starting conditions. In the comparison of education demand models for Spain, Ireland and Germany a strong interdependence of supply of schooling and parental demand for schooling is shown. This indicates a high 'coefficient of coupling' of the sphere of social background of pupils with both educational outcomes and labour market segment at entry. The second part of hypothesis 9, which suggests that a tight coupling of training and the labour market is more likely to reinforce the transmission of parental background to employment careers in the labour market, remains to be empirically investigated.

Hypothesis 10 argues that *the amount and quality of education/training, as well as the early experience of transitions, has lasting effects on entry into the labour market as well as most other subsequent labour market transitions, including exit decisions from the labour market.* This suggests that making and mastering transitions can be learned in the early stages of the life course and may be an important part of enhancing a person's potential. Our results, showing that educational attainment both reduces the risk of transitions from employment to unemployment and increases the rate of transition from employment to employment, provide support for the first part of the hypothesis (Chapters 6 to 9). People who have higher education degrees are also more likely in most countries to have changed schools at least once and made a further education-related transition to higher education. It is possible that early experience of transitions within the education system may provide additional 'transition' skills in successfully negotiating transitions which can subsequently reinforce the more formal learning associated with education or training. This involves learning to cope with new institutional arrangements and new environments, making new friends and, in the transition to university, becoming familiar with a new geographical location. All of these experiences are likely to teach 'communication skills' which could also be valuable on the labour market at later stages of the life course. However, a detailed empirical scrutiny of the additional impact of 'transition' skills is beyond the scope of the present volume.

Labour market segmentation sets in at first entry into the labour market (see Chapter 4) Indeed, in many countries such segmentation may take place within the vocational training system prior to labour market entry. Hypothesis 11 states that *segmentation tendencies early in the education system and particularly at the time of labour market entry will show severe persistence unless mitigated through transitional labour market arrangements and a conscious policy concentrating on the links between subsystems.* The available evidence points to the persistence of early segmentation at labour market entry, so we cannot reject this hypothesis. The involvement of networks of small and medium size enterprises (SMEs) in the organization of training of employees (*Verbundausbildung*) represents one promising transitional labour market arrangement which allows mobility between learning and working. In general, however, we found that industrial sectors which recruit labour market entrants with unstable non-standard employment contracts are more likely to be characterized by higher lay-off rates and less favourable conditions for early retirement. However, further research based on longitudinal data would be required to investigate long-term segmentation processes of this kind.

Hypothesis 12 argues that *labour market entry and mobility patterns are influenced by labour market exit patterns, including individual retirement policies, firms' early retirement programmes and legislative regulations governing retirement.* In Chapter 11, relating to the Netherlands, we find no evidence of a relationship between policies to encourage early labour market withdrawal and inflow rates of younger employees. The relationship between labour market outflows and inflows may be more complex than hypothesized, entailing additional intervening processes. Such processes seem to operate with time lags structures which we are unable to capture. Adequate empirical analysis of the impact of interventions to encourage various forms of early labour market withdrawal may have to await the availability of long-run longitudinal data on firms.

3. ADVANCING SOCIAL INTEGRATION DESPITE MARKET AND POLICY FAILURE

Labour markets can be regarded as obeying the same laws as commodity markets to the extent that there exists a pricing mechanism based on supply and demand for quality and quantity of labour. However, labour markets are more complex than simple commodity markets. Suppliers of labour are actors with basic human and social rights which restrict the working of a market-like price mechanism. Transitional labour markets attempt to develop institutional interventions designed to promote the social integration of those with marginal attachment to the labour market. In most industrial societies, social groups with marginal attachments to the labour market comprise young labour market entrants, women mainly engaged in household activities, the unemployed and older employees close to retirement age. These subgroups correspond to four transitional labour markets outlined by Schmid (2000). The theoretical framework developed in Chapter 2 emphasizes the importance of prevention of social exclusion and of reintegration as the two core pillars of labour market policies.

While those with higher levels of qualifications may face lower risks of unemployment, they are not immune, suggesting that transitional labour markets have a role to play in preventing social exclusion among all social groups, not only those disadvantaged in the labour market. Apprenticeship training systems represent one example of an institutional arrangement of a transitional labour market; arrangements that permit job-training rotations provide an alternative example which allows the combination of learning and working in a manner which promotes social integration (Kruhoffer, 1999). For economically inactive persons, including many women with caring obligations, the speed of technological innovation leads to deskilling if no links to the labour market, and thereby opportunities for continuing learning, can be sustained during phases of child care or caring for the elderly. In this case, transitional labour markets would allow for a combination of caring, work and training to promote labour market integration over the longer term.

One important element of policies for social integration is improving incentives for lifelong learning by facilitating training transitions throughout the life course, for example through sabbatical leaves or job rotation for training purposes. These forms build on existing mobility in the labour market and add a training component to job mobility which can be driven by either firms or individuals. Closer links between publicly supported training activities and skill needs in the labour market can enhance the effectiveness and the social integration potential of active labour market policies (see Chapter 5, by O'Connell and McGinnity). Job rotation is just one way to organize multiple transitions between working and learning. The combination of new working time arrangements and learning opportunities is another promising field for policy development which could allow more people, with varying market capacities, to participate in technological progress.

In recent years there has been a great deal of attention devoted to the importance of educational credentials for labour market success. Increased labour market participation has, however, also meant that those who fall below minimum educational thresholds are increasingly poorly equipped to compete in the labour market. Other groups confronting severe disadvantages in the labour market include ethnic minorities, migrants, women with long career interruptions and those with a disability. Interventions to promote social integration of such groups are more effective if programmes are aimed at their specific needs (Schmid *et al.*, 1996). The findings from Ireland (Chapter 5) and from the Netherlands (Chapter 11) suggest that relatively high net rates of return to such specific training investments can be achieved for these target groups, assuming that courses are completed. Since economic inactivity is frequently the costly alternative to interventions, the social returns to such programmes may be worthwhile even if gross placement rates in employment are relatively low for these 'hard-to-place' target groups (see de Koning, 2000; Gelderbloom and de Koning, 2000, in this volume).

Low participation in training of certain groups of employees may serve as an early warning of the risk of social exclusion. Part III of the volume suggests that older employees face a particular risk of adverse selection for training, which, in turn, may increase the risk of subsequent lay-off. Early identification of groups facing these risks and policies to provide training as a preventive form of labour market policy show some positive effects in France and the Netherlands. Of course dismissal of older employees is not to be equated with social exclusion, but the risk of downward spirals for older employees is higher than for younger employees. We were able to demonstrate social selectivity according to levels of qualifications and age in both the education/training system and the labour market. Overall, this can be attributed to market failure, but the real challenge is to overcome such market failure and also policy failure.

More generally, it is necessary to acknowledge that 'creaming', the selection for training of those who are already well equipped with skills and qualifications, is widespread in both publicly sponsored and enterprise-sponsored training policies. This suggests the need for monitoring of access to further education and training in both public and private training efforts. The state, the social partners, local governments and administrations all have an important role to play in the challenging task of expanding the scope and effectiveness of actions to promote social integration, most likely through transitional labour markets.

BIBLIOGRAPHY

Acemoglou, D. and Pischke, J.S. (1999), 'Beyond Becker: Training in Imperfect Labor Markets', *The Economic Journal*, February, 112–42.

Becker, G.S. (1964), *Human Capital*, New York: Columbia University Press.

Becker, S. (2000), 'Explaining University Enrolment in Italy and Germany', paper presented at the GSOEP Conference at the WZB, 5 July.

Bonmati, A.S. (2000), 'Labour Market Transitions of Youth in Germany, Italy and Spain', paper presented at the GSOEP Conference at the WZB, 5 July.

Borghans, L. and de Grip, A. (2000), *The Overeducated Worker? The Economics of Skill Utilization*, Cheltenham, UK and Northampton, MA, USA: Edward Elgar.

Büchel, F. (1998), *Zuviel gelernt? Ausbildungsinadäquate Erwerbstätigkeit in Deutschland*, Bielefeld: Bertelsmann.

Eurostat (2000), *European Social Statistics – Labour Force Survey Results 1999*, Luxembourg: Office for Official Publications of the European Communities.

Fondeur, Y. and Lefresne, F. (1999), 'Les jeunes sur le marché du travail, une comparaison européenne', *Revue de l'IRES*, 31, 5–22.

Gangl, M. (2000a), 'Education and Labour Market Entry across Europe: The Impact of Institutional Arrangements in Training Systems and Labour Market', Mannheimer Zentrum für Europäische Sozialforschung, working paper no. 25.

Gangl, M. (2000b), 'Changing Labour Markets and Early Career Outcomes: Labour market entry in Europe over the past decade', Mannheimer Zentrum für Europäische Sozialforschung, working paper no. 26.

Ichniowski, C., Shaw, K. and Prennushi, G. (1995), 'The Effects of Human Resource Management Practices on Productivity', working paper no. 5333, Cambridge, Mass.: National Bureau of Economic Research.

Kruhoffer, J. (1999), 'Job Rotation in Denmark – Status and Problems', in G. Schmid and K. Schömann (eds), *Learning from Denmark*, WZB Discussion Paper FS I 99-201, WZB, Berlin.

Lynch, L.M. (1994), *Training and the Private Sector: International Comparisons*, Chicago: University of Chicago Press.

Müller, W. and Shavit, Y. (1998), 'The Institutional Embeddedness of the Stratification Process: A Comparative Study of Qualifications and Occupations in Thirteen Countries', in Yossi Shavit and Walter Müller (eds), *From School to Work – A Comparative Study of Educational Qualifications and Occupational Destinations*, Oxford: Oxford University Press, pp. 1–48.

Neugart, M. (2000), The Supply of New Engineers in Germany, WZB Discussion Paper FS I 00-209, WZB, Berlin.

O'Connell, P.J. (1999), 'Adults in Training: An International Comparison of Continuing Education and Training', OECD Center for Educational Research and Innovation, WD(99)1, Paris.

OECD (1999), *Employment Outlook*, Paris: OECD.

Parkin, F. (ed.) (1974), *The Social Analysis of Class Structure*, London: Tavistock.

Schmid, G. (2000), 'Transitional Labour Markets: A New European Employment Strategy', in B. Marin, D. Meulders and D. Snower (eds), *Innovative Employment Initiatives*, Aldershot: Ashgate.

Schmid, G., O'Reilly, J. and Schömann, K. (eds) (1996), *International Handbook of Labour Market Policy and Evaluation*, Cheltenham, UK and Brookfield, US: Edward Elgar.

Schömann, K., Rogowski, R. and Kruppe, T. (1998), *Labour Market Efficiency in the European Union. Employment Protection and Fixed-term Contracts*, London: Routledge.

Serrano, A. (ed.) (2000), *Tackling Youth Unemployment in Europe*, Brussels: European Trade Union Institute.

Shavit Y. and Müller, W. (eds) (1998), *From School to Work – A Comparative Study of Educational Qualifications and Occupational Destinations*, Oxford: Oxford University Press.

Index